# Judgment of the Nephilim

Ryan Pitterson

Cover Illustration by: Teshingul - Pakistan
Edited by: Scott Stewart, christianbookeditor.com
Formatting by Polgarus Studio

# DEDICATION

Praise and thanks to my Lord and Savior Jesus Christ by whose Spirit and grace I was able to write this book. It is my sincere hope and prayer that this work be pleasing in His sight. I also thank my hero - my mother Olga Pitterson. You are a phenomenal woman of God who ignited the love of the Bible in me as a child. Thank you for your love, sacrifice, and constant encouragement for me to achieve all of my dreams. And for taking this journey with me from the time it was just a conversation until now. To my brother Sean for helping me be the man I am today and my brother Adam - the one person I can bounce any idea or concept off of and know if I am on the right track. To Pastor Matthew Recker of Heritage Baptist Church – thank you for your leadership, sound teaching and passion for the Gospel. And very special thanks to Erika, my beautiful, amazing wife and best friend - for all of your support, patience, and love during this process. You are an endless blessing. Finally, thanks to my two Boos - the greatest motivation and inspiration an author could ever ask for. I love you.

# Contents

# INTRODUCTION

"There were giants in the earth in those days; and also after that, when the sons of God came in unto the daughters of men, and they bare children to them, the same became mighty men which were of old, men of renown." – Genesis 6:4

Humanity is in a great war between God and His allies, righteous angels and saints, and the Devil and his army of fallen angels, demons, and human agents. This is the true Great War – a war to rule Heaven and Earth that dates all the way back to the Garden of Eden and the first two human beings created, Adam and Eve. In the Garden, God told Lucifer (Satan) that one day a woman would give birth to a male child who would defeat him. This male child (the Messiah) would have the power to redeem fallen humanity and destroy Satan and his armies forever.

*Who was this child?* Though Satan did not know, he was obsessed with preventing God from ever fulfilling His plan and redeeming humanity. That is why Pharaoh ordered that all male children be thrown into the river when Moses was an infant (Exodus 1:22). That is why Herod executed all male children in Bethlehem under the age of two when Jesus Christ was a newborn (Matthew 2:16). That is why 5,000 years ago Satan instigated a fallen angelic rebellion in which a group of angels broke off their allegiance to the Lord and entered the earthly realm. These fallen angels ("sons of God") took human wives ("daughters of men") and had children with them. Their offspring – hybrid half-human, half-angel beings known as the Nephilim – were superhuman giants who waged war against humanity and corrupted the human gene pool. The Devil knew that the Messiah would be human and would specifically redeem humanity. Thus, if he could taint human DNA with angelic DNA, the bloodline leading to the prophesied Messiah would be corrupted leaving humanity with no chance of salvation.

The Nephilim and their fallen angel fathers were the original "gods" of mythology. Their kingdoms before the Flood would later be known through myriad legends such as Atlantis, Lumeria, and many others. They ruled the planet, spawned genetic hybrid monstrosities, and led the population into sinful rebellion against God. Non-believers often wonder why a loving God would destroy humanity with a cataclysmic global flood. The answer is, because He *is* a loving God, for it was the only way the Lord could save us. Now, thousands of years later, many questions remain about what happened during that era of global history:

- How were angels able to reproduce with human women?
- What was the biblical location of the angelic arrival on Earth before the Flood?
- Who was the first human woman to marry the "sons of God"?
- Who was the leader of the antediluvian Nephilim kingdom?
- How did the Nephilim return after the Flood? Are there still Nephilim among us? Are they coming again?
- What happened to the souls of the giants once they died?
- Why did God order certain nations to be entirely **exterminated** – including women and children?

The answers to all these questions are in **the Holy Bible**. Using **only Scripture**, we are given a complete picture of the war between two bloodlines – the lineage of the Messiah and the seed of Satan. Far from being fringe characters in a "bizarre" chapter of Genesis, the Nephilim, their offspring, and their mission to corrupt the human gene pool were key factors in some of the principal themes throughout the Bible. A literal reading of Genesis 6 will enable us for the first time to fully understand Bible passages that have rarely been thought of as referring to giants. This is the story of God's enduring love for all people and His divine master plan to bring redemption through the Savior, Jesus Christ. This is the Judgment of the Nephilim.

# CHAPTER 1

# THE ULTIMATE PROPHECY

"For they have taken of their daughters for themselves, and for their sons: *so that the holy seed have mingled themselves with the people of those lands:* yea, the hand of the princes and rulers hath been chief in this trespass. And when I heard this thing, I rent my garment and my mantle, and plucked off the hair of my head and of my beard, and sat down astonied." – Ezra 9:2–3

Jesus Christ, the Son of God, is the central figure of the Bible, the universe, and human history. The angelic rebellion and the birth of the Nephilim and their ultimate judgment by God all come back to Jesus Christ. Christ is the fulfillment of "the holy seed" Ezra wrote of above. In the passage cited above, the reason Ezra was so distraught that he literally tore his hair and beard out was that he saw the threat that the genetic invasion of the Nephilim giants posed to the holy lineage of the Savior of humanity. The Devil, warned that a human child would one day conquer him, was hellbent on destroying the human race. Thus, this story cannot be fully comprehended without understanding that Jesus Christ is He on whom all the promises of God throughout Scripture and indeed the salvation of the world rests. As you read this book, keep this at the forefront of your thinking. It will make it far easier to comprehend the ongoing cosmic war between the Lord and Satan (and his angelic and Nephilim armies). Once the Devil was warned of a coming Messiah who would defeat him, he furiously waged war to prevent His birth and ultimate victory. And the prophetic warning of Satan's defeat was introduced in the Garden of Eden:

> "And the LORD God planted a garden eastward in Eden; and there he put the man whom he had formed. And out of the ground made the LORD God to grow every tree that is pleasant to the sight, and good for food; the tree of life also in the midst of the garden, and the tree of knowledge of good and evil... And the LORD God took the man, and put him into the garden of Eden to dress it and to keep it. And the LORD God commanded the man, saying, Of every tree of the garden thou mayest freely eat: But of the tree of the knowledge of good and evil, thou shalt not eat of it: for in the day that thou eatest thereof thou shalt surely die." – Genesis 2:8–9; 15–17

The creation of humanity was a momentous event. The Book of Job 38 confirms that the angels were created prior to humanity and even the creation of Earth:

> "Where wast thou when I laid the foundations of the earth? declare, if thou hast understanding. Who hath laid the measures thereof, if thou knowest? or who hath stretched the line upon it? Whereupon are the foundations thereof fastened? or who laid the corner stone thereof; When the morning stars sang together, and all the sons of God shouted for joy?"

The "sons of God" – angelic beings who are central figures in the present study – sang with joy at the creation of the planet Earth. Thus, we know with certainty that they were in existence and witnessed what must have been a shocking event – the birth of humanity. Satan and his fallen angels, who were already branded as rebels against the Lord, were watching the new race that would replace them in the heavenly ranks. The Bible confirms this in 1 Corinthians:

"Know ye not **that we shall judge angels?** how much more things that pertain to this life?" – 1 Corinthians 6:3

Born-again believers will take the place of the apostate angels who turned against the Creator, God. God Himself established this in creating the human race in His own image.

## HUMANITY WAS GOD'S SPECIAL CREATION

God created man in His own image. This special creation was the image bearer of the Lord on Earth. When the prophet Ezekiel saw a vision of God on His throne he wrote: "…and upon the likeness of the throne was the likeness as the appearance of a man above upon it" (Ezekiel 1:26). When Jesus rescued Shadrach, Meshach, and Abednego from the fiery furnace, King Nebuchadnezzar exclaimed: "…I see **four men** loose, walking in the midst of the fire…" (Daniel 3:25). The book of Hebrews states of Christ's incarnation: "For verily he took not on him the nature of angels; but he took on him the seed of Abraham" (Hebrews 2:16). Even before His incarnation on Earth, Jesus Christ looked like a man, or more aptly, humans resemble Jesus Christ.

## THE GARDEN OF EDEN –
## GOD AND MAN RULING THE EARTH

Adam, the first human, was given a very specific charge –to dress or care for the Garden and to protect it. Adam became an authority in a place where the Lord Himself manifested His presence. Genesis 2 informs us that God Himself planted the Garden of Eden. The Lord built it and set the Tree of Life – which provides immortality – in it. This was a supernatural place where the divine and earthly realms intersected, and in this regard the Garden itself was akin to the tabernacle or the temple. Even in the new Earth detailed in the book of Revelation, God once again "plants" His Holy dwelling:

> "And I saw a new heaven and a new earth: for the first heaven and the first earth were passed away; and there was no more sea. **And I John saw the holy city, new Jerusalem, coming down from God out of heaven, prepared as a bride adorned for her husband**. And I heard a great voice out of heaven saying, Behold, the tabernacle of God is with men, and he will dwell with them, and they shall be his people, and God himself shall be with them, and be their God." – Revelation 21:1–3

No surprise then that the end times New Jerusalem also contains the "tree of life" just as the Garden of Eden did (Revelation 22:2, Genesis 2:9), further confirming the Garden's special purpose.

The Septuagint (the oldest existing version of the Old Testament) refers to the Garden as "paradise," which means "next to God." And the first human being was assigned rulership over it. The Garden of Eden stood as a symbol of man's elevation over Satan and his rebel angels. A pastor in the 19th century wrote this about the Garden:

> "We should, however, seem justified, even were there no Scriptural statements to support the opinion, in supposing that the garden of Eden was something more than a scene of material loveliness, and that God invested its luxuriant foliage and sparkling flowers with a nobler power than that of merely gratifying the bodily sense. We know that he created man after his own image, and endowed him with powers which allowed of his holding communion with his Maker; and when God had arranged and planted Paradise as a dwelling place for his lofty and much honored creature, we can scarcely question that it must have been so disposed as to serve as a glorious temple, and that instruction

must have been conveyed by its trees and its fruits upon matters which it most behooved man to know." – *The Preacher In Print, Second Series, The Golden Lectures*, Henry Melvill, London: James Paul 1, Chapter House Court, 1854, p. 150.

The Garden of Eden was the original temple between God and humanity, and Adam was its priest. It was the portal between the heavenly and earthly realms. When God instructed Moses on how to construct the tabernacle – the place where God would manifest His presence before the people of Israel after the Exodus, He said: "And look that thou make them after their pattern, which was shewed thee in the mount" (Exodus 25:40). While on Mt. Sinai for 40 days Moses was literally given a vision of God's heavenly temple and instructed to use this as the basis for the design of the tabernacle. The temples of God on Earth are patterned after their heavenly counterparts. Adam even received access to the tree endowed with Divine power – the Tree of Life.

The Tree of Life gave humans eternal life – putting them on par with angels. It was a prefigure of salvation in Jesus Christ. The Lord Himself stated that if Adam continued to eat from the Tree he would "live forever" (Genesis 3:22). the Lord established a new race of beings to keep His holy temple on Earth. What made this even more perplexing was that Adam was inferior to angels. When speaking of the incarnation of Christ as a human being, the Bible underscores the superiority of angelic beings to humans:

> "But we see Jesus, who was made a little lower than the angels for the suffering of death, crowned with glory and honour; that he by the grace of God should taste death for every man." – Hebrews 2:9

So God took this earthly, inferior creature and appointed him as the steward of the temple of God on Earth. This is confirmed in Psalm 115:16: "The heaven, even the heavens, are the LORD's: but the earth hath he given to the children of men."

Humans did not possess angels' power or knowledge and yet they were given the earth. If humans could have a harmonious relationship with God and immortality, *they could replace and supplant the rebel angels.*

In addition, a second revolutionary event occurred after the creation of man – God established the institution of marriage:

> "And the LORD God said, It is not good that the man should be alone; I will make him an help meet for him. And out of the ground the LORD God formed every beast of the field, and every fowl of the air; and brought them unto Adam to see what he would call them: and whatsoever Adam called every living creature, that was the name thereof. And Adam gave names to all cattle, and to the fowl of the air, and to every beast of the field; but for Adam there was not found an help meet for him. And the LORD God caused a deep sleep to fall upon Adam, and he slept: and he took one of his ribs, and closed up the flesh instead thereof; And the rib, which the LORD God had taken from man, made he a woman, and brought her unto the man.
>
> "And Adam said, This is now bone of my bones, and flesh of my flesh: she shall be called Woman, because she was taken out of Man. Therefore shall a man leave his father and his mother, and shall cleave unto his wife: and they shall be one flesh. And they were both naked, the man and his wife, and were not ashamed." – Genesis 2:23–25

## MARRIAGE – FORESHADOW OF GOD'S PLAN TO CONQUER SATAN

The first recorded words in human history were about marriage (Genesis 1:23–24). This should underscore the importance God places on this institution. Adam, speaking under divine inspiration, established the principles of marriage in which a man and his wife become "one flesh." It is a spiritual union in God's eyes. In fact, until they were found in sin, Eve did not have a name. Both husband and wife were referred to as Adam. The unity of husband and wife is also powerfully seen through sexual relations in which a husband and wife (the "two") join in intimacy and create a child (the "one flesh"). For the angelic host in Heaven, this was an entirely new concept. After all, the Lord Jesus Christ explained that marriage was an institution reserved exclusively for humanity while in the earthly realm:

> "And Jesus answering said unto them, The children *of this world* marry, and are given in marriage: But they which shall be accounted worthy to obtain that world, and the resurrection from the dead, neither marry, nor are given in marriage: **Neither can they die any more: for they are equal unto the angels;** and are the children of God, being the children of the resurrection." – Luke 20:34–36

Humans are mortal, and thus marriage was necessary to propagate the race. God created angels directly with immortal, celestial bodies. They are of heavenly origin and do not die and are not permitted to marry. This prohibition was a pivotal issue in the war between God and Satan. For now, suffice it to say that angels, who observe and are very interested in the affairs of humanity, witnessed something in the Garden of Eden they had never experienced themselves. Though the angels did not know it at the time, marriage had far greater spiritual purposes related to Jesus Christ and salvation.

> "For the husband is the head of the wife, **even as Christ is the head of the church**: and he is the saviour of the body. Therefore **as the church is subject unto Christ**, so let the wives be to their own husbands in every thing. **Husbands, love your wives, even** as Christ also loved the church, and gave himself for it… For this cause shall a man leave his father and mother, and shall be joined unto his wife, and they two shall be one flesh. **This is a great**

> mystery: but I speak concerning Christ and the church." –
> Ephesians 5:23-25, 31–32

This "mystery" – revealed in the church age – is that marriage itself is a type and shadow of the spiritual relationship between Jesus Christ the Bridegroom and His Church – all born-again Christians, who are spiritually the Bride of Christ. By God's grace through faith in Christ, all born-again Christians enter a literal spiritual union with Christ, thus sharing in His atoning sacrifice on the cross, receiving the righteousness of perfect, sinless life and inheriting the universe He earned on their behalf. The Messiah would defeat Satan, and all who believed in Him would rule and reign in Heaven and Earth for eternity.

Thus, marriage served as the blueprint for the salvation of humanity from sin and eternal damnation. The Lord, anticipating humanity's fall into sin, foreshadowed the means by which He would restore all believers to right standing and forgiveness. So, it should come as no surprise that marriage was the first order of business for humanity under God's direction. Eve, Adam's wife, was created from Adam's rib – again signifying that she was an earthly being made from an Earth-born person. This was a stunning event for the angels watching humanity who did not realize the fuller and much greater purpose being wrought through this union.

The first man was appointed the steward of God's ancient temple and given a wife to start the expansion of the human race. Adam and Eve were free to enjoy the abundant fruit of every tree in the Garden except one: God forbade them to eat from the Tree of the Knowledge of Good and Evil: "And the LORD God commanded the man, saying, Of every tree of the garden thou mayest freely eat: But of the tree of the knowledge of good and evil, thou shalt not eat of it: for in the day that thou eatest thereof thou shalt surely die" (Genesis 2:16–17).

# SATAN AND HIS FALLEN ANGELS –
# THE ENEMIES OF HUMANITY

At this point in human history, Adam was without sin. He demonstrated his faith in God with his testimony towards his wife. Though he was asleep when God created his wife, Adam believed God's account and proclaimed it. And his union with Eve was a holy one: "Marriage is honourable in all, and the bed undefiled: but whoremongers and adulterers God will judge" (Hebrews 13:4). So how was there any "evil" in the world? Much less a tree from which one could obtain knowledge of evil? What did this all mean? Some of these mysteries can be clarified by examining the enemy of humanity and of all those who love the Lord Jesus Christ – Satan:

> "How art thou fallen from heaven, O Lucifer, son of the morning! how art thou cut down to the ground, which didst weaken the nations! For thou hast said in thine heart, I will ascend into heaven, I will exalt my throne above the stars of God: I will sit also upon the mount of the congregation, in the sides of the north: I will ascend above the heights of the clouds; I will be like the most High. Yet thou shalt be brought down to hell, to the sides of the pit. They that see thee shall narrowly look upon thee, and consider thee, saying, Is this the man that made the earth to tremble, that did shake kingdoms; That made the world as a wilderness, and destroyed the cities thereof; that opened not the house of his prisoners?" – Isaiah 14:12–17

This very well-known passage details the original aspirations of Lucifer, or Satan, the once-holy angelic being who committed the first sin in rebellion against God. While addressed to the "King of Babylon," this esoteric passage carries a greater reference to the Devil. Satan's goal is to usurp the Lord's position and authority. The following statements refer to the exalted status of the true God of the Bible: ascending into Heaven (which implies Satan was *looking up towards Heaven* when he had this thought), sitting on a throne above the "stars," or angels, of God, and sitting upon the "mount of the congregation, in the sides of the north." There are also other mysterious references, such as verse 17, which states that Satan "opened not the house of his prisoners" (which we will explore in a later chapter). But for our purposes we are going to focus on Satan's aspiration to be God.

## SATAN REBELLED BEFORE HUMANITY'S CREATION

A similar esoteric address is given in Ezekiel 28:

> "Son of man, take up a lamentation upon the king of Tyrus, and say unto him, Thus saith the Lord GOD; Thou sealest up the sum, full of wisdom, and perfect in beauty. **Thou hast been in Eden the garden of God; every precious stone was thy covering**, the sardius, topaz, and the diamond, the beryl, the onyx, and the jasper, the sapphire, the emerald, and the carbuncle, and gold: the workmanship of thy tabrets and of thy pipes was prepared in thee in the day that thou wast created. Thou art the anointed cherub that covereth; and I have set thee so: **thou wast upon the holy mountain of God; thou hast walked up and down in the midst of the stones of fire**. Thou wast perfect in thy ways from the day that thou wast created, till iniquity was found in thee...

> "By the multitude of thy merchandise they have filled the midst of thee with violence, and thou hast sinned: therefore I will cast thee as profane out of the mountain of God: and I will destroy thee, O covering cherub, from the midst of the stones of fire. Thine heart was lifted up because of thy beauty, thou hast corrupted thy wisdom by reason of thy brightness: I will cast thee to the ground, I will lay thee before kings, that they may behold thee. Thou hast defiled thy sanctuaries by the multitude of thine iniquities, by the

iniquity of thy traffick; therefore will I bring forth a fire from the midst of thee, it shall devour thee, and I will bring thee to ashes upon the earth in the sight of all them that behold thee. All they that know thee among the people shall be astonished at thee: thou shalt be a terror, and never shalt thou be any more." – Ezekiel 28:12–19

Looking at this passage in the Septuagint, the oldest extant form of the Old Testament, the version most quoted by Jesus Christ and His disciples (and the only translation from paleo-Hebrew, the form of Hebrew used in Old Testament times) provides a little more clarity on Satan's activities:

"From the day that thou wast created thou *wast* with the cherub: I set thee on the holy mount of God; thou wast in the midst of the stones of fire. Thou wast faultless in thy days, from the day that thou wast created, until iniquity was found in thee. Of the abundance of thy merchandise thou hast filled thy storehouses with iniquity, and hast sinned: therefore thou hast been cast down wounded from the mount of God, and the cherub has brought thee out of the midst of the stones of fire.

"Thy heart has been lifted up because of thy beauty; thy knowledge has been corrupted with thy beauty: because of the multitude of thy sins I have cast thee to the ground, I have caused thee to be put to open shame before kings. Because of the multitude of thy sins and the iniquities of thy merchandise, I have profaned thy sacred things; and I will bring fire out of the midst of thee, this shall devour thee; and I will make thee *to be* ashes upon thy land before all that see thee. And all that know thee among the nations shall groan over thee: thou art gone to destruction, and thou shalt not exist any more." – Ezekiel 28:14–19 LXX

Satan was a perfect, beautiful, brilliant being who was in the Garden of Eden during his time of obedient service to the Lord. The passage describes him bedecked with nine different jewels – "sardius, topaz, and the diamond, the beryl, the onyx, and the jasper, the sapphire, the emerald, and the carbuncle, and gold" – all worn on the breastplate of the High Priest of the temple in ancient Israel (Exodus 28:9–29). Satan had been the priest in the Garden of Eden administering worship to God in a generation before Adam. Following his rebellion against the Lord, Satan was removed from his position and replaced. The Garden he once presided over was given to Adam. The Devil, due to his exceeding angelic beauty, was "corrupted." In providing the guidelines for ordaining a pastor, the Apostle Paul referenced Satan's fall:

> "Not a novice, lest being lifted up with pride he fall into the condemnation of the devil." – 1 Timothy 3:6

## THE CORRUPTION OF ADAM AND EVE – SATAN'S FIRST ATTACK

Corrupted by pride and arrogant ambitions, the Devil soon conspired with a group of fallen angels to dethrone the Lord (Revelation 12:3–4, Matthew 25:41). This wicked confederacy despised humanity whom they perceived as a threat to the positions they once held. Scripture describes Satan and his apostate angels as the true enemy of every person:

> "Put on the whole armour of God, that ye may be able to stand against the wiles of the devil. For we wrestle not against flesh and blood, but against principalities, against powers, against the rulers of the darkness of this world, against spiritual wickedness in high places." – Ephesians 6:11–12

Principalities, powers, and the other titles are various rankings of angels in Heaven. The passage above confirms that these angels along with the Devil are waging war against the human race – all for the purpose of achieving Satan's ultimate goal, which is to rule Heaven and Earth. Escaping God's ultimate judgment (eternal torment in the Lake of Fire) is paramount in this agenda.

With this context, we return to the Garden of Eden in Genesis 3. the Lord's command to Adam – not to eat from the Tree of the Knowledge of Good and Evil – takes on even more meaning. There was an evil presence in the world, and God, in His love, was protecting His children from it. Up to this point humanity lived in sinless harmony with the Creator. Satan of course brought that to a quick end with his temptation of Eve:

> "Now the serpent was more subtil than any beast of the field which the LORD God had made. And he said unto the woman, Yea, hath God said, Ye shall not eat of every tree of the garden? And the woman said unto the serpent, We may eat of the fruit of the trees of the garden: But of the fruit of the tree which is in the midst of the garden, God hath said, Ye shall not eat of it, neither shall ye touch it, lest ye die. And the serpent said unto the woman, Ye shall not surely die: For God doth know that in the day ye eat thereof, then your eyes shall be opened, and ye shall be as gods, knowing good and evil. And when the woman saw that the tree was good for food, and that it was pleasant to the eyes, and a tree to be desired to make one wise, she took of the fruit thereof, and did eat, and gave also unto her husband with her; and he did eat." – Genesis 3:1–6

God established His Word with clarity: Eating from the sole forbidden tree in the Garden meant certain death. Satan deceived Eve by slandering God ("Yea, hath God said, Ye shall not eat of every tree of the garden?"), contradicting God's Word ("Ye shall not surely die"), and in fact promising her the wonders of being "as gods" if she partook of the forbidden fruit. Angels were more powerful, and Eve had the opportunity to be like them (or so Satan claimed). The Devil enticed Eve by shaking her faith in God.

Satan's offer enticed her to mistrust God's Word by deceiving her into believing that God was keeping hidden divine knowledge from her and that she could be like the heavenly beings she and Adam may have encountered in the Garden. Who would not marvel to some degree at Satan's abilities or those of the "gods"? Revelation 12:9 confirms that Satan appeared as a serpent in referring to the Devil as "that old serpent." He could have also appeared supernatural in nature. The "fiery serpents" of Numbers 21 is a translation of the Hebrew word *"saraph."* This term is used for the seraphim, winged creatures who surround the throne of God in Isaiah 6. So, when Satan appeared to Eve he was most likely a luminescent creature. The Apostle Paul alluded to this when he wrote that "Satan himself is transformed into an angel of light" (2 Corinthians 11:14).

In offering Eve godhood, this shiny, brilliant angel not only corrupted the woman but Adam as well when he partook of the forbidden fruit. Thus, Satan's motives from the beginning of Scripture were clear – to rebel against God, undermine His Word, and ultimately destroy humanity through sinful rebellion.

## SIN FORCED ADAM AND EVE FROM GOD'S PRESENCE

The Lord created a new race of beings and put them in His holy Garden with the authority to rule and protect it, and Satan responded by corrupting them with sin – bringing guilt into their lives as he had done for himself and his minions. With the first transgression, Adam died a spiritual death. He no longer enjoyed open communion with God or access to His full presence. The spiritual death of humanity is an extremely important aspect of the Devil's agenda. Scripture states repeatedly that in sinning the body, though functioning and living, is "dead":

"And you hath he quickened, who were dead in trespasses and sins; Wherein in time past ye walked according to the course of this world, according to the prince of the power of the air, the spirit that now worketh in the children of disobedience:" – Ephesians 2:1–2

"And you, being dead in your sins and the uncircumcision of your flesh…." – Colossians 2:13

"And if Christ be in you, **the body is dead because of sin**; but the Spirit is life because of righteousness." – Romans 8:10

The human body, made sinless in the image of the Creator, was corrupted and died spiritually. From that point on, Adam was changed. This goes to the heart of Satan's plan with the Nephilim. The giants were a tool to change and corrupt the very human body and spirit to prevent us from bringing forth God's will and our ultimate redemption. The spiritual death of Adam and Eve was evident in their immediate reaction to their sin:

"And the eyes of them both were opened, and they knew that they were naked; and they sewed fig leaves together, and made themselves aprons. And they heard the voice of the LORD God walking in the garden in the cool of the day: and Adam and his wife hid themselves from the presence of the LORD God amongst the trees of the garden. And the LORD God called unto Adam, and said unto him, Where art thou? And he said, I heard thy voice in the garden, and I was afraid, because I was naked; and I hid myself. And he said, Who told thee that thou wast naked? Hast thou eaten of the tree, whereof I commanded thee that thou shouldest not eat?" – Genesis 3:7–11

Their eyes opened, the sinful couple who had lived naked with no shame were now embarrassed by their lack of clothing. What changed to make their nakedness an issue was the spiritual corruption they suffered once they sinned. The book of Titus says, "Unto the pure all things are pure: but unto them that are defiled and unbelieving is nothing pure; but even their mind and conscience is defiled" (Titus 1:15). They could no longer stand before a pure, righteous God, so they vainly attempted to conceal their shame and themselves from the Lord. It is possible that their physical appearance changed as well. Extended time with God leads humans to reflect His divine light:

> "And [Moses] was there with the LORD forty days and forty nights … And it came to pass, when Moses came down from mount Sinai with the two tables of testimony in Moses' hand, when he came down from the mount, **that Moses wist not that the skin of his face shone while he talked with him**. And when Aaron and all the children of Israel saw Moses, **behold, the skin of his face shone; and they were afraid to come nigh him**. And Moses called unto them; and Aaron and all the rulers of the congregation returned unto him: and Moses talked with them. And afterward all the children of Israel came nigh: and he gave them in commandment all that the LORD had spoken with him in mount Sinai. And till Moses had done speaking with them, he put a vail on his face." – Exodus 34:27–33

If Adam and Eve had also experienced this divine light, the sinful rebellion in their hearts extinguished it. After the first sin, God judged Adam, whom He had previously honored with rulership of the Garden, by making him work on futile soil:

> "And unto Adam he said, Because thou hast hearkened unto the voice of thy wife, and hast eaten of the tree, of which I commanded thee, saying, Thou shalt not eat of it: cursed is the ground for thy sake; in sorrow shalt thou eat of it all the days of thy life; Thorns also and thistles shall it bring forth to thee; and thou shalt eat the

herb of the field; In the sweat of thy face shalt thou eat bread, till thou return unto the ground; for out of it wast thou taken: for dust thou art, and unto dust shalt thou return. And Adam called his wife's name Eve; because she was the mother of all living." – Genesis 3:17–20

The war between God and Satan took on a new dimension. The newly-created race of humans was then involved and had the choice to walk in godly faith or fall into sinful disobedience. Satan's wicked instigation of the Fall, however, was not overlooked. In punishing him, God responded with a prophecy that would forever change the course of history.

## A HUMAN SAVIOR WHO WOULD
## ONE DAY DEFEAT SATAN

"And the LORD God said unto the serpent, Because thou hast done this, thou art cursed above all cattle, and above every beast of the field; upon thy belly shalt thou go, and dust shalt thou eat all the days of thy life: And I will put enmity between thee and the woman, **and between thy seed and her seed; it shall bruise thy head, and thou shalt bruise his heel**." – Genesis 3:14–15

This was the ultimate prophecy. In punishing Satan, the Lord announced that he would not only have "enmity" or be at war with women (a prophecy Satan would fulfill three chapters later) but that "the seed of the woman" would one day bruise his (i.e., the serpent's) head. This was a prophecy of Satan's defeat. Rather than vanquishing Satan in that moment (which was well within His power), God the Father chose to defeat Satan through His Son, Jesus Christ, to whom this prophecy referred. But at that time thousands of years ago in the Garden, all Satan knew was that a male child, *born of a human woman*, would one day defeat him.

The Lord, in His Sovereignty, decided to not just tell Satan he was going to be destroyed but to reveal *who was going to do it*. From that point in history Satan knew the means of his destruction. It would not be 12 legions of holy angels battling him or a lightning strike from Heaven. Rather it would be a godly bloodline carried through a human woman. A male child – seemingly inferior to a being such as Satan in all aspects of power – was going to conquer him. Clearly this child would be endowed with divine power or nature in some form. Beginning with this pronouncement, the Devil's primary objective was to destroy this child or, better yet, prevent His birth. The Apostle John saw a vision of this in the book of Revelation:

> "And there appeared a great wonder in heaven; a woman clothed with the sun, and the moon under her feet, and upon her head a crown of twelve stars: And she being with child cried, travailing in birth, and pained to be delivered. And there appeared another wonder in heaven; and behold a great red dragon, having seven heads and ten horns, and seven crowns upon his heads. And his tail drew the third part of the stars of heaven, and did cast them to the earth: **and the dragon stood before the woman which was ready to be delivered, for to devour her child as soon as it was born.**"
> – Revelation 12:1–4

The woman in the vision represented the 12 tribes of Israel, from whom the Messiah ultimately descended (Genesis 37:9–11). From the moment he heard God's pronouncement in the Garden to the birth of Jesus Christ, Satan, the Dragon, was watching and scheming ways to destroy the Savior – confirming that he took God's prophecy seriously. By the third chapter of Genesis, **human marriage and genetics** were critical to the fate of the universe as the prophecy's fulfillment hinged on a future savior born from a woman.

# ANGELIC BEINGS INTERACTED WITH HUMANS IN THE ANTEDILUVIAN WORLD

Heavenly beings *interacted openly with humans* during this ancient era of history. When Satan approached Eve in the Garden (Genesis 3) she was neither frightened nor surprised. This contrasts with people's typical reaction – sheer terror such that they needed to be admonished to "fear not" – upon encountering an angel later in biblical history (Daniel 10:4–8; Matthew 28:2–4). Also, when God punished Adam and Eve for their sin, another being from the heavenly realm entered the story:

> "Unto Adam also and to his wife did the LORD God make coats of skins, and clothed them. And the LORD God said, Behold, the man is become as one of us, to know good and evil: and now, lest he put forth his hand, and take also of the tree of life, and eat, and live forever: Therefore the LORD God sent him forth from the garden of Eden, to till the ground from whence he was taken. So he drove out the man; **and he placed at the east of the garden of Eden** *Cherubims*, **and a flaming sword which turned every way, to keep the way of the tree of life**." – Genesis 3:21–24

After casting Adam and Eve out of the Garden, the Lord appointed Cherubim to guard the path that led to the Tree of Life. Cherubim are heavenly creatures normally stationed around the Lord's throne.

When King Hezekiah prayed for God's mercy as the wicked King Sennacherib and his armies were preparing to ransack Israel, he said: "O LORD God of Israel, which dwellest between the cherubims, thou art the God, even thou alone, of all the kingdoms of the earth; thou hast made heaven and earth" (2 Kings 19:15). The Psalms proclaim that God "rode upon a cherub, and did fly: yea, he did fly upon the wings of the wind" (Psalm 18:10).

The prophet Ezekiel witnessed a series of discussions among the Lord and His holy angels as He carried out a judgment upon Jerusalem for rampant idolatry occurring in the very temple of God. Ezekiel's eyes were opened to see the series of punishments the various angels carried out. And the cherubim appear again:

> "Then I looked, and, behold, in the firmament that was above the head of the cherubims there appeared over them as it were a sapphire stone, as the appearance of the likeness of a throne. And he spake unto the man clothed with linen, and said, Go in between the wheels, even under the cherub, **and fill thine hand with coals of fire from between the cherubims**, and scatter them over the city. And he went in in my sight… And the cherubims were lifted up. This is the living creature that I saw by the river of Chebar." – Ezekiel 10:1–2, 15

Note that "coals of fire" sit close to the throne of God. Before his fall, Satan was in "the midst of the stones of fire" among those same cherubim, which underscores his preeminent position before his descent into sinful rebellion. The cherubim are very important heavenly realm beings. They sit at God's very throne. They are mentioned more than 70 times in Scripture. In Genesis 3, God places several of these creatures in the Garden of Eden to guard the path that leads to the Tree of Life. The important point for our study of the Nephilim, and the wars of the two bloodlines, is that *heavenly realm beings were on Earth openly communicating and interacting with humans.* God appeared and spoke to Adam and Eve in person. Satan not only spoke to Eve to deceive her into sin but stood with her and Adam when the Lord pronounced their punishments. Cherubim served as guards in the Garden, and a supernatural fiery sword with the power to swing on its own was positioned to guard the path to the Tree of Life.

This was the state of the world before the Flood. Thus, based on a literal reading of Scripture it is quite conceivable that a *fallen angelic being* could interact with a human for evil purposes. This is important to keep in mind as we move on: The antediluvian world was a mixture of the natural (from a human perspective) and the supernatural. And Eden was the central place from which the Lord and heavenly beings communed with humanity and ruled (hence the presence of cherubim who, though normally stationed at God's throne, were readily available to guard the way of the Tree of Life).

## ADAM'S FAITH IN THE PROPHECY AND SATAN'S ULTIMATE DEFEAT

By the end of Genesis 3, man was banished from the Garden of Eden, spiritually dead from sin, and sentenced to hard labor – tilling a cursed, unfruitful soil until his inevitable physical death. But there was hope. God in His mercy promised Adam and Eve a "seed" who would one day conquer the very serpent who had seduced them into all this calamity in the first place. God also made coats of animal skins for them to wear, a type of the sacrificial system of using animal blood to cover sin in the Mosaic Law and a foreshadow of the sacrifice of Christ, the true Seed of the Woman, who would shed His blood to save humanity from their sins.

Upon hearing the Prophecy, Adam named his wife Eve meaning "the mother of all living." Both the timing and the choice of name are significant as they show that Adam believed God's merciful promise of a future Savior. It meant Eve would one day be a mother. The first man had hope that through his wife, whom he had followed into sin, would come the promised Redeemer who would save them from eternal punishment. Although humanity had lost that round, the fight was far from over, and victory would come through the child of the Prophecy.

Satan, after hearing of his impending defeat and death, began working feverishly to undo God's plan of judgment and redemption by any means possible. Satan knew that while the Prophecy predicted his demise, it also predicted he would have his own "seed" and these two lineages – the Divine and the Satanic – would wage war. So, there was an avenue through which he could formulate his plan. The next round in the battle was set to begin.

CHAPTER 2

# THE FIRST SEED

"And Adam knew Eve his wife; and she conceived, and bare Cain, and said, I have gotten a man from the LORD. And she again bare his brother Abel. And Abel was a keeper of sheep, but Cain was a tiller of the ground." – Genesis 4:1–2

Cain was the first son in human history. From Satan's perspective on the Prophecy of the coming Messiah, the infant Cain *could have been the prophesied Messiah*. Cain was, after all, the firstborn seed of the only woman on Earth, Eve. Thus, Satan set out to kill or corrupt Cain and used the same tactics on Cain that he had used on Eve – temptation into sinful rebellion. By the time we meet Cain in Genesis 4, his heart was not right with the Lord. His inferior offering clearly demonstrated his lack of faith in God:

"And in process of time it came to pass, that Cain brought of the fruit of the ground an offering unto the LORD. And Abel, he also brought of the firstlings of his flock and of the fat thereof. And the LORD had respect unto Abel and to his offering: But unto Cain and to his offering he had not respect. And Cain was very wroth, and his countenance fell." – Genesis 4:3–5

Abel's faith led him to make a more excellent sacrifice (one that involved blood, which God makes clear later in Scripture is required for every sacrifice, a precedent God set when He killed two animals to clothe Adam and Eve). Scripture makes it clear that Abel knew God's commands, and Romans 10:4 says "faith cometh by hearing, and hearing by the word of God." So, whether by Adam, Eve, or the Lord Himself, Abel clearly knew God's Word and was living his life according to his belief:

> "By faith Abel offered unto God a more excellent sacrifice than Cain, by which he obtained witness that he was righteous, God testifying of his gifts: and by it he being dead yet speaketh." – Hebrews 11:4

## CORRUPTING CAIN – THE POTENTIAL MESSIAH

Cain's offering of crops represented the work of his own hands and was a product of the very soil God had cursed in the Garden of Eden. Despite knowing firsthand about the Garden of Eden, the fall of humanity, the prophecy of the Redeemer, and the corrupting force that is the Devil (all of which involved his mother and father), Cain rejected God's own prophesied words and authority. Cain was not an atheist – after all God appeared openly to him. To not believe would deny reality he had experienced firsthand. Cain's religion, however, was of his own design and not based on believing and trusting the Lord. Sacrifices were offered for God's forgiveness. It was a work to call upon the Lord's mercy for atonement of sin. If a person made sacrifices not believing he was truly deserving of God's wrath or secretly justifying his iniquity, that person was not truly offering in the manner God desires: "For thou desirest not sacrifice; else would I give it: thou delightest not in burnt offering. The sacrifices of God *are a broken spirit: a broken and a contrite heart,* O God, thou wilt not despise" (Psalm 51:16–17). A heart that does not hold love for God will lead to empty offerings and rejected sacrifice.

Once Cain's faithless offering was rejected, he turned to greater evil:

"And Cain talked with Abel his brother: and it came to pass, when they were in the field, that Cain rose up against Abel his brother, and slew him." – Genesis 4:8

Again, consider this situation in light of the Prophecy. Satan had succeeded in luring Cain into sinful rebellion, thus removing one potential threat to his reign. With the older brother corrupted and effectively out of the picture, perhaps his younger twin, Abel, was the Messiah? By corrupting Cain so effectively that he would murder his own brother in spite and jealousy, Satan was in effect killing two threats with one deception. Scripture confirms that Cain was under satanic influence:

"For this is the message that ye heard from the beginning, that we should love one another. Not as Cain, **who was of that wicked one**, and slew his brother. And wherefore slew he him? Because his own works were evil, and his brother's righteous." – 1 John 3:11–12

The devil led the very lineage God ordained to redeem the world into sin. This is a recurring theme throughout biblical history. Cain was so depraved he was "of that wicked one" – a spiritual seed of Satan – and this fueled his hatred of Abel to the point of homicide. A prominent 19th-century commentary on this chapter of Scripture expounded on this tragic reality:

"The same devil that set enmity betwixt man and God, sets enmity betwixt man and man; and yet God said, *I will put enmity between thy seed and her seed.* Our hatred of the serpent and his seed is from God: their hatred of the holy seed is from the serpent. Behold here at once, in one person, the seed of the woman and of the serpent: Cain's natural parts are of the woman; his vicious qualities of the serpent: the woman gave him to be a brother, the serpent to be a man slayer, all uncharitableness all quarrels are of one author: we cannot entertain wrath, and not give place to the devil. Certainly so deadly an act must needs be deeply grounded." – *The Works of Joseph Hall, Successively Bishop of Exeter and Norwich: With Some Account of His Life And Sufferings, Written by Himself,* Joseph Hall, Vol. 1, Oxford: D.A. Talboys, 1837, p.16.

## GOD GEOGRAPHICALLY SEPARATED SATAN'S SEED FROM GOD'S CHILDREN TO PROTECT THE MESSIANIC BLOODLINE

Just as He responded swiftly to Adam and Eve's transgression, so God responded swiftly to Cain's sin:

"And the LORD said unto Cain, Where is Abel thy brother? And he said, I know not: Am I my brother's keeper? And he said, What hast thou done? the voice of thy brother's blood crieth unto me from the ground. And now art thou cursed from the earth, which hath opened her mouth to receive thy brother's blood from thy hand; When thou tillest the ground, it shall not henceforth yield unto thee her strength; a fugitive and a vagabond shalt thou be in the earth. And Cain said unto the LORD, My punishment is greater than I can bear. Behold, thou hast driven me out this day from the face of the earth; and from thy face shall I be hid; and I shall be a fugitive and a vagabond in the earth; and *it shall come to pass, that every one that findeth me shall slay me*. And the LORD said unto him, Therefore whosoever slayeth Cain, vengeance shall be taken on him sevenfold. And the LORD set a mark upon Cain, lest any

finding him should kill him. And Cain went out from the presence of the LORD, and dwelt in the land of Nod, on the east of Eden."
– Genesis 4:9–16

Fully perverted with sin, Cain had the audacity to lie to God's face about his brother's whereabouts. Although Adam obfuscated the truth in explaining his sin ("The woman whom thou gavest to be with me, she gave me of the tree, and I did eat"), Cain lied in brazen fashion. As He had done with Adam, the Lord banished Cain and beyond that cursed him. God in His sovereign judgment again separated the wicked from the righteous. Adam and Eve left the Lord's presence in the Garden but remained in the holy land of Eden. Cain, however, was removed from Eden altogether, sent eastwards (signaling that God's presence is approached from the east heading west as was the case with the tabernacle and temples throughout the Old Testament).

Cain showed no remorse or repentance for his crimes. His only concern was for his own safety. Though many assume that Cain feared *only humans'* seeking to avenge Abel's death, the Scriptures up to this point describe angels on Earth – certainly in the case of the cherubim and flaming sword in Eden – to serve the specific purposes of security and punishment. In the Septuagint, Cain is quoted: "My crime is too great for me to be forgiven" (Genesis 4:13 LXX). His heart was far removed from God, and thus his lineage would not be permitted to interact with and bring their sinful influence to Adam and Eve's other children. The first two "seeds of the woman," and their prophesied threat to Satan's reign, were effectively removed. The Prophecy appeared undone.

> "And Adam knew his wife again; and she bare a son, and called his name Seth: For God, said she, hath appointed me another seed instead of Abel, whom Cain slew. And to Seth, to him also there was born a son; and he called his name Enos: then began men to call upon the name of the LORD." – Genesis 4:25–26

Satan had struck a mighty blow at God's plan to redeem humanity, but the war was far from over. Adam and Eve conceived and gave birth to a third son, Seth. Eve, well aware of the Prophecy, knew that Seth was going to replace Abel as the continuation of the godly bloodline leading to the prophesied Seed of the Woman. Hence Seth's name in Hebrew means "compensation." Though Abel died, Eve was compensated by her third son who was "another seed instead of Abel" (Genesis 4:25). Seth begat Enos, which coincided with a spiritual revival. Faithful men of God were growing in number. This would lead to another turn in the ongoing battle between God and evil.

## THE DAUGHTERS OF MEN –
## GROWTH OF THE HUMAN POPULATION

Genesis 5 details Adam's lineage – a list of holy, God-fearing descendants leading to the Messiah. It also clarifies a point:

> "And Adam lived a hundred and thirty years, and begat a son in his own likeness, and after his image; and called his name Seth: And the days of Adam after he had begotten Seth were eight hundred years: **and he begat sons and daughters**: And all the days that Adam lived were nine hundred and thirty years: and he died." – Genesis 5:3–5

This passage marks the first time Scripture details the birth of daughters. Adam had Seth at 130 years of age (the rate of aging in the antediluvian era was quite different from today), and he and Eve subsequently bore many sons and daughters. The reference continued throughout the Genesis 5 genealogy.

> "And Seth lived after he begat Enos eight hundred and seven years, and begat sons and daughters: And all the days of Seth were nine hundred and twelve years: and he died. And Enos lived ninety years,

and begat Cainan: And Enos lived after he begat Cainan eight hundred and fifteen years, and begat sons and daughters: And all the days of Enos were nine hundred and five years: and he died. And Cainan lived seventy years and begat Mahalaleel: And Cainan lived after he begat Mahalaleel eight hundred and forty years, and begat sons and daughters…." – Genesis 5:7–13

The divine lineage in Genesis emphasizes the fact that females were born alongside the males of the Messianic line. The Bible never tells us how old Adam and Eve were when Cain and Abel were born. All we can discern from Scripture is that they were born before Adam was 130 years old (when he begat Seth). So, by the time God banished Cain it is very easy to see that over time it would "come to pass" (to use Cain's own words) that he would have siblings who would have their own children. Thus, the human population grew at a rate that would allow Cain to find a wife.

## THE IMPORTANCE OF GOD'S COMMAND TO "BE FRUITFUL AND MULTIPLY"

So, what are we to make of the details of this lineage? A line of godly men was born and having many children. Satan's direct approach of using one sibling to kill another or trying to corrupt one male child at a time was no longer effective because the number of families in the Messianic lineage was growing exponentially. With all the newborn males among Adam's descendants, the "potential messiahs" were numerous, and Cain, the Devil's main human agent, was geographically banished from the godly line and on the run for his life.

These circumstances allowed for a time of spiritual revival. God's countermove of commanding humanity to be fruitful and multiply rendered Satan's initial method of corruption futile. It was going to take *a large-scale attack* to ruin humanity and stop the promised Redeemer. This development was the backdrop for the invasion of the fallen angels who would be the fathers of the Nephilim.

# CHAPTER 3

# ENTER THE SONS OF GOD

"And it came to pass, when men began to multiply on the face of the earth, and daughters were born unto them, That the sons of God saw the daughters of men that they were fair; and they took them wives of all which they chose. And the LORD said, My spirit shall not always strive with man, for that he also is flesh: yet his days shall be an hundred and twenty years. There were giants in the earth in those days; and also after that, when the sons of God came in unto the daughters of men, and they bare children to them, the same became mighty men which were of old, men of renown. And God saw that the wickedness of man was great in the earth, and that every imagination of the thoughts of his heart was only evil continually." – Genesis 6:1–5

This is the passage that has generated a massive amount of discussion, debate, and controversy in the church. Books and movies such as *The DaVinci Code* have alluded to this mysterious lineage. There are video games and even a whole genre of romance fiction on this topic. But only the Bible explains its true importance. Genesis 6 details the greatest threat to human existence and the birth of the Messiah: *the corruption of the human genetic code through the Nephilim*. Many authors have examined this topic using a wide variety of Christian, secular, and pagan sources. Unfortunately, most have overlooked precious passages in many books of the Bible that shed the truth on this subject and its great importance in ancient times, in our day, and for the future.

## GENESIS 6 – A VERSE-BY-VERSE ANALYSIS

"…when men began to multiply…" – Genesis 6:1

The question of *when* angels had relations with human women is critical for understanding God's judgment in the Flood. Many assume the Nephilim appeared during the life of Noah, most likely because of Matthew 24:37 ("as it was in the days of Noah"). That verse, however, described the peak of the violence and damage the Nephilim caused, *not* its beginning. It was *during the life of Adam* not during the life of Noah when men began to multiply and give birth to the women whom the sons of God in Genesis 6 would seduce:

"And the days of Adam after he had begotten Seth were eight hundred years: and he begat sons and daughters…." – Genesis 5:4

The first daughters on Earth were born to Adam and Eve. They were sisters of Cain, Abel, and Seth. This took place centuries before the days of Noah. The timeline of Adam's descendants in Genesis 5 tells us that Adam, who died at 930 years old, lived to see seven generations of the Messianic bloodline. In fact, Adam was alive for more than 50 years of the life of Lamech, Noah's father. With the extended lifespans of the pre-Flood world, a husband and wife could conceive dozens of children, allowing for rapid population expansion.

This was the same period during which Cain committed the first murder and was banished:

*"And in process of time it came to pass,* that Cain brought of the fruit of the ground an offering unto the LORD." – Genesis 4:3 [emphasis added]

"Behold, thou hast driven me out this day from the face of the earth; and from thy face shall I be hid; and I shall be a fugitive and a vagabond in the earth; *and it shall come to pass*, that every one that findeth me shall slay me." – Genesis 4:14 [emphasis added]

*"And it came to pass,* when men began to multiply on the face of the earth, and daughters were born unto them." – Genesis 6:1 [emphasis added]

We are not told how old Cain was when he murdered Abel. But, Cain was well aware that there were other people on Earth besides just him and his parents – namely his siblings, nieces, and nephews who could come looking for him to avenge Abel's death. The phrase "come to pass" refers to the days of Adam and Cain, not to the days of Noah. **This is the time period when daughters were first born to men**. Thus, when Genesis 6:4 speaks of giants "in those days and after that" it is referring to the days of the daughters born of Adam all the way forward to the time of Noah. Many assume "and after that" refers to the time *before and after the Flood*, but that conclusion overlooks both the timing established in Genesis 6:1 and the grammatical and textual fact that the Flood had not yet been mentioned. Thus, the "that" in "after that" could not be a reference to the Flood. No angels took women as wives *after* the Flood. But, for several generations *before the Flood*, they indeed partook of this illicit relationship.

# GENESIS 6:2 –
# WERE THE "SONS OF GOD" REALLY ANGELS?

"That the sons of God saw the daughters of men that they were fair; and they took them wives of all which they chose." – Genesis 6:2

Were the "sons of God" angels or just normal human men? Continuing our verse-by-verse analysis of Genesis 6, we find that the Bible again confirms sexual relations between angels and humans. Rather than admitting the literal meaning, however, many use this verse as evidence that Nephilim never existed, arguing that "sons of God" were just godly human men. The Hebrew words for the "sons of God," however, are *B'nai ha Elohim*, a term used in Scripture exclusively of heavenly beings. The offspring of these mysterious sons of God and daughters of men were "mighty men" of "renown." They were also "giants" (Genesis 6:4). Something in their genetic make-up rendered the children born of this union larger and more powerful than average humans – and that "something" was their fallen angelic parentage.

Examining the use of the term *Elohim* in Scripture from a linguistic perspective leads to the same conclusion. Dr. Michael S. Heiser, adjunct Professor of Biblical Studies at Liberty University, who holds a PhD in Hebrew and Semitic studies, writes:

> "All beings called Elohim in the Hebrew Bible share a certain characteristic: they all inhabit the non – human realm. By nature, Elohim are not part of the world of humankind, the world of ordinary embodiment. Elohim – as a term – indicates residence, not a set of attributes; it identifies the proper domain of the entity it describes. Yahweh, the lesser gods of His council, angels, demons, and the disembodied dead all inhabit the spiritual world. They may cross over into the human world – as the Bible informs us – and certain humans may be transported to the non-human realm (e.g., prophets; Enoch). But the proper domains of each are two separate and distinct places." – The Divine Council, Dr. Michael Heiser. http://www.thedivinecouncil.com/ElohimAsGodsFSB.pdf

# SCRIPTURE CONFIRMS THE
# SONS OF GOD WERE ANGELS

The Bible is self-confirming, and one passage of Scripture can always be explained by another. The book of Job further confirms that the term "sons of God" refers to angels:

> "Now there was a day when the sons of God came to present themselves before the LORD, and Satan came also among them. And the LORD said unto Satan, Whence comest thou? Then Satan answered the LORD, and said, From going to and fro in the earth, and from walking up and down in it." – Job 1:6–7

This passage details God's literal meeting with the sons of God in Heaven. This is, to use a term popularized by Dr. Heiser, a "Divine Council" in which God presides over an assembly of holy and fallen angels to discuss worldly affairs, grant permission to carry out certain actions in the human realm, or assign various tasks.

Job 2 describes another Divine Council:

> "Again there was a day when the sons of God [*b'nai ha elohim*] came to present themselves before the LORD, and Satan came also among them to present himself before the LORD." – Job 2:1

From the clear reading of the text, the "sons of God" are not human men but in fact angels, who were meeting with the Lord in Heaven. The third reference to the sons of God in the Old Testament is also in the book of Job, in chapter 38. When God was posing questions to Job about the creation of the universe (to show Job how little understanding and knowledge he had compared to the Lord), He proclaimed:

"Where wast thou when I laid the foundations of the earth? declare, if thou hast understanding. Who hath laid the measures thereof, if thou knowest? or who hath stretched the line upon it? Whereupon are the foundations thereof fastened? or who laid the corner stone thereof; When the morning stars sang together, and all the sons of God [*b'nai ha Elohim*] shouted for joy?" – Job 38:4–7

Thus, the sons of God were not only in the presence of the Lord but existed even before the earth itself was created. Every use of the term *b'nai ha Elohim* in the Old Testament refers to angelic beings. The use of the phrase in the New Testament (which was written in Greek) has the same meaning.

## CHRISTIANS WILL ULTIMATELY BECOME "SONS OF GOD"

"Behold, what manner of love the Father hath bestowed upon us, that we should be called the sons of God: therefore the world knoweth us not, because it knew him not. Beloved, **now are we the sons of God,** and it doth not yet appear what we shall be: but we know that, when he shall appear, we shall be like him; for we shall see him as he is." – 1 John 3:1–2

Although a born-again Christian receives a new spirit from God at the moment of salvation, the body, with its sinful nature, remains. At the Rapture, all Christians receive glorified, heavenly bodies and thus become "sons of God." This is what the Apostle John explained in the verses above. Note that the passage is forward-looking. In the future, Christians will be fully born of the heavenly realm in body and spirit and thus equal to the angels (Matthew 22:30). This "translation" also allows Christians to see Jesus in His true glorified divine state, which humans today generally cannot do and the prophets of old were given only glimpses of.

So, in all contexts the term "sons of God" is clearly referring to angels. The notion of angels' taking human wives poses a big hurdle for many. But we should never fear a literal reading of the Word of God, which is our foundation. Within this context, one ought leave behind whatever presuppositions he may bring to the Bible and let the text and its corresponding passages speak for themselves. Angels from Heaven married human women and produced children with them.

## ANGELS LUSTED FOR HUMAN WOMEN

"… saw that they were fair and they took them wives of all which they chose." – Genesis 6:2

The book of Jude provides one of a handful of principal passages on the angelic seduction of human women and birth of the Nephilim:

"And the angels which kept not their first estate, but left their own habitation, he hath reserved in everlasting chains under darkness unto the judgment of the great day. Even as Sodom and Gomorrah, and the cities about them in like manner, giving themselves over to fornication, and going after strange flesh, are set forth for an example, suffering the vengeance of eternal fire." – Jude 1:6–7

Sinful lust led the once-holy sons of God to leave their heavenly position in service to the Lord and enter the earthly realm to interact directly with humanity and take human wives. The passage in Jude likens the desire for "strange flesh" to the homosexual fornication of Sodom and Gomorrah (interestingly, the men of Sodom *also wanted to have intimate relations with angels*) (Genesis 19:5).

2 Peter 2 is the second principal passage that describes the angelic-human illicit relations:

"For if God spared not the angels that sinned, but cast them down to hell, and delivered them into chains of darkness, to be reserved unto judgment; And spared not the old world, but saved Noah the eighth person, a preacher of righteousness, bringing in the flood upon the world of the ungodly; And turning the cities of Sodom and Gomorrha into ashes condemned them with an overthrow, making them an ensample unto those that after should live ungodly; And delivered just Lot, vexed with the filthy conversation of the wicked: (For that righteous man dwelling among them, in seeing and hearing, vexed his righteous soul from day to day with their unlawful deeds;) the Lord knoweth how to deliver the godly out of temptations, and to reserve the unjust unto the day of judgment to be punished...." – 2 Peter 2:4–9

In 1841, a highly-regarded Christian theologian wrote of the angelic fornication described in Jude and 2 Peter 2:

"This passage again holds us up the united instances of the impurity of the angels and of Sodom, and the example of their punishment, as a terror to all who should be inclined to act as they. He [Peter] also brings the angels' fall in juxtaposition with the flood, thus confirming us in the belief that they were nearly cotemporaneous events; – no light corroboration of the preceding comment. That he speaks of the same persons as St Jude, is clear from the remarkable parallelisms throughout, especially the words describing their punishment in 'chains of darkness' and its duration, until the judgment of the great day: while both Jude and Peter unite together as being of similar crimes and similar in their recompence, the angels, and the cities of the plain." – *Isaiah Unfulfilled: Being an Exposition of the Prophet, with New Version and Critical Notes*, Robert Govett, 1841, p. 349.

A very basic analysis of the Bible confirms that the sons of God were indeed angels who took human wives in an act of extreme rebellion against God. Recall that in the Garden the Lord prophesied that Satan also had a seed (Genesis 3:15). Thus, through the angelic invasion of Genesis 6, Satan sought to create his own bloodline to bring about humanity's destruction.

Satan did this by providing a system of temptation. For the once-righteous sons of God sexual pleasure was the bait to ensnare them in iniquity. These angels observed human beings – inferior to them in all respects – enjoying marital bliss and intimacy in ways angels were not permitted to (Matthew 22:30). This prohibition coupled with the sight of beautiful human women provoked lustful desires in the sinning angels. And that moral weakness was all the Devil needed to provoke a faction of the holy ones to fall into rebellion against the Lord God Almighty. This was a second angelic rebellion that took place well after the Devil's initial revolt against the Lord, which predated the creation of humanity. The Genesis 6 invaders were a fraction of the rebel angelic army who report to the Devil. Robert Govett affirmed this notion in his commentary:

> "Upon the supposition that the apostle is referring to the fallen angels in general, which is the notion generally entertained, how does the apostle's commentary agree with the fact on which he is commenting? Let us suppose that he is speaking of the general fall of the angels in the time of Satan's revolt. To these no pardon has been offered, no mercy shown. How then is the fact that God 'spared not angels' when taken by itself, (as an event which on this theory occurred hundreds, perhaps thousands of years before the flood,) a proof that God knows how to save as well as to destroy? For on this supposition three instances are given of mingled justice and mercy: in two of them this is apparent the destruction of the old world in justice; the saving of Noah and his family in mercy: the destruction of the cities of the plain in justice the sparing Lot and his daughters in mercy." – Ibid, p. 350.

# THE SETHITE VIEW – WERE THE SONS OF GOD HUMAN DESCENDANTS OF SETH?

The most popular theory opposing the idea that angelic beings came to Earth and took human wives holds that the "sons of God" were descendants of Seth, Adam and Eve's third son. In short, the "Sethite view," as it has come to be known, argues that the godly descendants of Seth married the sinful daughters of Cain and bore the Nephilim (who were not giants but very sinful, combative men). In addition to the biblical confirmation that the sons of God were angels (as we saw earlier), for several very clear reasons this notion does *not* work with the biblical narrative.

1) The Bible never identifies the lineage of Seth as "the sons of God" nor Cain's daughters as "the daughters of men." The Sethite view reads this connection into the text with no warrant.

2) The Scriptures provide a detailed lineage of Cain, and there is no mention of any of Seth's sons marrying into Cain's family. In fact, we are told that Noah, a descendant of Seth, was "perfect in his generations," and thus his lineage would not have had illicit genetic intermingling (Genesis 6:9).

3) The Sethite theory does not explain why the union of Seth's good sons and Cain's bad daughters would lead to giants being born and the entire earth becoming corrupt. If that were the case, then any Christian today who married an unbeliever could give birth to a giant. Nor does it explain what the passage from Jude is referring to when it says that certain angels went after "strange flesh" for the purpose of fornication and were subsequently imprisoned (Jude 1:6). This is perhaps the most glaring oversight of this view.

# CHURCH FATHERS BELIEVED
# THE SONS OF GOD WERE ANGELS

When we examine the writings of church fathers and other Christians of the first through third centuries, it is clear that the early church interpreted "the sons of God" of Genesis 6:2 as angels who took human wives and conceived children with them.

Irenaeus (c. early 2nd century – c. 202 AD) was the bishop or pastor of the church in what is now Lyons, France. He was a disciple of Polycarp, who was a disciple of the Apostle John. His treatise *Against Heresies* was a landmark work that challenged the heretical Gnostic Christianity that threatened the true faith at that time. On Genesis 6:2 he wrote:

> "And for a very long while wickedness extended and spread, and reached and laid hold upon the whole race of mankind, until a very small seed of righteousness remained among them and illicit unions took place upon the earth, since angels were united with the daughters of the race of mankind; and they bore to them sons who for their exceeding greatness were called giants." – *A Discourse in the Demonstration of Apostolic Preaching*, 18., as quoted in *St. Irenaeus The Demonstration Of The Apostolic Preaching,* Translated by J. Armitage Robinson, D.D., 1920, p. 85-86.

Athenagoras of Athens (c. 133 – 190 AD) was a Greek Christian apologist who wrote treatises on many topics regarding the Christian faith and defended it against Greek philosophy and religion. With respect to Genesis 6:2 he wrote:

> "Just as with men, who have freedom of choice as to both virtue and vice (for you would not either honour the good or punish the bad, unless vice and virtue were in their own power; and some are

diligent in the matters entrusted to them by you, and others faithless), so is it among the angels. Some, free agents, you will observe, such as they were created by God, continued in those things for which God had made and over which He had ordained them; but some outraged both the constitution of their nature and the government entrusted to them: namely, this ruler of matter and its various forms, and others of those who were placed about this first firmament (you know that we say nothing without witnesses, but state the things which have been declared by the prophets); these fell into impure love of virgins, and were subjugated by the flesh, and he became negligent and wicked in the management of the things entrusted to him. Of these lovers of virgins, therefore, were begotten those who are called giants." – *A Plea for the Christians*, Chapter 24, as quoted in *The Anti-Nicene Fathers: Translations of the Writings of the Fathers Down to AD 325*, Vol. II, translated by Rev. Alexander Roberts, D.D., James Donaldson, L.D., 1867, p. 406.

Justin Martyr (c. 100 – c. 165 AD) was an early Christian apologist. He was killed along with his students, and his surname became the term used for those who die for the Christian faith. He also wrote a commentary on the sons of God and the daughters of men:

"God, when He had made the whole world, and subjected things earthly to man, and arranged the heavenly elements for the increase of fruits and rotation of the seasons, and appointed this divine law – for these things also He evidently made for man – committed the care of men and of all things under heaven to angels whom He appointed over them. But the angels transgressed this appointment. and were captivated by love of women." – *Second Apology*, Chapter V, as quoted in *ibid*, p. 75-76.

Commodian was a Christian poet who lived in the third century AD. A convert to the faith late in life, he spent his elder years trying to instruct other lost souls on the Christian faith. He recorded this commentary on Genesis 6:

> "When Almighty God, to beautify the nature of the world, willed that that earth should be visited by angels, when they were sent down they despised His laws. Such was the beauty of women, that it turned them aside; so that, being contaminated, they could not return to heaven. Rebels from God, they uttered words against Him. Then the Highest uttered His judgment against them; and from their seed giants are said to have been born." – *Instructions of Commodianus in Favour of Christian Discipline. Against the Gods of the Heathens*; III., as quoted in *The Anti-Nicene Fathers: Translations of the Writings of the Fathers Down to AD 325*, Vol. IV, Rev. Alexander Roberts, D.D., James Donaldson, L.D., 1905, p. 203.

Clement of Rome (c. 35 - c. 99 AD) was a Christian bishop in Rome in the first century and was a contemporary of the Apostle John. His epistle to the Corinthian church is one of the oldest extant Christian writings outside of the New Testament. The Clementine Homilies are a series of writings from the 2nd and 3rd century purporting to record dialogue between Clement and the Apostle Peter. While its authorship may have not been from Clement, its details on the Nephilim again demonstrate that this concept was well established in the early church:

> "For of the spirits who inhabit the heaven, the angels who dwell in the lowest region, being grieved at the ingratitude of men to God, asked that they might come into the life of men, that, really becoming men, by more intercourse they might convict those who had acted ungratefully towards Him, and might subject every one to adequate punishment. When, therefore, their petition was

granted, they metamorphosed themselves into every nature; for, being of a more godlike substance, they are able easily to assume any form…yet having become in all respects men, they also partook of human lust, and being brought under its subjection they fell into cohabitation with women; and being involved with them, and sunk in defilement and altogether emptied of their first power, were unable to turn back to the first purity of their proper nature… But from their unhallowed intercourse spurious men sprang, much greater in stature than *ordinary* men, whom they afterwards called giants; not those dragon-footed giants who waged war against God, as those blasphemous myths of the Greeks do sing, but wild in manners, and greater than men in size, inasmuch as they were sprung of angels; yet less than angels, as they were born of women."
- Clementine Homilies, Homily VIII, Chapter XIII, As printed in *The Ante-Nicene Library, Translations of the Writings of the Fathers Down to A.D. 325*, Vol. XVII, Edited by Rev. Alexander Roberts and James Donaldson, LLD, 1870, p.142-144.

Tertullian (155 – 240 AD) was an African Christian theologian from the Roman province of Carthage. He was a prolific writer and his works are the foundation of Christian thought in the language of Latin. Outside of the Bible itself, he is the earliest believer on record to write about the concept of the trinity. On the Genesis 6 incursion he wrote:

"We are instructed, moreover, by our sacred books how from certain angels, who fell of their own free-will, there sprang a more wicked demon-brood, condemned of God along with the authors of their race, and that chief we have referred to. It will for the present be enough, however, that some account is given of their work. Their great business is the ruin of mankind. So, from the very first, spiritual wickedness sought our destruction. They inflict, accordingly, upon our bodies diseases and other grievous calamities, while by violent assaults they hurry the soul into sudden and extraordinary excesses." – *The Apology of Tertullian for the Christians*, translated by T. Herbert Bindley, M.A., Merton College Oxford, 1890, p. 75.

Sulpicius Severus (c. 363 – c. 425 AD) was a Chrsitian author and native of what is today France. His writings on the Old Testament were so well-regarded that over 1,000 years later they were used as textbooks at schools in Europe. A believer in the truth of angelic-human marriages in the days of Noah he wrote:

> "When by this time the human race had increased to a great multitude, certain angels, whose habitation was in heaven, were captivated by the appearance of some beautiful virgins, and cherished illicit desires after them, so much so, that falling beneath their own proper nature and origin, they left the higher regions of which they were inhabitants, and allied themselves in earthly marriages. These angels gradually spreading wicked habits, corrupted the human family, and from their alliance giants are said to have sprung, for the mixture with them of beings of a different nature, as a matter of course, gave birth to monsters." – *Chronicle*, Ch. 2, Sulpicius Severus, as printed in *A Select Library of the Nicene and Post Nicene Fathers*, Second Series, Vol. XI, translated by Philip Schaff, D.D., LL.D., and Henry Wace, D.D., The Christian Literature Company, 1894, p. 71-72.

In early church writings dating back to the days of the apostles the interpretation of Genesis 6:2 was that evil angels married human woman and produced children with them. Although this may seem like a bizarre and stunning conclusion, Scripture strongly supports it. And Moses, writing under inspiration of the Holy Spirit, also indicated exactly *who* were the first humans with whom this ungodly union took place.

# CHAPTER 4

# THE FIRST FAMILY OF THE NEPHILIM

A careful examination of the precious few verses on Cain's lineage reveals their connection to the birth of the Nephilim. Banished from the presence of God, Cain continued a life of wickedness and revolt against the Lord. His descendants, living in exile from believers and raised to seek worldly pleasure, were the perfect targets for the angelic invasion of Genesis 6.

> "And Cain went out from the presence of the LORD, and dwelt in the land of Nod, on the east of Eden." – Genesis 4:16

When Cain's parents (Adam and Eve) were punished, they left the Garden and took residence east of the Garden. After God banished him, Cain left the "presence of the Lord" altogether. God manifested His presence in specific locations in the pre-Flood world. He still appeared in Eden after the Fall of Adam and Eve. Cain and Abel knew the location at which to make sacrifices before God where God would appear to accept or reject them (Genesis 4:3–4). The Lord never abandons humanity. Only man's willful rejection of God's mercy leads to the ultimate separation between a sinner and God.

Cain ignored the Creator's loving reprimand regarding his offering. He killed Abel in jealous rage and then lied to God when questioned. He showed no remorse or repentance for murdering his own brother. He was a reprobate, and thus God separated him from the rest of the godly line that was to be continued through Seth. Cain moved farther east of Eden to a land that would become known as Nod, or *Nowd* in Hebrew, which means "wandering." The region was named for Cain, the first fugitive and wanderer of the earth. There he established the first family that would fall prey to angelic seduction.

## A FAMILY FOCUSED ON WORLDLY SUCCESS AND PLEASURES

"And Cain knew his wife; and she conceived, and bare Enoch: and he builded a city, and called the name of the city, after the name of his son, Enoch." – Genesis 4:17

Cain's wife was one of his sisters, a daughter of Abel, or a niece from another sibling. No other conclusions hold any logical weight. Also of note is that Cain was the *inventor of cities* (Genesis 4:17). Cities in the early part of Earth's history were centers of sinful rebellion. As we will discuss in more detail later, the first cities after the Flood were built by Nimrod, an infamous biblical tyrant and leader of the Tower of Babel rebellion. His wickedness is revealed in the stated goal of the coalition of rebels who planned the tower's construction:

"And they said, Go to, let us build us a city and a tower, whose top may reach unto heaven; and let us make us a name, lest we be scattered abroad upon the face of the whole earth." – Genesis 11:4

The goal of these schemers was not just to make a tower but "*a city* and a tower." They intended the Tower of Babel to be a metropolis that encompassed all or most of the world's inhabitants.

The next cities mentioned in Scripture are Sodom and Gomorrah, which were the gold standard of sinful wickedness in Scripture. In keeping with his selfish nature Cain named the first city after his son Enoch (who should not be confused with the righteous Enoch, the son of Jared, who was the seventh generation from Adam in the Messianic bloodline). Enoch means "dedicated," and the eldest son of Cain was dedicated to the sinful ways of the world. Rather than honoring God in naming the first city ever built, Cain honored his own lineage. Psalm 49 captures the depraved spiritual state of men like Cain:

> "They that trust in their wealth, and boast themselves in the multitude of their riches; None of them can by any means redeem his brother, nor give to God a ransom for him: (For the redemption of their soul is precious, and it ceaseth for ever:) That he should still live for ever, and not see corruption. For he seeth that wise men die, likewise the fool and the brutish person perish, and leave their wealth to others. Their inward thought is, that their houses shall continue for ever, and their dwelling places to all generations; **they call their lands after their own names**. Nevertheless man being in honour abideth not: he is like the beasts that perish. This their way is their folly: yet their posterity approve their sayings. Selah." – Psalm 49:6–13

## THE PERFECT TARGET FOR THE DEVIL

In arrogance, Cain used his city to celebrate his own bloodline. The name Enoch would later become synonymous with the word "city" in ancient Sumerian culture, and the term *unug* or *uruk* is often cited as the oldest Sumerian city. The Hebrew "n" is equivalent to the Sumerian "r," and after the Flood Nimrod, in the tradition of sinful rebels, would build a "New Erech" (Genesis 10:10). None of this sinful self-exaltation was lost on Satan of course. Cain's lineage was full of children born outside of God's presence and influence in Eden – children raised by Cain, a brazen rebel who had no faith. Cain's descendants were the perfect place for Satan to launch the next offensive in his plan to thwart the coming Seed of the Woman.

## LAMECH'S CORRUPTION OF MARRIAGE TEMPTED ANGELS TO FOLLOW SUIT

A literal reading of Scripture points to Cain's descendant Lamech and his immediate family as the first humans to interact and interbreed with the fallen angels who invaded Earth and fathered the antediluvian Nephilim:

> "And *Lamech took unto him two wives*: the name of the one was Adah, and the name of the other Zillah." – Genesis 4:19

> "That the sons of God saw the daughters of men that they were fair; and *they took them wives* of all which they chose." – Genesis 6:2

A renowned 18th-century sermon confirmed that the descendants of Cain were the first humans the angels mingled with:

> "The fall of the Angels here alluded to losing them their first [estate] could not be their Pride and Ambition. That was aspiring above them. This is rather described as a degeneracy and falling short of the dignity and excellency of their Nature which was exactly this ignoble sort of Marriages **whereby they mingled this Holy Seed of God with the unholy Posterity of the piacular Cain**." – *A Sermon Preach'd at Chester: Against Marriages in Different Communions*, Charles Leslie, Henry Dodwell, Printed by W.B. for Char. Brome at the West End of St. Paul's, 1702, p. 165.

# THE BIBLE USES SPECIAL REFERENCES TO HIGHLIGHT THE MOST NOTORIOUS FIGURES IN ITS HISTORY

Genesis 4:19 begins an important trend in Scripture. In recording a lineage, Moses, through inspiration of the Holy Spirit, occasionally recorded greater detail about certain infamous people whose wickedness would be well-known to ancient Israelite readers. Genesis 4:17–18 chronicles six generations of Cain's descendants in just two verses, listing the name of one patriarch "begetting" the next. Yet, when the genealogy reaches Lamech, *six full verses are devoted to discussing this one man* (Genesis 4:18–24). Lamech is the first of several nefarious biblical figures who received this exceptional level of detail.

In the spirit of his forefather Cain, Lamech's life was one of open rebellion against God. He was the first polygamist on record in Scripture, violating the Lord's decree that defined marriage as one man and one woman joined for life. This sin was an important point in history. The Lord previously issued severe punishment to Adam, Eve, and the Serpent for violating His commands. Cain was banished from Eden for murdering Abel. So, what would happen to Lamech for his transgression of the marital law?

In the Garden of Eden God established that in marriage one husband and one wife "shall be one flesh." Lamech took two wives in flagrant violation of the Lord's design for wedlock. Richard Watson, a 19th-century theologian who wrote one of the more comprehensive extant biblical dictionaries, provided an apt description of the rebellious Lamech:

> "He stands branded as the father of polygamy, the man who first dared violate the sacred command, Gen. ii. 24; giving way to his unbridled passion, and thus overleaping the divine mound raised by the wisdom of our Great Creator; which restraint is enforced by the laws of nature herself, who peoples the earth with equal

amounts of males and females, and thereby teaches foolish man that polygamy is incompatible with her regulations." – *A Biblical and Theological Dictionary: Explanatory of the History, Manners, and Customs of the Jews, and Neighboring Nations,* Richard Watson, Published by B. Waugh and T. Mason, 1833, p. 567.

For all humanity and the angelic world who were witnessing these events unfold, it was a time to see what would become of Lamech for his sinful behavior. Would God curse Lamech as He had Cain? Would He force Lamech to abandon his two wives? But instead of a thunderous pronouncement of judgment from the Most High, there was silence. Lamech received no immediate punishment for his polygamy. Nor did God visit or speak with Lamech after his brazen act of evil.

Lamech's polygamy was the first description of a person's *taking wives* unto oneself ("Lamech *took two wives* unto himself"). The next occurrence of this phrase referred to the sons of God who "*took them wives* of all which they chose" leading to the birth of the Nephilim (Genesis 6:2). Could Lamech's first violation of God's rules for marriage (which went unpunished) have been a part of the inspiration for the sinning angels? A 19th-century expositor supported this notion:

"The corruption of marriage as it was one of the earliest devices so was it a master work of Satan's. For in thus changing the divine law he directly struck at the hope of redemption which is so affectingly emblematized in the mystery of wedlock." – *Messias and Antimessias: A Prophetical Exposition,* Charles Ingham Black, Printed in London: Masters, 1853, p. 22.

# THE FIRST FAMILY'S DEAL WITH THE DEVIL

The Bible confirms that angels observe human affairs (1 Peter 1:12; 1 Corinthians 4:9). Also, certain angels are sent to monitor specific people (Matthew 18:10; Daniel 4:17). Seeing the unpunished sin of Lamech, combined with the allure of his daughter, could have served as the provocation for the sons of God to enter the human realm. They then offered divine knowledge in exchange for the first human bride of an angel – an attenuated version of Satan's original offer of hidden divine secrets to Eve. It is no coincidence that during the time of Lamech's marriage and childbearing humans made *enormous technological advances*:

> "And Lamech took unto him two wives: the name of the one was Adah, and the name of the other Zillah. And Adah bare Jabal: **he was the father of such as dwell in tents, and of such as have cattle.** And his brother's name was Jubal: **he was the father of all such as handle the harp and organ.** And Zillah, she also bare Tubalcain, **an instructer of every artificer in brass and iron**: and the sister of Tubalcain was Naamah." – Genesis 4:19–22

Lamech's son Jabal introduced tent dwelling and cattle grazing. His brother Jubal was the inventor of musical instruments. And Tubal-Cain was the Creator of metal works, such as tools and weapons. The name Tubal-Cain means "thou will be brought of Cain." This choice of name demonstrates Lamech's fierce loyalty and admiration of Cain. Lamech was a rebel against the Lord and had no fear of God. Psalm 36 speaks of people caught in such a deluded sinful state:

> "The transgression of the wicked saith within my heart, that there is no fear of God before his eyes. For he flattereth himself in his own eyes, until his iniquity be found to be hateful. The words of his mouth are iniquity and deceit: he hath left off to be wise, and

to do good. He deviseth mischief upon his bed; he setteth himself
in a way that is not good; he abhorreth not evil." – Psalm 36:1–4

Thinking oneself beyond God's judgment is a dangerous move. God's grace
and longsuffering are not to be taken for granted. Lamech thought he was
immune to God's wrath but was soon overwhelmed by a judgment beyond
his imagination. The book of Jude says this of false teachers who infiltrate the
church with heresy: "Woe unto them! for they have *gone in the way of Cain*"
(Jude 1:11). The way of Cain was one of trying to receive the Lord's blessings
without honoring Him. Those who were of Cain lived with jealousy and
hatred of faithful believers to the point of murder. The way of Cain embodied
a bold disregard for God's authority and wrath. Hence Lamech's naming his
son after the rebel patriarch and the first murderer of humanity. Lamech's
sinful boast to his wives recorded in Genesis 4 reflected both his callous
rejection of God's laws and his ancient artistic influence:

"And Lamech said unto his wives,
Adah and Zillah, Hear my voice;
ye wives of Lamech, hearken unto my speech:
for I have slain a man to my wounding,
and a young man to my hurt.
If Cain shall be avenged sevenfold,
truly Lamech seventy and sevenfold." – Genesis 4:23–24

The passage was laid out in this fashion to show that it is Hebrew poetry, a style
employed in various parts of Scripture. This was most likely a part of a greater
song Lamech composed to boast of his exploits in killing a man. This is the first
use of Hebrew poetry in the Bible – and it was done in the name of prideful,
human-centered justice. *Matthew Henry's Commentary* on this passage states:

"One of Cain's wicked race is the first recorded, as having broken
the law of marriage. Hitherto, one man had but one wife at a time;

but Lamech took two. Worldly things, are the only things that carnal, wicked people set their hearts upon, and are most clever and industrious about. So it was with this race of Cain. Here was a father of shepherds, and a father of musicians, but not a father of the faithful. Here is one to teach about brass and iron, but none to teach the good knowledge of the Lord: here are devices how to be rich, and how to be mighty, and how to be merry; but nothing of God, of his fear and service. Present things fill the heads of most. Lamech had enemies, whom he had provoked. He draws a comparison betwixt himself and his ancestor Cain; and flatters himself that he is much less criminal. **He seems to abuse the patience of God in sparing Cain, into an encouragement to expect that he may sin unpunished.**"

– http://biblehub.com/commentaries/genesis/4-23.htm

Lamech's arrogant poem reveled in admiration of Cain and Lamech's belief that his sin would also go without judgment. He was the first person on record not to be punished immediately for his sin. "Because sentence against an evil work is not executed speedily, therefore the heart of the sons of men is fully set in them to do evil" (Ecclesiastes 8:11). Though Lamech was a polygamist and murderer, God did not come looking for him as he had for Adam, Eve, the Serpent, and Cain. No sentence was pronounced. For all intents and purposes, Lamech appeared to have gotten away with his crimes (and certainly his boastful poem reinforced his delusion). Rather than give his Creator thanks for being spared a curse for his sin, his desire for iniquity only increased. Like Cain, he abused the common grace of God, the general time of probation God allows all people to repent despite their sinful acts: "the Lord is not slack concerning his promise, as some men count slackness; but is longsuffering to us-ward, not willing that any should perish, but that all should come to repentance" (2 Peter 3:9). Right after Lamech's polygamy, his family became inventors of art and science courtesy of the apostate sons of God.

## NAAMAH – MOTHER OF THE NEPHILIM

Genesis 4 describes Tubal-Cain's sister, Naamah: "…and the sister of Tubalcain was Naamah" (Genesis 4:22). Naamah was the second person in the Bible to receive a special reference in a lineage. Almost all genealogies in the Bible list only men. Naamah is *one of only four women mentioned by name* in the 1,656-year pre-Flood history of the Bible.[1] The others are Eve and Naamah's mother, Zillah, and her aunt/step-mother, Adah. Clearly the women in this family were of extreme historical importance to be named in Scripture. Hundreds if not thousands of women were born before Naamah. Yet, curiously Moses only mentioned her and the other women in her immediate family. An 18th-century Christian academic wrote of Naamah:

> "Moses seems to refer to some things that happened near the beginning of the world, as well-known in his time, as in Gen. iv. 22. where he says 'The Sister of Tubal-Cain was Naamah:' For no probable account can be given, why Naamah should be mentioned, but because her name was then well known among the Israelites, for some reason which it does not concern us to be acquainted with, but which served to confirm to them the rest of the Relation. Some have delivered that Naamah, by her beauty, enticed the Sons of God, or the Posterity of Seth, to commit idolatry (Genesis 6:2)." – *The Reasonableness and Certainty of the Christian Religion*, Volume 1, 5th Edition, Professor Robert Jenkin, 1721, p. 37.

While Jenkin subscribed to the Sethite view, he nevertheless connects Naamah to the Nephilim of Genesis 6. Naamah in Hebrew means "beauty." The beauty of the daughters of men is what served as the sinful temptation for the angels who sinned in the first place. They *saw* that the women were fair (Genesis 6:2). An article from a 19th century Christian publication came to a similar conclusion:

"He had also a daughter Naamah, who was beautiful, but she was not to be the mother of the promised seed, but rather the fountain whence sprang much of that fairness among the daughters of men, which not long after tempted the angels to "go after strange flesh" and brought on their defection from God and the fearful corruption of the world before the Flood."– *Satan's Parody of God's Kingdom*, as printed in The Rainbow, a Magazine of Christian Literature, Vol. XX, 1883, p. 438.

Namaah's brothers were all inventors in arts and sciences. This family experienced an intellectual explosion that is easily explained if heavenly beings delivered this knowledge as compensation for Naamah's becoming the first wife of an angel and first mother of the Nephilim.

## DIVINE TECHNOLOGY
## IN EXCHANGE FOR A HUMAN WIFE

"Seeing that in old time the parents and brothers claimed the right to dispose of their maidens, the brief statement that "The sons of God saw the daughters of men, that they were fair, and they took them wives of all which they chose," carries in it the conception that the consent of the families of men had been fully secured to those strange marriages." – *id.*, p. 439.

The apocryphal Book of Enoch is often cited for its passage in which sinning angels teach humanity various trades, arts, and occult practices:

"Moreover Azazyel taught men to make swords, knives, shields, breastplates, the fabrication of mirrors, and the workmanship of bracelets and ornaments…." – Book of Enoch 8:1

In the family of Cain, the angels who sinned found willing participants in their plan to violate God's prohibition on angelic marriage. Moses made yet another special reference in recording the genealogy of Lamech's sons. In the lineage of the patriarchs in Genesis 4 and 5 typically only one son from each generation is mentioned. In Lamech's generation *all three of his sons are listed*:

> "And Adah bare Jabal: he was the father of such as dwell in tents, and of such as have cattle. And his brother's name was Jubal: he was the father of all such as handle the harp and organ. And Zillah, she also bare Tubalcain, an instructer of every artificer in brass and iron: and the sister of Tubalcain was Naamah." – Genesis 4:20–22

The innovations from this rebel family are astounding. Jabal invented the nomadic herder lifestyle (raising cattle while living in tents) that many ancient biblical figures employed for several thousand years. Generations later we learn that Noah "was uncovered **within his tent**" (Genesis 9:21). Of Abraham it is said: "And the Lord appeared unto him in the plains of Mamre: **and he sat in the tent door in the heat of the day**" (Genesis 18:1). We know from Scripture that some form of raising sheep existed well before these three sons of Lamech were born. Abel, the second son of Adam, was a shepherd. So Jabal, father of "…such as have cattle," most likely invented a superior method of mass-herding. This of course would lead to commercial success.

Jubal was the "father" of music – not just the inventor of music but the instruction of music. His name became the Hebrew root for "trumpet." The Jubilee year, a semi-centennial musical celebration on the ancient Jewish calendar, shares the same name as this man. The notion that Lamech's sons were gatekeepers of angelic knowledge that they then disbursed in the world is the emphasis in the brief biblical history of this family. As Jabal had mastered a means of keeping wealth in the family, Jubal created entertainment – a mainstay for those whose chief goals in life are financial success and earthly desires. The prophet Job reflected on this:

> "Wherefore do the wicked live, become old, yea, are mighty in power? Their seed is established in their sight with them, and their offspring before their eyes. Their houses are safe from fear, neither is the rod of God upon them. **Their bull gendereth, and faileth not; their cow calveth, and casteth not her calf. They send forth their little ones like a flock, and their children dance. They take the timbrel and harp, and rejoice at the sound of the organ.** They spend their days in wealth, and in a moment go down to the grave. Therefore they say unto God, Depart from us; for we desire not the knowledge of thy ways. What is the Almighty, that we should serve him? and what profit should we have, if we pray unto him?" – Job 21:7–15

Luxurious, sensual living is an easy avenue to forgetting the Word of God. And this family was accelerating this descent into rebellion for all human society. Job describes this by referring to both abundant cattle (mastered by Jabal) and the enjoyment of instruments (two of which Jubal invented). Cain's descendants relished their earthly knowledge while rejecting the Word of God. James 3 states: "This wisdom descendeth not from above, but is earthly, sensual, devilish." And Lamech's third son brought this sensual, devilish pursuits of this family to another level entirely:

## "... TUBALCAIN, AN INSTRUCTER OF EVERY ARTIFICER IN BRASS AND IRON"

Tubal-Cain was the first teacher of metallurgy – the manipulation of metals through fire to forge weapons and tools.

> "The wicked, through the pride of his countenance, will not seek after God: God is not in all his thoughts." – Psalm 10:4

Tubal-Cain, who has taken on mythic status in the occult (his name is a password used in Freemasonry, and books of magic are dedicated to his name), was the inventor of blacksmithing. Tools and weapons gave man more confidence in his own might and less reliance on God. And this human arrogance led to Tubal-Cain himself being deified:

> "The smith god, Vulcan of the Greeks and Romans is no other person than Tubal Cain; and their Venus, the wife of Vulcan, is most probably the same as Naamah, the sister of Tubal Cain: for Naamah signifies beauty and gracious, and Venus was the goddess of beauty. The mythology of Vulcan and Venus shows that the origin of the whole matter is the history of Tu-bal Cain and Naamah." – *The Millennial Harbinger: A Monthly Publication Devoted to Primitive Christianity*, Alexander Campbell, New Series – Vol. II, 1838, p. 328.

Tubal-Cain was the son who mastered blacksmithing and taught others his trade. This underscores a major difference between the Bible and the pseudepigraphical texts that discuss the Nephilim: The Bible's emphasis is on God and humanity. It is the revelation of God's plan of redemption and reconciliation of the fallen human race through the sacrifice and resurrection of the Lord Jesus Christ. Apocryphal texts such as the Book of Enoch or Jubilees are devoted mostly to *chronicling angels and their activities.*

## INSTANCES IN THE BIBLE WHERE HUMANS SUPERNATURALLY RECEIVED KNOWLEDGE

Could Tubal-Cain and his brothers have been taught supernatural knowledge by angels? I contend that indeed they were. In the Bible, humans were aware of angelic beings' superior intellect. In 2 Samuel, the woman of Tekoah compared King David's wisdom to that of angels: "Then thine handmaid said, The word of my lord the king shall now be comfortable: *for as an angel of God, so is my lord the king to discern good and bad*: therefore, the LORD thy God will be with thee … my lord is wise, according to the wisdom of an angel of God, to know all things that are in the earth" (2 Samuel 14:17–20). The belief that angels possessed superior intelligence was well-known. If the sinning angels of the pre-Flood world did indeed teach Cain's lineage, it would not be the only time in Scripture that humans were taught via divine intervention. Following the Exodus from Egypt, God appointed certain men under Moses to serve as craftsmen to make the items for worship in the tabernacle:

> "And the LORD spake unto Moses, saying, See, I have called by name Bezaleel the son of Uri, the son of Hur, of the tribe of Judah: **And I have filled him with the spirit of God, in wisdom, and in understanding, and in knowledge, and in all manner of workmanship, To devise cunning works, to work in gold, and in silver, and in brass,** And in cutting of stones, to set them, and in carving of timber, to work in all manner of workmanship. And I, behold, I have given with him Aholiab, the son of Ahisamach, of the tribe of Dan: and **in the hearts of all that are wise hearted I have put wisdom, that they may make all that I have commanded thee**;

> "The tabernacle of the congregation, and the ark of the testimony, and the mercy seat that is thereupon, and all the furniture of the tabernacle, And the table and his furniture, and the pure candlestick with all his furniture, and the altar of incense, And the altar of burnt offering with all his furniture, and the laver and his foot, And the cloths of service, and the holy garments for Aaron the priest, and the garments of his sons, to minister in the priest's office, And the anointing oil, and sweet incense for the holy place: according to all that I have commanded thee shall they do." – Exodus 31:1–11

These craftsmen received divine wisdom and knowledge via the Holy Spirit to construct the tabernacle. God supernaturally endowed these men with intelligence to become expert craftsmen with gold, silver, brass, and wood in "all manner of workmanship." Interestingly, the first skills the Lord gave to a human being involved metalwork – the very craft that Tubal-Cain mastered.

# THE LAST FULLY HUMAN GENERATION IN CAIN'S LINEAGE

The Bible further indicates that Lamech's family was the original humans who interbred with fallen angels, in that, after Jabal, Jubal, Tubal-Cain, and Naamah were born, the record of their lineage abruptly ends. From the timeline provided in Genesis 5, Lamech and his sons lived approximately 700 years before the Flood. And yet after Jabal, Jubal, and Tubal-Cain, we hear nothing further of Cain's lineage. Although Lamech's three sons were all superior innovators and inventors, there is no mention of their children. In fact, the last person mentioned in the Cainite lineage is Naamah.

All signs point to the children of Lamech as *the last generation that was purely human*. If Naamah was the first Nephilim bride and her brothers received angelic knowledge in exchange for their sister's hand in marriage, it stands to reason that the Bible purposely excluded their corrupted, hybrid offspring from mention by name. None of the giants of the antediluvian world are mentioned by name or quoted in Scripture. While we cannot establish conclusively that Lamech and his children were the first to interact with angels and provided the first daughter an apostate angel taken as a wife, Scripture certainly provides some very strong and interesting evidence that this was the case. What we can know conclusively is that, like Lamech, the sinning angels of Genesis 6 wrongfully "took wives" from the human population, which led the Lord to render a cataclysmic judgment.

A commentary on this very question affirms this conclusion:

"Then we are told of another class, children of sons of God and daughters of men; such intermarriage is forbidden under the Mosaic law, and also in the Gospel dispensation; it is a confusion, a Babylon class, and God was displeased. This intermarriage did not take place in Noah's line, 'He was perfect in his generations' it must then have been the daughters of Cain who attracted the sons of God." – *The Sons of God and Their Inheritance*, Emma J. Penney, 1921, p. 42.

## THE ANGELIC INVASION OCCURRED DURING THE LIFETIME OF LAMECH'S FAMILY

Both the Bible and extra-biblical texts place the timing of the Genesis 6 invasion during the lifetime of Lamech – further suggesting that his daughter was the first bride of an angel and mother of a Nephilim. The Book of Enoch places the timing of the angelic invasion during the days of Jared:

"And they were in all two hundred; who descended in the days of Jared on the summit of Mount Hermon…." – 1 Enoch 6:6

Jared was the sixth generation of humanity in the Messianic bloodline. He lived for 962 years, making him a contemporary of Methusael and Lamech and his sons Jubal, Jabal, and Tubal-Cain, who comprised the fifth, sixth, and seventh generations in the line of Cain. The Bible chronology further indicates the exact time frame of the "days of Jared." The Flood occurred 1,656 years from Adam's creation. In Genesis 6:3, God warned Noah that there would be a 120-year probationary period before the flood judgment commenced. Going back those 120 years from the Flood to the year 1536 from Adam puts God's warning to Noah a few years after Jared's death.

Thus, going strictly by biblical chronology, we can know conclusively that the invasion of fallen angelic beings and the subsequent corruption of the earth by their Nephilim offspring reached its peak of wickedness during Jared's lifetime. Shortly after Jared's death God told Noah that "all flesh had corrupted itself" so much that He repented ever creating humanity. This explosion of evil led God to declare the 120-year probation for repentance before wiping out the world with the global flood. So, the invasion of the fallen angels and their seduction of human women started and reached its sinful apex in Jared's lifetime (which was concurrent with Lamech and his infamous children). The Bible's timing of the angelic invasion falls directly in line with the record in the Book of Enoch.

The Book of Jubilees, the other commonly cited extra-biblical text on the Nephilim, also puts the timing of the angelic invasion during the days of Jared:

> "Mahalalel took unto him to wife Dinah, the daughter of Barakiel the daughter of his father's brother, and she bare him a son in the third week in the sixth year [461 A.M.], **and he called his name Jared, for in his days the angels of the Lord descended on the earth**, those who are named the Watchers, that they should instruct the children of men, and that they should do judgment and uprightness on the earth." – Book of Jubilees 4:15–16

The name Jared or *yarad* in Hebrew means "descent." So, although the Bible does not explicitly state the year of the invasion of the "sons of God," the text supports the notion that during Jared's lifetime the corruption of the Nephilim was at its worst. In addition to providing the time frame, the Bible also provides the likely location where the sons of God entered the human realm to carry out their sinful intimate relations.

[1.] There is much debate over the length of the antediluvian era as the Septuagint and other sources detail 2,262 years before the flood. This however is beyond the scope of this study.

# CHAPTER 5

# MT. HERMON
# OR THE JORDAN RIVER?

"And they were in all two hundred; who descended in the days of Jared on the summit of Mount Hermon…" – 1 Enoch 6:6.

"Jordan means 'their going down.' The name 'Jared' is etymologically akin to it, if I may say so; it also yields the meaning 'going down'; for Jared was born to Maleleel, as it is written in the Book of Enoch – if any one cares to accept that book as sacred – in the days when the sons of God came down to the daughters of men." – *Commentary on John*, Origen, as recorded in *The Ante-Nicene Fathers*, Original Supplement to the American Edition 1896, p. 371.

The Book of Enoch cites Mount Hermon as the original landing point for the rebellious Watcher angels who would become the fathers of the Nephilim. But was this the case? The Bible gives no indication that Mt. Hermon was the "landing point" for the angelic invaders of the antediluvian world. Many passages in Scripture point instead to the Jordan River as being the far more likely landing point for the sons of God who left their first estate to fornicate with human women. The Jordan River was the "Area 51" of the ancient world, as numerous supernatural events took place in its waters and on its shores. It served as an ancient portal between the heavenly and earthly realms and a significant location for the Nephilim in Scripture.

# THE JORDAN RIVER
## COMPARED TO THE GARDEN OF EDEN

The name of the river implies a supernatural arrival. Jordan or *Yarden* in Hebrew means "descender" or "their going down." As Origen noted, its root, *yarad,* is the root of the name Jared, which means "descent." The Jordan River is mentioned 179 times in the Bible and is an extremely significant location throughout all Scripture. The first mention of the Jordan River alludes to divine presence:

> "And there was a strife between the herdmen of Abram's cattle and the herdmen of Lot's cattle: and the Canaanite and the Perizzite dwelled then in the land. And Abram said unto Lot, Let there be no strife, I pray thee, between me and thee, and between my herdmen and thy herdmen; for we be brethren. Is not the whole land before thee? separate thyself, I pray thee, from me: if thou wilt take the left hand, then I will go to the right; or if thou depart to the right hand, then I will go to the left. **And Lot lifted up his eyes, and beheld all the plain of Jordan**, that it was well watered every where, before the LORD destroyed Sodom and Gomorrah, **even as the garden of the LORD**, like the land of Egypt, as thou comest unto Zoar. Then Lot chose him all the plain of Jordan; and Lot journeyed east: and they separated themselves the one from the other." – Genesis 13:7–11

In Abraham's day, the plain adjacent to the Jordan River was compared to the Garden of Eden, signaling its divine connection. When Abraham's grandson Jacob was in Bethel, due west of the Jordan River, he saw in his dream *angels ascending and descending* on a ladder and God standing above it (Genesis 28:12). In the days of Moses, the Jordan River served as the gateway to the Promised Land (which was a foreshadow of Heaven) for the Israelites. It was the western border of the kingdom of notorious Nephilim ruler Og of Bashan

(Deuteronomy 4:47). Og's kingdom was "east of the Jordan," which separated him from the Promised Land in a way that paralleled the banishment of Adam, Eve, and Cain all of whom settled "East of Eden" as part of their respective divine punishments.

## MORE EXAMPLES OF THE JORDAN RIVER'S DIVINE IMPORTANCE

In the book of Joshua, when Israel was finally going to enter the Promised Land, God gave detailed instructions to Joshua for the crossing of the Jordan River:

> "And Joshua said unto the children of Israel, Come hither, and hear the words of the LORD your God. And Joshua said, Hereby ye shall know that the living God is among you, and that he will without fail drive out from before you the Canaanites, and the Hittites, and the Hivites, and the Perizzites, and the Girgashites, and the Amorites, and the Jebusites. **Behold, the ark of the covenant of the LORD of all the earth passeth over before you into Jordan**. Now therefore take you twelve men out of the tribes of Israel, out of every tribe a man. And it shall come to pass, as soon as the soles of the feet of the priests that bear the ark of the LORD, the LORD of all the earth, shall rest in the waters of Jordan, that the waters of Jordan shall be cut off from the waters that come down from above; and they shall stand upon an heap. And it came to pass, when the people removed from their tents, to pass over Jordan, and the priests bearing the ark of the covenant before the people;

> "And as they that bare the ark were come unto Jordan, and the feet of the priests that bare the ark were dipped in the brim of the water, (for Jordan overfloweth all his banks all the time of harvest,) That the waters which came down from above stood and rose up upon an heap very far

from the city Adam, that is beside Zaretan: and those that came down toward the sea of the plain, even the salt sea, failed, and were cut off: and the people passed over right against Jericho. **And the priests that bare the ark of the covenant of the LORD stood firm on dry ground in the midst of Jordan,** and all the Israelites passed over on dry ground, until all the people were passed clean over Jordan." – Joshua 3:9–17

God (who here is titled "Lord of all the Earth") supernaturally parted the Jordan River, creating a divine pathway for the Levite priests bearing the Ark of the Covenant to lead the nation across dry ground into the Promised Land. After crossing Joshua was instructed to perform two rituals – both involving 12 stones. The first was to take 12 stones from the floor of the Jordan River and erect a mound on the shores of Gilgal as a memorial of the great miracle God performed in parting the waters of the Jordan (Joshua 4:1-8).

The 12 stones on the shore represented God's blessing and salvation to those who believe. 1,500 years later, preaching in Bathabarra or the "house of the passage" – the very site where the Israelites crossed Jordan, John the Baptist referenced those very stones:

"Then went out to him Jerusalem, and all Judaea, and all the region round about Jordan, And were baptized of him in Jordan, confessing their sins. But when he saw many of the Pharisees and Sadducees come to his baptism, he said unto them, O generation of vipers, who hath warned you to flee from the wrath to come? Bring forth therefore fruits meet for repentance: And think not to say within yourselves, We have Abraham to our father: **for I say unto you, that God is able of these stones to raise up children unto Abraham.**" – Matthew 3:5-9.

John the Baptist, the forerunner to the Seed of the Woman, identified those who were of the seed of Satan (the sinful religious leaders of the day) and pointed to the stones commemorting God's Divine proclamation of His sovereignty and salvation. All on the shores of the Jordan River.

The second command was to take 12 stones and place them on the floor of the Jordan River. These stones were to remain at the bottom of the river to be covered by the Jordan's waters once the priests took the ark on the shore and the supernatural parting would cease (Joshua 4:9). These stones represented the judgment of those who rejected the Lord and salvation in the Promised Messiah. They would be covered by the Jordan's raging waters (**it was flooding** at that time of year – Joshua 3:15).

At the Jordan River God instructed the fugitive prophet Elijah to rest and then sent ravens, carnivorous birds, to supernaturally deliver him bread and meat:

> "And Elijah the Tishbite, who was of the inhabitants of Gilead, said unto Ahab, As the LORD God of Israel liveth, before whom I stand, there shall not be dew nor rain these years, but according to my word. And the word of the LORD came unto him, saying, Get thee hence, and turn thee eastward, **and hide thyself by the brook Cherith, that is before Jordan**. And it shall be, that thou shalt drink of the brook; and I have commanded the ravens to feed thee there. So he went and did according unto the word of the LORD: for he went and dwelt by the brook Cherith, that is before Jordan. And the ravens brought him bread and flesh in the morning, and bread and flesh in the evening; and he drank of the brook." – 1 Kings 17:1–6

Elijah later returned to the Jordan River to be transported literally to Heaven by God:

> "And the sons of the prophets that were at Jericho came to Elisha, and said unto him, Knowest thou that the LORD will take away thy master

> from thy head to day? And he answered, Yea, I know it; hold ye your peace. And Elijah said unto him, Tarry, I pray thee, here; *for the LORD hath sent me to Jordan.* And he said, As the LORD liveth, and as thy soul liveth, I will not leave thee. And they two went on. And fifty men of the sons of the prophets went, and stood to view afar off: **and they two stood by Jordan**. And Elijah took his mantle, and wrapped it together, and smote the waters, and they were divided hither and thither, so that they two went over on dry ground. And it came to pass, when they were gone over, that Elijah said unto Elisha, Ask what I shall do for thee, before I be taken away from thee. And Elisha said, I pray thee, let a double portion of thy spirit be upon me. And he said, Thou hast asked a hard thing: nevertheless, if thou see me when I am taken from thee, it shall be so unto thee; but if not, it shall not be so. **And it came to pass, as they still went on, and talked, that, behold, there appeared a chariot of fire, and horses of fire, and parted them both asunder; and Elijah went up by a whirlwind into heaven.**"
> – 2 Kings 2:5–11

By divine power Elijah and Elisha crossed over the Jordan River on dry ground, as the waters once again supernaturally parted for them to pass through. Angelic chariots and horses then took Elijah up into Heaven at the Jordan River, giving further evidence that there was some form of divine portal or passageway at this river. After Elijah's departure, Elisha, who succeeded him as the prophet to Israel, was also able to supernaturally part the waters of the Jordan again to return to the Promised Land:

> "He took up also the mantle of Elijah that fell from him, and went back, **and stood by the bank of Jordan**; And he took the mantle of Elijah that fell from him, and smote the waters, and said, Where is the LORD God of Elijah? **and when he also had smitten the waters, they parted hither and thither: and Elisha went over.**"
> – 2 Kings 2:13–14

When Naaman, the captain of the Syrian army, was seeking a cure for his deadly leprosy, his Hebrew servants advised him to contact Elisha to receive a supernatural healing. The prophet told Naaman to wash himself in the Jordan River seven times to be cured. The Syrian captain, revolted at the bizarre instructions, suggested other rivers he could dip himself in. His servants finally persuaded him to follow Elisha's commands, and two miracles soon took place:

> "Then went he down, **and dipped himself seven times in Jordan, according to the saying of the man of God**: and his flesh came again like unto the flesh of a little child, and he was clean. And he returned to the man of God, he and all his company, and came, and stood before him: and he said, Behold, now I know that there is no God in all the earth, but in Israel: now therefore, I pray thee, take a blessing of thy servant. But he said, As the LORD liveth, before whom I stand, I will receive none. And he urged him to take it; but he refused. – 2 Kings 5:14–16

## RIVERS WERE AREAS OF SUPERNATURAL MANIFESTATION IN THE BIBLE

Naaman was not only healed of leprosy but emerged from the Jordan River a true believer in God. In addition to being sites for the Lord's miracles, rivers were prime locations for angelic manifestation in the Bible. Although we rarely find angels mentioned near mountains (and not one is mentioned at Mt. Hermon), many accounts locate angelic beings near water and specifically rivers. The prophet Ezekiel encountered angels at a river:

> "Now it came to pass in the thirtieth year, in the fourth month, in the fifth day of the month, as I was among the captives **by the river of Chebar, that the heavens were opened, and I saw visions of**

**God**. In the fifth day of the month, which was the fifth year of king Jehoiachin's captivity, The word of the LORD came expressly unto Ezekiel the priest, the son of Buzi, in the land of the Chaldeans by the river Chebar; and the hand of the LORD was there upon him. And I looked, and, behold, a whirlwind came out of the north, a great cloud, and a fire infolding itself, and a brightness was about it, and out of the midst thereof as the colour of amber, out of the midst of the fire. Also out of the midst thereof came the likeness of four living creatures. And this was their appearance; they had the likeness of a man. And every one had four faces, and every one had four wings. And their feet were straight feet; and the sole of their feet was like the sole of a calf's foot: and they sparkled like the colour of burnished brass." – Ezekiel 1:1–7

The prophet literally witnessed a portal to Heaven open and four angelic beings descend to Earth at the river Chebar. Ezekiel later returned to the river Chebar and encountered God:

"Then I came to them of the captivity at Telabib, that dwelt by the river of Chebar, and I sat where they sat, and remained there astonished among them seven days. And it came to pass at the end of seven days, that the word of the LORD came unto me, saying, Son of man, I have made thee a watchman unto the house of Israel: therefore hear the word at my mouth, and give them warning from me." – Ezekiel 3:15–17

After being told to lie on his side for 430 days, Ezekiel was sitting in his home at the river Chebar when he again encountered the divine realm:

"And it came to pass in the sixth year, in the sixth month, in the fifth day of the month, *as I sat in mine house*, and the elders of Judah sat before me, that the hand of the Lord GOD fell there upon me.

Then I beheld, and lo a likeness as the appearance of fire: from the appearance of his loins even downward, fire; and from his loins even upward, as the appearance of brightness, as the colour of amber. And he put forth the form of an hand, and took me by a lock of mine head; and the spirit lifted me up between the earth and the heaven, and brought me in the visions of God to Jerusalem, to the door of the inner gate that looketh toward the north; where was the seat of the image of jealousy, which provoketh to jealousy. And, behold, the glory of the God of Israel was there, according to the vision that I saw in the plain." – Ezekiel 8:1–4

Ezekiel had more angelic and heavenly realm experiences *than any other prophet in the Bible* and, not surprising, the word "river" occurs more times in his amazing account than in the other 65 books of the Bible.

The prophet Daniel received some of the more startling end-time prophecies from angels situated near a river:

"In the third year of Cyrus king of Persia a thing was revealed unto Daniel, whose name was called Belteshazzar; and the thing was true, but the time appointed was long: and he understood the thing, and had understanding of the vision. In those days I Daniel was mourning three full weeks. I ate no pleasant bread, neither came flesh nor wine in my mouth, neither did I anoint myself at all, till three whole weeks were fulfilled. And in the four and twentieth day of the first month, *as I was by the side of the great river*, which is Hiddekel; Then I lifted up mine eyes, and looked, and behold a certain man clothed in linen, whose loins were girded with fine gold of Uphaz: His body also was like the beryl, and his face as the appearance of lightning, and his eyes as lamps of fire, and his arms and his feet like in colour to polished brass, and the voice of his words like the voice of a multitude. And I Daniel alone saw the vision: for the men that were with me saw not the vision; but a great quaking fell upon them, so that they fled to hide themselves." – Daniel 10:1–7

The "great river" called Hiddekel is another name for the eastern branch of the Tigris River, which in Daniel's day separated the Babylonian and Medo-Persian empires. In the Septuagint, the verse reads: "On the twenty-fourth day of the first month, I was near the great river, which is Tigris Eddekel" (Daniel 10:4 LXX). Hiddekel was one of the four original rivers of the Garden of Eden (Genesis 2:14) and flowed from beneath the first temple of God on Earth. Thus, it would no doubt be a suitable location for angels to manifest in the human realm.

In Daniel 12 the prophet encounters another pair of angels who suddenly appear on either side of the Tigris River:

> "Then I Daniel looked, and, behold, there stood other two, **the one on this side of the bank of the river, and the other on that side of the bank of the river**. And one said to the man clothed in linen, which was upon the waters of the river, How long shall it be to the end of these wonders? And I heard the man clothed in linen, which was upon the waters of the river, when he held up his right hand and his left hand unto heaven, and sware by him that liveth for ever that it shall be for a time, times, and an half; and when he shall have accomplished to scatter the power of the holy people, all these things shall be finished." – Daniel 12:5–7

In addition to the two new angels who appeared, Daniel also saw a "man clothed in linen" supernaturally *standing on the waters of the Tigris River*. This was an Old Testament manifestation of the Lord Jesus Christ (as only God can swear an oath in His Holy Name – Hebrews 6:13).

The other "great river" in Scripture, the Euphrates, is where four apostate angels are currently imprisoned:

"And the sixth angel sounded, and I heard a voice from the four horns of the golden altar which is before God, Saying to the sixth angel which had the trumpet, **Loose the four angels which are bound in the great river Euphrates**. And the four angels were loosed, which were prepared for an hour, and a day, and a month, and a year, for to slay the third part of men." – Revelation 9:13–15

In the New Testament an angel descended to the pool of Bethsaida periodically to "trouble the waters" and bestow them with supernatural properties:

"After this there was a feast of the Jews; and Jesus went up to Jerusalem. Now there is at Jerusalem by the sheep market a pool, which is called in the Hebrew tongue Bethesda, having five porches. In these lay a great multitude of impotent folk, of blind, halt, withered, waiting for the moving of the water. **For an angel went down at a certain season into the pool, and troubled the water**: whosoever then first after the troubling of the water stepped in was made whole of whatsoever disease he had." – John 5:1–4

The last chapter of the Bible describes the future New Jerusalem where a river will run directly under the throne of Jesus Christ:

"And he shewed me a pure river of water of life, clear as crystal, proceeding out of the throne of God and of the Lamb." – Revelation 22:1

Time and time again, rivers – not mountains – are the site of angelic and divine manifestations. No significant biblical events even took place at Mt. Hermon. The preeminent place where the heavenly realm intersected with the human was at the Jordan River. And its most famous supernatural event was the baptism of the Lord Jesus Christ:

> "**Then cometh Jesus from Galilee to Jordan** unto John, to be baptized of him. But John forbad him, saying, I have need to be baptized of thee, and comest thou to me? And Jesus answering said unto him, Suffer it to be so now: for thus it becometh us to fulfil all righteousness. Then he suffered him. And Jesus, when he was baptized, went up straightway out of the water: **and, lo, the heavens were opened unto him, and he saw the Spirit of God descending like a dove**, and lighting upon him: And lo a voice from heaven, saying, This is my beloved Son, in whom I am well pleased." – Matthew 3:13–17

Jesus Christ, God in the flesh, chose to be baptized in the Jordan River. And the skies opened to reveal a heavenly portal and the Holy Spirit *descended on Him* in the same divinely appointed location of the Jordan River. Immediately after this, God the Father spoke from Heaven to Earth for all to hear proclaiming that Jesus Christ was the Son of God. The pathway from Earth to the divine realm was on display at this mystical river.

The many Nephilim giant nations that appeared after the Flood all set up their kingdoms in proximity to the Jordan River with the mightiest being on its shores. Considering the numerous supernatural events that occurred there, Scripture provides much more evidence that the Jordan River was the likely location for the Genesis 6 invasion than Mt. Hermon as the Book of Enoch suggests. (As we will see, the Book of Enoch contains some glaring errors that demonstrate that, unlike the Bible, it is not inerrant.) The Jordan River is the "Roswell, New Mexico" of the Bible in terms of the sheer number of supernatural encounters that took place in its waters or adjacent to it.

Scriptural evidence suggests that angels choose to descend, manifest, and live near rivers. The name of the river also lends credence to the notion that the

Genesis 6 "landing spot" was at the Jordan. Why else would Moses and the Hebrew people call a well-known river "Jordan" ("their going down") unless there was a famous descent there in the first place? It seems then, to this author at least, that the Jordan River would be the most likely place the angels who sinned in Genesis 6 made their initial invasion. At the river of Their Descent – the Jordan.

## THE LORD GIVES HUMANITY TIME TO REPENT

"And the LORD said, My spirit shall not always strive with man, for that he also is flesh: yet his days shall be an hundred and twenty years." – Genesis 6:3.

The Lord pronounced His judgment on the genetic and moral corruption that occurred at the hands of these sinful angels. Human civilization, overrun with the invasion of the fallen angels and Nephilim, was going to reach a point where God's Spirit would cease to work on its behalf.

"…My spirit shall not always strive with man…"

The word "strive" in Hebrew is *diyn*, which means to "judge, contend or plead." God was not going to allow His Holy Spirit to judge the works of this corrupted pre-Flood world forever. The Lord set a time limit to extend man the opportunity to repent from the rampant wickedness and genetic corruption that was engulfing the world. For centuries, the Creator used His prophets – believers who received their words directly from Him – to preach His message and the Gospel of salvation through the coming Seed of the Woman. God uses His Word to provoke society to recognize their sinfulness before Him and turn to Him in faith and repentance. In Genesis 5 we are told that the Messianic bloodline carried on through the lineage of Seth. Many of these faithful patriarchs served as prophets of the Lord. In studying the Nephilim, it is critical to examine the first prophet in the Bible – Enoch.

# CHAPTER 6

# ENOCH – THE FIRST PROPHET

"And Jared lived an hundred sixty and two years, and he begat Enoch: And Jared lived after he begat Enoch eight hundred years, and begat sons and daughters: And all the days of Jared were nine hundred sixty and two years: and he died. And Enoch lived sixty and five years, and begat Methuselah: And Enoch walked with God after he begat Methuselah three hundred years, and begat sons and daughters: And all the days of Enoch were three hundred sixty and five years: And Enoch walked with God: and he was not; for God took him." – Genesis 5:18–24

In recent years, Enoch has attained celebrity status as the Book of Enoch experienced a massive resurgence in popularity among Bible students, scholars, UFO enthusiasts, and those involved in the occult and New Age movement. Some texts call Enoch the founder of modern Freemasonry. Others describe him serving as an advocate for fallen angels. A branch of witchcraft is known as "Enochian Magic." So, who was this mysterious figure whom so many different groups in society today are claiming? The son of Jared, Enoch lived during the high point of the fallen angelic-Nephilim kingdom of the antediluvian world. He witnessed the supernatural power of Satan's armies dazzle and subjugate the planet, threatening the very existence of the Holy Seed. And he posed the greatest threat to Satan's kingdom. Enoch was the first living human to become an immortal. His rapture proved that faith in God could overcome even death and the grave.

Enoch was a unique figure in the Bible. He is the first quoted prophet. He is one of the two people in the Bible who "walked with God." Enoch and the prophet Elijah were the only two people in the Bible who were raptured to Heaven and never died. Enoch was born when Adam was 622 years old. So he spent over 300 years with the patriarch of humanity. We should not underestimate the vast knowledge Adam possessed of Eden, the Fall, Satan, and God's judgment. Adam lived in the presence of the Lord and had direct conflict with Satan. He thus had incomparable experiences to share with his many sons and daughters. But the Scripture tells us that it was Enoch's own son who had a profound effect on Him:

> "And Enoch lived sixty and five years, and begat Methuselah: And Enoch walked with God after he begat Methuselah three hundred years, and begat sons and daughters." – Genesis 5:22

It is noteworthy that Enoch walked with God *after he begat Methuselah*. Something at that specific juncture in his life brought the prophet to a life of devotion to the Lord. Methuselah's name provides a clue. The name Methuselah in Hebrew means "When he is dead, it shall be sent." Such an ominous title was an indication that Enoch received divine revelation at the birth of Methuselah. And the prophetic message was of a coming judgment upon the earth. A closer look at the timelines of the genealogies of the patriarchs suggests that it is no coincidence that Methuselah died in the same year the Flood was sent upon the earth! Enoch knew centuries in advance that the destruction of the earth and human civilization was linked to the life and death of his child. Renowned theologian A. W. Pink wrote of this:

> "Suppose God should say to you, 'The life of that little one is to be the life of the world. When that child dies the world will be destroyed.'

What would be the effect upon you? Not knowing how soon that child might die, there would come before you the possibility that the world might perish at any time. Every time that child fell sick the world's doom would stare you in the face! Suppose further, that you were unsaved. Would you not be deeply exercised? Would you not realize as never before your urgent need of preparing to meet God? Would you not at once begin to occupy yourself with spiritual things? May not some such effects have been produced upon Enoch? Be this as it may—and it is difficult to escape such a conclusion it is certainly implied that from the time Methuselah was born, the world lost all its attractiveness for Enoch and from that time on, if never before, he walked with God." – *Gleanings in Genesis*, A. W. Pink, Moody Bible Institute of Chicago, 1922, p. 78.

The impact of this revelation was clear: From the year of Methuselah's birth, Enoch "walked with God." We should not take this short phrase lightly. Walking with God is a profound devotion that the Bible repeatedly implores and commands all people to do (though many fall quite short). The book of Micah says this on the matter:

"Wherewith shall I come before the LORD, and bow myself before the high God? shall I come before him with burnt offerings, with calves of a year old? Will the LORD be pleased with thousands of rams, or with ten thousands of rivers of oil? shall I give my firstborn for my transgression, the fruit of my body for the sin of my soul? He hath shewed thee, O man, what is good; and what doth the LORD require of thee, but to do justly, and to love mercy, and to walk humbly with thy God?" – Micah 6:6–8

Rather than performing good works to "impress" the Lord, walking with God involves humble obedience. And that can only come through faith. Enoch was a man of faith. Hebrews 11:5 states: "By faith Enoch was translated that he should not see death; and was not found, because God had translated him: for before his translation he had this testimony, that he pleased God." Enoch thus knew God's Word because "faith cometh by hearing, and hearing by the word of God." Enoch heard God's Word and believed it.

Enoch also "pleased God" as Hebrews 11:5 attests. But how did he do this? The subsequent verse in Hebrews 11 explains: "But without faith it is impossible to please him: for he that cometh to God must believe that he is, and that he is a rewarder of them that diligently seek him" (Hebrews 11:6). This first prophet of Scripture believed in the Lord as Creator and Ruler of all who would bless his efforts to seek His presence.

Walking with God also involves striving to live holy. While Cain's descendants were enjoying their high-tech city life and engaging in all sorts of wicked pleasure, Enoch rejected the sinful world to live for the Lord. Amos 3:3 states: "Can two walk together, except they be agreed?" A Christian who walks with the Lord lives a life that reflects it – striving for holiness in thought, word, and deed.

Having faith in God inspires action to serve, which Enoch also did. The book of Jude contains Enoch's prophecy:

> "And Enoch also, the seventh from Adam, prophesied of these, saying, Behold, the Lord cometh with ten thousands of his saints, To execute judgment upon all, and to convince all that are ungodly among them of all their ungodly deeds which they have ungodly committed, and of all their hard speeches which ungodly sinners have spoken against him." – Jude 1:14

These warnings are the earliest quoted words of a prophet in the Bible. Enoch was inspired by the Holy Spirit to issue a warning to the world. Naming his son Methuselah served as a doomsday clock for a rebellious, God-hating society, counting down to the Lord's judgment of the earth. These facts indicate that during the lifetime of Enoch and his father, Jared, the Genesis 6 invasion was well underway. After all, the wicked polygamist Lamech was Enoch's cousin and contemporary. Enoch witnessed the violence, unbridled lust, and global domination of the Nephilim as they polluted the human genetic code. The angels and their giant offspring controlled the power, wealth, and resources of the planet. And sinful humanity either succumbed to or deified them. In the face of this, Enoch enlisted in God's army as one of the chosen servants to warn the world of its sin and stir hearts to repentance and faith:

"This voice of Enoch must have sounded to the antediluvian sinners exactly as the warning of our Lord in the parable sounded to the fool while he was saying, 'I have much goods laid up for many years' – 'Thou fool, this night thy soul shall be required of thee.' In an age when dishonesty was promising gain, when vanity was promising distinction, when ambition was promising place and power, when unbelief was promising safety, God's word, louder and stronger than them all, proclaimed, 'the Lord cometh to execute judgment upon all the ungodly.' Now such a warning voice as this is no less needed now." – *The Church before the Flood*, Reverend John Cumming, London: Arthur Hall, Virtue and Co., 1853, pp. 449–450.

If Enoch's message seemed harsh, it was only reflecting the urgency of the situation. Humanity was on the brink of spiritual and genetic self-destruction. The world as they knew it was going to end. And souls were on the verge of being lost to Hell and God's wrath. The Apostle Paul cited God's wrath as a reason for such strong preaching: "Knowing therefore the terror of the Lord, we persuade men…" (2 Corinthians 5:11). It is better to repent in fear and live eternally then proudly go to judgment before God with no forgiveness for your sin.

# THE RAPTURE OF ENOCH –
# A MAN BECAME IMMORTAL

"And Enoch walked with God: and he was not; for God took him."
– Genesis 5:24

After 300 years of walking with God and prophesying the Lord's judgment, Enoch was translated or raptured to Heaven. Hebrews 11 states: "By faith Enoch was translated **that he should not see death;** and was not found, because God had translated him: for before his translation he had this testimony, that he pleased God." Enoch believed that the Lord would save him from the wrath to come, and God most certainly did. By no coincidence, Noah, the only other person who "walked with God" in the Bible, also believed the Lord would deliver him from divine judgment. This was evidence of God's mercy. So many skeptics and critics of Christianity attempt to describe God as an angry, vengeful tyrant who destroys innocents on a whim. Yet, time and time again throughout Scripture the Lord demonstrates His mercy and patience with wicked, sinful humanity.

Imagine the world's reaction when Enoch, the prophet of God who spent years pleading with his friends, neighbors, and anyone who would listen that the end of the world was near, was suddenly snatched from Earth to Heaven, soaring through the clouds and never seen again, and leaving behind a son whose death would be the sign that God's wrath was set to be unleashed on an unbelieving society. The rapture of Enoch served as stunning testimony that the God of the universe he proclaimed was real, thus giving people more reason to believe and turn back to the Lord.

The fallen angels awed humanity with their occult secrets, advanced technology, and mastery of the earthly elements. The Nephilim giants were unlike anything humanity had seen before. To the average person in Enoch's day, the apostate angels *appeared* to possess the keys to immortality and godhood. Satan's seductive false promise from the Garden of Eden regained its appeal with the descent of the sons of God and their half-human, godlike children. But amid their earthly domination, Enoch, a faithful servant of God, transformed into an immortal and flew to Heaven. Those foolish men and women who fell for the seduction of the fallen angels still eventually died. The giants of the antediluvian world – invincible, bloodthirsty warriors that they were – nevertheless perished. But Enoch, the prophet and teacher of the Lord's Word who warned of His wrath upon a rebellious world, was "translated," his earthly body shed in exchange for a divine, immortal, glorified body and raptured to Heaven.

## PEOPLE KNEW ENOCH WAS RAPTURED

The rapture of Enoch was not a secret event. Hebrews 11:5 states: "By faith Enoch was translated that he should not see death; *and was not found...*." This verse reveals that *people knew Enoch was supernaturally taken* and searched for him to confirm the Lord had truly removed him from Earth. His divine departure stood as evidence of God's power and truth. A similar search party effort occurred with the only other person in the Bible who was snatched into Heaven while alive and received immortality – the prophet Elijah.

"And it came to pass, when the LORD would take up Elijah into heaven by a whirlwind, that Elijah went with Elisha from Gilgal. And Elijah said unto Elisha, Tarry here, I pray thee; for the LORD hath sent me to Bethel. And Elisha said unto him, As the LORD liveth, and as thy soul liveth, I will not leave thee. So they went down to Bethel. And the sons of the prophets that were at Bethel came forth to Elisha, and said unto him, **Knowest thou that the LORD will take away thy master from thy head to day? And he said, Yea, I know it;** hold ye your peace.

"And Elijah said unto him, Elisha, tarry here, I pray thee; for the LORD hath sent me to Jericho. And he said, As the LORD liveth,

> and as thy soul liveth, I will not leave thee. So they came to Jericho. And the sons of the prophets that were at Jericho came to Elisha, and said unto him, **Knowest thou that the LORD will take away thy master from thy head to day? And he answered, Yea, I know it;** hold ye your peace. And Elijah said unto him, Tarry, I pray thee, here; for the LORD hath sent me to Jordan. And he said, As the LORD liveth, and as thy soul liveth, I will not leave thee. And they two went on. And fifty men of the sons of the prophets went, and stood to view afar off: and they two stood by Jordan." – 2 Kings 2:1–7

Elijah knew he was going to be raptured and shared the news with his protégé, Elisha, and the "sons of the prophets," men instructed in the Word of God to serve under Elijah and Elisha's authority. They also knew Elijah's ascent to Heaven would take place at the Jordan River (home, as we have seen, to many supernatural events):

> "And it came to pass, as they still went on, and talked, that, behold, there appeared a chariot of fire, and horses of fire, and parted them both asunder; and Elijah went up by a whirlwind into heaven. And Elisha saw it, and he cried, My father, my father, the chariot of Israel, and the horsemen thereof. And he saw him no more: and he took hold of his own clothes, and rent them in two pieces. He took up also the mantle of Elijah that fell from him, and went back, and stood by the bank of Jordan; And he took the mantle of Elijah that fell from him, and smote the waters, and said, Where is the LORD God of Elijah? and when he also had smitten the waters, they parted hither and thither: and Elisha went over.

> "And when the sons of the prophets which were to view at Jericho saw him, they said, The spirit of Elijah doth rest on Elisha. And they came to meet him, and bowed themselves to the ground before him. And they said unto him, **Behold now, there be with thy**

servants fifty strong men; let them go, we pray thee, and seek thy master: lest peradventure the Spirit of the LORD hath taken him up, and cast him upon some mountain, or into some valley. And he said, Ye shall not send. And when they urged him till he was ashamed, he said, Send. They sent therefore fifty men; and they sought three days, **but found him not**. And when they came again to him, (for he tarried at Jericho,) he said unto them, Did I not say unto you, Go not?" – 2 Kings 2:11–18

Elijah was escorted to Heaven by a divine chariot and horses of fire. Elisha witnessed the event along with the 50 sons of the prophets who stood on the other side of the Jordan River. And the sons of the prophets pressed Elisha to permit them to search for Elijah in the event that the elder prophet was not actually translated but instead supernaturally transported to a mountain or valley. Of course, as was the case with the search for Enoch, "they found him not."

It is no stretch to conclude that a similar set of circumstances occurred in the translation of Enoch. Perhaps Methuselah, Jared, and other godly men were aware of his coming translation. Certainly there were people who witnessed it and searched for him afterwards. Despite not having the technological trappings or angelic alliances that his cousin Lamech and his wicked brood possessed, Enoch was the only person in the history of the pre-Flood world to never die. He achieved true immortality and became "as the gods." He was able to reach Heaven by way of his faith and trust in the true and living God. In the ongoing battle for the hearts and minds of humanity, the Lord made the strongest statement yet. Enoch's translation was dazzling proof that death held no power over those who put their faith and trust in the Creator. For all their boasts and false promises, Satan and his seed could not stop the inevitable march to the grave. But God, in the twinkling of an eye, proved His power over death, the grave, and all things in Earth and Heaven.

Of this amazing event one commentator wrote:

"The miraculous translation of this, the best known and foremost, man of his day was adapted, and no doubt intended, to confirm the godly and convict the impious. It was God's seal on his mission, testimony, and character; just as Elijah's was on his, just as Christ's resurrection and ascension were, in a still higher sense, on his. Happy had it been for that godless antediluvian generation had they but caught the mantle of the ascending prophet, by drinking into his spirit, as did, long after, Elisha that of Elijah, and the disciples that of Jesus, and by improving the unspeakably solemn providential event. Long had the Spirit striven with them for this end. Long was He through Noah to strive with them still. It was in love He strove; but He strove in vain; and at last the flood had to come and overwhelm them all." – *Heroes of Faith as Delineated in Hebrews*, John Guthrie, Glascow: John S. Marr & Sons, 1878, p. 102.

## GOD USED THE FALLEN ANGELS AND NEPHILIM TO PROVE HE IS LORD

Time and time again God used the fallen angels and Nephilim to *demonstrate He was the true Creator and Almighty God of all.* Despite presenting themselves as gods and demigods to humanity, the fallen angels and their hybrid offspring were merely rebellious creatures who stood no chance of ever overthrowing God. For all their supposed power, the Lord repeatedly exposed their lies and established His superiority as Creator of all. Enoch was a powerful testimony to the true way to Heaven – faith in the Creator and His Promised Savior. Eternal life for Enoch did not begin at his rapture. It started once he believed God's Word and walked with the Lord for those 300 years. Just like Noah who also "walked with God" and was saved from the Flood, Enoch was spared from experiencing the punishment of the evil of the Nephilim hybrids who invoked the Lord's wrath to the point that He resolved to exterminate the entire creation.

# METHUSELAH'S LONG LIFE WAS A SYMBOL OF GOD'S PATIENCE AND MERCY

After Enoch's translation, his son Methuselah, the man whose death signaled the timing of God's wrath God unleashed on the world, went on to *live the longest life of any person in the Bible*. Methuselah died at 969 years old (Genesis 5:27), showing God provided close to 1,000 years for humanity to repent from its rebellion and reject the fallen angels who were interbreeding and corrupting the world.

1 Peter 3 describes the final decades before the Flood as a time of God's mercy:

> "For Christ also hath once suffered for sins, the just for the unjust, that he might bring us to God, being put to death in the flesh, but quickened by the Spirit: By which also he went and preached unto the spirits in prison; **Which sometime were disobedient, when once the longsuffering of God waited in the days of Noah**, while the ark was a preparing, wherein few, that is, eight souls were saved by water." – 1 Peter 3:18-20

God is longsuffering and will exercise patience with sinful rebellion. 2 Peter 3 states: "the Lord is not slack concerning his promise, as some men count slackness; but is longsuffering to us-ward, not willing that any should perish, but that all should come to repentance." In His great mercy and grace, God allows time before delivering judgment. But that time for repentance eventually comes to an end.

"My spirit shall not always strive with man" meant that God gave humanity time to repent. Through His Spirit, He inspired prophets to warn the world of coming judgment. He inspired Noah to preach the Gospel of salvation. He timed the Flood per the life of Methuselah to stand as a daily reminder of just how much in the balance was the life of the earth itself. He took Enoch directly to Heaven without dying, providing public, supernatural confirmation of the prophet's ministry and validation that eternal life could be obtained only through faith in the promised Seed of the Woman. The Lord instructed Noah to prepare the ark 120 years in advance of the Flood, thus giving the world an enormous sign as Noah, the preacher of God's Word, was openly preparing for the flood judgment. All this was God's longsuffering, waiting patiently on humanity to repent. God's Spirit strove with rebellious mankind, but the judgment was coming.

## "... FOR THAT HE ALSO IS FLESH..." – UNLOCKING A MYSTERIOUS PHRASE

"And the LORD said, My spirit shall not always strive with man, **for that he also is flesh**: yet his days shall be an hundred and twenty years." – Genesis 6:3

Often in the Bible a small verse holds a great deal of information. As God prepared to judge the world He noted that man "also is flesh." Bible commentator Watchman Nee provides insight into the meaning of this pronouncement:

"The passage in Genesis 6.3 is clear: 'for that he [man] also is flesh.' What is meant here by the word 'also'? It means the second time. For instance, You have eaten, but I also have eaten. This 'also' means the second time. God says that man also is flesh, indicating that before man somebody else has first become flesh. Who, aside from man, can be spoken in such parallel fashion to man? **None but the angel. Hence in saying that man also is flesh, it implies that the angels had already become flesh.** With such evidence as this, we can assuredly conclude that 'the sons of God' points to the angels." – *How to Study the Bible: Practical Advice for Receiving Light from God's Word*, Watchman Nee, Living Stream Ministry, p. 130. [emphasis added]

The sinning angels corrupted their holy nature to become "flesh," driven by sinful lust and wicked desires. In the beginning, all angels were godly, righteous creatures who witnessed the creation of the earth and humanity. But with the new creation of humans, God instituted something angels were not privy to – marriage:

> "And the rib, which the LORD God had taken from man, made he a woman, and brought her unto the man. And Adam said, This is now bone of my bones, and flesh of my flesh: she shall be called Woman, because she was taken out of Man. Therefore shall a man leave his father and his mother, and shall cleave unto his wife: and they shall be one flesh." – Genesis 2:22–24

The angels witnessed something revolutionary to them – marriage: the joining of a man and woman as "one flesh." For the sons of God who sinned in Genesis 6, the temptation to be joined with human women was so powerful that they abandoned their godly vocation and rebelled. Fornication is a special sin in Scripture because it involves *defiling one's body*:

> "Know ye not that your bodies are the members of Christ? shall I then take the members of Christ, and make them the members of an harlot? God forbid. **What? know ye not that he which is joined to an harlot is one body? for two, saith he, shall be one flesh**. But he that is joined unto the Lord is one spirit. Flee fornication. Every sin that a man doeth is without the body; but he that committeth fornication sinneth against his own body. What? know ye not that your body is the temple of the Holy Ghost which is in you, which ye have of God, and ye are not your own? For ye are bought with a price: therefore glorify God in your body, and in your spirit, which are God's." – 1 Corinthians 6:15–20

By having sexual relations with human women, the rebel angels became "one flesh" with sinful humanity, defiling their angelic bodies and corrupting their spirits that were previously "joined unto the Lord" (1 Corinthians 6:17).

> "And the angels which kept not their first estate, *but left their own habitation*, he hath reserved in everlasting chains under darkness unto the judgment of the great day. Even as Sodom and Gomorrah, and the cities about them in like manner, **giving themselves over to fornication, and going after strange flesh**, are set forth for an example, suffering the vengeance of eternal fire." – Jude 1:6–7

## PHYSICALLY CORRUPTED BEINGS CANNOT STAND BEFORE GOD

Like Enoch, all born-again Christians will one day receive a new, glorified body – a body-like substance of angelic beings. The angels who sinned in Genesis 6 went through a "reverse rapture" in which they descended to Earth and defiled and corrupted their once glorified bodies by joining themselves sexually to women who possessed a sinful flesh nature. They had thus disqualified themselves from full heavenly realm access. In the Garden of Eden, Adam was unable to remain in God's presence once he sinned. In his fallen flesh, he could not stand before God's full divine glory. This is an important concept in Scripture confirmed in the book of Exodus:

> "And the LORD said unto Moses, I will do this thing also that thou hast spoken: for thou hast found grace in my sight, and I know thee by name. And he said, I beseech thee, shew me thy glory. And he said, I will make all my goodness pass before thee, and I will proclaim the name of the LORD before thee; and will be gracious to whom I will be gracious, and will shew mercy on whom I will shew mercy. *And he said, Thou canst not see my face: for there shall no man see me, and live.*" – Exodus 33:17–20

Corrupted beings whose bodies have been tainted with sin cannot stand before the literal power and energy of God. Scripture says that upon His return in the end times Christ will destroy His enemies by the sheer force of His appearance:

> "And then shall that Wicked be revealed, whom the Lord shall consume with the spirit of his mouth, and shall destroy with the brightness of his coming." – 2 Thessalonians 2:8

The sons of God risked their very heavenly status by venturing into fornication with human women. Because of their sin, they became "flesh" – degraded and no longer in righteous harmony with the Creator. The notion that an angel can lose immortality, suffer corruption, and die is confirmed in Psalm 82, a "Divine Council" chapter where the Lord addressed fallen angels:

> "I have said, Ye are gods; and all of you are children of the most High. But *ye shall die like men*, and fall like one of the princes." – Psalm 82:6–7

The Genesis 6 rebels wagered their very immorality to satisfy sinful desires. The fallen angels who originally rebelled with Satan and even Satan himself retained heavenly access after their sin (Job 1:6–7; Job 2:1–2). But the sons of God who married human women were cast to the abyss – their defiled bodies kept in darkness of Hell until the Great Tribulation.

And most of humanity followed their lead into being consumed by lust.

Sinful rebellion is a process. The Lord endows part of His Spirit into every person from birth. Even fallen humanity retains some of God's goodness: "For when the Gentiles, which have not the law, do by nature the things contained in the law, these, having not the law, are a law unto themselves: Which shew the work of the law written in their hearts, their conscience also bearing witness..." (Romans 2:14–15). The human conscience is a law written on the heart by the Lord whereby a person even without biblical knowledge can know innately that lying, stealing, murder, and other sins are wrong.

But over time even that influence in a person's heart can leave him as he succumbs more and more to sinful desires. This leads the conscience to become "seared with a hot iron," meaning a person no longer cares about the consequence of his sin and lives life merely seeking to satisfy his lusts. Romans 1 describes this process in detail:

> "For the wrath of God is revealed from heaven against all ungodliness and unrighteousness of men, who hold the truth in unrighteousness; Because that which may be known of God is manifest in them; for God hath shewed it unto them. For the invisible things of him from the creation of the world are clearly seen, being understood by the things that are made, even his eternal power and Godhead; so that they are without excuse: Because that, when they knew God, they glorified him not as God, neither were thankful; but became vain in their imaginations, and their foolish heart was darkened. Professing themselves to be wise, they became fools...." – Romans 1:18–22

By denying God's existence and thus His authority over humanity, a person falls deeper into his own sinful imaginations of what is "right and wrong," becoming his own god and authority in his life. The text describes this as the "foolish heart" being "darkened." And the descent into depravity continues as Romans 1:18–28 makes clear.

Denial of God and His authority soon leads to idolatry and sinful lust. The consequence for a person in this downward spiral is God's giving "them over to a reprobate mind, to those things which are not convenient" (Romans 1:28). Once a person consistently rejects God and follows his own sinful lifestyle, the Lord removes His remaining influence (the conscience) and the person is now a reprobate – fully turned over to his own wicked desires. Note that the first example of reprobate sins in the passage above is illicit sexual behavior. This is precisely what humanity fell into in the days of Noah. The apostate angels who sinned gave themselves wholly over to carnal lust and became flesh, inciting humankind to succumb to their own wickedness in open rebellion against the Lord. A 19th-century commentary on this concept states:

> "Another argument arises from the expression 'My Spirit shall not always strive with man for that he also is flesh' from which word also it follows that some other nature beside that of man was become flesh but on the usual theory this word is useless and insignificant. Or if we give to flesh the signification of a corrupt nature which it afterwards attained the sentiment will probably be: 'As my Spirit has ceased to strive with these rebel angels so shall it also be with man for he too is become corrupt.'" – *Isaiah Unfulfilled: Being an Exposition of the Prophet, with New Version and Critical Notes*, Reverend R. Govett, 1841, p. 346.

This corruption necessitated the Messiah. As humanity genetically degraded itself, only the salvation of God would provide a chance of redemption. Because it was corrupted the flesh and blood of humanity could not enter Heaven. Thus, a person must be "born again" – in body and spirit – to get to Heaven. The Lord Jesus Christ explained this in a conversation with Nicodemus the Pharisee: "Jesus answered, Verily, verily, I say unto thee, Except a man be born of water and of the Spirit, he cannot enter into the kingdom of God. That which is born of the flesh is flesh; and that which is born of the Spirit is spirit. Marvel not that I said unto thee, Ye must be born again" (John 3:4–6). Even though humans gave into their carnal nature, the promised Seed of the Woman held the sole hope of redemption.

# "...YET HIS DAYS SHALL BE AN HUNDRED AND TWENTY YEARS" – COUNTDOWN TO JUDGMENT DAY

Thoroughly dismayed at the corruption occurring all over the world, the Lord set a 120-year probation period before executing His judgment. The logical conclusion from a plain reading of the text is that the Lord afforded those in rebellion against Him 120 years to repent before imposing the devastating flood judgment. The invasion of the fallen angels who sinned and their Nephilim progeny had accelerated sin, death, and corruption to such a level that God responded by wiping out over 99.9% of the human population. We must not overlook this. The sinful violation was so severe and grievous in the Lord's eyes that the entire planet needed to be wiped out.

Providing a period for sinners to repent is a part of the Lord's character. In Genesis 15 God told Abraham of his future inheritance of the Promised Land:

> "And he said unto Abram, Know of a surety that thy seed shall be a stranger in a land that is not theirs, and shall serve them; and they shall afflict them four hundred years; And also that nation, whom they shall serve, will I judge: and afterward shall they come out with great substance. And thou shalt go to thy fathers in peace; thou shalt be buried in a good old age. But in the fourth generation they shall come hither again: for the iniquity of the Amorites is not yet full." – Genesis 15:13–16

In this prophecy, God stated that the timing set for Abraham's descendants to take possession of the Promised Land was in part because the "iniquity of the Amorites is not yet full." God has a measure of patience with a sinful people before they reach the tipping point to incur His wrath.

"And the LORD passed by before him, and proclaimed, the Lord, the Lord God, merciful and gracious, longsuffering, and abundant in goodness and truth, Keeping mercy for thousands, forgiving iniquity and transgression and sin…" – Exodus 34:6–7

We find further confirmation of this in one of the principal Nephilim passages:

"For Christ also hath once suffered for sins, the just for the unjust, that he might bring us to God, being put to death in the flesh, but quickened by the Spirit: By which also he went and preached unto the spirits in prison; **Which sometime were disobedient, when once the longsuffering of God waited in the days of Noah, while the ark was a preparing**, wherein few, that is, eight souls were saved by water." – 1 Peter 3:18–20

This passage describes Christ's time in Hell during the three days following His crucifixion when He preached to the angels who sinned. And the Apostle Peter refers to the time "when once the longsuffering of God waited in the days of Noah, while the ark was a preparing," which confirms that that 120-year period was indeed an opportunity for humanity to repent before the devastation of the Flood.

CHAPTER 7

# HOW CAN ANGELS HAVE CHILDREN WITH HUMAN WOMEN?

"All reasoning and preconceived opinions must give way to opposing facts and these facts are plainly presented in the only legitimate interpretation of our passage. We find it stated that the Bne ha Elohim whom we cannot but conclude to be angels, for this point we regard as established even by what has been already advanced, did in the days before the Flood form such alliances with human beings as the objectors declare to be impossible and this being so we are bound to believe the fact however difficult it may be to understand or to explain how such an extraordinary union could take place." – *The Fallen Angels and the Heroes of Mythology*, Rev. John Fleming A.B., Dublin: Hodges, Foster, & Figgis, 1879, p. 85.

"There were giants in the earth in those days; and also after that, **when the sons of God came in unto the daughters of men, and they bare children to them**, the same became mighty men which were of old, men of renown." – Genesis 6:4

How can an angel from Heaven conceive a child with a human woman? A literal reading of Scripture explains. The principal passage in the book of Jude refers to these angels' literal and spiritual descent into sin:

"And the angels which kept not their first estate, but left their own habitation, he hath reserved in everlasting chains under darkness unto the judgment of the great day. Even as Sodom and Gomorrah, and the cities about them in like manner, giving themselves over to fornication, and going after strange flesh, are set forth for an example, suffering the vengeance of eternal fire." – Jude 1:6–7

The "first estate" translates as a "beginning" or "origin." The apostate angels abandoned their heavenly station and holy service to God. Also of interest is the phrase "but left their own habitation." The term "habitation," which is the Greek *oikētērion,* occurs only twice in the Bible. The only other instance is in 2 Corinthians 5:

"For we know that if our earthly house of this tabernacle were dissolved, we have a building of God, an house not made with hands, eternal in the heavens. For in this we groan, earnestly desiring to be clothed upon with our house (*oikētērion*) which is from heaven: If so be that being clothed we shall not be found naked. For we that are in this tabernacle do groan, being burdened: not for that we would be unclothed, but clothed upon, that mortality might be swallowed up of life. Now he that hath wrought us for the selfsame thing is God, who also hath given unto us the earnest of the Spirit. Therefore we are always confident, knowing that, whilst we are at home in the body, we are absent from the Lord." – 2 Corinthians 5:1–6

The Greek word *oikētērion* is used here metaphorically to describe the glorified, heavenly body a born-again believer will eventually receive as a "house" that believers "earnestly" desire to be clothed with. The Apostle Paul, under the Holy Spirit's inspiration, explains that for Christians the flesh bodies we are born with pale in comparison to the heavenly bodies we will receive at the Rapture when all believers are translated. This celestial body is immortal and does not contain the sin nature that all human beings have inherited from Adam. So, the "house" that Paul desires is the same "habitation", or *oikēterion,* that the angels who sinned chose to desecrate to pursue their sinful schemes. These apostate angels succumbed to evil desires, degraded their habitation in an immortal, heavenly body, and became "flesh" – stained with sin and destined for God's judgment.

The second half of Jude 1:6 references that very judgment ("… he hath reserved in everlasting chains under darkness unto the judgment of the great day"). These sinning sons of God are presently locked in chains in the abyss, under darkness awaiting their final judgment and punishment.

> "Even as Sodom and Gomorrah, and the cities about them in like manner, giving themselves over to fornication, and going after strange flesh…." – Jude 1:7

Sodom and Gomorrah are the preeminent symbols of unrestrained sin and wickedness in the Bible. Jude compares the rebel sons of God, consumed with fleshly lust for human women, to the people of these two cursed and damned cities. In Genesis 18 when God informed Abraham of His intention to judge and potentially destroy Sodom and Gomorrah we read: "And the LORD said, Because the cry of Sodom and Gomorrah is great, and because their sin is very grievous…" (Genesis 18:20). Concerned for his nephew Lot, who lived in Sodom, Abraham sought to bargain with the Lord. He first asked for clemency for Sodom and Gomorrah if 50 God-fearing people could be found in them; the Lord said yes. Abraham continued to whittle down the number of believers needed for a pardon to 10, and God, again showing His great mercy and compassion, agreed to spare the entire populations of both cities from judgment for their sin if even 10 faithful people could be found in them.

# THE MEN OF SODOM WANTED TO FORNICATE WITH ANGELS

Like the book of Jude, the book of Genesis describes the rampant fornication among the people of these two cities:

> "And there came two angels to Sodom at even; and Lot sat in the gate of Sodom: and Lot seeing them rose up to meet them; and he bowed himself with his face toward the ground; And he said, Behold now, my lords, turn in, I pray you, into your servant's house, and tarry all night, and wash your feet, and ye shall rise up early, and go on your ways. And they said, Nay; but we will abide in the street all night. And he pressed upon them greatly; and they turned in unto him, and entered into his house; and he made them a feast, and did bake unleavened bread, and they did eat. But before they lay down, the men of the city, even the men of Sodom, compassed the house round, both old and young, all the people from every quarter: And they called unto Lot, and said unto him, Where are the men which came in to thee this night? bring them out unto us, that we may know them. And Lot went out at the door unto them, and shut the door after him, And said, I pray you, brethren, do not so wickedly." – Genesis 19:1–7

The city of Sodom was so depraved that a mob consisting of all males in the city, young and old, tried to break into Lot's home to sexually molest the two angels staying with Lot. Consider their demand to Lot – that the two messengers of God come into the street so an entire group of lustful men could have their way with them publicly. This was a society whose moral fiber was absolutely destroyed. Open, rampant sexual immorality had become the norm. The men of Sodom, their consciences seared, were given over to the same reprobate mind and accompanying lusts described in Romans 1. The people of these cities were not merely consumed with lust but desired sexual relations that defied God's divinely-ordained order. The men of Sodom and Gomorrah engaged in homosexual activity and even attempted *to fornicate with angels*. Both Jude and Peter compare Sodom to the behavior of the angelic fathers of the Nephilim who invaded the human realm before the Flood.

A plain reading of the text reveals that the issue here *was sexual sin*. Physical attraction to human women sparked the initial thought of sin in the minds of the evil angels of Genesis 6 ("they saw that they were fair"). Some have suggested that the angels used some type of occult or scientific experimentation – instead of sexual relations – to impregnate human women and breed Nephilim giants. Scripture, however, leaves no room for such an interpretation in Genesis 6. The passage in Jude specifically says the angels were "as Sodom and Gomorrah, giving themselves over to fornication." Nothing could make it any clearer: The lustful fallen angels were having forbidden sex with human women. And both Sodom and Gomorrah and the incursion of fallen angels in Genesis 6 brought God's swift, devastating, and decisive punishment.

## BIBLICAL EVIDENCE OF
## ANGELIC-HUMAN RELATIONS

So how can an angel reproduce with a woman? How is this possible? While Genesis 6 does not provide the specific mechanics of these illicit relations, we can glean much from other passages of Scripture that confirm that angel-human reproduction was indeed possible.

Job, the earliest book of the Bible, was written by the patriarch Job who lived close to the time of the Flood (which is also reflected in his use of the term *B'nai ha Elohim* or "sons of God" to refer to angels just as Genesis 6 does). In Job 15 we read: "Behold, he [God] putteth no trust in his saints; yea, the heavens are not clean in his sight," indicating sin taking place in the heavenly realm. Another passage of Job not often cited refers directly to certain angels who were indeed involved in illicit relations with human women. It is found in the chapter where Eliphas, one of Job's friends, shared a vision he witnessed:

> "Now a thing was secretly brought to me, and mine ear received a little thereof. In thoughts from the visions of the night, when deep sleep falleth on men, Fear came upon me, and trembling, which made all my bones to shake. Then a spirit passed before my face; the hair of my flesh stood up: It stood still, but I could not discern the form thereof: an image was before mine eyes, there was silence, and I heard a voice, saying, Shall mortal man be more just than God? shall a man be more pure than his maker? Behold, he put no trust in his servants; **and his angels he charged with folly**...." – Job 4:13–18

The word "folly," which is translated from the Hebrew *nĕbalah,* is commonly defined as "senselessness; or disgraceful." While dictionary definitions are important, the primary source for the meaning of a word is the context in which it occurs. In the King James Version of the Old Testament (which is the primary Bible version used in this book), "folly" is most often used to describe sexual sin. Here are several examples:

> "And Dinah the daughter of Leah, which she bare unto Jacob, went out to see the daughters of the land. And when Shechem the son of Hamor the Hivite, prince of the country, saw her, he took her, and lay with her, and defiled her... And the sons of Jacob came out of the field when they heard it: and the men were grieved, and they were very wroth, **because he had wrought folly in Israel in lying with Jacob's daughter**: which thing ought not to be done." – Genesis 34:1–2, 7

> "Then they shall bring out the damsel to the door of her father's house, and the men of her city shall stone her with stones that she

die: **because she hath wrought folly in Israel, to play the whore in her father's house**: so shalt thou put evil away from among you." – Deuteronomy 22:21

"Now as they were making their hearts merry, behold, the men of the city, certain sons of Belial, beset the house round about, and beat at the door, and spake to the master of the house, the old man, saying, **Bring forth the man that came into thine house, that we may know him**. And the man, the master of the house, went out unto them, and said unto them, Nay, my brethren, nay, I pray you, do not so wickedly; seeing that this man is come into mine house, **do not this folly**." – Judges 19:22–23

"And it came to pass after this, that Absalom the son of David had a fair sister, whose name was Tamar; and Amnon the son of David loved her. And Amnon was so vexed, that he fell sick for his sister Tamar; for she was a virgin; and Amnon thought it hard for him to do anything to her... And when she had brought them unto him to eat, he took hold of her, and said unto her, Come lie with me, my sister. And she answered him, **Nay, my brother, do not force me**; for no such thing ought to be done in Israel: **do not thou this folly**." – 2 Samuel 13:1–2; 11–12

Rape, fornication, and incest are the three contexts for the term "folly" above. Rather than a reference to "silly behavior," folly in the King James Bible is used to describe serious, illicit sexual activity.

With the proper biblical connotation in mind, let's return to Job 4:18: "Behold, he put no trust in his servants; and his angels he charged with folly..." When we let Scripture interpret Scripture, the Bible confirms that certain untrustworthy angels were charged with the sin of "folly" for unholy sexual acts. In the Septuagint, the same verse from Job reads: "he perceives *perverseness* in his angels" confirming all the more that angels committed acts of fornication.

An 18th-century sermon referring to these sinning angels stated:

> "He tells us of their Fall: *Behold he put no trust in his Servants and his Angels he charged with folly,* Job iv.8. Again, *Behold he putteth no trust in his Saints Yea the Heavens are not clean in his sight* Job xv.15. This uncleanness in the Inhabitants of Heaven seems rather to allude to this Fall of the Angels by Incontinency, than that of Pride and Ambition. And I do not know why it may not intimate their polluting of the Holy Seed." – *A Sermon Preach'd at Chester: Against Marriages in Different Communion*, Charles Leslie, Henry Dodwell, 1702, p. 165.

The polluting of the Holy Seed was the sons of Gods' attempt to corrupt the Messianic bloodline. Job's description of the angels' folly corresponds with the principal passage from 2 Peter 2:

> "For if God spared not the angels that sinned, but cast them down to hell, and delivered them into chains of darkness, to be reserved unto judgment; And spared not the old world, but saved Noah the eighth person, a preacher of righteousness, bringing in the flood upon the world of the ungodly; And turning the cities of Sodom and Gomorrah into ashes condemned them with an overthrow, making them an ensample unto those that after should live ungodly; And delivered just Lot, vexed with the filthy conversation of the wicked…" – 2 Peter 2:4–7

The sinning sons of God who left their "habitation" are reserved in chains of darkness until Judgment Day. This was the punishment for those angels who left their heavenly office to "go after strange flesh," namely human women. Like Jude, 2 Peter also refers to Sodom and Gomorrah. Scripture gives ample evidence that angels did indeed fornicate with human women. The Bible also provides further information on how it could happen from a physiological standpoint.

*Angels Have Physical Bodies*

> "And the LORD appeared unto him in the plains of Mamre: and he sat in the tent door in the heat of the day; And he lift up his eyes and looked, and, lo, three men stood by him: and when he saw them, he ran to meet them from the tent door, and bowed himself toward the ground, And said, My LORD, if now I have found favour in thy sight, pass not away, I pray thee, from thy servant: **Let a little water, I pray you, be fetched, and wash your feet, and rest yourselves under the tree**: And I will fetch a morsel of bread, and comfort ye your hearts; after that ye shall pass on: for therefore are ye come to your servant. And they said, So do, as thou hast said. And Abraham hastened into the tent unto Sarah, and said, Make ready quickly three measures of fine meal, knead it, and make cakes upon the hearth. And Abraham ran unto the herd, and fetch a calf tender and good, and gave it unto a young man; and he hasted to dress it. And he took butter, and milk, and the calf which he had dressed, **and set it before them; and he stood by them under the tree, and they did eat**." – Genesis 18:1–8

In this passage, God comes to Abraham's home accompanied by two angels. All three heavenly guests have physical bodies. They eat Abraham's food (roasted calf and baked bread) and drink milk. Abraham's servants wash their feet. Thus, angelic beings not only have physical bodies but biological systems similar to humans (which enable them to eat human food).

Conversely, humans can eat the food angels eat in Heaven:

> "And had rained down manna upon them to eat, and had given them of the corn of heaven. **Man did eat angels' food**: he sent them meat to the full." – Psalm 78:24–25

In this passage the Psalmist describes the manna God gave the Israelites as "angels' food." So even in Heaven angels eat, and the physiology of humans and angels is similar because both can eat food from the other's realm. This passage provides further evidence that angels have actual physical bodies and are not just formless, disembodied beings like the common modern conception of ghosts.

On the notion of angels' assuming human form, Tertullian, the legendary second-century theologian, wrote:

> "It is evident that angels do not in their proper nature bear a fleshly body as being of a spiritual nature, and if possessed of a body at all certainly of a body *sui generis* yet such nevertheless that it may when occasion requires be converted to a fleshly substance like the human so that they can appear to and have intercourse with human beings. And as we are not informed from what source they derive this fleshly substance we are at liberty to suppose that it is one of the properties of angels…that is to acquire a fleshly body not from any matter foreign to themselves but simply from a change in their original corporeal forms…." *De Carne Christi* as quoted in *The Fallen Angels and the Heroes of Mythology*, Rev. John Fleming A.B., Dublin: Hodges, Foster, & Figgis, 1879, p. 93.

## Angels Can Physically Interact with Human Beings

> "Then the angel of the LORD went forth, and smote in the camp of the Assyrians a hundred and fourscore and five thousand: and when they arose early in the morning, behold, they were all dead corpses." – Isaiah 37:36

> "And it came to pass, when I, even I Daniel, had seen the vision, and sought for the meaning, then, behold, there stood before me *as*

*the appearance of a man.* And I heard a man's voice between the banks of Ulnae, which called, and said, Gabriel, make this man to understand the vision. So he came near where I stood: and when he came, I was afraid, and fell upon my face: but he said unto me, Understand, O son of man: for at the time of the end shall be the vision. Now as he was speaking with me, I was in a deep sleep on my face toward the ground: but he touched me, and set me upright." – Daniel 8:15–18

In the passages above a single angel kills 185,000 men, and the angel Gabriel, resembling a human man, touched Daniel to wake him and help him stand up straight, reinforcing the fact that angels have physical bodies that can directly interact with human beings.

## Angels Resemble Men

Several classes of angelic realm beings are mentioned in Scripture (such as cherubim, seraphim, sons of God, principalities, morning stars). Certain types of angels resemble or assume a form that resembles human men:

"And it came to pass, when I, even I Daniel, had seen the vision, and sought for the meaning, then, behold, there stood before me as the appearance of a man. And I heard a man's voice between the banks of Ulai, which called, and said, Gabriel, make this man to understand the vision. So he came near where I stood: and when he came, I was afraid, and fell upon my face: but he said unto me, Understand, O son of man: for at the time of the end shall be the vision." – Daniel 8:15–17

The prophet Daniel encountered the angel Gabriel face to face and described him as having "the appearance of a man." He quickly realized, however, that he was speaking with a heavenly being – hence his fear and respectful bow.

"Now upon the first day of the week, very early in the morning, they came unto the sepulchre, bringing the spices which they had prepared, and certain others with them. And they found the stone rolled away from the sepulchre. And they entered in, and found not the body of the Lord Jesus. And it came to pass, as they were much perplexed thereabout, **behold, two men stood by them in shining garments**: And as they were afraid, and bowed down their faces to the earth, they said unto them, Why seek ye the living among the dead? He is not here, but is risen: remember how he spake unto you when he was yet in Galilee, Saying, The Son of man must be delivered into the hands of sinful men, and be crucified, and the third day rise again." – Luke 24:17

Although they wore shining garments signifying their heavenly status, the two angels in the tomb of Jesus Christ appeared as "men." John 20, which recounts the same events, removes any doubt that they were more than mere men:

"But Mary stood without at the sepulchre weeping: and as she wept, she stooped down, and looked into the sepulchre, **And seeth two angels in white sitting**, the one at the head, and the other at the feet, where the body of Jesus had lain." – John 20:11-12

The Bible confirms that certain classes of angels assume the appearance of humans. The wicked men of Sodom referred to the angels as "men" as well. The book of Hebrews confirms this notion with an interesting passage: "Let brotherly love continue. Be not forgetful to entertain strangers: for thereby some have entertained angels unawares" (Hebrews 13:1–2). Certain angels so closely resemble humans that it is possible to have a visitor in your home and not even be aware that he or she is an angelic being. Whether it is an assumed or normal form, angels have physical bodies identical in appearance to humans.

# ANGELS HAVE A STRIKING APPEARANCE

When assuming human form, angels have distinct physical features that reveal their heavenly origin. In the book of Judges, Samson's mother acknowledged this difference in her encounter with an angel, whom she originally mistook for a mortal man:

> "And the angel of the LORD appeared unto the woman, and said unto her, Behold now, thou art barren, and bearest not: but thou shalt conceive, and bear a son… Then the woman came and told her husband, saying, A man of God came unto me, and his countenance was like the countenance of an angel of God, very terrible: but I asked him not whence he was, neither told he me his name…" – Judges 13:3, 6

The Apostle Stephen, the first martyr of the church, was filled with the Holy Spirit and performed miracles and supernatural acts while serving food as a deacon in the early church (Acts 6:5–8). He was soon framed via lying witnesses whom the Sanhedrin had ordered to lie. At Stephen's trial the Holy Spirit no doubt enhanced his appearance:

> "And all that sat in the council, looking stedfastly on him, saw his face as it had been the face of an angel." – Acts 6:15

Of Stephen's angelic visage, a 19th-century commentary stated:

> "If Acts vi 15 the face of Stephen appears as the face of an angel it follows from this that this face is conceived of after a human analogy but glorified by a heavenly glory." – *Biblical Theology of the New Testament, Translated from the Third Revised Edition*, Rev. James E. Duguid, Vol. II, 1883, p. 303.

# ANGELS HAVE "SEED"

Angels clearly have physical bodies that can touch, move, and taste in the human realm. But does this mean they can reproduce? And, if so, with a human? 1 Corinthians 15 explains that angels not only have bodies but also "seed":

> "But some man will say, How are the dead raised up? and with what body do they come? Thou fool, that which thou sowest is not quickened, except it die: And that which thou sowest, thou sowest not that body that shall be, but bare grain, it may chance of wheat, or of some other grain: **But God gives it a body as it hath pleased him, and to every seed his own body.** All flesh is not the same flesh: but there is one kind of flesh of men, another flesh of beasts, another of fishes, and another of birds. There are also celestial bodies, and bodies terrestrial: but the glory of the celestial is one, and the glory of the terrestrial is another." – 1 Corinthians 15:36–40

Note the initial questions the Apostle Paul was responding to: How are those who die in faith in Christ able to be resurrected? What body are they resurrected with? The Apostle responded with a beautiful illustration from agriculture. A farmer does not grow wheat by dropping wheat on the soil. He drops a wheat *seed*. As biology confirms, a seed must fall apart and release its genetic material into the soil to enable wheat or another grain to be born and grow from the ground. Every living creature that has a body *also has a seed*.

Paul reiterated the Lord's genetic order – that all creatures are not genetically the same. Humans and animals are different kinds of "flesh," just as fish are different from both. The apostle then contrasts the bodies of "celestial" or heavenly creatures with those of "terrestrial" or Earth-born creatures. As Pastor Michael Hoggard of Bethel Baptist Church (Festus, Missouri) has pointed out in his extensive study of this topic, Paul was contrasting opposites but driving home a consistent point – that all creatures God created, including angels and humans, have both bodies and seed. This contrast is emphasized in Job: "Behold, he put no trust in his servants; and his angels he charged with folly: *How much less in them that dwell in houses of clay*, whose foundation is in the dust, which are crushed before the moth?" (Job 4:18–19). Unlike angels who are made from heavenly substance and are "celestial," humans are wholly from the dust of the earth and thus "terrestrial."

British Bible scholar John Kitto expounded on this point:

> "When therefore the ancient Jews called angels spirits, they did not mean to deny that they were endued with bodies. When they affirmed that angels were incorporeal, they used the term in the sense in which it was understood by the ancients; – that is, as free from the impurities of gross matter. The distinction between a 'natural body' and a 'spiritual body' is indicated by St Paul (1 Corinthians xv44); and we may with sufficient safety, assume that angels are spiritual bodies, rather than pure spirits in the modern acceptation of the word." – *A Cyclopedia of Biblical Literature*, ed. by J. Kitto, Vol. 1, 1851, p. 148.

Human beings who have faith in Jesus Christ for the forgiveness of their sins will receive that new incorruptible, "spiritual body":

> "So also is the resurrection of the dead. It is sown in corruption; it is raised in incorruption: It is sown in dishonour; it is raised in glory: it is sown in weakness; it is raised in power: It is sown a natural body; it is raised a spiritual body. **There is a natural body, and there is a spiritual body**. And so it is written, The first man Adam was made a living soul; the last Adam was made a quickening spirit. Howbeit that was not first which is spiritual, but that which is natural; and afterward that which is spiritual. The first man is of

the earth, earthy; the second man is the Lord from heaven. As is the earthy, such are they also that are earthy: and as is the heavenly, such are they also that are heavenly. And as we have borne the image of the earthy, we shall also bear the image of the heavenly." – 1 Corinthians 15:42–49

Human beings have earthly, "natural" bodies. But, like the resurrected Christ, born-again Christians will one day be translated to a "spiritual body." The spiritual body, made from heavenly substance, is not immaterial or ghost-like. It can be touched and felt and function like a natural body. After His resurrection, Jesus Christ went out of His way to demonstrate this to His disciples:

"And as they thus spake, Jesus himself stood in the midst of them, and saith unto them, Peace be unto you. But they were terrified and affrighted, and supposed that they had seen a spirit. And he said unto them, Why are ye troubled? and why do thoughts arise in your hearts? Behold my hands and my feet, that it is I myself: handle me, and see; **for a spirit hath not flesh and bones, as ye see me have.** And when he had thus spoken, he shewed them his hands and his feet. And while they yet believed not for joy, and wondered, he said unto them, Have ye here any meat? And they gave him a piece of a broiled fish, and of an honeycomb. And he took it, and did eat before them." – Luke 24:36–43

In His glorified, spiritual body Jesus bore wounds and could be touched and eat human food. He specifically told His disciples that he had "flesh and bones" and was not a "spirit" or ghost. A glorified body has physical properties and functions. Unlike the earthly body, which suffers corruption, the spiritual body is immortal:

"And Jesus answering said unto them, The children of this world marry, and are given in marriage: But they which shall be accounted worthy to obtain that world, and the resurrection from the dead, neither marry, nor are given in marriage: *Neither can they die any more*: for they are equal unto the angels; and are the children of God, being the children of the resurrection." – Luke 20:34–36

Born-again Christians, upon receiving their eternal, glorified bodies, will be immortal and thus "equal to angels." Scripture establishes that angels do indeed have physical bodies, can interact in the human physical realm, eat food, touch, hold, and even physically kill human beings and that they have seed – the same genetic reproductive materials found in humans, plants, and animals. When the sinning sons of God "came in unto" the daughters of men, did the seed of a heavenly angel pass on to an earthly woman and impregnate her? This is precisely what Genesis 6 reports.

If this concept still seems difficult to accept, consider the birth of the Lord Jesus Christ:

"Now the birth of Jesus Christ was on this wise: When as his mother Mary was espoused to Joseph, before they came together, she was found with child of the Holy Ghost. Then Joseph her husband, being a just man, and not willing to make her a public example, was minded to put her away privily. But while he thought on these things, behold, the angel of the LORD appeared unto him in a dream, saying, Joseph, thou son of David, fear not to take unto thee Mary thy wife: **for that which is conceived in her is of the Holy Ghost**. And she shall bring forth a son, and thou shalt call his name JESUS: for he shall save his people from their sins." – Matthew 1:18–21

Jesus Christ was literally conceived in Mary, a human woman, by the Holy Ghost. A seed was placed in her through supernatural means and impregnated her. Scripture clearly establishes that heavenly beings, even the Holy Spirit

Himself, can pass on seed to a human woman to conceive a child. Satan, knowing a divine child of a woman was prophesied to conquer him, established his perverse imitation via wicked angels' fornicating with human women. A 19th-century commentary connected the biblical concept of "seed" to the angels who sinned:

> "All flesh is not the same flesh, (1 Cor. xv. 39). The next verse informs us that there is celestial as well as terrestrial flesh. Several instances of celestial flesh we have recorded. The angels who visited Abraham and partook of his fare; (Gen. xviii. 2, 8), and two of them pulled Lot in, and took hold of his hand, (xix. 10, 16). The angel also that wrestled with Jacob, (xxxii. 24, 30), **and the sons of God who begat the giants of the daughters of men**, (vi. 2. Jude 6), This appears to be the origin of the heathen mythology of the ancients. These were the angels that shouted for joy at the creation, before Adam was made, (Job xxxviii. 7), and amongst whom Satan appeared before God, (i. 6, ii. 1). They subsist upon substantial food like us, (Ps lxxviii. 25) and, we are only made a little lower than them, (Heb ii. 7)." – *The Wisdom of God Shown Forth by the Opening of the Books*, Thomas Stokes, Printed by J. Barker, Wortley, 1847, p. 67.

## BUT DOESN'T THE BIBLE SAY ANGELS CANNOT MARRY?

The biblical concept of angels' having intimate relations with human women is not often taught in churches or seminaries. It is frequently rejected out of hand as being too bizarre to possibly be true. But the biblical record supports it. The most common objection to the idea of angelic-human illicit relations is the following passage:

"The same day came to him the Sadducees, which say that there is no resurrection, and asked him, Saying, Master, Moses said, If a man die, having no children, his brother shall marry his wife, and raise up seed unto his brother. Now there were with us seven brethren: and the first, when he had married a wife, deceased, and, having no issue, left his wife unto his brother: Likewise the second also, and the third, unto the seventh. And last of all the woman died also. Therefore in the resurrection whose wife shall she be of the seven? for they all had her. Jesus answered and said unto them, Ye do err, not knowing the scriptures, nor the power of God. For in the resurrection they neither marry, nor are given in marriage, but are as the angels of God in heaven." – Matthew 22:23–31

In this passage Jesus states that humans after the resurrection do not marry, but "are as the angels of God in Heaven." Righteous angels do not marry despite the existence of female angels, as the prophet Zechariah witnessed:

"Then lifted I up mine eyes, and looked, and, behold, **there came out two women, and the wind was in their wings; for they had wings like the wings of a stork**: and they lifted up the ephah between the earth and the heaven." (Zechariah 5:9).

So how could the angels of Genesis 6 take wives as they chose? The answer is simple: The Lord was referring to *the obedient angels of God in Heaven*, denoting these are holy angels who do not marry. The angels who sinned "left their first estate." They were willing to forfeit their heavenly status to satisfy their lust. (We would do well to see the powerful lesson in this, as many people today are willing to give up salvation, eternal life, and Heaven to fulfill their sinful desires.) Thus, while it is true that righteous angels do not marry, the evil rebels of Genesis 6 certainly did.

# THE VIOLATION OF GOD'S GENETIC ORDER

"And God said, Let the earth bring forth grass, the herb yielding seed, and the fruit tree yielding fruit **after his kind**, whose seed is in itself, upon the earth: and it was so. And the earth brought forth grass, and herb yielding seed after his kind, and the tree yielding fruit, **whose seed was in itself, after his kind**: and God saw that it was good… And God said, Let the earth bring forth the living creature **after his kind**, cattle, and creeping thing, and beast of the earth **after his kind**: and it was so. And God made the beast of the earth **after his kind**, and cattle **after their kind**, and every thing that creepeth upon the earth **after his kind:** and God saw that it was good." – Genesis 1:11–12; 24–25

From the first week of creation, the Lord established a genetic order for the world. Plants, animals, birds, and creatures of all types were to be created and reproduce after their "kind." The Hebrew term *miyn*, which is translated "kind," in Scripture refers to a "species, family or race." God's specific desire was for the various species to reproduce along the lines of their given genetics. Maintaining genetic order was critical to the Lord's creative work and man, the pinnacle of the creation week, was designed with a genetic makeup that also bore the image of God in him.

## PSALM 139: THE BIBLICAL CHAPTER ON DNA

Psalm 139 is the most detailed passage on genetics in the Bible. In it King David provided a commentary on human DNA:

"For thou hast possessed my reins: thou hast covered me in my mother's womb. I will praise thee; for I am fearfully and wonderfully made: marvelous are thy works; and that my soul knoweth right well.

My substance was not hid from thee, when I was made in secret, and curiously wrought in the lowest parts of the earth. Thine eyes did see my substance, yet being unperfect; and in thy book all my members were written, which in continuance were fashioned, when as yet there was none of them." – Psalm 139:13–16

In the passage above, David marveled at God's power to create a human life in the womb. In verse 14, David states that God's "eyes did see my substance, yet being unperfect." In other words, God knew what David would look like before his body was even fully formed. He then writes "and in thy book all my members were written, which in continuance were fashioned, when as yet there was none of them." The "members" or David's body parts were written in "God's book" before they ever existed. This "book" is DNA. Human DNA is the blueprint of a person's body. In the womb, a baby's gender, race, height, hair, eye color, family relations, and a host of other physical attributes can be determined just from examining his DNA. Psalm 139 acknowledged this blueprint for the human body when David wrote that his body parts "in continuance were fashioned, when as yet there was none of them." Even before his hands, eyes, and hair were created, the design for them was already within the womb, recorded in the Lord's book – human DNA.

Only in recent decades have scientists discovered that DNA is indeed a book, with a code written on it that can be read and deciphered to know everything about a person's physiology:

> "Imagine a future where the amount of data on the Web could be saved to a thumb drive. A storage medium already exists that can hold this amount of information. It's call DNA.

> "DNA typically stores biological information in cells that direct structures like proteins do their jobs. But scientists are investigating ways to get DNA to store other kinds of information. This week, *Harvard researchers* reported in the journal *Science* that they

encoded an entire book into DNA. Not only that, they read back the text.

"How'd they do it? Well, it all boils down to letters and numbers.

"If you remember back to your middle school biology class, DNA is composed of two coiled strands consisting of four chemical bases: adenine (A), guanine (G), cytosine (C) and thymine (T).

"Using the zeros–and–ones of computer language, the Harvard team began with the digital version of the book. On paper, they translated the zeros into the A or C of the DNA base pair. Likewise, they translated the ones into the G or T.

"Then they created actual DNA — nearly 55,000 short strands that all included the new coded sequence that contained portions of the text.

"In this viscous-liquid or solid-salt form, researchers said that a billion copies of the book could easily fit into a test tube and that they could last for centuries, provided with the right conditions.

"It shows that the vast increase in capacity to synthesize and sequence DNA can be applied to store significant amounts of data," said synthetic biologist Drew Endy at Stanford University, who wasn't involved in the project. "If you wanted to have your library encoded in DNA, you could probably do that now." – Text Book Encoded In DNA, Nic Halverson, http://news.discovery.com/tech/biotechnology/entire–book–encoded–dna–120817.htm

Although Psalm 139 was written about 1000 BC, King David accurately described the way DNA functions to contain the instructions and design of the human body. Aside from demonstrating how amazing and truly divinely-inspired the Bible is, this also shows that genetics are a high priority to God. The importance of maintaining genetic purity is reemphasized in the Mosaic Law:

> "Ye shall keep my statutes. Thou shalt not let thy cattle gender with a diverse kind: thou shalt not sow thy field with mingled seed: neither shall a garment mingled of linen and woollen come upon thee. And whosoever lieth carnally with a woman, that is a bondmaid, betrothed to an husband, and not at all redeemed, nor freedom given her; she shall be scourged; they shall not be put to death, because she was not free." – Leviticus 19:19–20

God forbade the Israelites from "gendering" or cross-breeding any kind of cattle with a different species. "Cattle" in Scripture refers to cows, horses, donkeys, sheep, and other varieties of four-legged animals. So, a cow was not be cross-bred with a horse, for example. And mixing their genetic lines was a sin.

In his commentary on the Bible, Adam Clarke said of this passage:

> "These precepts taken literally seem to imply that they should not permit the horse and the she-ass, nor the he-ass and the cow, (as they do in the East), to couple together; nor sow different kinds of seeds in the same field or garden; nor have garments of silk and woolen, cotton and silk, linen and wool, etc. And if all these were forbidden, there must have been some moral reason for the prohibitions, because domestic economy required several of these mixtures, especially those which relate to seeds and clothing. With respect to heterogeneous mixtures among cattle, there is something very unnatural in it, and it was probably forbidden to prevent excitements to such unnatural lusts as those condemned in the preceding chapter, Leviticus 18:22, Leviticus 18:23." – *The Holy*

*Bible, Containing the Old and New Testaments: The Text Carefully Printed from the Most Correct Copies of the Present Authorized Translation. Including the Marginal Readings and Parallel Texts. With a Commentary and Critical Notes,* Vol. 1, Adam Clarke L.L.D., Published by Ezra Sergeant: New York, 1811.

Leviticus 18:22–23 deals with sexual sin, showing that Clarke understood that the principle regarding not mixing cattle or blending seeds was pointing to a moral evil. Ironically, today many who try to challenge the Bible will cite this very verse from Leviticus 19: *"After all,"* they say, *"the book of Leviticus says not to mix fabrics, so clearly it's an outdated text...."* When we examine this passage in context, however, we find a greater principle at work: God sought to maintain His original creation and protect it from corruption.

From the days of the Garden of Eden, the Lord pronounced that salvation would come via "seed." Satan, the enemy of mankind, would wage war through his own "seed." The battle shifted to one of competing lineages, and the corruption of the human bloodline was one of the worst, most abominable acts committed in human history. It threatened the very plan of salvation for all people. Satan knew that if he could corrupt human genetics and disrupt the intended nature of God's creation, he could potentially thwart the Lord's plan of redemption – ensuring all human beings would burn in Hell and the Lake of Fire. With this understanding, God's reaction to the Devil's Nephilim armies will make much more sense.

The wicked sons of God crossed a line that would bring unprecedented judgments of destruction and wrath. What they were doing was threatening the very existence of humanity itself and the coming of the Savior – the Seed of the Woman. In the days of Jared, Enoch, and Noah, human beings were literally being replaced and supplanted by an entirely new breed of being: the Nephilim.

# CHAPTER 8

# BIRTH OF THE GIANTS

"….and they bare children to them, the same became mighty men which were of old, men of renown." – Genesis 6:5

"For many angels of God accompanied with women, and begat sons that proved unjust, and despisers of all that was good, on account of the confidence they had in their own strength; for the tradition is, that these men did what resembled the acts of those whom the Grecians call giants." – *Antiquities of the Jews*, Book I, 3:1, Flavius Josephus, as recorded in *The Works of Flavius Josephus*, William Whiston, Vol. 1, 1843, p. 16.

"Unless a man is born from above he cannot enter the kingdom of heaven but he must be born of the Spirit of God not of the spirit of angels. The unnatural combination of two distinct species, of the angelic and the human; disturbed the whole order of things and broke down the barriers between heaven and earth. The Giants, half brothers to the angels, laid claim to half the privileges of heaven and would have brought heaven and earth into a [connection] both unholy and premature." – *The Last Vials: Being a Series of Essays on the Second Advent*, Volume 21, Robert Purdon, 1855, p. 15.

Genesis 6:5 on its own confirms that something unique took place in that era of biblical history: Giants were born. This is the first verse in Scripture that directly references the Nephilim, the giant offspring of the union of the angelic sons of God and the human daughters of men.

## THE ORIGIN OF THE TERM "NEPHILIM"

The term "Nephilim" is often translated "those who fall," "the fallen," or "those who descend to earth." Dr. Michael Heiser, however, provides a sound explanation based on the actual Hebrew grammar. The following is a quote from his critique of an author who defined Nephilim as "those who fall":

> "Sitchin assumes 'Nephilim' comes from the Hebrew word 'naphal' which usually means 'to fall.' He then forces the meaning 'to come down' onto the word, creating his 'to come down from above' translation. In the form we find it in the Hebrew Bible, if the word *Nephilim* came from Hebrew *naphal*, it would not be spelled as we find it. The form *Nephilim* cannot mean 'fallen ones' (the spelling would then be *nephulim*). Likewise Nephilim does not mean 'those who fall' or 'those who fall away' (that would be *nophelim*). The only way in Hebrew to get *Nephilim* from *naphal* by the rules of Hebrew morphology (word formation) would be to presume a noun spelled *naphil* and then pluralize it.

> "I say 'presume' since this noun does not exist in biblical Hebrew – – unless one counts Genesis 6:4 and Numbers 13:33, the two occurrences of *Nephilim* — but that would then be assuming what one is trying to prove! However, in Aramaic the noun naphil(a) does exist. It means 'giant,' making it easy to see why the Septuagint (the ancient Greek translation of the Hebrew Bible) translated *Nephilim* as *gigantes* ('giant') .... It is most likely that *Nephilim* is an Aramaic term imported into Hebrew during the final editing of

the Hebrew Bible in Babylon (where Aramaic was the lingua franca) and then the ending was corrected to Hebrew rules of word formation. Both phenomena are known in the Hebrew Bible."
– Michael Heiser,
http://www.sitchiniswrong.com/nephilim/nephilim.htm

A 19th-century commentary provides further confirmation:

"All the ancient versions translate nephilim, 'giants' and the modern exegetes do the same…In the Aramaic of the Targumim, Orion, or rather Sagittarius, the Kesil of the Hebrew is called *niphla* an expression rendered in the Syriac version by *gaeboro*, 'giant', and it calls the great constellations of the heavens *nephllin*, 'giants'. In the Medrash of the book of Ruth quoted by Castelli there is a question as to the progeny of the union of a *nephil* with a *nephila* a giant with a giantess. **All this shows plainly that *nephilim* is not the designation of a special race a particular people but is a general term to designate giants**." – *The Beginnings of History According to the Bible and the Traditions of Oriental Peoples: From the Creation of Man to the Deluge*, Translated from the French Second Edition, François Lenormant, 1844, p. 343–344.

So rather than originating from the Hebrew term *naphal*, "Nephilim" is an Aramaic term for giant that was adopted in ancient Hebrew. The King James Version translators seemed to be aware of this since they used the term "giants" in Genesis 6:4 (as opposed to calling them "the fallen" or "those who fall"; "attackers"; etc.). The Septuagint uses the Greek term *gigantes*, which also translates "giant."

The Nephilim were Satan's nuclear weapon in the war to disrupt the plan of God and place himself in authority over Earth and Heaven. The Nephilim threatened humanity because they had the potential to fully corrupt the gene pool. Additionally, the extreme violence of the giants extinguished much of humanity on its own. Genesis chapters 6 and 7 provides insight into the extent of the damage the giants wrought:

> "And God saw that the wickedness of man was great in the earth, and that every imagination of the thoughts of his heart was only evil continually. And it repented the LORD that he had made man on the earth, and it grieved him at his heart." – Genesis 6:5–6

The presence of the Nephilim giants so accelerated the moral decay of society that the human heart was focused on "…only evil continually." These giants corrupted the entire planet to the point that Scripture proclaims: "The earth also was corrupt before God, and the earth was filled with violence. And God looked upon the earth, and, behold, it was corrupt; for all flesh had corrupted his way upon the earth" (Genesis 6:11–12). The Nephilim that were taking over the world degraded all the creatures on Earth.

This was the gravest threat yet to the survival of the human race and the prophecy of the seed of the woman. If there were no people left on Earth, how could the Savior be born? If human beings were no longer human, where could their redemption come from? This is why God's reaction to this violation of His genetic order for all creatures to reproduce after their "kind" was so harsh. On this subject, the renowned 20th-century theologian A.W. Pink wrote:

> "The reference in Jude 6 to the angels leaving their own habitation, appears to point to and correspond with these 'sons of God' (angels) coming in unto the daughters of men. Apparently, by this means, Satan hoped to *destroy* the human race (the channel through which the woman's Seed was to come) *by producing a race of monstrosities.* How nearly he succeeded is evident from the fact, that with the exception of one family, 'all flesh had *corrupted his* way upon the

earth' (Gen. 6:12). That monstrosities *were* produced as the result of this unnatural union between the 'sons of God' (angels) and the daughters of men, is evident from the words of Genesis 6:4: 'There were *giants* in the earth in those days.'" – *Gleanings in Genesis*, A.W. Pink, Moody Bible Institute of Chicago, 1922, p. 93.

## THE LORD PRESERVED THE LAST PURE HUMAN BEINGS ON EARTH

Many Bible scholars, pastors, and Sunday School teachers attempt to explain the flood judgment by saying that God decided to flood the world as a punishment because humanity was just "sinning too much." Far greater evils were taking place, however, that led to such a destructive judgment. The Scriptures make clear the moral depravity, violence, and genetic corruption the Nephilim posed to the earth. The Lord's response was to destroy the entire polluted human population but for Noah and seven of his family members. Noah was singularly suited to carry on the human race after the flood judgment:

> "But Noah found grace in the eyes of the LORD. These are the generations of Noah: Noah was a just man **and perfect in his generations**, and Noah walked with God." – Genesis 6:8–9

Noah was chosen to carry on and restart humanity after the Flood because he was a believer in God. He was "perfect in his generations" – part of a genetic ancestry that was 100% human. Noah's lineage was not corrupted by the Nephilim hybridization plaguing humanity. The Hebrew word for "perfect" in Genesis 6:9 is *tamiym*, which means "complete, whole" regarding health and physical condition. This is the same word used to prescribe the condition of animals sacrificed to the Lord:

> "And whosoever offereth a sacrifice of peace offerings unto the LORD to accomplish his vow, or a freewill offering in beeves or sheep, it shall be perfect (*tamiym*) to be accepted; there shall be no blemish therein." – Leviticus 22:21

Noah was not a morally perfect person. We need only to look a few chapters ahead to see Noah's own sinful rebellion on display. The Bible is clear that "all have sinned and fall short of the glory of God" (Romans 3:23). The "perfection" Noah possessed was that he was *completely and wholly human.*

The importance of returning the earth to its original state of genetic purity was also evident in the preparatory instructions God gave to Noah:

> "And of every living thing of all flesh, two of every sort shalt thou bring into the ark, to keep them alive with thee; they shall be male and female. Of fowls after their kind, and of cattle after their kind, of every creeping thing of the earth after his kind, two of every sort shall come unto thee, to keep them alive." – Genesis 6:19–20

The Lord commanded Noah to bring fowls, cattle, and creeping animals "after their kind" onto the ark. The purpose was to restore the original genetic order that God had implemented in the creation week of Genesis 1. This is reemphasized in Genesis 7:

> "And the LORD said unto Noah, Come thou and all thy house into the ark; for thee have I seen righteous before me in this generation. Of every clean beast thou shalt take to thee by sevens, the male and his female: and of beasts that are not clean by two, the male and his female. Of fowls also of the air by sevens, the male and the female; **to keep seed alive upon the face of all the earth**." – Genesis 7:1–3

By "keeping seed alive" on Earth God rescued the DNA of the human race and animal kingdom from extinction. The Flood served three main purposes: 1) to destroy the Nephilim giants; 2) to punish the angels who partook of illicit relations with women – making an example of them so no other angels would ever again attempt it; and 3) to save humanity from certain destruction. Much more than the "overreaction of an angry God" as skeptics like to paint it, the global flood was God's way of preserving humanity before it suffered complete corruption at the hands of the Nephilim.

This is an important point: Many people today point to the Flood as "proof" that the God of the Bible (especially as He is revealed in the Old Testament) is cruel and angry with humanity all the time and willing to kill millions on a whim. The biblical truth is that God sent the Flood to preserve humanity and to make sure we could still receive the promised Redeemer who could save our souls. Without Jesus Christ, there is no hope, no future, and no forgiveness, meaning every last person would spend eternity in Hell and the Lake of Fire. The Flood was the Creator's loving way to keep that blessed hope for all.

## WHY WERE THE NEPHILIM SO EVIL?

"And the Philistine said, I defy the armies of Israel this day; give me a man, that we may fight together." – The Giant Goliath, 1 Samuel 17:10

"For what were those results? 'There were Giants on the earth in those days.' Such was the result, and nothing more marvellous has ever been revealed, except the Incarnation itself. Not giants only, but SEMI–CELESTIAL giants. Half human, by the mother's side, half angelic, by the Father's side; but altogether earthly, and without one trace of the purity of heaven." – *The Last Vials: Being a Series of Essays on the Second Advent*, Vol. 21, Robert Purdon, 1855, p. 7.

Why were the Nephilim so wicked? What was it about the giants that caused such an acceleration of sin that God repented making humanity at all? The Bible explains that in addition to physical genetic traits, a *spiritual nature* is passed on to a child in the womb. When the apostate sons of God chose to have children with human women, the fallen angelic spirit raging within them led to an unprecedented wicked nature in their Nephilim offspring.

## FATHERS PASS ON THE SIN NATURE TO THEIR CHILDREN

"Wherefore, **as by one man sin entered into the world**, and death by sin; and so death passed upon all men, for that all have sinned...." – Romans 5:12

All people are born with a sin nature, which is a corrupted spirit that seeks to fulfill fleshly lusts and sin against God. This is the reason the Bible boldly proclaims "all have sinned." Notice in the verse above that death – the by-product of sin – was "passed upon all men." Children inherit their spiritual nature from their parents, specifically their fathers.

In the Garden of Eden *Eve sinned first* as 1 Timothy 2 says: "For Adam was first formed, then Eve. And Adam was not deceived, but the woman being deceived was in the transgression" (1 Timothy 2:13–14). Eve was not only the first sinner but the only one actually deceived by Satan's lies. Adam did not believe in the false promises of Satan when he *chose* to sin. Yet, *it is through Adam* that the corrupted sinful nature of man is passed on. In Scripture this "spiritual inheritance" from the father to his children is referred to as "begetting":

"And Adam lived an hundred and thirty years, **and begat a son in his own likeness, and after his image**; and called his name Seth...." – Genesis 5:3

A 19th-century Christian magazine expounded on the notion that the sin nature is inherited from the father:

> "'By one man's disobedience all men were constituted sinners,' 'in Adam all died', spiritually died, lost the life and image of God: that fallen, sinful Adam then 'begat a son in his own likeness:' nor was it possible he should beget him in any other; for 'who can bring a clean thing out of an unclean?' That consequently we as well as other men 'were, by nature, dead in trespasses and sins, without hope, without God in the world,' and therefore 'children of wrath;' that every man may say, 'I was shapen in wickedness and in sin did my mother conceive me:' that 'there is no difference, in that all have sinned, and come short of the glory of God,' of that glorious image of God wherein man was originally created.
>
> "… It remains then that the only true and rational way of accounting for the general wickedness of mankind in all ages and nations is pointed out in these words: "In Adam all die. "In and through their first parent, all his posterity died in a spiritual sense; and they remain 'wholly dead in trespasses and sins' till the second Adam makes them alive. **By this one man 'sin entered into the world and passed upon all men.' And through the infection which they derive from him all men, are and ever were by nature entirely 'alienated from the life God without hope without God in the world.'**" –*The Methodist Magazine and Monthly Review*, Volume XIV, New Series – Volume 3; 1832, p. 51.

Adam begat a son in his own likeness, confirming that the fallen spiritual state of mankind would continue until the promised Messiah redeemed it. Through Adam, all human fathers pass on the corrupt sinful nature to their children. The original breath of life that God breathed into Adam to make him a "living soul" was corrupted, and it was passed on to his sons and daughters. This is confirmed in the book of Job: "The spirit of God hath made me, and the breath of the Almighty hath given me life" (Job 33:4). After God made Adam, He never personally breathed life into an individual person again. Instead, they inherited this spirit nature from Adam. Thus, in conception, just as the woman produces the physical body of the child, the man produces the spirit nature. This is also confirmed in Scripture:

> "For the man is not of the woman: but the woman of the man.... For as the woman is of the man, **even so is the man also by the woman**; but all things of God." (1 Corinthians 11:8; 12)

Eve was "of Adam" in the sense that she was literally made from his body and received the spirit of life once breathed into him. But a male is "also by the woman" in that the physical body of a baby is formed in a woman's body. In the past decade, scientists have confirmed that the Y chromosome (passed down through males) does not recombine or change through generations. Thus, a Y chromosome of a man today would be the same as his paternal ancestors' 6,000 years ago. **The genetic inheritance of sin nature from fathers is why God ordained that the Messiah would come through "the seed of *the woman*."** The prophesied Savior would have a human mother *but God as His father*. Therefore, the corrupted spiritual nature inherited from Adam would not pass on to Him. Jesus Christ did not bear the corrupted flesh all other people in human history possess. He was not begotten of Adam. He was the "only begotten" Son of God – *His spiritual nature was wholly divine.*

Suddenly, the term "only begotten" in John 3:16 takes on much greater meaning. Jesus Christ was obviously not the only baby God formed in a womb. Certain angels hold the title "sons of God." But what made Christ different in His incarnation is that His Spirit was wholly "begotten of God" and thus not subject to the corruption and spiritual wickedness inherited from Adam. And in Jesus' sinless life, death, and resurrection, all believers receive a new birth through which they also receive the incorruptible spirit from God. Hence, 1 Corinthians 15 calls Christ "the last Adam":

"And so it is written, The first man Adam was made a living soul; *the last Adam was made a quickening spirit.* Howbeit that was not first which is spiritual, but that which is natural; and afterward that which is spiritual. The first man is of the earth, earthy; the second man is the Lord from heaven. As is the earthy, such are they also that are earthy: and as is the heavenly, such are they also that are heavenly. **And as we have borne the image of the earthy, we shall also bear the image of the heavenly.**" – 1 Corinthians 15:45–49

The first Adam was the father of corrupt, fallen humanity. Jesus Christ, the "last Adam," is the father of redeemed, incorruptible humanity. Adam passed on sin and mortality. Jesus passes on sinlessness and immortality. In salvation, Jesus can pass on His perfect, righteous spiritual nature to all who believe upon His name for the forgiveness of their sins. This is why it is of paramount import that Christ was the *only begotten* Son of God. In this unique position, He stands as the only person in the universe born with the perfect, righteous Holy Spirit of God in Him. "For in him dwelleth all the fulness of the Godhead bodily" (Colossians 2:9).

This is how Christ justly bestows the Spirit of God upon those who are "in Him":

"Whosoever believeth that Jesus is the Christ is born of God: **and every one that loveth him that begat loveth him also that is begotten of him**." – 1 John 5:1

In a similar sense, the spiritual nature of the fallen angelic fathers was passed on to their Nephilim offspring. This powerful, evil angelic spirit filled the Nephilim with a superhuman desire for iniquity. Their fathers, departed from their first estate and now "flesh" in their nature, produced offspring conceived entirely out of the earthly realm. As we will see, even the distant descendants of the Nephilim possessed the giants' unrelenting desire to sin and, specifically, to inflict violence upon the innocent. Already birthed outside of God's creation, these beings were intent on defying God, killing His believers, and dominating Earth for themselves. For their many sins, they more than earned God's wrath.

## GOLIATH – PRIME EXAMPLE OF
## THE EVIL NATURE OF THE NEPHILIM

"And he [Goliath] stood and cried unto the armies of Israel, and said unto them, Why are ye come out to set your battle in array? am not I a Philistine, and ye servants to Saul? choose you a man for you, and let him come down to me. If he be able to fight with me, and to kill me, then will we be your servants: but if I prevail against him, and kill him, then shall ye be our servants, and serve us. And the Philistine said, I defy the armies of Israel this day; give me a man, that we may fight together." – 1 Samuel 17:8–10

The Lord in His infinite wisdom gave voice to only one giant in Scripture, Goliath. The Philistine champion was a distant descendant of the antediluvian Nephilim. And though he was a much more genetically diluted and inferior specimen of Nephilim, he still epitomized brazen defiance against God. First we see his motive – to enslave God's people. He exhibited extreme arrogance. Earlier in 1 Samuel 17, Goliath left the Philistine camp with just his armor bearer to confront the armies of Israel alone. He was so confident in his fighting prowess that he wagered his entire nation's freedom on his victory in battle. He disrespectfully referred to the armies of Israel as "servants of Saul."

Goliath presumed authority. Every time he opened his mouth, it was to bark orders and control the situation. He told the Israelites the terms of the battle and repeated his demand for blood for 40 days until they were met. A 19th-century commentary on the Nephilim agreed with the notion that the giants routinely ruled over the humans they dwelled among:

> "Those men with angelic blood in their veins became the leaders and rulers of mankind. The fire, the genius, the beauty, the strength and the strong will descended from birth to birth from the ancestral Angels to their earth born posterity." – *The Last Vials: Being a Series of Essays on the Second Advent*, No. X, 22nd year, Sept. 1st, 1867, Robert Purdon, p. 6.

The depraved spirit of his angelic ancestors filled Goliath with the violent bloodlust that raged in the days of Noah. His appearance and brashness struck the Israelites with trepidation:

> "When Saul and all Israel heard those words of the Philistine, they were dismayed, and greatly afraid." – 1 Samuel 17:11

> "**And all the men of Israel**, when they saw the man, fled from him, and were sore afraid." – 1 Samuel 17:24

Soldiers abandoned their positions at the mere sight of Goliath. King Saul was frightened as well, even though Scripture tells us Saul was far taller than any other person in Israel (1 Samuel 9:2). The Septuagint places Goliath's height at 4 cubits and a span whereas the King James Bible says six cubits (the ancient Egyptian cubit was 22 inches). Thus, this Nephilim descendant was between 8 and 11 feet tall. His armor, described in vivid detail in Scripture for the obvious purpose of highlighting his supernatural strength, weighed approximately 272 pounds (*Calmet's Dictionary of the Holy Bible: With the Biblical Fragments*, Vol. 1, Augustin Calmet, 1832, p. 584). The Bible goes out of its way to emphasize the Philistine warrior was superhuman in both size and strength. To move, much less fight, in such a massive suit of armor required extraordinary strength. It is no wonder the soldiers in Israel's army dared not confront this hybrid creature.

When young King David volunteered to take the giant's challenge, Goliath responded with disgust. "And the Philistine said unto David, Am I a dog, that thou comest to me with staves? And the Philistine cursed David by his gods" (1 Samuel 17:43). This passage reinforced Goliath's satanic nature as he cursed God's anointed king and called out to his own pagan gods. "And the Philistine said to David, Come to me, and I will give thy flesh unto the fowls of the air, and to the beasts of the field" (1 Samuel 17:44). Goliath perceived no threat from David and prepared to claim another victim. Of course, David, trusting in the Lord, proved the victor.

This account provides a lot of information on the nature of the Nephilim. Though one of the last of the giants to walk the earth, Goliath retained the hyper-depraved nature of his ancestors. The seed of Satan may not have been as tall or as numerous in the days of King David, but they were as bent on opposing God, the Holy Seed, and the human race as ever. Though corrupted with the sin nature inherited from Adam, humans still maintained "the residue of the spirit" – a tainted version of the breath of the life God breathed into Adam (Malachi 2:15). The Nephilim were given spiritual life from degenerated, fallen angels and were thus bred absent God's Spirit and acted without conscience.

## MEN OF RENOWN – THE NEPHILIM WERE THE BASIS OF ANCIENT MYTHOLOGY

Many cultures contain myths of ancient races of giants. Some of the themes we find in Greek mythology and the legends of ancient cultures include gods' taking human women as wives, giant offspring, and a global flood. All of this mythology was a spin on the account of sons of God, daughters of men, and the birth of the Nephilim. Ancient church fathers and theologians for centuries were aware that pagan cultures borrowed from the account of Genesis 6 to make their own version of the antediluvian angelic invasion. Justin Martyr, writing about 125 AD, made this very observation:

"Whence also the poets and mythologists, not knowing that it was the angels and those demons who had been begotten by them that did these things to men, and women, and cities, and nations, which they related, ascribed them to god himself, and to those who were accounted to be his very offspring, and to the offspring of those who were called his brothers, Neptune and Pluto, and to the children again of these their offspring. For whatever name each of the angels had given to himself and his children, by that name they called them." – *The Second Apology of Justin, For the Christians, Addressed to the Roman Senate*, Justin Martyr, Chapter V, as quoted in *The Ante–Nicene Fathers, Justin Martyr, Ireneaus*, Vol. 1, 1903, p. 190.

More modern theologians and academics arrived at the same conclusion:

"Lastly, it should be observed that the general view here taken is corroborated by Gentile records, and the traditions of profane writers. As the story of Deucalion, with other traditions, present manifest traces of the reality of the Scripture history of the deluge, so the poetic fables and early historic traditions of the war of the giants or Titans against Saturn, the fables of the Cyclops, of Hercules, and other mystic heroes, manifest the truth of the Scripture declarations, respecting the fall of the angels, their strength, their violence, their pride, their destruction. Their celestial origin was noticed in the tradition that represented them as sons of Ouranus. Their vastness, and their war against heaven, are celebrated by Homer, Hesiod, Ovid, Plato, Lucan, Seneca, and others." – *Isaiah Unfulfilled: Being an Exposition of the Prophet, with New Version and Critical Notes*, Robert Govett, 1841, pp. 362–363.

One 19th century commentary quotes Hesiod and Plato as confirming the connection to Genesis 6:

"'The tradition of the existence of giants in the earliest ages of the world is common both to the historians and poets of the ancients. Hesiod, speaking of the offspring of earth and heaven, which signifies, perhaps, 'the sons of God and the daughters of men," says: –

'Other sons

Were born of earth and heaven; three mighty sons

And valiant; dreadful but to name.

A vigor strong,

Immeasurable, filled each mighty frame.

Of all the children sprung from earth and heaven

The fiercest these; and they e'en from the first,

Drew down their father's hate.' – Hesiod, Theog v 147

'Socrates. Do you not know that heroes are demigods?

Hemogenes. What then?

Socrates. All of them were doubtless begotten, either from a god falling in love with a mortal woman, or from a mortal man falling in love with a goddess.'" – *Cratylus*, Plato, about 370 BC, as quoted in *The Testimony of the Heathen to the Truths of Holy Writ*, Rev. Thomas S. Millington, 1854, p. 19.

Hesiod and Plato, two of the earliest Greek poets and scholars, respectively, both detail the ancient mythology as an era of gods' taking human wives and begetting giants who dominated the world with violence in a manner startlingly similar to the biblical account. This was not lost on Christian scholars who correctly identified that Moses and the Greek writers were referring to the same era of history:

"The children of these unlawful connections before the flood were the renowned heroes of old: the subsequent repetition of the crime doubtless gave rise to the countless legends of the loves of the gods, and explains the numerous passages in the classics, as well as in ancient literature of other languages, in which human families are traced to a half Divine origin." – *Earth's Earliest Ages*, G. H. Pember, 1884, p. 212.

"We do not assert that there were ever such individuals as Theseus, Hercules, or Achilles; but those men, and those names, we believe to have been typical. They represented the actual heroes of the heroic age, and they exhibit the impressions left upon the minds of the great poets by the traditions of that age. There were once upon earth a race of heroes of supernatural powers. Those heroes were descended from "the sons of God," and their wonderful prowess and achievements left an impression upon the mind which broke out into light in the poetry of Homer." – *The Last Vials: Being a Series of Essays on the Second Advent*, No. X, 22nd year, Sept. 1st, 1867, Robert Purdon, p. 8.

Hercules and Perseus, two of the more famous figures in Greek mythology, were both the offspring of a god who came down to Earth and impregnated a human woman. In the legend of Atlantis, the island metropolis was populated by both gods and humans, filled with luxury and advanced technology, and ultimately destroyed by a flood to punish the wickedness of its inhabitants. We already pointed out that the Roman god Vulcan was based on Tubal-Cain. Also of note is the Greek god Prometheus who stole fire from the gods and delivered it to benefit mankind. The forging of metals, invented by Tubal-Cain, requires the manipulation of fire. In Greek mythology Prometheus was deemed the creator of mankind and its greatest benefactor. From the Bible we learn that Prometheus was an allusion to the first sons of

God who offered Lamech and his family advanced technology in exchange for Naamah's hand in marriage.

Considering that Homer, Hesiod, Ovid, and the great Greek poets lived anywhere from 800–1500 years *after* Genesis was written, it should be quite clear why biblical commentators from the first century AD through the 1800s were convinced that Greek, Roman, and other pagan mythologies were derivative of the ancient events first recorded in Genesis 6.

## THE GIANTS WERE FAMOUS FOR THEIR SIZE

Church fathers and Jewish historians remarked on the giants' fame on account of their supernatural size. Even in the first century AD the skeletons and bones of giants were displayed in exhibits like museum artifacts for people to view:

> "For which reason they removed their camp to Hebron; and when they had taken it, they slew all the inhabitants. There were till then left the race of giants, who had bodies so large and countenances so entirely different from other men, that they were amazing to the sight and terrible to the hearing. The bones of these men are still shown to this very day, unlike any credible relations of other men." – *Antiquities of the Jews*, Book I, 5:2.3, Flavius Josephus, as recorded in *The Works of Flavius Josephus*, William Whiston, Vol. 1, 1843, p.136.

> "The giants [were] men of immense bodies, whose bones of enormous size are still shown in certain places for confirmation of their existence." – *Recognitions 1.29*, Clement of Rome, (ca. AD 96) as quoted in *The First Fossil Hunters: Dinosaurs, Mammoths, and Myth in Greek and Roman Times*, Adrienne Mayor, Princeton University Press. Kindle Edition.

> "There are the carcasses of the giants of old time; it will be obvious enough that they are not absolutely decayed, for their bony frames

are still extant. We have already spoken of this elsewhere." – *On the Resurrection of the Flesh*, 42, Tertullian, (ca. AD 200) as quoted in *The Ante-Nicene Fathers. Translations of the Writings of the Fathers down to AD 325,* American Reprint of the Edinburgh Edition, Vol. 1, ed. by The Rev. Alexander Roberts and James Donaldson, LLD, 1903, p. 576.

These writings attest that the Nephilim were of such extraordinary size that their bones were kept on display as "attractions" for the public to view. Scripture records a similar fact about King Og of Bashan:

"For only Og king of Bashan remained of the remnant of giants; behold his bedstead was a bedstead of iron; is it not in Rabbath of the children of Ammon? nine cubits was the length thereof, and four cubits the breadth of it, after the cubit of a man."
– Deuteronomy 3:9

King Og was a giant whose bed measured nine cubits or 13 feet long. And his size was so impressive that his bed was on display in Rabbath, which was the royal city of the Ammonite kingdom in the days of King David (2 Samuel 12:26). Even in death the giants inspired awe and fascination.

## THE GIANTS DEFIED GOD

Basil the Great (329–379AD), a renowned fourth-century pastor, wrote of the Nephilim's rebellious nature:

"Strength of arm, swiftness of foot and comeliness of body – the spoils of sickness and the plunders of times – also awaken pride in man, unaware as he is that 'All flesh is grass and all the glory of man as the flower of the field. The grass is withered and the flower is fallen.' Such was the arrogance of the giants because of their strength. Such was also the God-defying pride of witless Goliath." – *Homily 20, Of Humility*, as quoted in *Genesis 1–11*, Andrew Louth, Marco Conti, InterVarsity Press, Apr 3, 2001, p. 126.

Eusebius (ca 260–339 AD) was a fourth-century Christian historian and regarded as one of the most knowledgeable theologians of his era. He wrote of Genesis 6:

"They gave themselves wholly over to all kinds of profanity, now seducing one another, now slaying one another, now eating human flesh, and now daring to wage war with the Gods and to undertake those battles of the giants celebrated by all; now planning to fortify earth against heaven, and in the madness of ungoverned pride to prepare an attack upon the very God of all. 20. On account of these things, when they conducted themselves thus, the all-seeing God sent down upon them floods and conflagrations as upon a wild forest spread over the whole earth." – *Church History* 1.2.19–20, Eusebius, ca. 324AD, as quoted in *A Select Library of the Nicene and Post–Nicene Fathers of the Christian Church, A New Series*, Vol. 1, Henry Wace, Philip Schaff, 1890, p. 84.

## THE APOCRYPHA – ANCIENT JEWISH WRITINGS: THE ACCOUNT OF THE NEPHILIM

The biblical Apocrypha were books written between the time of the Old and New Testaments. For centuries, they were included with printed Bibles as "recommended reading." These books are never quoted in the New Testament, and the Lord Jesus Christ implicitly omitted them as Scripture when He gave an overview of the entire canon of Scripture: "That the blood of all the prophets, which was shed from the foundation of the world, may be required of this generation; From the blood of Abel unto the blood of

Zacharias which perished between the altar and the temple: verily I say unto you, It shall be required of this generation" (Luke 11:50–51). In the ancient Hebrew Bible, Genesis was the first book and 2 Chronicles was the last. Thus, Jesus excluded the Apocrypha from accepted Scripture.

Though not divinely-inspired, these books reflect ancient Jewish thought in the centuries before the birth of Christ. Several of the apocryphal books mention the Nephilim giants.

"It was thou who didst destroy the former workers of unrighteousness, among whom were the giants, who trusted in their strength and hardihood, by covering them with a measureless flood." – III Maccabees 2:4

"There were the giants famous from the beginning, that were of so great stature, and so expert in war. Those did not the Lord choose, neither gave he the way of knowledge unto them: But they were destroyed, because they had no wisdom, and perished through their own foolishness." – Baruch 3:26–28

"For in the old time also, when the proud giants perished, the hope of the world governed by thy hand escaped in a weak vessel, and left to all ages a seed of generation." – Wisdom 14:6

## THE NEPHILIM CORRUPTED THE PLANET

Interestingly, the Book of Enoch, with its heavy emphasis on angels, does not say much about the giants of the antediluvian world.

"¹ And all the others together with them took unto themselves wives, and each chose for himself one, and they began to go in unto them and to defile themselves with them, and they taught them charms [2] and enchantments, and the cutting of roots, and made them acquainted with plants. And they [3] became pregnant, and they bare great giants, whose height was three thousand ells: Who consumed [4] all the acquisitions of men. And when men could no longer sustain them, the giants turned against [5] them and devoured mankind. And they began to sin against birds, and beasts, and reptiles, and [6] fish, and to devour one another's flesh, and drink the blood. Then the earth laid accusation against the lawless ones." – 1 Enoch 7:1–6

The Bible provides this same information when the Lord decried the damage the incursion of fallen angels had wrought and the wickedness of the Nephilim:

"The earth also was corrupt before God, and the earth was filled with violence. And God looked upon the earth, and, behold, **it was corrupt; for all flesh had corrupted his way upon the earth**. And God said unto Noah, The end of all flesh is come before me; **for the earth is filled with violence through them**; and, behold, I will destroy them with the earth." – Genesis 6:11–13

Interestingly, when Noah and his family exited the ark after the Flood ended, the first law the Lord issued was a *prohibition on drinking blood*:

"And God blessed Noah and his sons, and said unto them, Be fruitful, and multiply, and replenish the earth. And the fear of you and the dread of you shall be upon every beast of the earth, and upon every fowl of the air, upon all that moveth upon the earth, and upon all the fishes of the sea; into your hand are they delivered. Every moving thing that liveth shall be meat for you; even as the green herb have I given you all things. **But flesh with the life thereof, which is the blood thereof, shall ye not eat.**" – Genesis 9:1–4

So, although the text in Genesis does not explicitly say the Nephilim were eating flesh and drinking blood, it was enough of an issue for the Creator to mention as soon as the earth's population restarted. Other Bible passages involving the Nephilim allude to the eating of humans. The 12 spies Moses sent to scout the Promised Land saw the infamous sons of Anak, giants living among the people there. The sight of these Nephilim so scared 10 of the unbelieving spies that they no longer believed the Lord could deliver the land to them. In their frightened account they stated:

> "But the men that went up with him said, We be not able to go up against the people; for they are stronger than we. And they brought up an evil report of the land which they had searched unto the children of Israel, saying, The land, through which we have gone to search it, **is a land that eateth up the inhabitants thereof**; and all the people that we saw in it are men of a great stature." – Numbers 13:31–32

Not satisfied with assaulting the human gene pool, the giants also defiled animals – a point recorded in the extra-biblical Book of Jasher:

> "And their judges and rulers went to the daughters of men and took their wives by force from their husbands according to their choice, and the sons of men in those days took from the cattle of the earth, the beasts of the field and the fowls of the air, and taught the mixture of animals of one species with the other, in order therewith to provoke the Lord; and God saw the whole earth and it was corrupt, for all flesh had corrupted its ways upon earth, all men and all animals. And the Lord said, I will blot out man that I created from the face of the earth, yea from man to the birds of the air, together with cattle and beasts that are in the field for I repent that I made them." – Book of Jasher 3:18–19

Although the Bible does not specifically report angels' teaching humanity "the mixture of animals of one species with the other," Scripture provides sufficient evidence to conclude that something sinful took place with animals in addition to human beings during the reign of the sons of God and their Nephilim offspring. When God pronounced judgment during the days of Noah, He specifically included animals:

> "And the LORD said, I will destroy man whom I have created from the face of the earth; **both man, and beast, and the creeping thing, and the fowls of the air**; for it repenteth me that I have made them." – Genesis 6:7

> "And, behold, I, even I, do bring a flood of waters upon the earth, to destroy all flesh, wherein is the breath of life, from under heaven; and every thing that is in the earth shall die." – Genesis 6:17

In the above verses God stressed that all flesh – both human and animal – was polluted by the angelic-Nephilim invasion. Just as God repented of making humanity, He also repented of making beasts, creeping things, and birds. Recall that in the Mosaic Law the Lord specifically outlawed the "gendering" or cross-breeding of animals, precisely what the Book of Jasher accused the sons of God of teaching humanity. And as we saw in the chapter on God's genetic order, the instructions God gave to Noah in Genesis 6 and 7 specifically called for only animals after their kind to be taken into the ark:

> "But with thee will I establish my covenant; and thou shalt come into the ark, thou, and thy sons, and thy wife, and thy sons' wives with thee. And of every living thing of all flesh, two of every sort shalt thou bring into the ark, to keep them alive with thee; they shall be male and female. **Of fowls after their kind, and of cattle after their kind, of every creeping thing of the earth after his**

**kind**, two of every sort shall come unto thee, to keep them alive."
– Genesis 6:18–20

The Lord returned the animal world to its original genetic state. Just as animals were originally created "after their kind," God told Noah to include only those animals who remained genetically pure "to keep seed alive."

We find yet another confirmation of the satanic hybridization that took place before the Flood in the book of Revelation. When the fallen angelic hordes are released from the abyss or *tartarus,* the current prison of the wicked sons of Gods, they appear as hybrid creatures:

> "And the fifth angel sounded, and I saw a star fall from heaven unto the earth: and to him was given the key of the bottomless pit. And he opened the bottomless pit; and there arose a smoke out of the pit, as the smoke of a great furnace; and the sun and the air were darkened by reason of the smoke of the pit. And there came out of the smoke locusts upon the earth: and unto them was given power, as the scorpions of the earth have power… And the shapes of the locusts were like unto horses prepared unto battle; and on their heads were as it were crowns like gold, and their faces were as the faces of men. And they had hair as the hair of women, and their teeth were as the teeth of lions. And they had breastplates, as it were breastplates of iron; and the sound of their wings was as the sound of chariots of many horses running to battle. And they had tails like unto scorpions, and there were stings in their tails: and their power was to hurt men five months." – Revelation 9:1–3; 7–10

The bizarre description of these creatures who are freed from their prison to torment sinners on Earth is reminiscent of minotaurs, centaurs, and other hybrid creatures of mythology. These "locusts" have faces like men, hair like women, and the ferocious teeth of lions. They have scorpion tails and can fly. These demonic hordes will no doubt frighten the world living in the Great

Tribulation just as the giants frightened the humans living in the days of Noah. The preponderance of biblical evidence points to the conclusion that the genetic corruption brought on by the sons of God and the Nephilim affected humanity and animals alike.

The Nephilim, murderous cannibals who hated God and anything related to the prophesied Messiah, were unbridled evil. They corrupted the antediluvian world to the point that humanity's very existence was in peril. Even the animal kingdom was victimized and turned into monstrosities. The world was literally transforming into Satan's kingdom. But there was one man who trusted in the True and Living God and knew the seed of Satan would not win this cosmic war. Heeding the prophecies handed down from his father, grandfather, and great-grandfather, this man knew the Lord was going to strike back in a manner the world had never seen before. And only the handful of believers left on Earth would survive. Noah, a preacher in a sinful world, knew the reign of the fallen angels and Nephilim was coming to an earth-shattering and unexpected end.

# CHAPTER 9

# THE END OF THE WORLD

Imagine knowing the precise day the world would end. A day of truly cataclysmic destruction when hundreds of millions, if not billions, of people would perish. Your entire, town, state, and nation wiped out. Imagine what it would be like knowing for decades that the dreadful day was approaching – each sunset winding the clock closer to doomsday – and that only you and your immediate family would survive. How would you live your life? What would you do? This was Noah's reality. He was not a perfect man. But he had faith in the Creator. Like Enoch, Noah walked with God. He believed the Lord's Word and lived out his faith through obedience based on trust. In Hebrews 11, right after honoring the faith of Enoch, the Scriptures mention Noah:

> "But without faith it is impossible to please him: for he that cometh to God must believe that he is, and that he is a rewarder of them that diligently seek him. By faith Noah, being warned of God of things not seen as yet, moved with fear, prepared an ark to the saving of his house; by the which he condemned the world, and became heir of the righteousness which is by faith." – Hebrews 11:6–7

# NOAH BELIEVED GOD WOULD SAVE HUMANITY FROM TOTAL DESTRUCTION

Noah prepared the ark believing God's warning of the coming judgment. As was the case with Enoch, Noah was "moved with fear" after being "warned of God." In his obedience and preaching he "condemned the world." The earth was so depraved that only one man stood as righteous in God's eyes and thus only his family was spared judgment. Noah serves as a reminder of the moral degradation of the antediluvian world and God's mercy in the midst of it. Noah did not earn his salvation. It was a gift for having faith to turn from the idolatry and excess of the world and look to God.

## THE ARK – A SUPERNATURAL VESSEL

Following divine instruction, Noah spent the last 120 years of the antediluvian era building this majestic ship:

> "Make thee an ark of gopher wood; rooms shalt thou make in the ark, and shalt pitch it within and without with pitch. And this is the fashion which thou shalt make it of: The length of the ark shall be three hundred cubits, the breadth of it fifty cubits, and the height of it thirty cubits. A window shalt thou make to the ark, and in a cubit shalt thou finish it above; and the door of the ark shalt thou set in the side thereof; with lower, second, and third stories shalt thou make it. And, behold, I, even I, do bring a flood of waters upon the earth, to destroy all flesh, wherein is the breath of life, from under heaven; and every thing that is in the earth shall die.
>
> But with thee will I establish my covenant; and thou shalt come into the ark, thou, and thy sons, and thy wife, and thy sons' wives with thee. And of every living thing of all flesh, two of every sort shalt thou bring into the ark, to keep them alive with thee; they shall be male

and female. Of fowls after their kind, and of cattle after their kind, of every creeping thing of the earth after his kind, two of every sort shall come unto thee, to keep them alive. And take thou unto thee of all food that is eaten, and thou shalt gather it to thee; and it shall be for food for thee, and for them. Thus did Noah; according to all that God commanded him, so did he." – Genesis 6:14–22

The world Noah knew was going to be destroyed. Subterranean waters bursting through the planet's surface would cause great earthquakes to shift the mountains and crumble whole cities. The Garden of God, along with all the land of Eden, would be lost. But in the ark the Lord provided hope. Like the Garden of Eden, the ark was designed by God. It served as a temporary temple and picture of God's salvation for those who believe. There are striking similarities between the ark, Solomon's temple, and the Millennial temple described in the book of Ezekiel:

- The precise dimensions of the ark, the tabernacle, Solomon's temple, and the Millennial temple were all given by God.
- The length of the ark was 300 cubits (Genesis 6:15). The length of the inner court of Ezekiel's Millennial temple is 300 cubits (Ezekiel 40:23, 27, 47).
- The height of the ark was 30 cubits. The inner temple of the most holy place in Solomon's temple, where the Ark of the Covenant was kept, was 30 cubits in height (1 Kings 6:2).
- The Lord instructed Noah "… rooms shalt thou make in the ark" (Genesis 6:14). Both the temple of Solomon and the Millennial temple had side rooms as part of their design (1 Kings 6:8, Ezekiel 41:16).
- The ark was three stories high. The temple of Solomon and the Millennial temple are three stories high (1 Kings 6:8, Ezekiel 41:16).

- The ark's design provided for a window at the top of the vessel. The temple of Solomon had windows on its ceiling of "narrow light" (1 Kings 6:4).

The ark was a picture of the Lord's salvation in the midst of the judgment of the ungodly. While the waves crashed, millions perished, and whole cities sank to the ocean floor, Noah and his family rested safely in the ark. This floating temple was also a foreshadow of the Messiah, Jesus Christ. All who trust in Jesus are protected from Satan, his angels, and Hell itself. Jesus acknowledged this symbolism:

> "Jesus answered and said unto them, Destroy this temple, and in three days I will raise it up. Then said the Jews, Forty and six years was this temple in building, and wilt thou rear it up in three days? **But he spake of the temple of his body**." – John 2:19–21

The supernatural aspects of the ark continue in Scripture after the flood waters subsided. The ark rested "in the seventh month, on the seventeenth day of the month, upon the mountains of Ararat" (Genesis 8:4). During the first Passover, God established the seventh month as the start of the new year on the Hebrew spiritual calendar (Exodus 12:2). The seventh month represented a new beginning for both Noah and the Israelites. The 14th day of the seventh month was the feast of Passover. Jesus Christ died on the day of Passover and rose three days later, on the 17th day of the seventh month – the precise day on which the ark rose above the earth and the floodwaters and came to rest on Mount Ararat.

## NOAH PREACHED BEFORE THE FLOOD

Noah spent those final decades of the old world not only building the ark but boldly proclaiming God's Word:

"For if God spared not the angels that sinned, but cast them down to hell, and delivered them into chains of darkness, to be reserved unto judgment; And spared not the old world, but saved Noah the eighth person, **a preacher of righteousness**, bringing in the flood upon the world of the ungodly…" – 2 Peter 2:4–5

Noah was a preacher. He spent his time warning the world of the need for repentance and salvation in the coming Messiah. Righteousness in the Bible is attained only through faith in the Messiah, by trusting in the saving power of the Seed of the Woman. This was the good news Noah shared with a world driven mad with sinful lusts. Although Satan had overrun the world with the accelerated sin of the fallen angels and giants, God provided the lost with a beacon of hope in Noah. And in rejecting this God-fearing preacher, humanity confirmed its own condemnation.

# THE FLOOD

It never rained before the Flood. A literal reading of the biblical text confirms that the Lord provided moisture through a mist from the ground: "And every plant of the field before it was in the earth, and every herb of the field before it grew: for the LORD God had not caused it to rain upon the earth, and there was not a man to till the ground. But there went up a mist from the earth, and watered the whole face of the ground" (Genesis 2:5–6). A noted 19th-century clergyman affirmed this interpretation:

"… or more probably, the whole earth was watered by a *mist*; for doubtless there was no rain before the Flood, since we read in Genesis ii 5, 6. 'the Lord God had not caused it to rain upon the earth and there was not a man to till the ground: but there went up a mist from the earth and watered the whole face of the ground.'"
– *An Analysis of Scripture History with Examination Questions,*

*Intended for Readers of Old Testament History*, Seventh Edition, William Henry Pinnock, 1855, p. 12.

Given that there had been no rain on Earth, Noah's warnings about flood waters wiping out all civilization must have sounded far-fetched to the antediluvian rebels. Like modern scoffers today who mock every aspect of the Christian faith, Noah likely faced laughter and derision as he preached and built his giant boat. In the postdiluvian world, however, the Flood was taken extremely seriously. Memory of the destructive power of God's wrath in the Flood became symbolic of the worst kind of death and suffering in ancient writings. Throughout the Bible, floods are referred to repeatedly as a symbol of the worst that can happen to humanity:

"I will call on the LORD, who is worthy to be praised: so shall I be saved from mine enemies. When the waves of death compassed me, the floods of ungodly men made me afraid; The sorrows of hell compassed me about; the snares of death prevented me...." – 2 Samuel 22:4–6

"For this shall every one that is godly pray unto thee in a time when thou mayest be found: surely in the floods of great waters they shall not come nigh unto him. Thou art my hiding place; thou shalt preserve me from trouble; thou shalt compass me about with songs of deliverance. Selah." – Psalm 32:6–7

"So shall they fear the name of the Lord from the west, and his glory from the rising of the sun. When the enemy shall come in like a flood, the Spirit of the Lord shall lift up a standard against him." – Isaiah 59:19

"Who is this that cometh up as a flood, whose waters are moved as the rivers? Egypt riseth up like a flood, and his waters are moved like the rivers; and he saith, I will go up, and will cover the earth; I will destroy the city and the inhabitants thereof." – Jeremiah 46:7–8

"But with an overrunning flood he will make an utter end of the place thereof, and darkness shall pursue his enemies." – Nahum 1:8

"Save me, O God; for the waters are come in unto my soul." – Psalm 69:1

## GOD CLOSED THE DOOR OF THE ARK

It is interesting to note that once Noah, his family, and the animals were aboard the ark, *God shut the door Himself*. The time of probation had expired. Having given the earth 120 years to repent, God's longsuffering gave way to judgment. The Flood was indeed global:

> "And the flood was forty days upon the earth; and the waters increased, and bare up the ark, and it was lift up above the earth. And the waters prevailed, and were increased greatly upon the earth; and the ark went upon the face of the waters. And the waters prevailed exceedingly upon the earth; and all the high hills, that were under the whole heaven, were covered. Fifteen cubits upward did the waters prevail; and the mountains were covered." – Genesis 7:17–20

The Flood destroyed all living creatures on the earth:

> "And all flesh died that moved upon the earth, both of fowl, and of cattle, and of beast, and of every creeping thing that creepeth upon the earth, and every man: All in whose nostrils was the breath of life, of all that was in the dry land, died. And every living substance was destroyed which was upon the face of the ground, both man, and cattle, and the creeping things, and the fowl of the heaven; and they were destroyed from the earth: and Noah only remained alive,

and they that were with him in the ark. And the waters prevailed upon the earth an hundred and fifty days." – Genesis 7:21–24

The strongest evidence for the utter catastrophe humanity had plunged into through the angelic-Nephilim invasion was that the only remedy was the wholesale eradication of the creation. A commentary on the Flood noted:

"All this sheds wondrous light upon the Flood and its necessity. It was a drowning not of natural men alone but, with them also, of *unnatural* men, of giants, of half demons, of a world which obliged just such a catastrophe." – *The Doctrines of Grace: And Kindred Themes,* Rev. George Sayles Bishop, Gospel Publishing House, 1910, p. 351.

A worldwide destruction was needed to remove the genetic contamination of the Nephilim from Earth. The Bible provides details about the specific group of Nephilim who wrought havoc in the antediluvian era.

# CHAPTER 10

# THE REPHAIM – GIANTS OF THE ANTEDILUVIAN WORLD

The Bible refers to the giants of the antediluvian world with one specific designation – Rephaim. This was the racial identity of the original Nephilim, direct offspring of the sinning sons of God and the daughters of men, their human wives. This conclusion is properly deduced from a literal reading of Scripture.

## UNDERSTANDING SHEOL – ABODE OF THE DEAD

To understand the term "rephaim" in Scripture, it is critical that we examine the concept of the afterlife in the Old Testament. After their spectacular destruction by God's global flood, the name "Rephaim" [*rapha'* in Hebrew] was adopted to refer to the ghosts of any unbeliever who was sent to Hell. Rather than being just an abode for the damned, Hell, or more accurately *Sheol* or *Hades*, before the resurrection of Christ was the destination for both believers and unbelievers. The Lord Jesus Christ provided the most succinct description of what happened to the souls of all the dead who perished before His First Coming to Earth in the account of the Rich Man and Lazarus:

> "There was a certain rich man, which was clothed in purple and fine linen, and fared sumptuously every day: And there was a certain

beggar named Lazarus, which was laid at his gate, full of sores, And desiring to be fed with the crumbs which fell from the rich man's table: moreover the dogs came and licked his sores. And it came to pass, that the beggar died, and was carried by the angels into Abraham's bosom: the rich man also died, and was buried; *And in hell* he lift up his eyes, being in torments, **and seeth Abraham afar off, and Lazarus in his bosom**. And he cried and said, Father Abraham, have mercy on me, and send Lazarus, that he may dip the tip of his finger in water, and cool my tongue; for I am tormented in this flame.

But Abraham said, Son, remember that thou in thy lifetime receivedst thy good things, and likewise Lazarus evil things: but now he is comforted, and thou art tormented. And beside all this, between us and you there is a great gulf fixed: so that they which would pass from hence to you cannot; neither can they pass to us, that would come from thence. Then he said, I pray thee therefore, father, that thou wouldest send him to my father's house: For I have five brethren; that he may testify unto them, lest they also come into this place of torment. Abraham saith unto him, They have Moses and the prophets; let them hear them. And he said, Nay, father Abraham: but if one went unto them from the dead, they will repent. And he said unto him, If they hear not Moses and the prophets, neither will they be persuaded, though one rose from the dead." – Luke 16:19–31

The first thing to note is that the Lord's account here was not a parable. Jesus stated "there was a *certain* rich man," indicating that He was referring to a real person, not an object lesson or fictional character. Jesus also gives the name of the beggar – another detail we never find in a parable. **All people before the resurrection of Christ went to *Sheol* at death** (after Christ's resurrection, the souls of born-again believers could rightly and justly access Heaven, emptying Abraham's Bosom permanently; Psalm 68:18, Ephesians

4:8). The Hebrew term *sheol* is the name of a series of spiritual holding areas for the souls *of the righteous and unrighteous alike.*

Jesus explained very clearly that the Rich Man, who died an unbeliever, could see Abraham and the beggar Lazarus in Hell. They were separated, however, by a great gulf. Thus, we have a picture of the arrangement of *Sheol*. There was a place of comfort for those who were believers and saved (Abraham's bosom) and a place of punishment and temporary holding cell for the wicked (the "place of torment") until God's final judgment of all unbelievers in the end times when they will be cast into the Lake of Fire (Revelation 20:12–15). This is very important for our study because the Nephilim before the Flood are constantly linked to *Sheol* in Scripture.

In the Old Testament *Sheol* is referred to as "hell," "the pit," or "the grave." In addition to Jesus' account of Lazarus and the Rich Man, the Bible refers several times to the different areas of *Sheol*.

## SHEOL HAD SEPARATE SECTIONS FOR THE RIGHTEOUS AND THE WICKED

"I will praise thee, O Lord my God, with all my heart: and I will glorify thy name for evermore. For great is thy mercy toward me: **and thou hast delivered my soul from the lowest hell.**" – Psalm 86:12–13

In this passage David remarks that God has delivered his soul from "the lowest hell." Jesus Christ confirmed that prior to His resurrection (when he earned the right for believers to enter Heaven upon death), both *believers and unbelievers* went to Hell. David agreed with this as he wrote: "For thou wilt not leave my soul in hell" (Psalm 16:10). So, if David acknowledged that he would be in Hell for an interim period, what are we to make of the notion of being delivered from the "lowest hell"? It refers to the place of the souls of the wicked. It is their temporary prison until the Great White Throne judgment.

And it is to this lowest Hell that the souls of the pre-Flood Nephilim were sentenced after God's great flood judgment.

King Solomon provided compelling evidence of this in the book of Proverbs. Speaking of the foolish, adulterous woman in chapter 9 he writes:

> "For she sitteth at the door of her house, on a seat in the high places of the city, To call passengers who go right on their ways: Whoso is simple, let him turn in hither: and as for him that wanteth understanding, she saith to him, Stolen waters are sweet, and bread eaten in secret is pleasant. But he knoweth not that the dead [*rapha*] are there; **and that her guests are in the depths of hell** [*sheol*]." – Proverbs 9:14–18

*Rapha* is the Hebrew singular form of Rephaim. In the passage above, the Rephaim are identified as inhabiting Sheol and specifically in "the depths of hell [*sheol*]" or, as David called it, "the lowest hell." Solomon made a similar reference in Proverbs 2:

> "To deliver thee from the strange woman, even from the stranger which flattereth with her words; Which forsaketh the guide of her youth, and forgetteth the covenant of her God. For her house inclineth unto death, and her paths unto the dead [*rapha*]." – Proverbs 2:16–18

Note that the text connects the sin of fornication with the deceased giants (who were the product of extreme fornication). Solomon issued a stern warning that although the pleasures of fornication might be the greatest of all temptations, the house of an adulterous woman leads to Hell and the abode of the Rephaim.

In Proverbs 21, we find another verse linking the Rephaim with souls in Hell:

"It is joy to the just to do judgment: but destruction shall be to the workers of iniquity. The man that wandereth out of the way of understanding shall remain in the congregation of the dead [*rapha*]." – Proverbs 21:15–16

The pre-Flood giants were so legendary that their very punishment and descent made them synonymous with the dead and Hell itself. The Lord never issued a sweeping cataclysmic judgment on humanity until the Flood. But the evil of the giants was so monumental that even their deaths were memorialized. A popular 19th-century Christian dictionary confirmed this notion:

"An attentive consideration seems to leave little room for doubt that the dead were called Rephaim, from some notion of *Sheol* (A.V. 'hell') being the residence of the fallen spirits or buried giants." – *A Comprehensive Dictionary of the Bible*, Mainly Abridged from WM. Smith's Dictionary of The Bible, edited by Rev. Samuel W. Barnum, 1888, p. 333.

The warnings Solomon issued would have struck a chord with any reader in ancient times as all were familiar with the account of the Flood and the corruption brought on by the angels who sinned. In effect Solomon was saying: *"Yes, a woman may entice you with her beauty and make adultery seem like an exciting, amazing pleasure. But do not forget that same temptation once brought the entire world to ruin. Quietly sneaking into the doorway of an adulteress is truly leading you on the path to sit right next to the dead armies of the Rephaim giants in the depths of Hell."*

The book of Job, which makes many references to the pre-Flood world, the Sons of God, and giants, makes the same connection:

> "But Job answered and said, How hast thou helped him that is without power? how savest thou the arm that hath no strength? How hast thou counselled him that hath no wisdom? and how hast thou plentifully declared the thing as it is? To whom hast thou uttered words? and whose spirit came from thee? **Dead things [*rephaim*] are formed from under the waters, and the inhabitants thereof.** Hell [*sheol*] is naked before him, and destruction hath no covering." – Job 26:1–6

In the Septuagint, verses 5 and 6 are even more explicit:

> "**Shall giants be born from under the water** and the inhabitants thereof? Hell is naked before him, and destruction has no covering." – Job 26:5-6, LXX.

The implication of the passage is that God is ruler over all. The Lord punished the giants with the Flood and sent them to the lowest parts of Sheol, beneath the deepest of waters, where they will not be able to be "reborn." God still has authority over them in Hell. He sees all the dead there just as He sees humans on the earth's surface.

An 18th-century British rector wrote of this connection in Job:

> "For this was properly the place of the *rephaim*; the word originally denoting those giants in impiety, that were overwhelmed by the flood; and from thence it came afterwards to [signify] the names of wicked men, or men of violence like them, who as they died, were gathered to their [assembly]." – *A Critical Dissertation on the Book of Job*, The Second Edition – corrected, Charles Peters, 1757, p. 360.

We find another compelling reference in Isaiah 14 (which contains a passage that esoterically addresses Satan and the Antichrist):

"Hell [*sheol*] from beneath is moved for thee to meet thee at thy coming: it stirreth up the dead [*Rephaim*] for thee, **even all the chief ones of the earth; it hath raised up from their thrones all the kings of the nations**." – Isaiah 14:9

The Rephaim were the dominant power of that ancient era, waging violent wars and taking human women as prizes for procreation. Isaiah calls them "the chief ones of the earth." Their destruction was so spectacular and devastating that the term "rephaim" in the ancient world symbolized the dead, unrepentant sinners and Hell itself. A 20th-century commentary links the Rephaim giants with the souls of dead men:

"These celebrated Rephaim 'these men of renown' are thus seen to be closely connected with the cast down giants, the fallen ones. The story of the giants who had been cast down to *tartarus* was current among the Israelites, and it had, even at this early date, reached the stage where *tartarus* had become a place inside the earth where men kept on living; hence they began to call all the dead 'Rephaim.' This fact positively connects these Rephaim with the cast down giants; they were not the fallen ones, but they were the men of renown, the children of those who afterwards became the fallen one's children of the sons of God and daughters of men." – *The Sons of God and Their Inheritance*, Emma J. Penney, 1921, p. 69.

The Rephaim, the original ethnic identity of the Nephilim, once ruled the earth and plunged it into violent, sinful rebellion against God. Though they viewed themselves as gods walking the earth, they died like mortal, human men. God in His wisdom and love for humanity provided salvation from this era of unprecedented evil. And as we will see in the next chapter, *how the Nephilim died* in the Flood leaves little doubt about how close the Nephilim brought humanity to the brink of genetic and spiritual destruction.

# CHAPTER 11

# THE JUDGMENT OF THE NEPHILIM

The Bible contains a series of rarely-discussed passages that shed a great deal of light on the history of the Nephilim. Ezekiel 31 and 32 chronicle the rise and fall of the supreme angel who ruled the antediluvian kingdom of fallen angels and their Rephaim children. This king, referred to as "the Assyrian," was the first global ruler and the most powerful of all the Genesis 6 apostate angels. The book of Ezekiel chronicles his rise to prominence, the destruction of his kingdom, and one of the main reasons the Lord administered such a catastrophic flood judgment.[1] Unlike the extra-biblical texts, the Bible provides specific details regarding the means and timing of the judgment of the sinning angels and the Nephilim and how they ended up deep in the abyss. It also contains prophetic references to the future return of the angels who sinned and the fate of the giants in Hell.

## Understanding Esoteric Passages

Certain sections of the Bible are addressed to a specific person (typically a king) or group but contain a deeper, hidden message and are directed to a heavenly realm or angelic being. The most famous of these passages is Isaiah 14:

> "That thou shalt take up this proverb against the king of Babylon, and say, How hath the oppressor ceased! the golden city ceased! the Lord hath broken the staff of the wicked, and the sceptre of the rulers. He who smote the people in wrath with a continual stroke, he that ruled

the nations in anger, is persecuted, and none hindereth. The whole earth is at rest, and is quiet: they break forth into singing. Yea, the fir trees rejoice at thee, and the cedars of Lebanon, saying, Since thou art laid down, no feller is come up against us. Hell from beneath is moved for thee to meet thee at thy coming: it stirreth up the dead [Rephaim] for thee, even all the chief ones of the earth; it hath raised up from their thrones all the kings of the nations.

All they shall speak and say unto thee, Art thou also become weak as we? art thou become like unto us? Thy pomp is brought down to the grave, and the noise of thy viols: the worm is spread under thee, and the worms cover thee. How art thou fallen from heaven, O Lucifer, son of the morning! how art thou cut down to the ground, which didst weaken the nations! For thou hast said in thine heart, I will ascend into heaven, I will exalt my throne above the stars of God: I will sit also upon the mount of the congregation, in the sides of the north: I will ascend above the heights of the clouds; I will be like the most High." – Isaiah 14:4–14

This passage, while addressed to the king of Babylon, is commonly accepted as also addressing Lucifer, one of the original titles of Satan. [Some Bible scholars believe the passage is addressing the Antichrist, which does not conflict with the former interpretation because Satan and the Antichrist, who is the seed of Satan, will be unified in spirit, power, and purpose in the end times.] We find a similar esoteric passage in Ezekiel 28:

"Son of man, take up a lamentation upon the king of Tyrus, and say unto him, Thus saith the Lord GOD; Thou sealest up the sum, full of wisdom, and perfect in beauty. **Thou hast been in Eden the garden of God;** every precious stone was thy covering, the sardius, topaz, and the diamond, the beryl, the onyx, and the jasper, the sapphire, the emerald, and the carbuncle, and gold: the workmanship of thy tabrets and of thy pipes was prepared in thee in the day that thou wast created. **Thou art the anointed cherub that covereth; and I have set thee so: thou wast upon the holy mountain of God; thou hast walked up and down in the midst of the stones of fire**. Thou wast perfect in thy ways from the day that thou wast created, till iniquity was found in thee.

By the multitude of thy merchandise they have filled the midst of thee with violence, and thou hast sinned: therefore I will cast thee as profane out of the mountain of God: and I will destroy thee, O covering cherub, from the midst of the stones of fire. Thine heart was lifted up because of thy beauty, thou hast corrupted thy wisdom by reason of thy brightness: I will cast thee to the ground, I will lay thee before kings, that they may behold thee. Thou hast defiled thy sanctuaries by the multitude of thine iniquities, by the iniquity of thy traffick; therefore will I bring forth a fire from the midst of thee, it shall devour thee, and I will bring thee to ashes upon the earth in the sight of all them that behold thee." – Ezekiel 28:12–19

Although this passage is directed to the king of Tyrus, much in the text suggests that an angel is the true intended recipient of the message. God pronounced that the king of Tyrus "sealest up the sum, full of wisdom, perfect in beauty," which is not a compliment that would be paid to a pagan king. The passage further states that this being "has been in Eden the garden of God" – a major indication that we are now transitioning from the earthly realm to a heavenly being. The passage continues to say that this being (whom many identify as Satan in his glory as a righteous angel before his descent into sinful rebellion) wore jewels in the manner of a high priest. All the jewels Satan wore in Eden were worn by the high priest of the Israelites (Exodus 28:17–20). The Devil served in a priesthood capacity prior to his fall. The mention of the "stones of fire" (which were before the throne of God and used by the cherubim as we saw earlier) and the other attributes prove that this passage is truly intended for Satan as a rebuke of his evil ways and a prophecy of his future judgment and destruction.

# EZEKIEL 31 – A VERSE-BY-VERSE ANALYSIS

Isaiah 14 and Ezekiel 28 are very well-known passages and familiar territory for students of the Bible. Two other esoteric passages are *not* as well-known but shed an amazing amount of light on the judgment of the Nephilim – Ezekiel 31 and 32. It is important to note that Ezekiel had more interaction with angelic, heavenly-realm beings than any other person in Scripture. From Ezekiel 1, the prophet encounters cherubim by the river Chebar (Ezekiel 1:1–4). He was transported through the skies by angels and God (Ezekiel 3:12–14, Ezekiel 8:3). The Lord provided Ezekiel special vision to see through the walls of the holy temple in Jerusalem to watch the secret occult practices of the Levite priests in charge of its care. Ezekiel witnessed conversations between angels and God. And in the final eight chapters of the book an angel gave Ezekiel a supernatural tour of the future Millennial temple from which the Lord Jesus Christ will rule after the Second Coming. If you are seeking a greater understanding of the angelic realm, read the book of Ezekiel.

# THE ASSYRIAN – ANGELIC KING OF THE PRE-FLOOD WORLD

Ezekiel 31 and 32 are an esoteric address to "the Assyrian," the angelic emperor who ruled the antediluvian world, and his fallen angelic-Nephilim kingdom. Although the text appears to be referring to "Pharaoh of Egypt," it is truly directed to the apostate angel who reigned over all of the fallen sons of God and Nephilim before the Flood:

> "And it came to pass in the eleventh year, in the third month, in the first day of the month, that the word of the LORD came unto me, saying, Son of man, speak unto Pharaoh king of Egypt, and to his multitude; Whom art thou like in thy greatness? **Behold, the Assyrian was a cedar in Lebanon with fair branches, and with a**

shadowing shroud, and of an high stature; and his top was among the thick boughs." – Ezekiel 31:1–3

Some Bible students will recognize parallels between this passage and the other, more popular esoteric Scriptures. "Pharaoh" or "the Assyrian" was incomparable in his level of "greatness." A similar lofty compliment is given at the beginning of Isaiah 14 and Ezekiel 28. The Assyrian was a "cedar in Lebanon with fair branches." The Lebanese cedar is an extremely tall tree that reaches heights of 130 feet. There is rich biblical imagery in this passage as well. The cedar tree is frequently used in Scripture as a metaphor for mighty beings.

## NEPHILIM ARE COMPARED TO CEDAR TREES IN SCRIPTURE

In Amos 2 the Amorites, a race of people ruled by Nephilim kings Og and Sihon, are compared to cedar trees:

"**Yet destroyed I the Amorite before them, whose height was like the height of the cedars**, and he was strong as the oaks; yet I destroyed his fruit from above, and his roots from beneath. Also I brought you up from the land of Egypt, and led you forty years through the wilderness, to possess the land of the Amorite." – Amos 2:9–10

In this chapter Amos rebuked the Israelites for their idolatry during the days of King Rehoboam. God testified to His faithfulness to Israel and His might by reminding the Israelites that He personally destroyed the Amorites who had superhuman height – *and whom the Lord Himself compared to cedar trees*. Like the Nephilim kings Og and Sihon, the Assyrian was also a "cedar."

## ANGELS ARE ALSO COMPARED TO
## CEDAR TREES IN SCRIPTURE

Isaiah 2 details God's pouring out His wrath during the Great Tribulation on those in sinful rebellion on Earth *and in the heavens*. With respect to the punishment of sinful angels, the chapter states:

> "For the day of the LORD of hosts shall be upon every one that is proud and lofty, and upon every one that is lifted up; and he shall be brought low: **And upon all the cedars of Lebanon, that are high and lifted up, and upon all the oaks of Bashan....**" – Isaiah 2:12–13

The Nephilim king Og resided in Bashan – another confirmation that the heavenly realm is in view. Like his Nephilim descendant Og, the Assyrian had "high stature" as a mighty being who towered over all the trees around him. Not only was the Assyrian a ruler, he was preeminent over all the kings in the world. The Assyrian had "fair branches," noting his beautiful and large family. The verse invokes the word "fair," the same term that described the "daughters of men" in Genesis 6 whom the sinning angels took as wives. A great deal of biblical precedent supports interpreting the descriptive language of this great tree as a metaphor for a powerful king of angelic origin and his branches and boughs as his family and kingdom.

## DANIEL 4 DECODES THE "TREE" SYMBOLISM

If the metaphoric language of a supreme monarch described as a tree still seems to be a stretch, consider the dream of King Nebuchadnezzar in Daniel 4. This passage serves as a Rosetta stone to decipher Ezekiel 31:

> "O Belteshazzar [Daniel], master of the magicians, because I know that the spirit of the holy gods is in thee, and no secret troubleth

thee, tell me the visions of my dream that I have seen, and the interpretation thereof. [10] Thus were the visions of mine head in my bed; I saw, **and behold a tree in the midst of the earth, and the height thereof was great.** [11] **The tree grew, and was strong, and the height thereof reached unto heaven, and the sight thereof to the end of all the earth:** [12] **The leaves thereof were fair, and the fruit thereof much, and in it was meat for all: the beasts of the field had shadow under it, and the fowls of the heaven dwelt in the boughs thereof, and all flesh was fed of it.**

[13] I saw in the visions of my head upon my bed, and, behold, a watcher and an holy one came down from heaven; [14] He cried aloud, and said thus, Hew down the tree, and cut off his branches, shake off his leaves, and scatter his fruit: let the beasts get away from under it, and the fowls from his branches: [15] Nevertheless leave the stump of his roots in the earth, even with a band of iron and brass, in the tender grass of the field; and let it be wet with the dew of heaven, and let his portion be with the beasts in the grass of the earth: [16] Let his heart be changed from man's, and let a beast's heart be given unto him; and let seven times pass over him. [17] **This matter is by the decree of the watchers, and the demand by the word of the holy ones:** to the intent that the living may know that the most High ruleth in the kingdom of men, and giveth it to whomsoever he will, and setteth up over it the basest of men. [18] This dream I king Nebuchadnezzar have seen. Now thou, O Belteshazzar, declare the interpretation thereof, forasmuch as all the wise men of my kingdom are not able to make known unto me the interpretation: but thou art able; for the spirit of the holy gods is in thee.

[19] Then Daniel, whose name was Belteshazzar, was astonied for one hour, and his thoughts troubled him. The king spake, and said, Belteshazzar, let not the dream, or the interpretation thereof, trouble thee. Belteshazzar answered and said, My lord, the dream

> be to them that hate thee, and the interpretation thereof to thine enemies. <sup>20</sup> **The tree that thou sawest, which grew, and was strong, whose height reached unto the heaven, and the sight thereof to all the earth;** <sup>21</sup> **Whose leaves were fair, and the fruit thereof much, and in it was meat for all; under which the beasts of the field dwelt, and upon whose branches the fowls of the heaven had their habitation:** <sup>22</sup> **It is thou, O king, that art grown and become strong: for thy greatness is grown,** and reacheth unto heaven, and thy dominion to the end of the earth." – Daniel 4:9–22

Nebuchadnezzar, ruler of the entire known world at that time, *was the tree in his dream.* And just like the Assyrian of Ezekiel 31, his height, leaves, and branches were all symbolic of his great power and dominion over the entire world. Thus, this is biblical confirmation (by letting Scripture interpret Scripture) that the metaphor of Ezekiel 31 is valid. The Assyrian was the preeminent angel among the sons of God who assumed rulership over the earth and was the angelic patriarch and High Chief of the Nephilim.

## THE ASSYRIAN WAS THE FIRST EMPEROR

With proper biblical context established, we return to a verse-by-verse analysis of Ezekiel 31:

> "The waters made him great, the deep set him up on high with her rivers running round about his plants, and sent her little rivers unto all the trees of the field. **Therefore his height was exalted above all the trees of the field, and his boughs were multiplied, and his branches became long because of the multitude of waters,** when he shot forth." – Ezekiel 31:4–5

The waters and rivers gave the Assyrian his strength. As we saw earlier, angels in the biblical account manifested near water *and rivers in particular*. That rivers could provide certain powers and strategic advantage is a reasonable conclusion. With this strategic location, the Nephilim hybrid empire of the Assyrian became great and his "boughs"– or Nephilim children – "multiplied," a term similar to the one the Lord used for begetting sons who carry the spiritual nature of their father ("be fruitful and multiply," Genesis 1:28). With numerous giant offspring, the Assyrian conceived his own army of superhuman warriors.

> "**All the fowls of heaven** made their nests in his boughs, and under his branches did **all the beasts of the field bring** forth their young, **and under his shadow dwelt all great nations**. Thus was he fair in his greatness, in the length of his branches: for his root was by great waters." – Ezekiel 31:6–7

This passage uses language almost identical to Daniel's description of Nebuchadnezzar (Daniel 4). The key word in this passage is "all": whether it was the fowls of heaven (angels), the beasts of the field (Nephilim hybrids), or the great nations (humanity), all were in the boughs, branches, and shadow of the Assyrian, symbolizing worldwide authority. Like Nebuchadnezzar, the Assyrian was the head of a global kingdom. Verse 7 again emphasizes how vast his empire and mighty family were because of his proximity to "great waters."

## THE ASSYRIAN ASSUMED CONTROL OF THE GARDEN OF EDEN

> "The cedars **in the garden of God** could not hide him: the fir trees were not like his boughs, and the chestnut trees were not like his branches; **nor any tree in the garden of God was like unto him** in his beauty." – Ezekiel 31:8

Verse 8 gives the true spiritual revelation as we see a reference to Eden, the garden of God. This is another biblical confirmation that the true referent of this chapter is the fallen angelic king who lived before the Flood destroyed the Garden of Eden and not Pharaoh of Egypt (who of course would never have been in the Garden of Eden). In fact, **Ezekiel 31 contains more references to the Garden of Eden than any other chapter of the Bible** (including the early chapters of the book of Genesis). Thus, in this passage the Bible provides the most details about the Garden's history. When humans vacated the Garden of Eden, the apostate angels moved in. The Assyrian usurped the holy temple of Eden and ruled the nations. The Assyrian was the most powerful of all the Genesis 6 invaders of Earth to the point that the "cedars in the garden of God could not hide him." He stood above them all. No angel approached his level of authority. He also exceeded other angels in beauty, the preeminent trait Satan possessed as detailed in Ezekiel 28:

> "Thine heart was lifted up because of thy beauty. Thou hast corrupted thy wisdom by reason of thy brightness…" – Ezekiel 28:17

The Devil's divine magnificent beauty was no doubt connected to his superior power among his fellow angels. Satan's pride in his beauty was part of his downfall into sin. Similarly, the Assyrian was puffed up in vanity over being the first global monarch. But his ascent to power and calamitous fall were all under the Lord's control and will:

> "I have made him fair by the multitude of his branches: so that all the trees of Eden, that were in the garden of God, envied him. Therefore thus saith the Lord GOD; Because thou hast lifted up thyself in height, and he hath shot up his top among the thick boughs, and his heart is lifted up in his height; I have therefore delivered him into the hand of the mighty one of the heathen; he shall surely deal with him: I have driven him out for his wickedness." – Ezekiel 31:9–11

Nothing being done in Earth or Heaven, by human or angel, is outside of God's control and authority. Because of the Assyrian's arrogance and self-exultation, God punished him. Verse 10 states "and his heart is lifted up in his height," indicating a sinful heart that rejected God's rule. The Lord used this phrase as a warning to the ancient Israelites about falling into sin:

> "*Then thine heart be lifted up*, and thou forget the LORD thy God, which brought thee forth out of the land of Egypt, from the house of bondage...." – Deuteronomy 8:13

God issued a similar command to the kings of Israel to remain in good fellowship with Him. Every king was required by divine law to write his own personal copy of the first five books of the Bible and read it daily to prevent his heart from being lifted up:

> "And it shall be, when he sitteth upon the throne of his kingdom, that he shall write him a copy of this law in a book out of that which is before the priests the Levites: And it shall be with him, and he shall read therein all the days of his life: that he may learn to fear the LORD his God, to keep all the words of this law and these statutes, to do them: *That his heart be not lifted up above his brethren, and that he turn not aside from the commandment*, to the right hand, or to the left: to the end that he may prolong his days in his kingdom, he, and his children, in the midst of Israel." – Deuteronomy 17:18–20

The Assyrian's heart was lifted up and he rejected God's authority. By populating the world with Nephilim, the Assyrian violated God's prohibition on angelic marriage and genetic purity and threatened the prophecy of the Seed of the Woman. This evil angel's incursion was a willful rebellion aimed at thwarting God's very plan of salvation. And the Lord punished the Assyrian severely for it. His power would be his undoing. He was permitted to become so powerful that "all of the trees in Eden, that were in the garden of God, envied him." This led to dissension in the ranks of the other sinning angels and Nephilim under his rule.

## THE DESTRUCTION OF THE ASSYRIAN'S KINGDOM

Just as quickly as the Assyrian abused his angelic authority and left his first estate to pursue fornication and world dominance, he was delivered to destruction. Verse 11 states that the Assyrian was delivered "into the hand of the mighty one of the heathen; he shall surely deal with him. I have driven him out for his wickedness." The Septuagint renders the verse: "therefore I delivered him into the hands of the prince of the nations, and he wrought his destruction." So, who is this "mighty one of the heathen" or "prince of the nations"? It was Satan, who after the events of Genesis 6 was responsible for initiating the Assyrian's destruction.

The Lord Jesus Christ referred to Satan as "the prince of this world" three times in Scripture:

> "Now is the judgment of this world: now **shall the prince of this world** be cast out." – John 12:31

> "Hereafter I will not talk much with you: **for the prince of this world cometh**, and hath nothing in me." – John 14:30

> "Of judgment, because **the prince of this world is judged**." – John 16:11

Although Satan is identified even by the Lord as the temporary ruler of this age, he remains beholden to the authority of God. In the book of Job, the Bible clearly shows that Satan can act only within boundaries set by God. And God can authorize Satan to harm others as He did in the case of Job:

"Again there was a day when the sons of God came to present themselves before the LORD, and Satan came also among them to present himself before the LORD. And the LORD said unto Satan, From whence comest thou? And Satan answered the LORD, and said, From going to and fro in the earth, and from walking up and down in it. And the LORD said unto Satan, Hast thou considered my servant Job, that there is none like him in the earth, a perfect and an upright man, one that feareth God, and escheweth evil? and still he holdeth fast his integrity, although thou movedst me against him, to destroy him without cause. And Satan answered the LORD, and said, Skin for skin, yea, all that a man hath will he give for his life. But put forth thine hand now, and touch his bone and his flesh, and he will curse thee to thy face. **And the LORD said unto Satan, Behold, he is in thine hand; but save his life.** So went Satan forth from the presence of the LORD, and smote Job with sore boils from the sole of his foot unto his crown." – Job 2:1–7

Although Job was a faithful believer, God permitted Satan to harm him to prove Job's faith was not dependent on his wealth (and to provide an example and instruct all of humanity). Similarly, a rebel such as the wicked Assyrian could be "delivered to the Devil" as a punishment. The idea of "delivering someone to Satan" for God's judgment occurs twice in the New Testament:

"This charge I commit unto thee, son Timothy, according to the prophecies which went before on thee, that thou by them mightest war a good warfare; Holding faith, and a good conscience; which some having put away concerning faith have made shipwreck: Of whom is Hymenaeus and Alexander; **whom I have delivered unto Satan, that they may learn not to blaspheme.** "– 1 Timothy 1:18–20

"In the name of our Lord Jesus Christ, when ye are gathered together, and my spirit, with the power of our Lord Jesus Christ,

**To deliver such an one unto Satan** for the destruction of the flesh, that the spirit may be saved in the day of the Lord Jesus." – 1 Corinthians 5:4–5

In both passages above someone who was supposed to be a follower of God defected from the faith or were in deep sin and was "delivered" to the Devil for bodily destruction as judgment. The Assyrian received the same punishment.

"And strangers, the terrible of the nations, have cut him off, and have left him: upon the mountains and in all the valleys his branches are fallen, and his boughs are broken by all the rivers of the land; and all the people of the earth are gone down from his shadow, and have left him. Upon his ruin shall all the fowls of the heaven remain, and all the beasts of the field shall be upon his branches." – Ezekiel 31:12–13

On the cusp of the global flood, a war broke out among the Angelic-Nephilim kingdoms. The Assyrian and his giant offspring were defeated just as the flood waters were about to be unleashed. His power and might destroyed, the Assyrian's kingdom was in ruin. Thus, in the final days before God's wrath the world was in chaos because of widespread warfare, as Genesis 6 reports:

"The earth also was corrupt before God, and **the earth was filled with violence.**" – Genesis 6:10

The final century of the antediluvian era descended into world war. The once-magnificent, sprawling kingdom of the Assyrian and his Nephilim spawn was torn apart by violence as the lower angels and their children attacked and defeated the Assyrian. In this light, it seems even more appropriate that the Lord told Noah to enter the ark for seven days before the heavy rains began.

JUDGMENT OF THE NEPHILIM • 181

Not only would the Assyrian fall but his "branches" (his many fair wives) and "boughs" (his Nephilim offspring) were destroyed as well. We should be careful not to overlook the reference to "fowls of heaven" and "beasts of the field." A similar judgment was pronounced on the Nephilim Goliath:

> "Then said David to the Philistine, Thou comest to me with a sword, and with a spear, and with a shield: but I come to thee in the name of the LORD of hosts, the God of the armies of Israel, whom thou hast defied. This day will the LORD deliver thee into mine hand; and I will smite thee, and take thine head from thee; and I will give the carcases of the host of the Philistines this day unto the fowls of the air, and to the wild beasts of the earth; that all the earth may know that there is a God in Israel." – 1 Samuel 17:45–46

## THE END OF ANGELIC-HUMAN MARRIAGE AND ILLICIT INTIMATE RELATIONS

Ezekiel 31:14 explains one of the ultimate purposes of the Flood:

> "To the end that none of all the trees by the waters exalt themselves for their height, neither shoot up their top among the thick boughs, neither their trees stand up in their height, all that drink water: for they are all delivered unto death, to the nether parts of the earth, in the midst of the children of men, with them that go down to the pit."

The Flood was a judgment of humanity and destroyed the Nephilim. But it also served as a stunning and devastating deterrent to all angels to never again attempt to repeat the sexual sins of the sons of God of Genesis 6. The Lord used the Flood to plunge the sinning angels down to Hell ("the nether parts of the earth") alive, where they were then bound with chains and remain until judgment day (Jude 1:6). Ezekiel uses the phrase "drink water" to describe those who were sucked through the raging waters into the subterranean abyss during the Flood. The passage distinguishes the Assyrian and his kingdom (his branches and boughs) from "the children of men" or normal human beings, referred to as "them that go down to the pit." Up to this point, there was no scriptural account of *angels being sent to Sheol.* But the Genesis 6 rebels were sentenced to imprisonment with the many souls of dead humans who are in Hell today.

The deterrent purpose of the flood judgment is made clear as the text states: "To the end that none of all the trees by the water exalt themselves." The Flood guaranteed that no other angels ever again attempted this type of rebellion. **This is why there are no further accounts of angels' taking human women as wives and having sexual relations after the Flood.** Distinguished 19th-century Irish pastor John Fleming agreed:

> "An insuperable objection appears to lie against the notion that demon intercourse of the kind in question was carried on subsequently to the Deluge. The purpose of God in bringing on the world that widespread destruction was, we believe, not merely to punish transgressors **but quite as much or more to put a period to the unnatural intercourse of angels with daughters of men,** to prevent the further commingling of different classes of creatures, to obliterate all traces of such intercourse and to exterminate the monstrous offspring to which it had given rise." – *The Fallen Angels and the Heroes of Mythology*, Rev. John Fleming A.B., Dublin: Hodges, Foster, & Figgis, 1879, pp. 108–109.

The floodwaters dragging angels into the abyss to be chained in darkness sent shockwaves through the angelic realm (Ezekiel 31:15). The Lord administered an extreme punishment for their attempt to pollute the Messianic bloodline. Psalm 29 praises the Creator for using the Flood to demonstrate His power and might over the Genesis 6 angels:

"Give unto the LORD, O ye mighty, give unto the LORD glory and strength. Give unto the LORD the glory due unto his name; worship the LORD in the beauty of holiness. The voice of the LORD is upon the waters: the God of glory thundereth: the LORD is upon many waters. The voice of the LORD is powerful; the voice of the LORD is full of majesty. **The voice of the LORD breaketh the cedars; yea, the LORD breaketh the cedars of Lebanon.** He maketh them also to skip like a calf; Lebanon and Sirion like a young unicorn. **The voice of the LORD divideth the flames of fire. the Lord sitteth upon the flood**; yea, the LORD sitteth King for ever… the Lord will give strength unto his people; the LORD will bless his people with peace." – Psalm 29:1–7; 11

In the Septuagint, verse 1 reads "bring to the Lord, **ye sons of God…**" – confirming the passage is *an address to angels*. And the purpose was to exhort the sons of God to give their Creator the respect and honor He is due. God "broke the cedars of Lebanon" and made them run in fear like baby animals. How did He do this? By the Flood. The "flames of fire" are a reference to angels (Hebrews 1:7). God divided the angels by sending the sinning Sons of God to Sheol in the Flood. The Psalm concludes that God "sits on the flood," symbolizing His supreme dominion over Heaven and Earth. The Flood was the Lord's proof that He reigns over all angels, Nephilim, and creation.

## THE BIBLICAL TIMING OF THE ASSYRIAN'S DESCENT INTO HELL

Ezekiel 31 also provides *the timing of the destruction of the Assyrian's kingdom:*

"Thus saith the Lord GOD; **In the day when he went down to the grave** I caused a mourning: I covered the deep for him, **and I restrained the floods thereof, and the great waters were stayed:**

and I caused Lebanon to mourn for him, and all the trees of the field fainted for him." – Ezekiel 31:15

After day 150 of the Flood, the waters finally started to "abate":

"And God remembered Noah, and every living thing, and all the cattle that was with him in the ark: and God made a wind to pass over the earth, and the waters assuaged; The fountains also of the deep and the windows of heaven were stopped, **and the rain from heaven was restrained; And the waters returned from off the earth continually: and after the end of the hundred and fifty days the waters were abated**." – Genesis 8:1–3

Both passages point to the same time in the Flood, the moment God "restrained" or stopped the rain showers from above and "stayed" the massive subterranean waters shooting up from "the deep." The divine force pushing water through the earth's surface ceased and the waters of the deep returned to beneath the earth's crust. The Assyrian was forced to fight for his survival in his ruined kingdom among the raging flood waters for 150 days. He watched his kingdom crumble and all his wives and Nephilim children perish. And once God stopped the Flood, the waters of the deep returned underground ("And the waters returned from off the earth continually"), sucking the Assyrian and the other sinning angels down to the abyss, alive.

The Assyrian, the apostate sons of God, and the corpses of their Nephilim offspring were engulfed by the flood waters and sent to the "nether parts of the earth" (Ezekiel 31:14). This was the completely unexpected and stunning punishment of the sinning angels. All "the trees of the field" – the angels who did not participate in illicit relations with human women – witnessed God's cataclysmic judgment of the Assyrian and the pre-Flood Angelic-Nephilim kingdoms and "fainted" in horror (Ezekiel 31:15).

This was not the only instance in Scripture in which a person was literally sucked down to Hell while alive. A similar judgment is found in the account of the rebellion of Korah in Numbers 16:

> "Now Korah, the son of Izhar, the son of Kohath, the son of Levi, and Dathan and Abiram, the sons of Eliab, and On, the son of Peleth, sons of Reuben, took men: And they rose up before Moses, with certain of the children of Israel, two hundred and fifty princes of the assembly, famous in the congregation, men of renown: And they gathered themselves together against Moses and against Aaron, and said unto them, Ye take too much upon you, seeing all the congregation are holy, every one of them, and the LORD is among them: wherefore then lift ye up yourselves above the congregation of the LORD? And when Moses heard it, he fell upon his face: And he spake unto Korah and unto all his company, saying, Even to morrow the LORD will shew who are his, and who is holy; and will cause him to come near unto him: even him whom he hath chosen will he cause to come near unto him." – Numbers 16:1–5

Korah, a Levite, challenged God's selection of Moses and Aaron as the leader and high priest of the 12 tribes of Israel. By this point in the wilderness journey God had demonstrated repeatedly that Moses was His chosen prophet and Aaron His chosen high priest. But Korah's heart was lifted up in arrogance and he sought to defy the Lord by making himself leader of the fledgling nation. He challenged Moses with a group of princes whom the Bible interestingly calls "men of renown."

Moses then arranged a contest in which both he and Korah would offer incense to God in front of the entire nation and see whose offering was received by the Lord – and thus who truly was the Creator's choice to be the prophet to the nation:

"And Korah gathered all the congregation against them unto the door of the tabernacle of the congregation: and the glory of the LORD appeared unto all the congregation. And the LORD spake unto Moses and unto Aaron, saying, Separate yourselves from among this congregation, that I may consume them in a moment. And they fell upon their faces, and said, O God, the God of the spirits of all flesh, shall one man sin, and wilt thou be wroth with all the congregation? And the LORD spake unto Moses, saying, Speak unto the congregation, saying, Get you up from about the tabernacle of Korah, Dathan, and Abiram. And Moses rose up and went unto Dathan and Abiram; and the elders of Israel followed him. And he spake unto the congregation, saying, Depart, I pray you, from the tents of these wicked men, and touch nothing of theirs, lest ye be consumed in all their sins." – Numbers 16:19–26

God's plan of salvation always involves warning His faithful believers of the judgment to come. Just as God warned Noah of the Flood, so He revealed to Moses that Korah was going to be consumed and that the people should move as far from him as possible:

"And Moses said, Hereby ye shall know that the LORD hath sent me to do all these works; for I have not done them of mine own mind. If these men die the common death of all men, or if they be visited after the visitation of all men; then the LORD hath not sent me. But if the LORD make a new thing, and the earth open her mouth, and swallow them up, with all that appertain unto them, and they go down quick into the pit; then ye shall understand that these men have provoked the LORD. And it came to pass, as he had made an end of speaking all these words, **that the ground clave asunder that was under them: And the earth opened her mouth, and swallowed them up, and their houses, and all the men that appertained unto Korah, and all their goods. They, and all that** appertained to them, went down alive into the pit, and the earth closed upon them: and they perished from among the congregation. And all Israel that were round about them fled at the cry of them: for they said, Lest the earth swallow us up also." – Numbers 16:28–34

Korah and his sinful cohorts were swallowed into the abyss of Hell alive. The earth supernaturally opened and swallowed them down to Hell. Just as angels "fainted" at the sight of the Assyrian being swallowed into Hell alive, the people of Israel ran in fear at the sight of Korah's punishment and the sound of his screams. In both instances the judgment served as both punishment of the rebel and a deterrent to anyone who might consider such defiance in the future. The Assyrian and the rest of the angels who sinned were then chained in the abyss where they remain until the end times judgment of God (2 Peter 2:4).

## BIBLICAL REFERENCES TO THE JUDGMENT OF THE NEPHILIM

Several passages of Scripture refer to the specific punishment of the Assyrian and his Angelic-Nephilim kingdom and use the Flood as a metaphor for the worst possible judgment a person could endure:

- "Let not the waterflood overflow me, neither let the deep swallow me up, and let not the pit shut her mouth upon me." – Psalm 69:15

This verse describes the exact sequence of the judgment of the Nephilim and the angels who sinned. The Flood overwhelmed them and they were swallowed by the waters of the deep, sucking all of them into "the pit" or the abyss of Hell.

- "Let us swallow them up alive as the grave; and whole, as those that go down into the pit…" – Proverbs 1:12

- Ezekiel 26 contains a very interesting prophecy of judgment against the kingdom of Tyre. The Lord rebuked the coastal city for its wickedness and predicted that it would sink into the sea:

"For thus saith the Lord GOD; When I shall make thee a desolate city, **like the cities that are not inhabited**; when I shall bring up the deep upon thee, and great waters shall cover thee; **When I shall bring thee down with them that descend into the pit, with the people of old time**, and shall set thee in the low parts of the earth, in places desolate of old, with them that go down to the pit, that thou be not inhabited; and I shall set glory in the land of the living...." – Ezekiel 26:19–20

Ezekiel, who recorded the history of the Assyrian, also refers to the destruction of the antediluvian world in this passage, describing them as "the people of old time." The passage refers also to "cities that are not inhabited," a possible reference to the cities of the Assyrian and his empire's sinking to the sea floor in the destructive tectonic activity of the Flood.

- "For if God spared not the angels that sinned, but cast them down to hell, and delivered them into chains of darkness, to be reserved unto judgment; And spared not the old world, but saved Noah the eighth person, a preacher of righteousness, bringing in the flood upon the world of the ungodly...." – 2 Peter 2:4–5
- "And the angels which kept not their first estate, but left their own habitation, he hath reserved in everlasting chains under darkness unto the judgment of the great day." – Jude 1:6

## 150 DAYS OF TORMENT

Unlike the Book of Enoch *or any other extra-biblical text or historical source*, Ezekiel 31 details the precise day when the Assyrian and the pre-Flood angelic-Nephilim kingdoms were judged. After a century of world war, his empire crumbled under the flood waters for 150 days. Then, in an instant, the Assyrian, his fellow fallen angels, and the corpses of their Nephilim sons were swallowed down to the pit of Hell. The sinning angels, still alive, were then bound in chains, where they remain (even today) until the end-times judgment of God.

Genesis 8 reveals that the flood waters were "restrained" after 150 days. This time frame runs parallel with a Great Tribulation judgment in the book of Revelation:

"And the fifth angel sounded, and I saw a star fall from heaven unto the earth: **and to him was given the key of the bottomless pit. And he opened the bottomless pit;** and there arose a smoke out of the pit, as the smoke of a great furnace; **and the sun and the air were darkened by reason of the smoke of the pit**. And there came out of the smoke locusts upon the earth: and unto them was given power, as the scorpions of the earth have power. And it was commanded them that they should not hurt the grass of the earth, neither any green thing, neither any tree; but only those men which have not the seal of God in their foreheads. **And to them it was given that they should not kill them, but that they should be tormented five months:** and their torment was as the torment of a scorpion, when he striketh a man.

And in those days shall men seek death, and shall not find it; and shall desire to die, and death shall flee from them. And the shapes of the locusts were like unto horses prepared unto battle; and on their heads were as it were crowns like gold, and their faces were as the faces of men. And they had hair as the hair of women, and their teeth were as the teeth of lions. And they had breastplates, as it were breastplates of iron; and the sound of their wings was as the sound of chariots of many horses running to battle. And they had tails like unto scorpions, and there were stings in their tails: and their power was to hurt men five months. **And they had a king over them,** which is the angel of the bottomless pit, whose name in the Hebrew tongue is Abaddon, but in the Greek tongue hath his name Apollyon." – Revelation 9:1–11

# THE RETURN OF THE FALLEN ANGELS OF THE ABYSS

Revelation 9 describes events of the Great Tribulation, the final years before the Second Coming of Christ. During this time, the Lord pours out supernatural punishments on the unbelieving world. At the fifth trumpet judgment of Revelation, the bottomless pit or abyss will open and "locusts" will emerge from the smoke of the pit. These are the angels of Genesis 6 who were imprisoned for millennia. Note that the smoke of the pit is so strong it darkens the sun and the air above ground. **This is the same "darkness" under which the Sons of God were imprisoned (Jude 1:6).** The Great Tribulation or Day of the Lord is the "Great Day" of Judgment (Zephaniah 1:14) that Jude refers to as the time when the sons of God would finally be released from their chains. The fallen angels emerge with a bizarre appearance. They have bodies like horses. They wear crowns and have the "faces of men." They have women's hair, teeth like lions, wings, and tails. This bizarre description is like the description of the cherubim who surround the throne of God or even that of the minotaurs or centaurs of Greek mythology. The locusts will be unleashed from the pit with the charge to torment unbelieving humans during the Great Tribulation. They will cause so much agony and pain that people will want to die but not be able to. This torment lasts five months.

The Bible records time according to the Hebrew calendar in which every month is 30 days. Thus, these locusts are released from Hell for 150 days to torment the earth as part of God's judgment – *the exact amount of time the Assyrian, the sinning angels, and their Nephilim sons were tormented by the Flood in the days of Noah.* In the end times, these grotesque, apostate angels will be released, and their king, who is called Abaddon or Apollyon, is also mentioned. The term "Abaddon," or *'abaddown* in Hebrew, is used only six times in the Old Testament. The first use is in Job:

> "Shall giants [*repahim*] be born from under the water and the inhabitants thereof? Hell is naked before him, and destruction [*'abaddown*] has no covering." – Job 26:5–6

Just as the Rephaim giants became synonymous with the dead, so too their antediluvian king took on the name for the bottomless pit – Abaddon. In the passage from Job above, the prophet explained that the giants, fallen angels, and their leader, the Assyrian, also known as Abaddon or Apollyon, are exposed before God in Hell – attesting to the fact that God sees all in every realm. But during the Great Tribulation, these sinful angels will be released to torment the earth.

## THE ASSYRIAN AND THE SONS OF GOD WILL RETURN IN THE END TIMES

Joel 2 gives warnings about this same event:

> "Blow ye the trumpet in Zion, and sound an alarm in my holy mountain: let all the inhabitants of the land tremble: for the day of the LORD cometh, for it is nigh at hand; A day of darkness and of gloominess, **a day of clouds and of thick darkness,** as the morning spread upon the mountains: **a great people and a strong; there hath not been ever the like, neither shall be any more after it, even to the years of many generations**. A fire devoureth before them; and behind them a flame burneth: **the land is as the garden of Eden before them,** and behind them a desolate wilderness; yea, and nothing shall escape them. The appearance of them is as the appearance of horses; and as horsemen, so shall they run." – Joel 2:1–4

This supernatural army of the fallen sons of God who are locked in the abyss is unlike anything the world has seen. When the bottomless pit is opened, the thick black smoke from Hell darkens the sky (Revelation 9:2). Joel confirms this by referring to the "clouds and thick darkness" (Joel 2:2). Released from their prison, they see the earth like "the garden of Eden before them" – another biblical clue that angelic beings and the pre-Flood world are in view. These beings who dominated the world and captured Eden 5,000 years earlier will be released with the same voracity to wage war on the earth. Both Revelation and Joel describe their general appearance as horses prepared for battle.

> "Like the noise of chariots on the tops of mountains shall they leap, like the noise of a flame of fire that devoureth the stubble, as a strong people set in battle array." – Joel 2:5

The wicked sons of God are dressed in battle armor and make noise of "a flame of fire," which is another reference to angels (Hebrews 1:7). The verse parallels Revelation 9: "And they had breastplates, as it were breastplates of iron; and the sound of their wings was as the sound of chariots of many horses running to battle" (Revelation 9:9) – right down to the sounds of their wings being as horse-drawn chariots.

> "Before their face the people shall be much pained: all faces shall gather blackness. They shall run like mighty men; they shall climb the wall like men of war; and they shall march every one on his ways, and they shall not break their ranks...." – Joel 2:6–7

The Nephilim giants were "mighty men" and "men of renown" for their prowess in warfare.

> "Neither shall one thrust another; they shall walk every one in his path: and when they fall upon the sword, they shall not be

wounded. They shall run to and fro in the city; they shall run upon the wall, they shall climb up upon the houses; they shall enter in at the windows like a thief. The earth shall quake before them; the heavens shall tremble: the sun and the moon shall be dark, and the stars shall withdraw their shining: And the LORD shall utter his voice before his army: for his camp is very great: for he is strong that executeth his word: for the day of the LORD is great and very terrible; and who can abide it?" – Joel 2:8–11

For 150 days Hell will literally be unleashed upon Earth. These passages affirm why Jesus Christ prophesied the final years on Earth would be "as the days of Noah" (Matthew 24:37). No extra-biblical text provides any details on the specific punishment of the Nephilim and the angels who sinned, the duration of their torment in the Flood, or their eventual return as a tool of God's wrath in the end-times judgment of the Great Tribulation. But the Bible provides great detail on all of this and is the superior source for the history of the antediluvian world.

## CONTINUING THE VERSE-BY-VERSE STUDY OF EZEKIEL 31

"I made the nations to shake at the sound of his fall, when I cast him down to hell with them that descend into the pit: and all the trees of Eden, the choice and best of Lebanon, all that drink water, shall be comforted in the nether parts of the earth. They also went down into hell with him unto them that be slain with the sword; and they that were his arm, that dwelt under his shadow in the midst of the heathen." – Ezekiel 31:16–17

The earth shook and convulsed when the frenzied floodwaters of the deep burst through the earth's crust. The Angelic-Nephilim kingdoms of the antediluvian world suffered cataclysmic destruction. This judgment of the Lord caused "all the trees of Eden" to be "comforted in the nether parts of the earth." The term "comforted" is derived from the Hebrew word *nacham,* which means "to be sorry, console oneself, repent." All the sinning angels or "trees of Eden" felt sorrow over their sin as they suffered in the depths of the abyss. It took such an overwhelming judgment of the Lord to bring these arrogant, rebellious apostates to even consider the grave sinfulness of their actions.

The Septuagint rendering of Ezekiel 31:16–17 provides deeper insight into the judgment:

> "At the sound of his fall the nations quaked, when I brought him down to Hades with them that go down to the pit: and all the trees of Delight comforted him in the heart, and the choice of *plants* of Libanus, all that drink water. **For they went down to hell with him among the slain with the sword; and his seed, *even* they that dwelt under his shadow, perished in the midst of their life**." – Ezekiel 31:16–17 LXX

Verse 16 in the Septuagint confirms that all the angels who sinned were dragged down to Hell (*Hades* in Greek). Verse 17 distinguishes the "trees of Delight" from those "slain with the sword," emphasizing that these angels (who went to Hell alive) are different from mortal human beings who go down to Hell. Unrepentant human beings, of course, die by the sword every day and are the normal group who go to the lowest level of Sheol. The text goes out of its way to highlight that this was a unique punishment. Sheol is the domain of the *human dead,* but in this particular instance certain angels would be cast into Hell as well.

Verse 17 in the Septuagint references "his seed," meaning the many Nephilim offspring of the Assyrian, who "perished in the midst of their life." So, all of the children of the Assyrian and the many other evil angelic rulers of the pre-

Flood world saw their Nephilim children, wives, and human subjects perish in the waters of the Flood.

> "To whom art thou compared? descend, and be thou debased with the trees of paradise to the depth of the earth: thou shalt lie in the midst of the uncircumcised with them that are slain by the sword. Thus shall Pharao be, and the multitude of his host, saith the Lord God." – Ezekiel 31:18 LXX

Ezekiel 31 closes with a taunt also found in Ezekiel 28's address to the Devil: "To whom are thou compared?" For a time, the Assyrian, like Satan before him, was an angel in a position of preeminent rulership over Earth. But eventually he fell and was punished. He was to be "debased" along with his other rebel angel to Hell. He was sentenced to imprisonment in the middle of the graves of the heathen humans. This was the fate of the Assyrian and "his multitude," the rebel angels and Nephilim offspring who overran and defiled the antediluvian earth.

## EZEKIEL 32 – RETURN OF THE SONS OF GOD IN THE END TIMES

Ezekiel 32 chronicles the final days of the Assyrian after he is released from Hell. His chains removed, the Assyrian will rule over the "Egypt" of the end times. Of course this "Egypt" is Mystery Babylon, the prophetic title for Jerusalem under the rule of Antichrist in the end times.

The Great Tribulation will be a time when the fallen angelic beings will openly manifest on Earth. And the Assyrian, the king and "angel of the bottomless pit," will be their leader:

> "And when they shall have finished their testimony, **the beast that ascendeth out of the bottomless pit shall make war against**

> them, and shall overcome them, and kill them. And their dead
> bodies shall lie in the street of the great city, which spiritually is
> called Sodom and Egypt, where also our Lord was crucified." –
> Revelation 11:7–8

All Bible scholars agree that the Lord Jesus Christ was crucified on the
outskirts of Jerusalem. The Bible uses titles like "Pharaoh" and "Egypt" to
foreshadow future events and people. The "Pharaoh" of the Great Tribulation
will be the Assyrian and "Egypt" will be his headquarters in Jerusalem (which
he will no doubt capture via conquest). Ezekiel 32 describes these prophetic
events:

> "And when I shall put thee out, I will cover the heaven, and make
> the stars thereof dark; I will cover the sun with a cloud, and the
> moon shall not give her light. All the bright lights of heaven will I
> make dark over thee, and set darkness upon thy land, saith the Lord
> GOD." – Ezekiel 32:7–8

This "double eclipse" is a consistent signpost of the end times. Joel 2, covered
above, referred to the sun's turning dark and the moon to "blood" before the
Great Tribulation (Joel 2:31). Jesus Christ cited it as sign preceding his
Second Coming (Matthew 24:29).

## EZEKIEL 31 RECORDS THE HISTORY OF THE
## PRE-FLOOD ERA WHILE EZEKIEL 32 CONTAINS
## FUTURE PROPHECY

Ezekiel 31 recorded the history of the fall of the Assyrian and the sinning
angels in the Flood. Ezekiel 32 is a prophecy detailing *the return of the Assyrian*
and the sinning angels during the Great Tribulation. The Bible further
confirms this in the language of Ezekiel 32, which is repeatedly *forward*

*looking*. The chapter contains phrases such as "I shall" and "I will" over and over throughout. This is distinctly different from chapter 31, where God spoke in the *past tense*:

> "…the Assyrian was a cedar in Lebanon with fair branches…"

> "The waters made him great…."

> "Therefore his height was exalted above all the trees of the field, and his boughs were multiplied, and his branches became long because of the multitude of waters, when he shot forth."

> "I have therefore delivered him into the hand of the mighty one of the heathen; he shall surely deal with him: I have driven him out for his wickedness."

> "Thus saith the Lord GOD; In the day when he went down to the grave I caused a mourning: I covered the deep for him, and I restrained the floods thereof, and the great waters were stayed: and I caused Lebanon to mourn for him, and all the trees of the field fainted for him."

Ezekiel 31 details the Lord's *looking back into the past* at the first reign of the Assyrian before the Flood. Ezekiel 32 is looking prophetically to the future end-times reign of the Assyrian after he is released from his captivity in the abyss:

> "Thus saith the Lord GOD; *I will therefore* spread out my net over thee with a company of many people; *and they shall bring* thee up in my net."

> "*Then will I leave thee upon the land, I will* cast thee forth upon the open field, and will cause all the fowls of the heaven to remain upon

thee, *and I will fill* the beasts of the whole earth with thee."

*"And I will* lay thy flesh upon the mountains, and fill the valleys with thy height."

*"I will also water* with thy blood the land wherein thou swimmest, even to the mountains; and the rivers shall be full of thee."

*"And when I shall put thee out,* I will cover the heaven, and make the stars thereof dark; I will cover the sun with a cloud, and the moon shall not give her light."

"All the bright lights of heaven *will I make* dark over thee, and set darkness upon thy land, saith the Lord GOD."

This is not an end-times study, so we will not examine in detail the numerous prophetic revelations contained in the first portion of Ezekiel 32, which will be covered in a future study on the Nephilim in end-times prophecy. For our purposes, we need only understand that the angels who sinned in Genesis 6 will be released in the end times and the Assyrian will once again assume a role of preeminence on the earth. And, once again, they will all be conquered by the hand of the Lord.

## THE NEPHILIM WHO DIED IN THE FLOOD ARE REFERENCED IN EZEKIEL 32

The second half of Ezekiel 32 contains a lamentation for the "multitude" of Pharaoh. The angels who foolishly pledge their allegiance to the Assyrian in the end times will be defeated and sent to Hell in judgment:

"**Son of man, wail for the multitude of Egypt, and cast them down, even her, and the daughters of the famous nations, unto** the nether parts of the earth, with them that go down into the pit. Whom dost thou pass in beauty? go down, and be thou laid with the uncircumcised. They shall fall in the midst of them that are slain by the sword: she is delivered to the sword: draw her and all her multitudes." – Ezekiel 32:18–20

The "multitude" – angelic soldiers of the Assyrian in the end times – will be cast down to Hell once again as the Lord's judgment. They will be delivered to "the nether parts of the earth" with "them that go down to the pit" (i.e., mortal human beings). The Septuagint offers a rendering of the text that provides interesting insights into these apostate angels:

"Son of man, lament over the strength of Egypt, for the nations shall bring down her daughters dead to the depth of the earth, to them that go down to the pit. They shall fall with him in the midst of them *that are* slain with the sword, and all his strength shall perish: **the giants also shall say to thee, Be thou in the depth of the pit: to whom art thou superior?** yea, go down, and lie with the uncircumcised, in the midst of them *that are* slain with the sword." – Ezekiel 32:18–21 LXX

As they enter into the depths of Hell, the angelic multitude will encounter the Nephilim giants! Their dead offspring will be astonished that angels have been conquered and sent to Hell alongside them. They will question the power of the rebel angels whom they mistakenly viewed as gods.

"**And they are laid with the giants that fell of old, who went down to Hades with *their* weapons of war: and they laid their swords under their heads, but their iniquities were upon their bones, because they terrified all men during their life.** And thou shalt lie in the midst of the uncircumcised, with them that have been slain by the sword." – Ezekiel 32:27–28 LXX

Right alongside these once-great nations are the "giants that fell of old." Genesis 6:4 describes the Nephilim giants as "mighty men which were of old." The term "of old" is a biblical reference to the antediluvian era:

> "Knowest thou not this of old, since man was placed upon earth…." – Job 20:4

> "I have considered the days of old, the years of ancient times." – Psalm 77:5

> "Of old hast thou laid the foundation of the earth: and the heavens are the work of thy hands." – Psalm 102:25

Thus, when Ezekiel 32 speaks of "the giants that fell of old" it further confirms that the Nephilim of the pre-Flood world went down to Hell.

In Ezekiel 32:27 the sinning angels are laid aside the souls of their Nephilim offspring who went down to the abyss "with their weapons of war." The giants' weapons went down to Hell with them, giving credence to the notion that a whirlpool in the midst of the floodwaters sucked the Nephilim and all people down into Hell in rapid fashion. Recall that when Korah led a revolt against Moses he and his rebels were swallowed into the pit along with "their houses, and all the men that appertained unto Korah, **and all their goods**."

The once-mighty hybrid creatures were consumed with war and violence. Their war was interrupted by the Flood as they sank to their death with weapons in hand. The Nephilim warriors terrified "all men" during their time on Earth until God conquered them. During the Great Tribulation rebel angels will see these giants as they descend to the lowest parts of Hell.

Continuing in Ezekiel 32:

"There are laid the princes of Assur, who yielded their strength to a wound of the sword: these are laid with the slain, with them that go down to the pit. There are the princes of the north, *even* all the captains of Assur, who go down slain *to Hades*: they lie uncircumcised among the slain with the sword together with their terror and their strength, and they have received their punishment with them that go down to the pit. King Pharao shall see them, and shall be comforted over all their force, saith the Lord God. **For I have caused his fear to be upon the land of the living yet he shall lie in the midst of the uncircumcised with them that are slain with the sword, *even* Pharao, and all his multitude with him, saith the Lord God.**" – Ezekiel 32:29–32 LXX

Ultimately, the Lord will judge all who oppose Him – the Assyrian, the rebel angels, the Nephilim, sinful humanity, and Satan himself – for their iniquity. Satan thought he had found his way to victory when corrupting humanity's genetics led to hell on Earth. The human race itself was almost destroyed and the prophecy appeared to be in peril. But God brought it all to a stunning and decisive end. God may allow sin to continue for a season to give sinners an opportunity to repent. And even though God will permit the Assyrian to return to the earth's surface and torment the world again in the end times, the fallen angel's ultimate punishment has already been determined.

## THE ATLANTIS CONNECTION

Right alongside the heroes of Greek mythology was Plato's legend of Atlantis, a story that is still well-known today. Atlantis was a mythical island populated by gods and humans, full of wealth and advanced technology. As that society grew more evil, it was ultimately destroyed by a flood. First recorded in two dialogues by Plato called *Critia and Timaeus*[2], upon close examination it is apparent that the Atlantis myth was ultimately derived from the accounts of the Garden of Eden, Genesis 6, and the rise and fall of the Assyrian's hybrid kingdom as described in Ezekiel 31.

In Plato's account, the Greek God Poseidon was ruler of the island of Atlantis. *He then fell in love with a human woman and impregnated her*:

> "...Poseidon fell in love with her and had intercourse with her and breaking the ground ... He also begat and brought up five pairs of male children dividing the island of Atlantis into ten portions."

Like the Sons of God in Genesis 6, Poseidon *begat* half-god, half-human children. These offspring were an allusion to the Nephilim. Atlas, the eldest son, was proclaimed king, and Atlantis and the Atlantic Ocean were named after him. He and his brothers were military warriors who ruled Atlantis. In the biblical account the Nephilim were militaristic tyrants who ruled the world (Isaiah 14, Ezekiel 32).

The gods and demigods of Atlantis possessed abundant natural resources and extreme wealth and were master builders:

> "For because of the greatness of their empire, many things were brought to them from foreign countries, and the island itself provided much of what was required by them for the uses of life. In the first place, they dug out of the earth whatever was to be found there, mineral as well as metal, and that which is now only a name, and was then something more than a name – orichalcum was dug out of the earth – in many parts of the island, and, with the exception of gold, was esteemed the most precious of metals among the men of those days."

In the biblical account, Eden was rich in precious metals as well:

"And a river went out of Eden to water the garden; and from thence it was parted, and became into four heads. The name of the first is Pison: that is it which compasseth the whole land of Havilah, where there is gold; And the gold of that land is good: there is bdellium and the onyx stone." – Genesis 2:10–12

## THERE WERE NUMEROUS SPECIES OF ANIMALS

"… there was provision for animals of every kind, both for those which live in lakes and marshes and rivers, and also for those which live in mountains and on plains, and therefore for the animal which is the largest and most voracious of them." - Plato.

In Genesis, God brought every species of animal to the Garden for Adam to name them (Genesis 2:19–20).

## POSEIDON SUPERNATURALLY FORMED THE CENTER ISLAND OF ATLANTIS

"He himself, as he was a god, found no difficulty in making special arrangements for the centre island, bringing two streams of water under the earth, which he caused to ascend as springs, one of warm water and the other of cold, and making every variety of food to spring up abundantly in the earth." –Plato.

"And the LORD God planted a garden eastward in Eden; and there he put the man whom he had formed. And out of the ground made the LORD God to grow every tree that is pleasant to the sight, and good for food; the tree of life also in the midst of the garden, and the tree of knowledge of good and evil. And a river went out of Eden to water the garden; and from thence it was parted, and became into four heads." – Genesis 2:8–10

In Scripture God personally planted the Garden of Eden and provided water for the plants and trees from the mist that emanated from underground springs (Genesis 2:5).

## SIMILAR ARCHITECTURE TO THE NEPHILIM

"He to secure his love enclosed the mountain with rings or zones varying in size, two of land and three of sea, which his divine power readily enabled him to excavate and fashion, and, as there was no shipping in those days no man could get into the place."

According to Plato's tale, Atlantis was made up of a series of five concentric circles of ring-shaped islands and water. This layout is strikingly similar to an ancient megalith discovered in Israel in 1967. Known as "Gilgal Repahim" or "Wheels of the Giants" – it a monument comprised of a series of 5 concentric circles atop a large hill. The circles are made from thousands of thousands of basalt stones weighing over 40,000 tons. In the center of the circles is a 15-foot high burial chamber. In addition to its massive size, the concentric formation cannot be properly viewed from the ground. It is only from aerial view that one can appreciate the structure. It was not until military jets during the Six Day War captured images that Israeli archeologists were even aware of its existence. The megalith is believed to be anywhere from 4,000-5,500 years old - dating it back to the same era or even earlier than Stonehenge (which is commonly believed to be the oldest megalithic strucute in the world).

Below is an image of Gilgal Rephaim next to a 19th century rendering of Atlantis based on Plato's description:

רפאא.צ/wikicommons

The similarities are striking. And what is even more compelling is that Gilgal Rephaim is located in the Golan Heights, which in ancient times was Bashan

- the kingdom of legendary Nephilim king Og (Deuteronomy 3:1). On the June and December solstices, the light from the sunrise aligns with the circular openings in the rock walls, only adding to its mysery. Some archelogists even suggest the entire structure was built in accordance with an astral alignment.

## THE ATLANTEAN NEPHILIM BENEFITTED FROM THEIR STRATEGIC LOCATION AMONG ABUNDANT WATERS AND SPRINGS

> "In the next place they used fountains both of cold and hot springs; these were very abundant, and both kinds wonderfully adapted to use by reason of the sweetness and excellence of their waters."– Plato.

The Atlanteans used these springs to construct all sorts of buildings and structures. Some of the excess waters were used to water the grove of Poseidon while a portion was channeled through aqueducts. Plato went out of his way to emphasize the advantages of being near the excellent waters of Atlantis.

The Assyrian received similar advantages from his proximity to the rivers of Eden:

> **"The waters made him great, the deep set him up on high with her rivers running round about his plants,** and sent her little rivers unto all the trees of the field. Therefore his height was exalted above all the trees of the field, and his boughs were multiplied, and his branches became long **because of the multitude of waters**, when he shot forth… Thus was he fair in his greatness, in the length of his branches: **for his root was by great waters**." – Ezekiel 31:4–5; 7.

# THE INTIMATE RELATIONS OF
# GODS AND HUMANS CORRUPTED SOCIETY

Repeated comingling of gods and humans caused the entire race of Atlanteans to become morally corrupted:

> "By such reflections and by the continuance in of a divine nature all that which we have described and increased in them but when this divine portion to fade away in them and became diluted too often with too much of the mortal admixture and the nature got the upper hand then they being unable to their fortune became unseemly and to him who had eye to see they began to appear base and had lost fairest of their precious gifts but to those who had no to see the true happiness they still appeared glorious blessed at the very time when they were filled with unrighteous avarice and power." - Plato.

Fornicating with human women corrupted the gods of the Atlantis myth, just as the Sons of God of Genesis 6 left who their first estate suffered corruption. And the more Nephilim who were born, the greater the moral and physical degradation.

The whole purpose of the Genesis 6 incursion was to corrupt the human race. Once the angels of Genesis 6 fornicated with human women both races suffered spiritual and physical degradation. The number of similarities between Plato's very short account and the biblical account of the pre-Flood world make it clear that the account of Atlantis was based on the scriptural details of the antediluvian world.

Nineteenth-century researchers of the myth of Atlantis determined that it was based on the biblical account:

"The Apaturia it will be remembered was the feast of the registration of youth at which Plato tells us he was told the legend of the subsidence of Atlantis which as I contend was only a form of the tradition of the universal Deluge." – *The Secret of Plato's Atlantis*, Lord Arundell of Wardour, London: Burns & Oates, 1885, p. 43.

"Atlantis was probably the original nursery and home of the human race. Here was a suitable site for the 'Garden of Eden'; here too were the four great rivers which watered the garden, one of which was called the Euphrates." – *The Church Eclectic*, Vol XL, The Rev. Arthur Lowndes, p. 187.

1. For further study on this topic please see the comprehensive study by Paradox Brown and Guy Malone: "The Case Against The Book of Enoch." http://paradoxbrown.com/the-case-against-book-first-enoch/

2. All quotes of Plato are as quoted in *Atlantis: The Antediluvian World*, 7th Edition, Ignatius Donnely, 1882, p. 5-21.

CHAPTER 12

# ARE "EXTRA-BIBLICAL" TEXTS REALLY BIBLICAL?

The Bible is the primary and authoritative source for the history of the Nephilim and their angelic forefathers. It contains answers and details found in no other book. It would be remiss not to comment on some of the inherent contradictions, errors, and even false doctrines found in the "extra–biblical texts" often cited on this topic, such as the Book of Enoch and the Book of Jasher. Although we should be grateful to the many writers who have helped reignite research into Genesis 6 and the giants using these writings, these books are not beyond criticism and their teachings at times directly contradict Scripture.

## THE MANY FLAWS IN THE BOOK OF ENOCH

It is important to note that no modern scholar or theologian has ever asserted that the text presently called "The Book of Enoch" was actually written by the prophet Enoch. It is classified as pseudepigrapha – books that falsely use the name of a biblical figure to draw more attention and lend them an air of credibility they would not otherwise have. The earliest extant copy of the Book of Enoch is composed of six fragments found with the Dead Sea Scrolls, placing its origin at about 350–200 BC. A version of the Book of Enoch was in circulation in the first century AD as several church fathers commended it (Tertullian, Augustine) while a number disapproved of it (Athanasius, Origen, Jerome).

There is no doubt that the Book of Enoch was accepted as at least informative (if not inspired) by some church members going back to the first century. However it was never considered a part of the Biblical canon by Jews or Christians in the first century AD. The Book of Enoch was not even included in the collection of Apocryphal books that were written in the two centuries before Christ on Earth. Endorsement or rejection by church fathers, however, is not the test of a text's validity. The pivotal criterion is whether a book is in line with Holy Scripture. Below is just a short list of the passages in the Book of Enoch (or Pseudo–Enoch, as it should be properly called) that directly contradict the Bible.

## IT FALSELY CLAIMS TO BE WRITTEN BY ENOCH

"**The words of the blessing of Enoch**, wherewith he blessed the elect and righteous, who will be living in the day of tribulation, when all the wicked and godless are to be removed." – Pseudo–Enoch 1:1

"**The second vision which he saw**, the vision of wisdom – which Enoch the son of Jared, the son [2] of Mahalalel, the son of Cainan, the son of Enos, the son of Seth, the son of Adam, saw. And this is the beginning of the words of wisdom **which I lifted up my voice to speak and say** to those which dwell on earth…" – Pseudo–Enoch 37:1

From its very first verse, the author (or authors - as most historians conclude the "Book of Enoch" is actually a series of 5 books written over several centuries) of the Book of Enoch do not indicate that they are penning their own summary of events that they had heard or believed happened to Enoch. Instead they write the text as if it were from the pen of Enoch himself. As noted above, archeologists and biblical scholars date the earliest fragments of the book to 350 BC, thousands of years after Enoch was raptured to Heaven.

The notion that Enoch wrote a book is a troubling one after even a basic review of the Old Testament. There is not a single mention of a book of Enoch throughout the entire history recorded in the Old Testament. This becomes even more glaring when we consider that Enoch's "book" would have been the first biblical text recorded in history.

## THE BIBLE NEVER REFERS TO A "BOOK OF ENOCH"

When the Bible refers to its individual books, it never mentions Enoch. The early books of the Bible contain several references to the Scriptures' being written, read, or preserved. The first person instructed to write Scripture was Moses:

"And the Lord said unto Moses, Write this for a memorial in a book, and rehearse it in the ears of Joshua: for I will utterly put out the remembrance of Amalek from under heaven." – Exodus 17:14

In Exodus 24 Moses held a public reading of all written Scripture in his possession (at that point in history) to the nation of Israel and made no mention of the Book of Enoch:

"**And Moses came and told the people all the words of the LORD, and all the judgments**: and all the people answered with one voice, and said, All the words which the LORD hath said will we do. **And Moses wrote all the words of the LORD**, and rose up early in the morning, and builded an altar under the hill, and twelve pillars, according to the twelve tribes of Israel. And he sent young men of the children of Israel, which offered burnt offerings, and sacrificed peace offerings of oxen unto the LORD. And Moses took half of the blood, and put it in basons; and half of the blood he sprinkled on the altar. **And he took the book of the covenant, and** read in the audience of the people: and they said, All that the LORD hath said will we do, and be obedient." – Exodus 24:3–7

The "book of the covenant" Moses read **were his own writings as contained in the first five books of the Bible**. This was "the Bible" for many centuries of ancient Hebrew history. God required all ancient Jewish kings to draft their own personal copy of the Mosaic writings and read it every day:

> "And it shall be, when he sitteth upon the throne of his kingdom, **that he shall write him a copy of this law in a book** out of that which is before the priests the Levites: And it shall be with him, and he shall read therein all the days of his life: that he may learn to fear the LORD his God, to keep all the words of this law and these statutes, to do them: That his heart be not lifted up above his brethren, and that he turn not aside from the commandment, to the right hand, or to the left: to the end that he may prolong his days in his kingdom, he, and his children, in the midst of Israel." – Deuteronomy 17:18–20

There is no reference to the Book of Enoch in any of the above passages. The books of Moses, or the book of the law, was the only Scripture in ancient Israel. The Ark of the Covenant contained only the books of Moses, with no mention of the Book of Enoch (Deuteronomy 31:26). When Joshua, Moses' protégé, read the Bible to all of Israel during the wars for the Promised Land, he read only from the writings of Moses:

> "Then Joshua built an altar unto the LORD God of Israel in mount Ebal, As Moses the servant of the LORD commanded the children of Israel, as it is written in the book of the law of Moses, an altar of whole stones, over which no man hath lift up any iron: and they offered thereon burnt offerings unto the LORD, and sacrificed peace offerings. **And he wrote there upon the stones a copy of**

the law of Moses, which he wrote in the presence of the children of Israel.

And all Israel, and their elders, and officers, and their judges, stood on this side the ark and on that side before the priests the Levites, which bare the ark of the covenant of the LORD, as well the stranger, as he that was born among them; half of them over against mount Gerizim, and half of them over against mount Ebal; as Moses the servant of the LORD had commanded before, that they should bless the people of Israel. **And afterward he read all the words of the law, the blessings and cursings, according to all that is written in the book of the law. There was not a word of all that Moses commanded, which Joshua read not before all the congregation of Israel**, with the women, and the little ones, and the strangers that were conversant among them." – Joshua 8:30–35

Joshua used this very special occasion to honor the Word of God. First, he wrote down the law of Moses in the sight of all 12 tribes of Israel. He then read all the books of Moses to the Israelites. This was a time of spiritual dedication and worship. Joshua's clear intent was to *read all of God's Word to his people.* The book of Enoch was not included. In the Old Testament, the book is never referred to as either existing or recited, much less a prized, divinely-inspired possession like the writings of Moses or other prophets.

After His resurrection, the Lord personally sat down with the disciples to teach them about Himself and the many prophecies of His Coming in the Old Testament. And this passage specifically identifies the first books of the Bible:

"Then he said unto them, O fools, and slow of heart to believe all that the prophets have spoken: Ought not Christ to have suffered these things, and to enter into his glory? **And beginning at Moses** and all the prophets, he expounded unto them in all the scriptures the things concerning himself." – Luke 24:25–27

The first books of the Old Testament were the books of Moses. Had the Book of Enoch been a treasured epistle, carried on Noah's ark and containing such amazing biblical history, why would Jesus not teach from it? The most likely reason is that the book of Enoch circulating in Jesus' day was not actually a part of Scripture. Based solely on the history of the writings of the Bible *as recorded in Scripture*, there were no books before the writings of Moses.

## THE ALLEGED QUOTE FROM THE BOOK OF ENOCH FOUND IN JUDE

The most cited and strongest evidence supporting the validity of the Book of Enoch is that the book of Jude quotes from it:

> **"And Enoch also, the seventh from Adam, prophesied of these, saying**, Behold, the Lord cometh with ten thousands of his saints, To execute judgment upon all, and to convince all that are ungodly among them of all their ungodly deeds which they have ungodly committed, and of all their hard speeches which ungodly sinners have spoken against him." – Jude 1:14–15

> "And behold! He cometh with ten thousands of His holy ones to execute judgment upon all, and to destroy all the ungodly: and to convict all flesh of all the works of their ungodliness which they have ungodly committed, and of all the hard things which ungodly sinners have spoken against Him." – Book of Enoch 1:9

Undoubtedly this is the best argument for the Book of Enoch's validity. After all, if Jude, under divine inspiration, used the book to quote Enoch, then it must have some credibility. But did Jude reference the Book of Enoch? In the verse above, Jude refers to *the prophecy* of Enoch, but not to any book written by him. While this may seem like a minor distinction, the Bible uses the phrase "it is written" or "that the Scripture might be fulfilled" – when quoting a verse from another part of Scripture, over 100 times.

The Bible was written by divine inspiration. Biblical authors did not have to comb through older parts of the Bible to write their own books. The Apostle Paul wrote "All scripture is given by inspiration of God" (2 Timothy 3:16) and the Apostle Peter wrote "For the prophecy came not in old time by the will of man: but holy men of God spake as they were moved by the Holy Ghost" (2 Peter 1:21). Recall that in Genesis, Moses quoted God, Adam, Eve, and the serpent in the Garden of Eden. He quoted the final conversation Cain had with Abel before killing him. He recorded the words of the Lord when sentencing Cain. How did Moses have this knowledge? By inspiration of the Holy Spirit. God spoke to Moses to inspire his writings. Thus, when Jude wrote his epistle, he did not necessarily have to read the quote from Enoch in a text to be inspired to write it; the Holy Ghost could have simply given him Enoch's words.

## ENOCH'S PROPHECY COULD HAVE BEEN IN A NON-CANONICAL BOOK

If we assume that the Apostle Jude did indeed obtain the words of Enoch from a book, we must then ask where he got such a book. The most likely answer is that there was a non-canonical text in circulation in Jude's day that contained the prophecy of Enoch amidst other non-biblical writings. In the first century, many writings based on the Bible were in circulation – some were commentaries while others were heretical, "fan fiction"-type accounts about biblical characters. *The Ascension of Isaiah, Jannes and Jambres, The Apocalypse of Paul and The Apocalypse of Elijah* are just a few examples of non-canonical books falsely puporting to be the testimony of prophets or apostles.[1]

If Jude did consult one of these texts, it would not be the only time in Scripture that a biblical writer under inspiration of the Holy Spirit cited a secular source in a passage of the Bible.

When the Apostle Paul, moved by the Holy Spirit, preached the Gospel in the city of Athens, he cited a pagan poet: "For in him we live, and move, and have our being; as certain also of your own poets have said, For we are also his offspring" (Acts 17:28). This was a quote of the Greek poet Aratus. In 1 Corinthians 15:33, Paul wrote: "Be not deceived: evil communications corrupt good manners," a quote from *Thais*, a work by the Greek poet Menander. Titus 1:12 states: "One of themselves, even a prophet of their own, said, the Cretians are always liars, evil beasts, slow bellies. This witness is true," quoting the poem *Paradox* by Epimenides, a Cretian poet. In all these instances, the Holy Spirit used truths from uninspired, non-biblical texts to compose Scripture. When Paul quoted Greek poets, he was not endorsing these writings as divinely inspired in their entirety; rather, he was citing an excerpt containing a solitary truth from fables and fiction to make a biblical point.

Which takes us back to the quotation in Jude. If Jude did indeed cite Enoch's prophecy from a text in his possession, that book, although not a part of the canon of Scripture, nevertheless recorded an accurate account of Enoch's words. This is far different from using that quote to assert that an entire book was written by the prophet Enoch (which, as we have seen, has no secular or biblical support).

Jude's reference to an account about the body of Moses gives further evidence that Jude may have had access to writings that are no longer extant:

> "Yet Michael the archangel, when contending with the devil he disputed about the body of Moses, durst not bring against him a railing accusation, but said, the Lord rebuke thee." – Jude 1:9

This very fascinating account is not recorded in the Old Testament, the Book of Enoch, or any other extra-biblical text in existence today. So where did Jude get this information? The most logical conclusion is that if it was something he read he got it from an ancient text that was not itself Scripture but contained certain Jewish historical accounts that were accurate and thus worthy of inclusion in the Bible. A 17th-century clergyman concurred:

> "It is therefore the opinion of some learned men, that if there were in Jude's time any writing which went under Enoch's name, it was written by some Jews, who mixed some things good and true, which peradventure they received by tradition concerning the prophecies of Enoch, with other things false and fabulous; which book of theirs might be more and more in the progress of time corrupted, and was deservedly rejected as apocryphal. Possibly out of this book Jude might take this passage." – *An Exposition Upon the Epistle of Jude: Delivered in Christ-Church, London*, Williams Jenkyn, originally published in 1652–1658, Compiled and republished by Samuel Holdsworth, 1839, p. 301.

There is no manuscript evidence or biblical account to support the notion that Enoch wrote a book. And if Jude did quote the "Book of Enoch" in circulation in his day, he very selectively chose a prophecy that was likely well known and an instance of truth in a non-canonical book. Therefore, the fact that Pseudo-Enoch claims to be written by the prophet Enoch makes it a highly dubious source at best, even more importantly, the Book of Enoch has doctrinal issues as well.

# THE BOOK OF ENOCH'S MANY CONTRADICTIONS WITH THE BIBLE

*Its Timeline Contradicts Scripture*

In the Book of Enoch, Enoch is still on Earth when Noah was born:

> "And now, my son, go and make known to thy son Lamech that this³ son, which has been born, is in truth his son, and that (this) is no lie.' And when Methuselah had heard the words of his father Enoch – for he had shown to him everything in secret – he returned and showed (them) to him and called the name of that son Noah; for he will comfort the earth after all the destruction." – Pseudo-Enoch 107:2–3

Following the biblical timeline in Genesis 5, Noah was born 1,056 years from Adam and Eve. This was *69 years after Enoch was translated* and taken to Heaven. The Bible confirms that after Enoch was taken to Heaven he "was not found, for God translated him" (Hebrews 11:5). There is no way in which Enoch would have been on Earth speaking to Lamech at the time of Noah's birth. Additionally, note that the verse above says that Noah received his name because he would "comfort the earth after all the destruction." That is *not* why Noah received his name according to the Bible, which says: "And he called his name Noah, saying, This same shall comfort us concerning our work and toil of our hands, because of the ground which the LORD hath cursed" (Genesis 5:29). Lamech, knowing that a judgment on the earth was coming (as prophesied by his grandfather Enoch and by the naming of his father, Methusaleh), prophesied that Noah would bring comfort *to them* regarding the curse upon humanity to till the soil. Noah would live to see the new world and the new start for humanity.

1 Enoch 60 begins: "In the year 500, in the seventh month, on the fourteenth day of the month in the life of Enoch." Enoch lived on Earth for only 365 years. He was born 622 years after the creation of humanity. So, by any measure, "the year 500" as a time in Enoch's life would be an incorrect statement. He was not alive in the year 500 and did not live to be 500 years old. The erroneous and illogical chronological errors refute any claim of divine inspiration for this text.

### It Changes the Role Of Enoch

The Book of Enoch turns Enoch, a prophet to humanity according to the Bible, into an advocate for the fallen angels of Genesis 6:

> "And Enoch went and said: 'Azazel, thou shalt have no peace: a severe sentence has gone forth [2] against thee to put thee in bonds: And thou shalt not have toleration nor request granted to thee, because of the unrighteousness which thou hast taught, and because of all the works of godlessness [3] and unrighteousness and sin which thou hast shown to men.' Then I went and spoke to them all [4] together, and they were all afraid, and fear and trembling seized them. **And they besought me to draw up a petition for them that they might find forgiveness, and to read their petition in the presence [5] of the Lord of heaven.** For from thenceforward they could not speak (with Him) nor lift up their [6] eyes to heaven for shame of their sins for which they had been condemned. Then I wrote out their petition, and the prayer in regard to their spirits and their deeds individually and in regard to their [7] requests that they should have forgiveness and length." – Pseudo-Enoch 13:1–7

Nowhere in Scripture does any human being ever intercede on behalf of a fallen angel. In Genesis 6, God condemned the sinning sons of God to the abyss. This was centuries after Enoch was translated and "found not" and thus would not have been on Earth for the angels to beseech. Pseudo-Enoch has the First Prophet not only found on Earth by sinful angels but told to draft a petition of their plea for forgiveness to God. Human beings, who are lower than angels, do not have to write letters to God but can simply open our mouths and speak in prayer. Why would an angel ever need a letter written by a human? This is a wildly unbiblical passage.

Even more disturbing is the claim in chapter 15 that God supposedly suggests to Enoch that angels are to intercede for humanity:

> "And He answered and said to me, and I heard His voice: 'Fear not, Enoch, thou righteous [2] man and scribe of righteousness: approach hither and hear my voice. And go, say to the Watchers of heaven, who have sent thee to intercede for them: "You should intercede" for men, and not men [3] for you.'" – Pseudo-Enoch 15:1–2

The Bible informs us that "there is one God, and one mediator between God and men, the man Christ Jesus" (1 Timothy 2:5). People are supposed to bring their prayers and petitions to Jesus, not to any angel. Applying a proper interpretation of Scripture, there is just no way that the Lord would make such a suggestion. This type of false doctrine is not only confusing to a student of the Bible but also serves to generate sympathy for fallen angels, playing on the natural fascination humanity has with them – something the Bible warns against (Colossians 2:18).

### The Book of Enoch Distorts the Account of the Garden of Eden

Scripture identifies Satan as the serpent who tempted and deceived Eve in the Garden of Eden:

> "And there was war in heaven: Michael and his angels fought against the dragon; and the dragon fought and his angels, And

prevailed not; neither was their place found any more in heaven. **And the great dragon was cast out, that old serpent, called the Devil, and Satan**, which deceiveth the whole world: he was cast out into the earth, and his angels were cast out with him." – Revelation 12:7–9

In the Book of Enoch an angel named "Gadreel" was responsible for deceiving Eve:

> "And the third was named Gadreel: he it is who showed the children of men all the blows of death, **and he led astray Eve**."– 1 Enoch 69:6

It is important to note that in the Book of Enoch, the angel Gadreel is distinct from Satan, thus this extra-biblical text contradicts the Bible, which very clearly identifies Satan as the deceiver of Eve: "But I fear, lest by any means, **as the serpent beguiled Eve through his subtilty**, so your minds should be corrupted from the simplicity that is in Christ" (2 Corinthians 11:3). The Devil is the serpent, not Gadreel (a being never mentioned in the Bible). This is a major contradiction.

### The Book of Enoch Names "Azazel" as the Source of All Sin

In addition to the above false doctrine, the Book of Enoch attributes all human sin to Azazel, one of the angels who allegedly led the invasion that gave birth to the Nephilim:

> "And the whole earth has been corrupted [9] through the works that were taught by Azazel: to him ascribe all sin." – Pseudo-Enoch 10:8–9

Scripture tells us that Adam's sin is what corrupted the image of God within all people and thus rendered all his descendants with a sinful nature: "For as by one man's disobedience many were made sinners, so by the obedience of one shall many be made righteous" (Romans 5:19). Adam and Eve were already fallen sinners centuries before the invasion of the sinning sons of God in Genesis 6. Cain had already killed Abel by then. Lamech was already committing polygamy. Thus, there is no possible scenario in which the Genesis 6 angels could have caused the first sin of humanity.

## Pseudo-Enoch Teaches Prayer to Angels

Rather than detailing the Nephilim, the Book of Enoch spends much more time documenting the alleged activities of angels. This is a spiritual danger as it can deceive the reader into believing the Bible condones communication with angels. In the following passage, righteous believing people pray to angels for help before the flood:

> "And then Michael, Uriel, Raphael, and Gabriel looked down from heaven and saw much blood being shed upon the earth, and all lawlessness being wrought upon the earth. And they said one to another: 'The earth made without inhabitant cries the voice of their crying up to the gates of heaven. And now to you, the holy ones of heaven, the souls of men make their suit, saying, "Bring our cause before the Most High."'" – Pseudo-Enoch 9:1-3.

This passage is heretical for two reasons. First, the Bible describes the antediluvian world as a wicked place devoid of the worship of God, save for Noah and his family (Genesis 6:5). Second, in this passage from Enoch, men pray to angels to intercede on their behalf to the Lord. This is brazen sin and in direct contradiction to Scripture. The Bible specifically warns:

> "Let no man beguile you of your reward in a voluntary humility

**and worshipping of angels**, intruding into those things which he hath not seen, vainly puffed up by his fleshly mind…" – Colossians 2:18

Note the passage from Pseudo-Enoch attempts to paint the praying men as pious and God-honoring, thus deceitfully sanctioning prayer to angels in the exact manner Colossians warns Christians to avoid. This is the one of the greatest dangers of Pseudo-Enoch as it subtly fuels the human fascination with the angelic realm while moving our eyes away from Jesus Christ, who is the true Intercessor and Advocate for humanity:

"For there is **one** God, and **one mediator** between God and men, the man Christ Jesus…" – 1 Timothy 2:5

No prayers should ever be made to angels or humans. Rather, they should be directed to God alone, through Jesus Christ alone. This blatant doctrinal error disqualifies Pseudo-Enoch from consideration as a "supplement" to the Holy Bible.

### Elevating the Tree of the Knowledge of Good and Evil

In Pseudo-Enoch, Enoch's travels take him to the Garden of Eden where he marvels not at the Tree of Life, which gives immortality, but instead the Tree of the Knowledge of Good and Evil – the same tree that ushered sin into the world and that the Lord warned Adam not to eat of or lest he "surely die":

"And I came to the Garden of Righteousness, and from afar off trees more numerous than these trees and great—two trees there, very great, beautiful, and glorious, and magnificent, and the tree of knowledge, whose holy fruit they eat and know great wisdom. 4. That tree is in height like the fir, and its leaves are like (those of) the Carob tree: and its fruit is like the clusters of the vine, very beautiful: and the fragrance of the tree penetrates afar.

> "5. Then I said: 'Ho beautiful is the tree, and how attractive is its look!' 6. Then Raphael the holy angel, who was with me, answered me and said: 'This is the tree of wisdom, of which thy father old (in years) and thy aged mother, who were before thee, have eaten, and they learnt wisdom and their eyes were opened, and they knew that they were naked and they were driven out of the garden.'" – Pseudo-Enoch 32:3-6

In stunning fashion, Enoch praises the forbidden tree that brought death to humanity. And Raphael's commentary actually reinforces Satan's original lie to Adam and Eve: namely, that the Tree of the Knowledge of Good and Evil provided "wisdom" that God was presumably trying to withhold from them. This is an indictment of the Lord and blasphemy. Adam and Eve gained no special "wisdom" after eating the fruit. They instead became acutely aware of their guilt, shame, and sin before God.

In Genesis 3, the Bible states that after banishing Adam and Eve from the Garden, God placed a cherubim and a flaming sword to guard the entry so no human could access the Garden again (Genesis 3:24). The Book of Enoch gives no explanation for how Enoch was permitted to enter and view it.

### In Pseudo-Enoch Angels – Not God – Warn Noah of the Flood Judgment

> "Then said the Most High, the Holy and Great One spake, and sent Uriel to the son of Lamech, [2] and said to him: 'Go to Noah and tell him in my name "Hide thyself!" and reveal to him the end that is approaching: that the whole earth will be destroyed, and a deluge is about to come [3] upon the whole earth, and will destroy all that is on it. And now instruct him that he may escape [4] and his seed may be preserved for all the generations of the world." – Pseudo-Enoch 10:1–4

In the Bible, the Lord speaks to Noah personally to warn him of the Flood:

> "**And God said unto Noah,** The end of all flesh is come before me; for the earth is filled with violence through them; and, behold, I will destroy them with the earth… **But with thee will I establish my covenant**; and thou shalt come into the ark, thou, and thy sons, and thy wife, and thy sons' wives with thee." – Genesis 6:13; 18

Rather than telling Noah "hide thyself," God reassured him that He would make a covenant with Noah and his family to protect them from the judgment to come. Scripture makes no mention of an angel named Uriel, nor was any angel involved in delivering a message to Noah. The Lord spoke to Noah directly. Furthermore, Noah did not live in hiding but rather preached to his neighbors and built the ark out in public as part of his prophetic warning to society (Hebrews 11:7; 2 Peter 2:5). Thus, Pseudo-Enoch has blatant inaccuracies that falsely attribute words and actions to God that never occurred.

## Angels Built the Ark in the Book of Enoch

One of the most brazen contradictions and errors in the Book of Enoch is its declaration that angels – not Noah – built the ark:

> "And in those days the word of God came unto me, and He said unto me: 'Noah, thy lot has come ² Up before Me, a lot without blame, a lot of love and uprightness. **And now the angels are making a wooden (building), and when they have completed that task I will place My hand upon it and preserve it, and there shall come forth from it the seed of life,** and a change shall set in so that the ³ earth will not remain without inhabitant. And I will make fast thy seed before me for ever and ever, and I will spread abroad those who dwell with thee: it shall not be unfruitful on the

face of the earth, but it shall be blessed and multiply on the earth in the name of the Lord.'" – Pseudo-Enoch 67:1–3

The "extra-biblical" text states that angels built the ark while Noah simply waited on standby for its completion and the Lord's stamp of approval. Scripture soundly refutes this false claim. Noah built the ark under divine instruction from God:

> **"And God said unto Noah,** The end of all flesh is come before me; for the earth is filled with violence through them; and, behold, I will destroy them with the earth. **Make thee an ark of gopher wood**; rooms shalt thou make in the ark, and shalt pitch it within and without with pitch. And this is the fashion which thou shalt make it of: The length of the ark shall be three hundred cubits, the breadth of it fifty cubits, and the height of it thirty cubits. A window shalt thou make to the ark, and in a cubit shalt thou finish it above; and the door of the ark shalt thou set in the side thereof; with lower, second, and third stories shalt thou make it... **Thus did Noah; according to all that God commanded him, so did he."** – Genesis 6:13–16; 22

The Lord spoke to Noah directly and commanded him to make the ark. The New Testament confirms that in faithful obedience Noah built the ark himself. That the Book of Enoch contains such a glaring contradiction is extremely alarming at best and absolute heresy at worst. We can reject the Book of Enoch as a divinely-inspired or "biblically harmonious" text on this basis alone.

*Pseudo-Enoch Calls the Act of Writing a Sin*

> "And the fourth was named Penemue: he taught the children of men the bitter and the sweet, and he taught them all the secrets of

their wisdom. And he instructed mankind in writing with ink and paper, and thereby many sinned from eternity to eternity and until this day. **For men were not created for such a purpose, to give confirmation to their good faith with pen and ink**. For men were created exactly like the angels, to the intent that they should continue pure and righteous, and death, which destroys everything, could not have taken hold of them, but through this their knowledge they are perishing, and through this power it is consuming me." – 1 Enoch 69:8–12

In the Bible God told Moses to write His words (Exodus 17:14). The Lord Himself wrote the original tablets containing the Ten Commandments (Exodus 31:18). All throughout Scripture prophets were instructed to write down God's Word. Yet the Book of Enoch says humans were never intended to write. Jesus Christ said, "Then said I, Lo, I come (in the volume of the book it is written of me,) to do thy will, O God" (Hebrews 10:7), and that the Scriptures testified of Him (John 5:39). The book of Revelation promises a blessing to all who read it (Revelation 1:3). Clearly, the written Word of God is not only good but our way to salvation.

### The Book of Enoch Mentions Rain Before the Flood

"Behold the summer and the winter, how the whole earth is filled with water, and clouds and dew and rain lie upon it." - Pseudo Enoch 2:3.

This is one of several instances in which the Book of Enoch references rain falling before the flood - a direct contradiction to Scripture which says no rain fell and the plants were watered by a mist (Genesis 2:5).

*The Book of Enoch Teaches Pagan Doctrines*

The Book of Enoch, supposedly quoting God, teaches occult doctrines that involve making "offerings" to the sun, moon and stars:

> "10 And now, know ye that from the angels **He will inquire as to your deeds in heaven, from the sun and from the moon and from the stars in reference to your sins** because upon the earth ye execute judgement on the righteous. 11. And He will summon to testify against you every cloud and mist and dew and rain; for they shall all be withheld because of you from descending upon you, and they shall be mindful of your sins. 12. **And now give presents to the rain that it be not withheld from descending upon you, nor yet the dew, when it has received gold and silver from you that it may descend.** 13. When the hoar-frost and snow with their chilliness, and all the snow-storms with all their plagues fall upon you, in those days ye shall not be able to stand before them" - Pseudo-Enoch 100:10-13

Not only does God purportedly seek counsel from the sun, moon and stars to know the sins of humanity, Enoch is commanded to "give presents" to the rain in the form of gold and silver offerings in order for rainfall to return to the land (this again contradicting Genesis 2:5 which states it never rained before the flood). This is flagrant heresy and strictly forbidden in Scripture:

> "Lest ye corrupt yourselves, and make you a graven image, the similitude of any figure, the likeness of male or female... And lest thou lift up thine eyes unto heaven, and when thou seest the sun, and the moon, and the stars, even all the host of heaven, shouldest be driven to worship them, and serve them, which the LORD thy God hath divided unto all nations under the whole heaven." - Deuteronomy 4:16-19

These are just some of the many erroneous doctrines and flagrant contradictions in the Book of Enoch. These heretical teachings and horrendous inaccuracies disqualify the version of Pseudo-Enoch in existence today from being considered divinely inspired, "complementary to," or in line with Scripture.

# CONTRADICTIONS AND HERESIES IN THE BOOK OF JASHER

The Book of Jasher is probably the second-most popular extra-biblical text commonly cited to support and explain the account of the Nephilim. It does not have the same manuscript support as the Book of Enoch. The earliest manuscripts date to 1552 AD. Like Pseudo-Enoch, however, the Book of Jasher is riddled with mistakes, false doctrines, and heresies that prove it is not a supplement to God's Holy Word.

*Incorrect Timeline*

Like the Book of Enoch, the Book of Jasher's historical timeline is inaccurate when compared to the Bible:

> "Arise now, take thy wife and all belonging to thee and go to the land of Canaan and remain there, and I will there be unto thee for a God, and I will bless thee. And Abram rose and took his wife and all belonging to him, and he went to the land of Canaan as the Lord had told him; **and Abram was fifty years old when he went from Haran**." – Jasher 13:5

The Book of Jasher states that Abram left Haran at age 50. The Bible says he did so at age 75: "So Abram departed, as the LORD had spoken unto him; and Lot went with him: **and Abram was seventy and five years old when he departed out of Haran**" (Genesis 12:4).

*Mistaking God for a Ministering Angel*

In Jasher, God sends three ministering angels to visit Abraham's home and announce that he and Sarah would have a child:

> "And the Lord appeared to him in the plain of Mamre, **and sent three of his ministering angels to visit him, and he was sitting at the door of the tent,** and he lifted his eyes and saw, and lo three men were coming from a distance, and he rose up and ran to meet them, and he bowed down to them and brought them into his house… And when they had done eating one of them said to him, I will return to thee according to the time of life, and Sarah thy wife shall have a son." – Jasher 18:4; 9

In the biblical account, the Lord *personally visits Abraham in his home* accompanied by two angels (the same two angels who would later rescue Lot from Sodom) and tells Abraham that he would have a son:

> "And he [God] said, I will certainly return unto thee according to the time of life; and, lo, Sarah thy wife shall have a son. And Sarah heard it in the tent door, which was behind him. Now Abraham and Sarah were old and well stricken in age; and it ceased to be with Sarah after the manner of women. Therefore Sarah laughed within herself, saying, After I am waxed old shall I have pleasure, my lord being old also? **And the LORD said unto Abraham, Wherefore did Sarah laugh, saying, Shall I of a surety bear a child, which am old? Is any thing too hard for the LORD?** At the time appointed I will return unto thee, according to the time of life, and Sarah shall have a son." – Genesis 18:10–14

In the Bible God visited Abraham and Sarah in their home (Genesis 18:1, 13). The Book of Jasher, though supposedly "in sync with Scripture," gets this story wrong. This is not only a contradiction but completely misses one of the main points of the account from a doctrinal standpoint – that nothing is impossible with God. Abraham and Sarah were in their nineties and well beyond child-bearing years. Yet God promised Abraham that he and Sarah would not only have a son but that the child would be the heir to the Messianic prophecy. This is a powerful foreshadow of the birth of Christ. Humanity could not save itself from its sin and damnation. It took a supernatural birth of the divine Savior to do the impossible – earn our forgiveness on the cross. All of this is omitted in the false teachings of the Book of Jasher.

*Enoch As Ruler Of Angels?*

In the Book of Jasher, an angel of the Lord requests that Enoch rule over the angels:

> "And in some time after, when the kings and princes and the sons of men were speaking to Enoch, and Enoch was teaching them the ways of God, behold an angel of the Lord then called unto Enoch from heaven, and wished to bring him up to heaven to make him reign there over the sons of God, as he had reigned over the sons of men upon earth." – Jasher 3:23

In the Bible, the Lord Jesus Christ is the ruler over angels:

> "For unto which of the angels said he at any time, Thou art my Son, this day have I begotten thee? And again, I will be to him a Father, and he shall be to me a Son? And again, when he bringeth in the first begotten into the world, he saith, **And let all the angels of God worship him**." – Hebrews 1:5–6

> "And I beheld, **and I heard the voice of many angels round about the throne** and the beasts and the elders: and the number of them

was ten thousand times ten thousand, and thousands of thousands; **Saying with a loud voice, Worthy is the Lamb that was slain to receive power, and riches, and wisdom, and strength, and honour, and glory, and blessing**. And every creature which is in heaven, and on the earth, and under the earth, and such as are in the sea, and all that are in them, heard I saying, Blessing, and honour, and glory, and power, be unto him that sitteth upon the throne, and unto the Lamb for ever and ever." – Revelation 5:11–13

Angels surround the throne of Jesus worshiping Him. He is called the "captain" of the angelic host (Joshua 5:14). Given the clear proclamation of the Bible, would a righteous angel of the Lord ever request that Enoch, a human being, rule all over all heavenly angels? Scripture soundly refutes such a heretical notion.

## Fictional Additions to the Exodus

The Book of Exodus describes in great detail the 10 plagues the Lord inflicted upon the Egyptians to force Pharaoh to free the Israelites. The Book of Jasher adds extra plagues that were never mentioned in the Bible including fiery serpents, scorpions, mice, and weasels (Jasher 80:14), attacks by reptiles and winged animals (Jasher 80:16), a sea monster called the Sulanuth, which used its 10-cubit-long arms to unlock the doors of Egyptians so animals could enter their homes and attack them (Jasher 80:19–21), and inflammation (Jasher 80:27). The Book of Jasher almost doubles the number of plagues and introduces more flagrant contradictions to the Bible.

Another error occurs with the description of the plague of darkness. Here is the biblical account:

"And the LORD said unto Moses, Stretch out thine hand toward heaven, that there may be darkness over the land of Egypt, even darkness which may be felt. And Moses stretched forth his hand toward heaven; and there was a thick darkness in all the land of Egypt three days: They saw not one another, neither rose any from his place for three days: **but all the children of Israel had light in their dwellings**." – Exodus 10:21–23

While the Egyptians suffered under supernatural darkness so thick they could not see one another, the Israelites had light in their homes in Goshen (the city they occupied that was supernaturally protected from all the plagues). The Book of Jasher changes this account dramatically:

"And God sent darkness upon Egypt, that the whole land of Egypt and Pathros became dark for three days, so that a man could not see his hand when he lifted it to his mouth. At that time died many of the people of Israel who had rebelled against the Lord and who would not hearken to Moses and Aaron, and believed not in them that God had sent them. And who had said, We will not go forth from Egypt lest we perish with hunger in a desolate wilderness, and who would not hearken to the voice of Moses. **And the Lord plagued them in the three days of darkness, and the Israelites buried them in those days, without the Egyptians knowing of them or rejoicing over them**." – Jasher 80:36–39

In the Book of Jasher, not only do the Israelites also suffer the plague of darkness but God executes a group of rebellious Israelites who are then buried during the three days of plague. This is an extreme contradiction of the biblical account. It also undermines the running Gospel theme of the plagues of Exodus: the salvation for those who are believers in God (Israelites) versus judgment for unbelievers (Egypt). So, the Jasher account is not only a factual error but a doctrinal one as it opposes critical biblical doctrine.

In the Jasher version of the Exodus, once the Israelites leave Egypt for the wilderness, Egyptian military forces pursue and engage the 12 tribes in battle:

"And all the nobles of Pharaoh rose up in the morning, and with them about seven hundred thousand men, and they went forth from Egypt on that day, and came to the place where the children of Israel were. And all the Egyptians saw and behold Moses and Aaron and all the children of Israel were sitting before Pi–hahiroth, eating and drinking and celebrating the feast of the Lord. And all the Egyptians said to the children of Israel, Surely you said, We will go a journey for three days in the wilderness and sacrifice to our God and return. Now therefore this day makes five days since you went, why do you not return to your masters?

And Moses and Aaron answered them, saying, Because the Lord our God has testified in us, saying, You shall no more return to Egypt, but we will betake ourselves to a land flowing with milk and honey, as the Lord our God had sworn to our ancestors to give to us. **And when the nobles of Egypt saw that the children of Israel did not hearken to them, to return to Egypt, they girded themselves to fight with Israel. And the Lord strengthened the hearts of the children of Israel over the Egyptians, that they gave them a severe beating, and the battle was sore upon the Egyptians, and all the Egyptians fled from before the children of Israel, for many of them perished by the hand of Israel.**" – Jasher 81:11–17

This is wildly inconsistent with the inspired Word. In the Bible, the Israelites **never engaged in armed combat with the Egyptians**. Once Pharaoh instructed his forces to chase after the Israelites, God performed one of the greatest miracles in history – the parting of the Red Sea. Moses' words of encouragement to his people before this miraculous moment not only glorified the Lord but expose the Book of Jasher's heresy:

"And when Pharaoh drew nigh, the children of Israel lifted up their eyes, **and, behold, the Egyptians marched after them; and they** were sore afraid: and the children of Israel cried out unto the LORD. And they said unto Moses, Because there were no graves in Egypt, hast thou taken us away to die in the wilderness? wherefore hast thou dealt thus with us, to carry us forth out of Egypt? Is not this the word that we did tell thee in Egypt, saying, Let us alone, that we may serve the Egyptians? For it had been better for us to serve the Egyptians, than that we should die in the wilderness. **And Moses said unto the people, Fear ye not, stand still, and see the salvation of the LORD, which he will shew to you to day: for the Egyptians whom ye have seen to day, ye shall see them again no more for ever. The LORD shall fight for you, and ye shall hold your peace.**" – Exodus 14:10–14

Rather than fighting valiantly against the Egyptians, the people of Israel were frightened and cried out to God. Moses reassured them that the Lord would fight for them. They were specifically told "hold your peace" because God was going to conquer Pharaoh before their eyes. Thus, Jasher's account is once again at odds with Scripture and omits one of the great foreshadows of salvation – namely, that just as the Lord fought Egypt, so He also fights our sin and guilt for us by the death and resurrection of Jesus Christ, the prophesied Seed of the Woman.

## Moses an African King?

In the book of Exodus, Moses was 40 years old when he saw the plight of the Israelite slaves and killed an Egyptian man who was harassing an Israelite. This was the point when Moses abandoned his position as Egyptian royalty to suffer alongside his people, the Israelites. Soon, word spread that he had committed the crime. A fugitive from the law, he fled to Midian where he remained until God called him to confront Pharaoh: "Now when Pharaoh heard this thing, he sought to slay Moses. But Moses fled from the face of Pharaoh, and dwelt in the land of Midian: and he sat down by a well."

In the Book of Jasher, an 18-year-old Moses leaves Egypt for Cush, where he became king for many years:

> "At that time that the war and the siege were against Cush, Moses fled from Egypt from Pharaoh who sought to kill him for having slain the Egyptian. **And Moses was eighteen years old when he fled from Egypt from the presence of Pharaoh,** and he fled and escaped to the camp of Kikianus, which at that time was besieging Cush. And Moses was nine years in the camp of Kikianus king of Cush, all the time that they were besieging Cush, and Moses went out and came in with them… And they wished to choose on that day a man for king from the army of Kikianus, and they found no object of their choice like Moses to reign over them." – Jasher 72:21–23, 34

Note that Jasher completely changes the chronology. Rather than killing a man and fleeing Egypt at 40 years of age, Moses does so at 18. Additionally, Scripture states very clearly that once he was suspected of murder, Moses went to Midian (where he lived 40 more years). In Jasher, a teenage Moses goes on a wild adventure in Cush, waging war, advising the king, and eventually becoming king himself.

This is a very important contradiction because in the New Testament, the Apostle Stephen, preaching on the life of Moses, directly refuted Jasher's account:

> "And Moses was learned in all the wisdom of the Egyptians, and was mighty in words and in deeds. And when he was full forty years old, it came into his heart to visit his brethren the children of Israel. And seeing one of them suffer wrong, he defended him, and avenged him that was oppressed, and smote the Egyptian: For he supposed his brethren would have understood how that God by his hand would deliver them: but they understood not.

Then fled Moses at this saying, and was a stranger in the land of Madian, where he begat two sons. And when forty years were expired, there appeared to him in the wilderness of mount Sinai an angel of the Lord in a flame of fire in a bush." - Acts 7:22-25; 29-30.

Clearly, the Apostle was not reading the Book of Jasher as he states that Moses was in Egypt until age 40. The Book of Jasher is once again, wildly incorrect.

Hebrews 11 recounts the life of Moses and refutes the Book of Jasher:

"By faith Moses, when he was come to years, refused to be called the son of Pharaoh's daughter; Choosing rather to suffer affliction with the people of God, than to enjoy the pleasures of sin for a season; Esteeming the reproach of Christ greater riches than the treasures in Egypt: for he had respect unto the recompence of the reward. By faith he forsook Egypt, not fearing the wrath of the king: for he endured, as seeing him who is invisible." – Hebrews 11:24–27

The foundation of Moses' faith was his willingness to relinquish his status as Egyptian royalty in order to suffer alongside his enslaved Israelites brothers and sisters, the "people of God." Moses valued suffering for the name of Christ over earthly power, wealth, and fame. This is a powerful biblical teaching and proof that Moses held no position of king, as Jasher would have us believe. Moses was focused on the throne of the Lord God Almighty – not any earthly throne for himself.

## In Jasher Pharaoh Survives the Red Sea Judgment

There are too many preposterous, fantastic details in the Jasher version of the Exodus that disqualify it as a Bible "supplement" to explore here. One of the final errors in Jasher's corrupted version of the Exodus is the fate of Pharaoh. In the Bible, Pharaoh drowns in the Red Sea along with his armies.

"And when Pharaoh drew nigh, the children of Israel lifted up their eyes, and, behold, the Egyptians marched after them; and they were sore afraid: and the children of Israel cried out unto the LORD… And I, behold, I will harden the hearts of the Egyptians, and they shall follow them: and I will get me honour upon Pharaoh, and upon all his host, upon his chariots, and upon his horsemen. **And the Egyptians shall know that I am the LORD, when I have gotten me honour upon Pharaoh, upon his chariots, and upon his horsemen**… And Moses stretched forth his hand over the sea, and the sea returned to his strength when the morning appeared; **and the Egyptians fled against it; and the LORD overthrew the Egyptians in the midst of the sea.** And the waters returned, and covered the chariots, and the horsemen, and all the host of Pharaoh that came into the sea after them; **there remained not so much as one of them.**" – Exodus 14:10; 17–18; 27–28.

Not only did Pharaoh perish in the Red Sea but no one from his armies survived. The conquest of Pharaoh and his armies is recalled in the book of Psalms:

"To him which divided the Red sea into parts: for his mercy endureth for ever: And made Israel to pass through the midst of it: for his mercy endureth for ever: **But overthrew Pharaoh and his host in the Red sea:** for his mercy endureth for ever." – Psalm 136:13–15

This passage leaves no doubt that Pharaoh himself died in the Red Sea. But the Book of Jasher has a completely different spin on the story:

"And when the children of Israel had entered the sea, the Egyptians came after them, and the waters of the sea resumed upon them, and they all sank in the water, and not one man was left excepting Pharaoh, who gave thanks to the Lord and believed in him, therefore the Lord did not cause him to perish at that time with the Egyptians. And the Lord ordered an angel to take him from amongst the Egyptians, who cast him upon the land of Ninevah and he reigned over it for a long time." – Jasher 81:40–41

So, in this fictional account Pharaoh not only survives the Red Sea judgment but repents and receives an angelic escort to Nineveh where he resumes the role of king. These spurious embellishments cast serious doubt on the character of the authors of the book of Jasher. Were they "Bible believers" or faithful students of God's Word? If so, we would not find so many horrendous inaccuracies and false teachings.

### The Book of Jasher Teaches Witchcraft

One of the worst and most heretical passages in the Book of Jasher is a tale in which Joseph speaks to the spirit of his dead mother. This is necromancy – a sin sternly forbidden in Scripture (Deuteronomy 18:11) and akin to witchcraft:

"And Joseph reached his mother's grave, and Joseph hastened and ran to his mother's grave, and fell upon the grave and wept. **And Joseph cried aloud upon his mother's grave, and he said, O my mother, my mother, O thou who didst give me birth, awake now, and rise and see thy son, how he has been sold for a slave, and no one to pity him.** O rise and see thy son, weep with me on account of my troubles, and see the heart of my brethren. Arouse my mother, arouse, awake from thy sleep for me, and direct thy battles against my brethren. O how have they stripped me of my coat, and sold me already twice for a slave, and separated me from my father, and there is no one to pity me.

"Arouse and lay thy cause against them before God, and see whom God will justify in the judgment, and whom he will condemn. Rise, O my mother, rise, awake from thy sleep and see my father how his soul is with me this day, and comfort him and ease his heart. And Joseph continued to speak these words, and Joseph cried aloud and wept bitterly upon his mother's grave; and he ceased speaking, and from bitterness of heart he became still as a stone upon the grave. **And Joseph heard a voice speaking to him from beneath the ground, which answered him with bitterness of heart, and with a voice of weeping and praying in these words:**

"My son, my son Joseph, I have heard the voice of thy weeping and the voice of thy lamentation; I have seen thy tears; I know thy troubles, my son, and it grieves me for thy sake, and abundant grief is added to my grief. Now therefore my son, Joseph my son, hope to the Lord, and wait for him and do not fear, for the Lord is with thee, he will deliver thee from all trouble." – Jasher 42:30–39

In the Book of Jasher, Joseph not only speaks to his dead mother but prays to her to intercede with the Lord on his behalf. This again is outrageous heresy. Scripture is clear that born-again believers are to pray to God and God alone: "For there is one God, and one mediator between God and men, the man Christ Jesus" (1 Timothy 2:5). In Deuteronomy 18, the Lord warned the Israelites against necromancy or speaking to the dead:

"When thou art come into the land which the LORD thy God giveth thee, thou shalt not learn to do after the abominations of those nations. There shall not be found among you any one that maketh his son or his daughter to pass through the fire, or that useth divination, or an observer of times, or an enchanter, or a witch. Or a charmer, or a consulter with familiar spirits, or a wizard, **or a necromancer. For all that do these things are an** abomination unto the LORD: and because of these abominations the LORD thy God doth drive them out from before thee. Thou shalt be perfect with the LORD thy God." – Deuteronomy 18:9–13

To attribute such abominable actions to Joseph when the Bible does not even hint of such things but explicitly forbids them is an utter contradiction of God's Word. Furthermore, the Book of Jasher is spiritually dangerous as it can actually entice an unwitting reader to commit occult practices thinking they are endorsed by God. We must therefore flatly reject any notion that the Book of Jasher is somehow on par with the Bible, provides "extra details the Bible left out," or harmonizes with Scripture.

Like Pseudo-Enoch, the Book of Jasher is rife with heresies, inaccuracies, and flagrant contradictions of Scripture. Could the Holy Spirit possibly have had any role in the writing of two texts filled with so many errors? God forbid. While the rediscovery of these texts has ignited study of the Nephilim giants and opened a great deal of fruitful, positive research and discourse in the Christian community, they cannot be taken seriously as "supplements" to the inerrant Word of God. They are clearly man-made texts, that expounded upon the Biblical account with extensive artistic liberty, mixing in Jewish thought and actual ancient theology. The Bible is truth. It is the one source on the history of the Christian faith that is beyond reproach because it is divinely-inspired. It provides more details on the Nephilim than any other source, as we will continue to see.

1. The *Canon of the Holy Scriptures Examined in the Light of History*, Prof. Louis S. Gassen, Translated from French and Abridged by Edward N. Kirk, D.D., 1862, p. 398-402.

# CHAPTER 13

# HOW DID THE NEPHILIM RETURN AFTER THE FLOOD?

Now that we have examined the Angelic-Nephilim kingdoms of the pre-Flood world, we turn our attention to the *Nephilim who appeared after the Flood*. How did they return? I contend that first-generation Nephilim – direct offspring of the angelic sons of God and daughters of men – never returned to Earth. *Their DNA,* however, passed on through the Flood on the ark, allowing giants to be born in the newly-restarted human population. Through a literal reading of the Bible and basic reasoning it becomes clear how this came to pass. A 19th-century Bible scholar concurs:

> "For my own part, however, I see no reason why Ishbi benob may not have been personally and lineally descended from the 'Sons of God' whosoever they may have been. Some people were, I suppose, and why not he? We must consider, that though the Ark contained only one family, consisting of but eight souls yet in all probability that family represented five lines of pedigree. The Patriarch Noah, it may be remembered, was himself of the family of Seth. Whatever idea we may have of his personal holiness, and of the antediluvian piety of his sons, we are not, I suppose, authorised to assume that by something amounting almost to a miracle, the several lines of Noah himself, of his wife, and of his three daughters-in-law – lines going back perhaps through many ages and generations – were all

kept pure from any mixture of giant blood." – *False Worship: An Essay*, Rev. Dr. Samuel Maitland, Published in London: Rivingtons, Waterloo Place, 1856, pp. 21–23.

# NOAH'S FAMILY LED A
# NEW BEGINNING FOR HUMANITY

"And God blessed Noah and his sons, and said unto them, Be fruitful, and multiply, and replenish the earth. And the fear of you and the dread of you shall be upon every beast of the earth, and upon every fowl of the air, upon all that moveth upon the earth, and upon all the fishes of the sea; into your hand are they delivered. Every moving thing that liveth shall be meat for you; even as the green herb have I given you all things. But flesh with the life thereof, which is the blood thereof, shall ye not eat. And surely your blood of your lives will I require; at the hand of every beast will I require it, and at the hand of man; at the hand of every man's brother will I require the life of man. Whoso sheddeth man's blood, by man shall his blood be shed: for in the image of God made he man." – Genesis 9:1–6

In the ongoing battle between God and the Devil, the Flood was a powerful counterstrike. Satan, who seemingly had the entire world entangled in the sinful rebellion of the Angelic-Nephilim kingdoms, witnessed his global system of iniquity destroyed before his eyes. On top of this, the human race and the Messianic Seed were preserved through a tiny remnant on the ark. Righteous Noah, a true believer in the coming Messiah and a pure human, would restart the population as the patriarch of the earth.

# PARALLELS TO ADAM IN THE GARDEN OF EDEN

There are many striking parallels between the account of Noah entering the newly restarted Earth and Adam in the Garden of Eden:

- Both Genesis 9 and the creation week start with the earth covered in water. Both stories involved animals supernaturally gathered to God's chosen servant (Genesis 2:19; 7:9).
- In the Creation week, the Holy Spirit (who in the New Testament took the form of a dove – Matthew 3:16) hovered above the waters of the earth before land appeared. In Genesis 8, Noah released a dove to fly above the waters in search for land.
- Humanity was once again granted dominion over those animals (Genesis 1:26; Genesis 9:2).
- The Lord reinforced to Adam and Noah the creation truth that man was unique from all other creatures as he was made in the image of God (Genesis 1:26; 9:6).
- Humans were to be fruitful and multiply to replenish the earth.
- Both stories include sin involving fruit (the forbidden fruit, the wine drunk by Noah).
- Both stories involve nakedness that needed to be covered (Genesis 3:7; Genesis 9:23).

These similarities underscore that the Lord's intention – to give his new race the earth to rule in righteous harmony with Him – never changed. Although the Garden of Eden was lost in the destructive effects of the Flood, God's plan to dwell with His creation was undisturbed.

# HAM'S SIN AND THE CURSE OF CANAAN

Always the relentless adversary, Satan went back on the attack with sinful temptation to disrupt God's order and further corrupt the image of God in humanity. As usual, he looked for the one person who would listen to sinful temptation and exploited that weakness. In this case it was Noah's son Ham, who would carry Satan's agenda into the postdiluvian world. Ham's son, Canaan, received the third special reference in the Bible:

> "And the sons of Noah, that went forth of the ark, were Shem, and Ham, and Japheth: **and Ham is the father of Canaan.** These are the three sons of Noah: and of them was the whole earth overspread. And Noah began to be an husbandman, and he planted a vineyard: And he drank of the wine, and was drunken; and he was uncovered within his tent. **And Ham, the father of Canaan**, saw the nakedness of his father, and told his two brethren without.
>
> And Shem and Japheth took a garment, and laid it upon both their shoulders, and went backward, and covered the nakedness of their father; and their faces were backward, and they saw not their father's nakedness. And Noah awoke from his wine, and knew what his younger son had done unto him. **And he said, Cursed be Canaan; a servant of servants shall he be unto his brethren.** And he said, Blessed be the LORD God of Shem; and Canaan shall be his servant. God shall enlarge Japheth, and he shall dwell in the tents of Shem; and Canaan shall be his servant." – Genesis 9:18–27

Twice in Genesis 9 we are told that Ham was "the father of Canaan" – affirming Canaan's infamy in ancient Hebrew society. One of the greater mysteries of the Bible was why Noah cursed Canaan for Ham's sin. Canaan was the father of all the postdiluvian giants (as we will see). From a literal reading of Scripture, it is clear that Ham's wife must have carried the corrupted DNA that passed through the Flood. The presence of the Nephilim gene may have caused Canaan to appear different from his siblings and cousins to the point that Noah knew some trace of the antediluvian genetic corruption was in him – something the Bible noted with respect to other siblings who were descendants of giants (2 Samuel 21:20). This would explain both the special reference to Canaan and the curse placed upon him rather than upon his father, Ham.

Although this passage has evoked massive speculation and all sorts of exotic racial and sexual theories, it seems best to simply take it at face value. Noah, a believer in Christ, was still human and inherited the same sinful nature in his flesh that all people have inherited from Adam. He succumbed to the sin of drunkenness and left himself naked in his tent:

> "And he drank of the wine, and was drunk, and was naked in his house." – Genesis 9:21 LXX

As is often the case in Scripture and in life, one sin begets more sin. Ham, aware of his father's condition, chose to view the patriarch naked rather than respect his authority and privacy. In an act of mockery, he then went and told his brothers of their drunken father's condition. Here Ham's nature was revealed. He did not seek to honor his father who was not only a prophet of God but had just saved them from certain death. Shem and Japheth, out of respect, entered their father's tent backwards and covered him. Once Noah awoke and realized what Ham had done, he cursed Ham's son Canaan.

Josephus, the first-century Jewish historian, agreed with this interpretation in his recording of the event:

> "Noah, when after the deluge, the earth was resettled in its former condition, set about its cultivation: and when he had planted it with vines, and when the fruit was ripe, and he had gathered the grapes in their season, and the wine was ready for use, he offered sacrifice, and feasted: and being drunk, he fell a-sleep, and lay naked in an unseemly manner. When his youngest son saw this, he came laughing, and shewed him to his brethren: but they covered their father's nakedness. And when Noah was made sensible of what had

been done, he prayed for prosperity to his other sons; but for Ham, he did not curse him, by reason of his nearness in blood, but cursed his posterity. And when the rest of them escaped that curse, God inflicted it on the children of Canaan." – *Antiquities*, Josephus, Book I, Ch. 3.

## WHY WOULD THE LORD ALLOW NEPHILIM DNA ON THE ARK?

The Bible provides no details about Noah's sons' wives. From Scripture we deduce that Shem, Ham, and Japheth were of Noah's purely human lineage. But *the timing of their births* is very informative. Noah was 500 years old when he had his children.

> "**And Noah was five hundred years old**: and Noah begat Shem, Ham, and Japheth." – Genesis 5:32

The birth of Noah's first child *was 20 years after God pronounced the 120-year probation* for the earth to repent before he would destroy the planet:

> "And Noah begat three sons, Shem, Ham, and Japheth. **The earth also was corrupt before God**, and the earth was filled with violence. And God looked upon the earth, and, behold, it was corrupt; **for all flesh had corrupted his way upon the earth**." – Genesis 6:10–12

By the time Noah's sons were born, the earth was already corrupted genetically. Unlike all his ancestors who had their first children by 200 years old, at the latest, Noah did not have children until he was 500 (Genesis 5:32). Why did Noah wait so long to have a child? Perhaps it was because he knew of Enoch's prophecy of the end of the world. Or because he knew that

Methuselah, his grandfather, was a literal walking doomsday clock, whose very lifespan was the signal of the last days. Perhaps Noah found it too awful to consider having children he knew would perish with the entire global population. Then, once God assured him that he would carry on the human population, he started a family. Unfortunately, by that point, the options for finding a godly woman with no trace of Nephilim DNA for his sons to marry were severely limited as all people outside of Noah's lineage were corrupted by giant blood to some degree (Genesis 6:10–12).

It stands to reason that Noah, a true believer in the midst of the sinful antediluvian society, had the wisdom to marry a woman who was not a descendant of the fallen angels and the Nephilim. But Ham, a reprobate, would have no such concerns. And the greatest evidence of this is that the Nephilim giants after the Flood all descended from his son Canaan. One commentator wrote on this fact:

> "As Noah was 'perfect in his generations,' it would seem he was not of this line of mighty ones; but how about the wives of his sons? We read that Nimrod a mighty one in the earth; he was the grandson of Noah's second son Ham. Was Ham's wife of this line of mighty ones? In some way a miracle working spirit has come down the stream of time and the Bible calls it 'the spirit demons'; and we have seen that the demons were the gods – the giants who were cast down." – *The Sons of God and Their Inheritance*, Emma J. Penney, 1921, pp. 73–74.

## NIMROD – THE FIRST POSTDILUVIAN EMPEROR

Genesis 10 lists the table of nations after the world was divided at the tower of Babel. The lineages of the sons of Noah are listed to document the successful preservation of the Holy Seed. Alternatively, when Ham's lineage is listed, one name immediately stands out: Nimrod.

"And the sons of Ham; Cush, and Mizraim, and Phut, and Canaan. And the sons of Cush; Seba, and Havilah, and Sabtah, and Raamah, and Sabtechah: and the sons of Raamah; Sheba, and Dedan. **And Cush begat Nimrod: he began to be a mighty one in the earth. He was a mighty hunter before the LORD: wherefore it is said, Even as Nimrod the mighty hunter before the LORD** And the beginning of his kingdom was Babel, and Erech, and Accad, and Calneh, in the land of Shinar." – Genesis 10:6–10

Just as Lamech, Naamah, and Canaan received special distinction in genealogies, Nimrod is the fourth person in Scripture with an exceptional reference. Several verses record his infamy. Nimrod was the first murderer and conqueror in the post-Flood world. He was the founder of the city of Babylon, which became a center of pagan, satanic idolatry, many versions of which featured Nimrod himself being worshiped as a god. His name, which means "to rebel" or "let us rebel," indicated his disposition. He was an enemy of God and Satan's main servant on Earth at that time. He is credited with leading the effort to build the Tower of Babel, a religious temple of worship for false gods and the first attempt to form a global government. The ancient king aspired for man to reach the spiritual realm and "godhood" without the Lord (to which God swiftly responded by destroying the tower, confusing the languages of all the people of the world, and scattering them all over the earth).

## WAS NIMROD A NEPHILIM?

It is interesting to note that verse 9 states that Nimrod "began to be a mighty one in the earth." "Mighty one" is translated from the Hebrew *gibbowr* or *gibborim*, which is also used to describe the Nephilim giants in Genesis 6 who were also "mighty men" (Genesis 6:4) and the giant Goliath (1 Samuel 17:51). *Gibborim* was also used in the Bible to describe human men:

"So Joshua arose, and all the people of war, to go up against Ai: and Joshua chose out thirty thousand mighty *[gibbowr]* men of valour, and sent them away by night." – Joshua 8:3

"These *be* the names of the mighty men *[gibbowr]* whom David had: The Tachmonite that sat in the seat, chief among the captains; the same *was* Adino the Eznite: **he lift up his spear against eight hundred, whom he slew at one tim**e." – 2 Samuel 23:8

Rather than designating a giant, *gibbowr* or *gibborim* referred to someone with exceptional, almost superhuman, fighting ability. The description fits Adino the Eznite in 2 Samuel 23:8 above who singlehandedly killed 800 enemies. Nimrod was the first of the post-Flood *gibborim*, far exceeding his contemporaries in combat. Although that would not necessarily mean he was a Nephilim giant, it is clear that he was so imposing and so dominant in warfare that he was the starkest reminder of the giants who once terrified humanity with their weapons of war.

The final interesting hint of evidence to consider is that in the Septuagint, the oldest version of the Old Testament, the same verse from Genesis reads:

"And [Cush] begot [Nimrod]: **he began to be a giant upon the earth.** He was *a giant hunter* before the Lord God; therefore they say, As **[Nimrod] the giant hunter** before the Lord. – Genesis 10:8, 9 LXX

Three times the text uses the word "giant" to describe Nimrod. A 17th-century biblical commentary acknowledged the seeming connection between this conqueror and the Nephilim:

"This principle took its ground in Nimrod, that great monarch and first establisher of idolatry, and the first grand persecutor of God in his select seed, therefore called the mighty hunter before the Lord… This Nimrod, having the fullness of the Angels nature in him, made him exceeding proud, thinking himself equal with God….” – *Truth's Triumph: Or a Witness to the Two Witnesses*, Thomas Tomkinson, Printed by W. Smith, King Street, London, 1690, pp. 19–20.

By combination of his genetics, fighting prowess, and defiance of God, Nimrod became the first postdiluvian on par with the Rephaim of the ancient world. If Nimrod did indeed undergo some sort of supernatural transformation, it would not be the only such occurrence recorded in Scripture. In Daniel 4, King Nebuchadnezzar of Babylon, was literally transformed into a “beast” and lived as an animal for seven years:

> “At the end of twelve months he walked in the palace of the kingdom of Babylon. The king spake, and said, Is not this great Babylon, that I have built for the house of the kingdom by the might of my power, and for the honour of my majesty? While the word was in the king's mouth, there fell a voice from heaven, saying, O king Nebuchadnezzar, to thee it is spoken; The kingdom is departed from thee. And they shall drive thee from men, and thy dwelling shall be with the beasts of the field: they shall make thee to eat grass as oxen, and seven times shall pass over thee, until thou know that the most High ruleth in the kingdom of men, and giveth it to whomsoever he will. **The same hour was the thing fulfilled upon Nebuchadnezzar: and he was driven from men, and did eat grass as oxen, and his body was wet with the dew of heaven, till his hairs were grown like eagles' feathers, and his nails like birds' claws.**” – Daniel 4:29–33

In Nebuchadnezzar's dream, one of the Watchers (the same class of angels the Book of Enoch refers to) announces judgment of the king saying: “Let his heart be changed from man's, and let a beast's heart be given unto him; and let seven times pass over him." Nebuchadnezzar was literally transformed from a man into a human-animal hybrid via angelic powers. So, could the same process have happened to Nimrod who already carried Nephilim genes via his grandmother?

## "HE WAS A MIGHTY HUNTER BEFORE THE LORD"

Hunting often carried a negative connotation in the Old Testament. The only other hunter mentioned by name in the Old testament was Esau, the son of the patriarch Isaac and a man whom Scripture says God "hated" (Malachi 1:3). Other verses about hunting often refer to *hunting people* rather than animals. After sparing the deranged King Saul's life, David told the monarch "yet thou huntest my soul to take it" (1 Samuel 24:11). Other examples of hunting as a reference to hunting people in Scripture include:

> "For by means of a whorish woman a man is brought to a piece of bread: and the adultress will hunt for the precious life." – Proverbs 6:26

> "They hunt our steps, that we cannot go in our streets: our end is near, our days are fulfilled; for our end is come." – Lamentations 4:18

> "The good man is perished out of the earth: and there is none upright among men: they all lie in wait for blood; they hunt every man his brother with a net." – Micah 7:2

Nimrod's hunting and military prowess was "before the Lord," meaning in opposition and defiance of God. The men of Sodom were similarly described as "wicked and sinners before the LORD exceedingly" (Genesis 13:13). Nimrod carried out rebellion against God. That Nimrod was a conqueror and renowned for his wars against his own extended family members is supported by the next part of his description: "… wherefore it is said, Even as Nimrod the mighty hunter before the LORD." Nimrod was so famous that he was the basis for an ancient metaphor. A person who acted in sinful rebellion was described as "even as Nimrod the mighty hunter before the Lord." The Bible emphasizes Nimrod's notorious legend. His life of conquest was a return to the violence, brazen sin, and bloodshed of the pre-Flood era.

Matthew Henry, author of perhaps the most popular biblical commentary of all time (and one that is still commonly used today), wrote of Nimrod:

> "Whereas those that went before him, were content to stand on the same level with their neighbors, and every man bare rule in his own house, nor pretended further; Nimrod resolved to tower above his neighbors, and not only so; but to lord it over them. The same spirit that actuated the giants before the flood, now revived in him; so soon was that tremendous judgment, which the pride and tyranny of those mighty men brought on the world, forgotten." – *The Comprehensive Commentary of the Bible, Containing Matthew Henry's Commentary*, edited by William Jenks, published by J.P. Lippincott & Co., 1847, p. 65.

Nimrod's kingdom started at Shinar, the location of what would one day be Babylon, and it was there he attempted to construct the Tower of Babel.

> "And the whole earth was of one language, and of one speech. And it came to pass, as they journeyed from the east, that they found a plain in the land of Shinar; and they dwelt there. And they said one to another, Go to, let us make brick, and burn them thoroughly. And they had brick for stone, and slime had they for mortar. And they said, Go to, let us build us a city and a tower, whose top may reach unto heaven; and let us make us a name, lest we be scattered abroad upon the face of the whole earth." – Genesis 11:1–4

The tower was intended to achieve spiritual greatness apart from God. Like the giants before the Flood who were "men of renown," Nimrod instigated his followers in creating a "name" for themselves. Babel represented another attempt to achieve immortality. This was the first open rebellion of the postdiluvian era.

Josephus, the first-century Jewish historian, wrote of the tower:

> "Now it was [Nimrod] who excited them to such an affront and contempt of God. He was the grand–son of Ham, the son of Noah: a bold man, and of great strength of hand. He persuaded them not to ascribe it to God, as if it was through his means that they were happy; but to believe that it was their own courage which procured that happiness. He also gradually changed the government into tyranny; seeing no other way of turning men from the fear of God, but to bring them into a constant dependence on his own power. He also said, 'He would be revenged on God, if he should have a mind to drown the world again: for that he would build a Tower too high for the waters to be able to reach; and that he would avenge himself on God for destroying their fore-fathers.'" – *Antiquities*, Flavius Josephus, Book 1, 4.2.

In making the tower, the people used brick and "slime." The slime, or *chemar* in Hebrew, was bitumen, the same sealant material God instructed Noah to use in building the ark (referred to as "pitch" in Genesis 6:14). The tower was built to withstand rising floodwaters. It is important to remember that these events were taking place 100–150 years after the Flood. Noah, Shem, Japheth, and Ham were all still alive. So, their knowledge of the pre-Flood world, and its superhuman angelic and Nephilim rulers, was well-known. Nimrod's perspective would be informed by his wicked grandfather, Ham. Thus, he would certainly have known of the flood judgment from the Lord. Second-century historian Herodotus wrote of the construction at Babel:

> "The earth of the trench was first of all laid in heaps, and when a sufficient quantity was obtained, made into square bricks, and baked

in a furnace. They used as cement a composition of heated bitumen, which, mixed with the tops of reeds, was placed between every thirtieth course of bricks. Within an eight days journey from Babylon is a city called Is; near which flows a river of the same name, which empties itself into the Euphrates. With the current of this river particles of bitumen descend towards Babylon, by means of which its walls were constructed." – Herodotus, ca. 179 AD, as quoted in *The Testimony of the Heathen to the Truths of Holy Writ: A Commentary on the Old and New Testaments*, Reverend Thomas Street Millington, Printed by Seeley, Jackson and Halliday, 1863, p. 80.

The Tower of Babel embodied Nimrod's arrogance and mockery of God's Word. The Lord promised never to flood the world again, but Nimrod encouraged his subjects to doubt God and construct the tower to survive a second deluge. Satan needed a human agent to carry out his agenda and found it in the grandson of Ham. Rather than spreading out to replenish the planet, Nimrod consolidated the global population in one city dedicated to pagan worship.

The Lord responded in swift fashion:

"And the LORD came down to see the city and the tower, which the children of men builded. And the LORD said, Behold, the people is one, and they have all one language; and this they begin to do: and now nothing will be restrained from them, which they have imagined to do. Go to, let us go down, and there confound their language, that they may not understand one another's speech. So the LORD scattered them abroad from thence upon the face of all the earth: and they left off to build the city. Therefore is the name of it called Babel; because the LORD did there confound the language of all the earth: and from thence did the LORD scatter them abroad upon the face of all the earth." – Genesis 11:5–9

A people united without God will always wind up in chaos. After examining the tower project, the Lord concluded that "nothing will be restrained from them, which they have imagined to do." This hearkened back to the days of Noah when "God saw that the wickedness of man was great in the earth, and that *every imagination* of the thoughts of his heart was only evil continually" (Genesis 6:5).

The Scriptures proclaim in Psalm 2:1–3: "Why do the heathen rage, **and the people imagine a vain thing**? The kings of the earth set themselves, and the rulers take counsel together, against the LORD, and against his anointed, saying, Let us break their bands asunder, and cast away their cords from us."

The human imagination, fueled by the sinful flesh, is a fast track to rebellion. The Tower of Babel exposed some yet-untapped potential for evil that Nimrod was close to achieving by unifying the global population. The Devil's seed was once again attempting to thwart God's plan of redemption by spiritually corrupting the entire human population. But the Lord countered Satan's emissary by confusing the languages. People soon formed new nations all over the world based on the many different languages, and the Lord's will was done.

## CANAAN'S OFFSPRING WERE GIANTS WHO DOMINATED THE PROMISED LAND

"And Canaan begat Sidon his first born, and Heth, And the Jebusite, and the Amorite, and the Girgasite, And the Hivite, and the Arkite, and the Sinite, And the Arvadite, and the Zemarite, and the Hamathite: and afterward were the families of the Canaanites spread abroad. And the border of the Canaanites was from Sidon, as thou comest to Gerar, unto Gaza; as thou goest, unto Sodom, and Gomorrah, and Admah, and Zeboim, even unto Lasha. These are the sons of Ham, after their families, after their tongues, in their countries, and in their nations." – Genesis 10:15–20

Canaan, the cursed child of Ham, was the father of the many giant-populated nations that opposed God's chosen people for centuries in the Bible:

> "When the Lord thy God shall bring thee into the land whither thou goest to possess it, and hath cast out many nations before thee, **the Hittites, and the Girgashites, and the Amorites, and the Canaanites, and the Perizzites, and the Hivites, and the Jebusites, seven nations greater and mightier than thou**; – [2] And when the LORD thy God shall deliver them before thee; thou shalt smite them, and utterly destroy them; thou shalt make no covenant with them, nor shew mercy unto them: [3] Neither shalt thou make marriages with them; thy daughter thou shalt not give unto his son, nor his daughter shalt thou take unto thy son." – Deuteronomy 7:1–3

## NATIONS WITH NEPHILIM GENES WERE PUT UNDER *CHEREM*

During this epoch of world history God decreed that several Nephilim-infested nations were to be shown no mercy and destroyed entirely. The "ban," or *cherem* in Hebrew, is one of the most controversial aspects of the Bible (and one we will explore in greater detail in a later chapter). Canaan's descendants comprised all of the postdiluvian peoples God targeted specifically for *cherem*.

Consider the prominence of Noah's cursed grandson Canaan. There are 157 references to Canaan in the Bible – a staggering number for a person whose *words and actions are never recorded in Scripture.* Aside from his being cursed by Noah (Genesis 9:25), the Bible records no other events in Canaan's life, and yet his name is one of the most famous. Such an omission is eerily similar to the abrupt end of the lineage of Cain in Genesis 4 after the family of Lamech and his children Jabal, Jubal, Tubal-Cain, and Naamah. Scripture has no interest in promoting the Nephilim or their life stories. Their presence is mentioned only as it serves to reveal God's glory and plan of salvation. This gives greater weight to the notion that the Nephilim gene survived the Flood through Ham's wife and then his sons, particularly Canaan.

Following the Tower of Babel dispersion, Canaan's offspring occupied all of the Promised Land – the prophesied location for Israel, God's chosen nation. Their rapid expansion led to the Promised Land's being dubbed "the land of Canaan." How is it that the first person cursed after the Flood was able to capture such a vast expanse, much less have his children and grandchildren inhabit the very area that God had proclaimed was His land? This is where Satan made his next move in the ongoing battle to prevent fulfillment of God's Seed of the Woman prophecy.

## THE DEVIL PLOTTED TO SECURE THE PROMISED LAND FOR HIMSELF

Even though the Flood had destroyed his hybrid empire, Satan remained relentless in his quest to prevent the birth of the Messiah. After the Lord scattered the people of the world over the Tower of Babel debacle, Canaan's corrupted offspring occupied the Promised Land. This was no coincidence. The Devil, who had witnessed all the events of human history since the Garden of Eden, knew the location was important to the Lord. Therefore, he placed his minions there to preempt the arrival of God's faithful servants. So, the Devil planted the lineage that contained the trace remnants of Nephilim DNA precisely in the most important piece of land on the planet Earth. Thus, the stage was set for the next battle between the Messianic bloodline and the seed of the Serpent.

# CHAPTER 14

# ONE MAN AGAINST THE WORLD

## AFTER BABEL, GOD DIVIDED THE
## UNBELIEVING WORLD INTO 70 NATIONS

"**Unto Shem also, the father of all the children of Eber**, the brother
of Japheth the elder, even to him were children born. The children of
Shem; Elam, and Asshur, and Arphaxad, and Lud, and Aram. And the
children of Aram; Uz, and Hul, and Gether, and Mash. And Arphaxad
begat Salah; and Salah begat Eber. And unto Eber were born two sons:
**the name of one was Peleg; for in his days was the earth divided;
and his brother's name was Joktan**." – Genesis 10:21–25

After Nimrod's failed revolution at Babel God divided the world into 70
nations (listed in Genesis 11). Nimrod and his fellow rebels dispersed all over
the globe. Shem, Noah's first son, carried on the Messianic bloodline and
remained in the Middle East. Those who opposed the Lord wanted to "make
a name" for themselves. Shem, the son of Noah, was called "the name" (the
Hebrew meaning of his name). In Jewish writing, the Lord is referred to as
"Hashem" or "the Name." Faithful believers such as Shem would bear the
blessing of God that the heathen world so desperately longed for.

In Genesis 10:25 the sons of Eber – Peleg and Joktan – were born. Peleg was
born during the time of God's judgment of the Tower of Babel rebellion and

subsequent division of the nations. God divided the population, the physical land of the earth, *and the angelic order as well.* The Lord gave the Devil numerical advantage by granting control of the 70 nations that would form "the Gentile world." Meanwhile the Lord would use His own chosen human lineage to carry the Holy Seed to effect His plan of salvation.

## ANGELS WERE GIVEN AUTHORITY OVER THE GENTILE NATIONS

"When the Most High divided the nations, when he separated the sons of Adam, **he set the bounds of the nations according to the number of the angels of God. And his people Jacob became the portion of the Lord, Israel was the line of his inheritance.**" – Deuteronomy 32:8–9 LXX

"And lest thou lift up thine eyes unto heaven, and when thou seest the sun, and the moon, and the stars, even all the host of heaven, shouldest be driven to worship them, and serve them, which the LORD thy God hath divided unto all nations under the whole heaven." – Deuteronomy 4:19

In the aftermath of the Tower of Babel rebellion, the faithless sinners who followed King Nimrod were divided into 70 nations according to the "the number of the angels of God." Dr. Michael Heiser summarizes these two passages on the angelic rule over Gentile countries:

"Deuteronomy 4:19–20 and 32:8 present two sides of the same coin. In Deuteronomy 32:8–9, God apportions the nations to the sons of God; here [in Deuteronomy 4:19], however, God allots the gods to the nations. Israelites, in other words, believed that Yahweh, their own supreme, unique God, sentenced the nations and their gods to each other. At Babel, God, like a father dismissing and disinheriting his children, judges all the nations for their disobedience (Gen 11:1–9). Then, in the very next chapter, He calls Abraham (Gen 12:1–3), effectively starting over in creating an earthly human family for Himself."

– http://www.thedivinecouncil.com/Deuteronomy32OTWorldview.pdf

God essentially permitted a select group of angels to have spiritual dominion over the entire known world. In turn, the Lord would create His own nation, not from any pagan country but from one man – Abraham. The battle lines were redrawn, and though the odds appeared stacked against the Lord's faithful, the planned path to the Messiah was going precisely according to God's will.

## ABRAHAM – ONE MAN SELECTED TO START GOD'S NATION

"Now the LORD had said unto Abram, Get thee out of thy country, and from thy kindred, and from thy father's house, unto a land that I will shew thee: **And I will make of thee a great nation, and I will bless thee, and make thy name great; and thou shalt be a blessing**: And I will bless them that bless thee, and curse him that curseth thee: and in thee shall all families of the earth be blessed." – Genesis 12:1–3

In the face of this global rebellion by the very angels and humans He gave life to, the Lord formed His own chosen people through whom the Messiah would come. He chose Abraham, a faithful believer in God, to be the father of that nation, which would later be named Israel.

Abraham was not only a believer but a descendant of Adam, Enoch, Noah, and Shem, a continuation of the line of pure humanity that would eventually lead to the birth of the Messiah, Jesus Christ. The genealogies in the Bible record God's preservation of humanity to ultimately fulfill His plan of salvation through Jesus Christ. Many who study the Nephilim wonder if there is a racial aspect to the Nephilim. Yes, there is: God was preserving one specific race – the *human* race. Israel carried the Holy Seed and would be the messengers of God's Word to the planet. Deuteronomy distinguishes Israel as "God's portion." The nation of Israel was literally the portion of the earth from which God would bring forth His means of redeeming humanity who had fallen under the curse of sin and deception of Satan and his fallen angels. The Lord presented humanity with a choice for their spiritual destiny. The pagan nations put their trust in occult practices and religions (many of which the Nephilim introduced to the world), while the nation of Israel offered the light of God's Word to unbelievers, rescuing them from Satanic influence and Nephilim interbreeding to the hope of living a holy life of belief in the true and living God.

## THE FALLEN ANGELS WHO HAVE DOMINION OVER GENTILE NATIONS WILL BE JUDGED

In Psalm 82, the angels overseeing the 70 nations are rebuked for their wickedness:

> "God standeth in the congregation of the mighty; **he judgeth among the gods**. How long will ye judge unjustly, and accept the persons of the wicked? Selah. Defend the poor and fatherless: do justice to the afflicted and needy. Deliver the poor and needy: rid them out of the hand of the wicked. They know not, neither will they understand; they walk on in darkness: all the foundations of the earth are out of course. I have said, **Ye are gods; and all of you are children of the most High**. But ye shall die like men, and fall like one of the princes. Arise, O God, judge the earth: **for thou shalt inherit all nations**." – Psalm 82

The "gods" are the fallen angels who pledged their allegiance to the Devil before the fall of Adam and Eve in the first wave of angelic revolt. Satan employed these rebels to influence the spiritual state of every nation in the world, except one. And he could use them to launch his assault on God's people and their fledgling country. We find a very clear example of this spiritual warfare in Daniel 10.

## THE ANGELS OF PAGAN NATIONS FIGHT BATTLES WITH HOLY ANGELS OVER THE AFFAIRS OF HUMANITY

In this very interesting chapter, the prophet Daniel is visited by a holy angel in response to his prayers. This angel tells Daniel he was delayed in reaching him by a fallen angel:

"Then I lifted up mine eyes, and looked, and behold a certain man clothed in linen, whose loins were girded with fine gold of Uphaz: His body also was like the beryl, and his face as the appearance of lightning, and his eyes as lamps of fire, and his arms and his feet like in colour to polished brass, and the voice of his words like the voice of a multitude… And he said unto me, O Daniel, a man greatly beloved, understand the words that I speak unto thee, and stand upright: for unto thee am I now sent. And when he had spoken this word unto me, I stood trembling. Then said he unto me, Fear not, Daniel: for from the first day that thou didst set thine heart to understand, and to chasten thyself before thy God, thy words were heard, and I am come for thy words.

But the prince of the kingdom of Persia withstood me one and twenty days: but, lo, Michael, one of the chief princes, came to help me; and I remained there with the kings of Persia. Now I am come to make thee understand what shall befall thy people in the latter days: for yet the vision is for many days... Then said he, Knowest thou wherefore I come unto thee? and now will I return to fight with the prince of Persia: and when I am gone forth, lo, the prince of Grecia shall come. But I will shew thee that which is noted in the scripture of truth: and there is none that holdeth with me in these things, but Michael your prince." – Daniel 10:5–6; 11–14; 20–21

In this passage, the holy angel explains the reason for his delay in bringing his message to Daniel: The "prince of the kingdom of Persia withstood" him. This Prince of Persia was an evil angelic being assigned to spiritually govern the nation of Persia (modern-day Iran) and was literally fighting with the holy angel. It was not until Michael, one of the "chief princes," and clearly more powerful than the two intervened that the holy angel could complete his mission and reach the prophet. Michael is called "your prince," indicating his office as angelic Prince of Israel.

After delivering the prophecy to Daniel, the angel would return to the fight with the Prince of Persia who would eventually be replaced by the "prince of Grecia," accurately prophesying that the Greek empire would succeed Persia as the dominant world power. The key conclusion from this passage is that heavenly beings are indeed assigned to nations and wage battles that directly affect affairs in the human realm.

To form his nation, God called Abraham (then known as Abram) out of the area of "Ur of the Chaldees," the same region where Nimrod began his rebellion. Abraham was to travel to the Land of Canaan, which was God's "portion." Like Noah before him, Abraham was a faithful believer chosen by God. The Lord used one man against the world to carry on the Messianic line that would bring salvation to humanity.

# IN ABRAHAM, SATAN HAD A SINGULAR TARGET TO DESTROY THE HOLY SEED

The fate of the world rested on the shoulders of Abraham, founder of God's nation. But he was not alone, for the Lord would guide and lead him every step of his life. From the Devil's perspective, this provided a new opportunity. Abraham was a lone target Satan could focus on to thwart God's plan. If Satan could somehow corrupt or destroy Abram he would score a major victory. And if he could not corrupt Abraham, the Devil could attack his children. During this same time, the Nephilim-tainted nations were migrating to the land of Canaan, usurping the very place God planned on establishing his country.

# THE LORD DISPATCHED ABRAHAM INTO NEPHILIM TERRITORY

"And Abram passed through the land unto the place of Sichem, unto the plain of Moreh. **And the Canaanite was then in the land**. And the LORD appeared unto Abram, and said, Unto thy seed will I give this land: and there builded he an altar unto the LORD, who appeared unto him." – Genesis 12:6–7

"Go your ways: behold, I send you forth as lambs among wolves." – Jesus Christ, Luke 10:3

In Genesis 12, God descended to Earth to speak to Abram in person, the first such appearance in the Bible. The Lord commissioned Abram to settle in the land of the Canaanites and live among the postdiluvian giants and their rebellious human cohorts. Surrounded by people just punished for rebelling against God, Abram could rely only on the prophetic words of the Lord who assured him that the land he was entering would indeed ultimately be given to him. Abraham demonstrated his faith and gratitude by building an altar in the heart of enemy territory.

In the next city he came to, Bethel (which at that time was named Luz), Abram continued his reliance on God:

> "And he removed from thence unto a mountain on the east of Bethel, and pitched his tent, having Bethel on the west, and Hai on the east: and there he builded an altar unto the LORD, and called upon the name of the LORD." – Genesis 12:8

In constructing this altar, Abraham was planting the flag of God's religion in enemy territory. Just as Noah claimed the renovated earth after leaving the ark, so Abram declared the land of Canaan "God's country." Those who would humbly turn from their sin and seek the Lord would find Him, while the enemies of the Creator were warned that their time was coming to an end.

## SATAN'S ATTEMPT TO CORRUPT ABRAHAM'S MARRIAGE

With Abram's faith growing as he continued to trust and follow the Lord, it took a famine for Satan to seize an opportunity to corrupt the Messianic bloodline:

> "And there was a famine in the land: and Abram went down into Egypt to sojourn there; for the famine was grievous in the land. And it came to pass, when he was come near to enter into Egypt, that he said unto Sarai his wife, Behold now, I know that thou art a fair woman to look upon: Therefore it shall come to pass, when the Egyptians shall see thee, that they shall say, This is his wife: and they will kill me, but they will save thee alive. Say, I pray thee, thou

art my sister: that it may be well with me for thy sake; and my soul shall live because of thee. **And it came to pass, that, when Abram was come into Egypt, the Egyptians beheld the woman that she was very fair. The princes also of Pharaoh saw her, and commended her before Pharaoh: and the woman was taken into Pharaoh's house.** And he entreated Abram well for her sake: and he had sheep, and oxen, and he asses, and menservants, and maidservants, and she asses, and camels." – Genesis 12:11–16

Facing a famine, Abraham made the mistake of not seeking God for a solution. The Lord never told him to go to Egypt. He chose to go on his own initiative. This decision took him away from God's command to inhabit Canaan. The situation only grew worse in Egypt when Abraham, out of fear of Pharaoh, lied and called his wife Sarai his "sister." Satan knew that the prophecy of the Seed of the Woman would be fulfilled through this one man. God narrowed the field and Satan could thus focus his attention on corrupting Abraham. If the lure of pagan worship would not work, Satan would resort to simpler temptations, such as fear. Had Pharaoh taken Sarai as his wife, the prophesied plan of God to bring a nation through Abraham would have been in jeopardy. So, the Lord intervened directly to thwart the Devil's attack:

"**And the LORD plagued Pharaoh and his house with great plagues because of Sarai Abram's wife.** And Pharaoh called Abram and said, What is this that thou hast done unto me? why didst thou not tell me that she was thy wife? Why saidst thou, She is my sister? so I might have taken her to me to wife: now therefore behold thy wife, take her, and go thy way. And Pharaoh commanded his men concerning him: and they sent him away, and his wife, and all that he had." – Genesis 12:17–20

Pharaoh was romantically attracted to Sarah and wanted to make her his wife. But the Lord intervened by striking Pharaoh and all his family with plagues, frightening the Egyptian king completely out of that idea. As is the case throughout Scripture, God intervened directly to protect the Messianic bloodline.

In Genesis 13, the servants of Abram and his nephew Lot were locked in conflict, and the two Hebrew men decided to divide their land and end the strife. Note that in the midst of this labor conflict the Bible introduces another Canaanite nation:

> "And there was a strife between the herdmen of Abram's cattle and the herdmen of Lot's cattle: and the Canaanite and the Perizzite dwelled then in the land. And Abram said unto Lot, Let there be no strife, I pray thee, between me and thee, and between my herdmen and thy herdmen; for we be brethren." – Genesis 13:7–8

This is the first mention in Scripture of the Perizzites, but they are mentioned in later verses when God lists the nations of usurpers from whom Abram would receive the Promised Land (Genesis 15:20). The Canaanites and Perizzites threatened the safety of Abram and Lot. Abram sought a peaceful resolution with Lot appealing to the fact that they were "brethren." The two men were ambassadors of the religion of the true and living God, and quarreling was a terrible witness to the pagan nations of the world and made them vulnerable to attack.

> "And Abram said unto Lot, Let there be no strife, I pray thee, between me and thee, and between my herdmen and thy herdmen; for we be brethren. Is not the whole land before thee? separate thyself, I pray thee, from me: if thou wilt take the left hand, then I will go to the right; or if thou depart to the right hand, then I will go to the left. And Lot lifted up his eyes, and beheld all the plain of Jordan, that it was well watered every where, before the LORD destroyed Sodom and Gomorrah, even as the garden of the LORD,

like the land of Egypt, as thou comest unto Zoar. Then Lot chose him all the plain of Jordan; and Lot journeyed east: and they separated themselves the one from the other. Abram dwelled in the land of Canaan, and Lot dwelled in the cities of the plain, and pitched his tent toward Sodom. But the men of Sodom were wicked and sinners before the LORD exceedingly." – Genesis 13:8–13

This reconciliation reveals the character of Abram. Although he had seniority over Lot and was the possessor of the land and the blessing of the Messianic bloodline, in humility Abram deferred to Lot when it was time to choose the land. Lot, thinking of potential wealth, desired the land in the cities in the plain of Jordan whose appearance was as "the garden of the Lord." This is another confirmation that they were in the area of Eden, which Satan wanted for himself. Sure enough, the inhabitants of Sodom adjacent to Lot's territory were "wicked and sinners before the Lord exceedingly" (Genesis 13:13). Their rebellion, like Nimrod's, was directed against God, and they were going beyond normal human capacity for sin in their behavior. Like Cain and Nimrod before them, they erected cities in which to consolidate the population and multiply sinful rebellion.

"And the LORD said unto Abram, after that Lot was separated from him, Lift up now thine eyes, and look from the place where thou art northward, and southward, and eastward, and westward: For all the land which thou seest, to thee will I give it, and to thy seed for ever. And I will make thy seed as the dust of the earth: so that if a man can number the dust of the earth, then shall thy seed also be numbered. Arise, walk through the land in the length of it and in the breadth of it; for I will give it unto thee. Then Abram removed his tent, and came and dwelt in the plain of Mamre, which is in Hebron, and built there an altar unto the LORD." – Genesis 13:14–18

After Abram made his generous peacemaking gesture with his nephew, God reaffirmed the covenant with him. The patriarch would not only receive the entire Promised Land (which included all of Lot's land as well) but it would also pass on to his "seed." Additionally, Abram's seed would become impossible to number. Abram responded by building an altar of worship to God. This was yet another pronouncement that this very specific individual was carrying the future of the Holy Seed. Abraham, who did not have a child at this time, was literally carrying all humanity's blessed hope within him. And this fact was not lost on Satan who would send the new generation of giants into action.

# CHAPTER 15

# GENESIS 14 – THE NEPHILIM WORLD WAR

"And it came to pass in the days of Amraphel king of Shinar, Arioch king of Ellasar, Chedorlaomer king of Elam, and Tidal king of nations; That these made war with Bera king of Sodom, and with Birsha king of Gomorrah, Shinab king of Admah, and Shemeber king of Zeboiim, and the king of Bela, which is Zoar. All these were joined together in the vale of Siddim, which is the salt sea. Twelve years they served Chedorlaomer, and in the thirteenth year they rebelled." – Genesis 14:1–4

## HUMANS WAGED WAR AGAINST THE POSTDILUVIAN GIANTS

Genesis 14 records the Bible's first major war, fought by two powerful coalitions. King Chedorlaomer led a confederacy of four kings from the north of the Promised Land (near modern-day Lebanon and Iraq) in a campaign against five kings who led vassal states in the southwestern region of the Promised Land, in the area of the Dead Sea. By prior arrangement the vassal states were required to pay tribute to Chedorlaomer, who most likely distributed some of this wealth to the other three kings in his alliance. These types of agreements were a form of "protection money," allowing the inferior five kings to carry on their affairs with no threat of attack from the more powerful King Chedorlaomer and his armies. In year 13 of the agreement, however, the vassal states "rebelled" prompting Chedorlaomer to marshal his forces to battle and punish the vassals. Sandwiched between the five vassal states and their mightier counterparts of the north was a region full of Nephilim giants. As he traveled south to wage war against the King of Sodom and the other cities of the plain, Chedorlaomer would have to do battle with the giants.

Of this battle Josephus wrote:

> "Now every part of the army had its own commander; and when the battle was joined, the Assyrians were conquerors, and imposed a tribute on the kings of the Sodomites, who submitted to this slavery twelve years; and so long they continued to pay their tribute: but on the thirteenth year they rebelled, and then the army of the Assyrians came upon them, under their commanders Amraphel, Arioch, Chodorlaomer, and Tidal. These kings had laid waste all Syria, and overthrown the offspring of the giants." – *Antiquities of the Jews Antiquities of the Jews*, Book I, Chapter 9, Flavius Josephus, as recorded in *The Works of Flavius Josephus*, William Whiston, Vol. 1, 1843, p. 39.

The Genesis 14 world war involved a series of three military campaigns. In the first campaign, Chedorlaomer led his powerful confederacy southwards to attack Sodom. Sodom was the wealthiest and most desirable of the cities of the vassal states of high strategic value. It was an ancient trade hub and metropolis that controlled most of the commerce heading west into ancient Israel. For Chedorlaomer's armies to reach it, however, they would have to pass through Ashteroth Karnaim, the city of Ham and Shaveh Kiriathaim, areas filled with Nephilim. This campaign pitted Chedorlaomer *against the giants of the region*. Humans were waging war against giants.

Chedorlaomer fought victoriously against them:

> "And in the fourteenth year came Chedorlaomer, and the kings that
> were with him, and smote the Rephaims in Ashteroth Karnaim,
> and the Zuzims in Ham, and the Emins in Shaveh Kiriathaim...."
> – Genesis 14:5

## THE POST-FLOOD GIANTS WERE ALL DIFFERENT ETHNIC BRANCHES OF THE REPHAIM

Genesis 14 contains the first reference to Nephilim giants after the Flood.
And the Rephaim, *the dominant tribe of the pre-Flood giants*, receive the first
mention. In the Septuagint, the verse reads:

> "And in the fourteenth year came [Chedorlaomer] the kings with
> him, and cut to pieces the giants [Rephaim] in Astaroth, and
> Carnain, and strong nations with them, and the [Emims] in the
> city Save." – Genesis 14:5 LXX

Scripture confirms that the giants were principal parties in this world war.
Additionally, they were settled due east of the land of Canaan. The Bible
repeatedly confirms that it was Ham's lineage that produced the giant
offspring after the Flood. The location also confirms the territory of the
Rephaim – Ashteroth Karnaim, the same area where Og, one of the final
Rephaim descendants, resided: "Og the king of Bashan, which dwelt at
Astaroth in Edrei" (Deuteronomy 1:4). Genesis 14 confirms the Repahim
lineage survived the Flood. Their genes having passed through the offspring
of Ham and his wife, the Rephaim returned in a genetically diluted, but still
powerful, state. And they were situated on the east bank of the Jordan River,
site of the original descent of their angelic ancestors.

Geographic locations were very important in ancient times. The Lord directed Abraham to specific territories to live and start the nation of Israel. Later in Scripture, God designated sacred locations for the tabernacle and Solomon's temple. Satan, always mimicking the true and living God, does the same for his servants and minions, reserving primary areas for pagan worship and idolatry. The Rephaim descendants acquired this territory after Babel.

## THE ZUZIM GIANTS WERE NEPHILIM DESCENDANTS OF HAM

Ham's offspring usurped the Promised Land to such an extent that a city was called "Ham." Genesis 14 helps us understand the ethnic groups of the post-Flood Nephilim. Genetically, **they were all Rephaim**. But after the Tower of Babel dispersal and the development of numerous languages, the postdiluvian giants received different ethnic titles based on where they migrated to and the people they mingled with. Johnathan Gill's *Exposition of the Bible* says of this people:

> "They are thought to be the same with the Zuzims in (Genesis 14:5) who had their name, as Hillerus [F3] thinks, from Mezuzah, a door post, from their tall stature, being as high as one; and for a like reason Saph the giant might have his name, (2 Samuel 21:18). The word Zamzummims, according to him, signifies contrivers of evil and terrible things; they were inventors of wickedness, crafty and subtle in forming wicked and mischievous designs, which struck terror into people, and made them formidable to them." - http://www.studylight.org/commentaries/geb/genesis-14.html

The Zuzims were also called Zamzummims. Deuteronomy 2 helps clear up the identities of these various giant tribes. With respect to the Zuzims or Zamzummims we read:

"That also was accounted a land of giants [repahaim]: giants dwelt therein in old time; and the Ammonites call them Zamzummims; A people great, and many, and tall, as the Anakims; but the LORD destroyed them before them; and they succeeded them, and dwelt in their stead...." – Deuteronomy 2:20–21

An early-20th-century commentary confirms:

"Probably the same as the Zamzummim according to the archaeological note Dt ii 20 21 the Ammonite name of a giant people the original inhabitants of the region NE of the Dead Sea afterwards occupied by the Ammonites. (Not mentioned elsewhere but conjectured from the context to have been the ancient name of the Ammonite capital Rabbath Ammon [2 Samuel 12:26], [25 miles NE] of the upper end of the Dead Sea.)" – *The Book of Genesis, with Introduction and Notes*, S.R. Driver, D.D., Second Edition, Printed by Methuen & Co. 36 Essex Street, W.C., London, 1904, p. 160.

Like the Anakim, the Zuzims or Zamzummims were Rephaim. They were dispersed among the territory of the Ammonites, who in their own language called them "Zuzims." Their unique titles were just a shorthand reference from the local culture they lived in. Many studies on the Nephilim describe the Anakim, Zuzims, Emims, and other giant groups as if they were all separate races with no relation to each other. On the contrary, these giants were descendants of the same stock – Rephaim. Because of the forced division of nations and tongues after the Babel incident, the various Nephilim remnants were called by different ethnic titles based on where they settled and the language or dialect of that particular area. Those still called Rephaim proper represented the most ethnically pure of the giants born after the Flood through Canaan, and their demise is specifically noted in Scripture (Deuteronomy 3).

# A NOTE ON THE OUTRAGEOUS "NEPHILIM WERE AFRICAN OR BLACK" THEORIES

The Zuzims lived in Ham, which scholars believe was the early name of the Ammonite capital Rabbath. This city was located due east of the Jordan River and Israel. Many authors, pastors, and Bible teachers claim that after Noah's family left the ark, Ham went directly to north and central Africa. This notion is then used to conclude that the major racial groups emerged in the world (with Ham being the father of all people of African descent). There is absolutely no support for this contention in Scripture, which nowhere mentions Ham in Africa. This notion is further refuted by **the fact that shortly after the Flood the entire global population** lived together and no doubt married one another in Babel (Genesis 11). All the races of humanity lived among each other for generations before the Lord dispersed them after the Tower of Babel's destruction. And in that division the Lord assigned languages to people randomly, not according to their ethnicity or family. So, any notion that Noah's three sons divided the world by racial lines is false.

Ham and his children (particularly Canaan) occupied what today is the Middle East, and his descendants were heavily populated in the same area. Ham's son Cush did eventually occupy north Africa and what is now Ethiopia. The notion that Ham was the "black child of Noah" is biblically inaccurate. Israel, Jordan, Lebanon, Iran, and Iraq are all modern nations that were originally populated by Ham's descendants after the Flood. While most who teach the "Ham went to Africa" theory have no ill intent, sadly this notion has been used to perpetuate the idea that the Nephilim were Africans and therefore that people of African descent are cursed and a host of other wildly heretical, bigoted ideas.

# THE EMIMS – THE REPHAIM
# WHO DWELLED IN MOAB

Deuteronomy 2 describes these giants: "The Emims dwelt therein in times past, a people great, and many, and tall, as the Anakims; *Which also were accounted giants [rapha], as the Anakims*; but the Moabites called them Emims." The term Emim in Hebrew means "terrible ones," reflecting the fear and fright these giant beings inspired in their enemies. A 20th-century theologian wrote of the Emims:

> "The word here rendered 'tall,' may also be translated 'haughty,' or great in their own estimation. The passage is suggestive of the awe-inspiring character of these Nephilim, who, although they were dispossessed and probably exterminated by the more numerous descendants of Moab, yet produced such an impression upon the conquerors that they could record them by no other names than the 'terrible ones.' Concerning them we are told in the Writings that they 'were of a similar kind to the Nephilim.'" – *Correspondences of Canaan: A Study of the Spiritual Geography and History of the Land and Nations of the Word*, Carl Theophilus Odhner, Academy Book Room, Bryn Athyn, PA, 1911, p. 58.

Like the Zuzims, the Emims were also "accounted Rapha" or Rephaim (which is the Hebrew plural of *rapha*). In the Moabite language they were called "Emim" and, not surprising, they were of the same height as the Anakim. The Emims were yet another group of giants who settled in an area near the Jordan River.

The Zuzims and Emims were both considered "great people." The post-Flood giants were the preeminent tribes in Abraham's day, and conquering them was no small feat. But as Scripture demonstrates, most of these tribes were killed by God Himself:

"And when thou comest nigh over against the children of Ammon, distress them not, nor meddle with them: for I will not give thee of the land of the children of Ammon any possession; because I have given it unto the children of Lot for a possession. (That also was accounted a land of giants: giants dwelt therein in old time; **and the Ammonites call them Zamzummims; A people great, and many, and tall, as the Anakims; but the LORD destroyed them before them**; and they succeeded them, and dwelt in their stead: As he did to the children of Esau, which dwelt in Seir, **when he destroyed the Horims from before them**; and they succeeded them, and dwelt in their stead even unto this day...." – Deuteronomy 2:19–22

When it came to conquering the Nephilim, the Lord repeatedly took matters into His own hands. God demonstrated His position as the true and living God and creator of all by single-handedly wiping out the post-Flood Nephilim. According to one commentary:

"We have here again another instance of the way in which the Shemites were especially favoured. The Moabites and Ammonites being descendants of Lot were permitted to destroy the Hamites who occupied the land before them and even received especial assistance from God to enable them to do what otherwise would have been impossible for them." – *Cambridge Essays, Vol. 4*, John W. Parker, Cambridge University, 1858, p. 142.

In Genesis 14 Chedorlaomer was God's tool to exact punishment on the Nephilim who lived north of Sodom and Gomorrah. From the details provided in Scripture, however, God had already vanquished most of the giants before the Genesis 14 war even commenced.

# THE AMORITES

The Amorites were a powerful Nephilim-infested nation. In the book of Amos, recalling the victory over the Amorites during the days of Moses, the Lord said through the prophet Amos: "Yet destroyed I the *Amorite before them, whose height was like the height of the cedars, and he was strong as the oaks*; yet I destroyed his fruit from above, and his roots from beneath" (Amos 2:9).

The description of their massive height came *from God*, not a human observing the Amorites. And once again the Lord personally intervened to conquer them. Also note in this passage that God *compares the Amorites to cedar trees* – the same tree used in Ezekiel 31 to describe the Assyrian, the antediluvian king who fathered a Nephilim empire.

The lineage of the Amorites is stated clearly in Genesis 10: "And Canaan begat Sidon his first born, and Heth, And the Jebusite, and the Amorite…" (Genesis 10:15–16). The Amorites were direct descendants of Canaan. **Scripture provides a very clear lineage for all the giants after the Flood that can be traced back to Canaan.**

# CHEDORLAOMER WIPED OUT THE NEPHILIM AND CONQUERED SODOM

The Nephilim giants, dwelling at this time in the area north of Sodom and Gomorrah, were slaughtered by Chedorlaomer, Amraphel, and their four-king confederacy as they headed south to deal with the rebellious vassal states. This powerful coalition wiped out scores of giants on their march to Sodom, evidence of the overwhelming military forces at their disposal. After the slaughter of the Nephilim giants and the four vassal kings, a second campaign took place:

> "And they returned, and came to Enmishpat, which is Kadesh, and smote all the country of the Amalekites, and also the Amorites, that

> dwelt in Hazezontamar. And there went out the king of Sodom, and the king of Gomorrah, and the king of Admah, and the king of Zeboiim, and the king of Bela (the same is Zoar;) and they joined battle with them in the vale of Siddim; With Chedorlaomer the king of Elam, and with Tidal king of nations, and Amraphel king of Shinar, and Arioch king of Ellasar; four kings with five." – Genesis 14:7–9

With their Nephilim protectors defeated, the vassal kings were forced to enter the battle with Chedorlaomer's forces. And like the giants before them, the vassal kings were easily conquered:

> "And the vale of Siddim was full of slimepits; and the kings of Sodom and Gomorrah fled, and fell there; and they that remained fled to the mountain. And they took all the goods of Sodom and Gomorrah, and all their victuals, and went their way. And they took Lot, Abram's brother's son, who dwelt in Sodom, and his goods, and departed." – Genesis 14:10–12

In the conquest of Sodom, Lot was kidnapped. His hasty decision to take the profitable land near Sodom had proved a grave error. But God, ever merciful, provided a means of rescue for Abram's nephew:

> "And there came one that had escaped, and told Abram the Hebrew; for he dwelt in the plain of Mamre the Amorite, brother of Eshcol, and brother of Aner: and these were confederate with Abram. $^{14}$ And when Abram heard that his brother was taken captive, he armed his trained servants, born in his own house, three hundred and eighteen, and pursued them unto Dan." – Genesis 14:13–14

# WITH THE LORD'S SUPERNATURAL ASSISTANCE, ABRAHAM NEEDED ONLY 318 MEN TO DEFEAT THE MIGHTY CHEDORLAOMER

Unlike the frightened man he was in Egypt, Abraham sprang into action. This is the great theme of this very mysterious chapter in Scripture. Chedorlaomer commanded a massive army that ran roughshod through the Middle East, slaughtering Nephilim and human alike. Despite these odds, Abraham attacked this entire coalition with just 318 men! Abraham armed only his trained servants "born in his own house" (an indication that they were raised as believers in the true and living God) for the third and climactic battle of this chapter:

> "And he [Abram] divided himself against them, he and his servants, by night, and smote them, and pursued them unto Hobah, which is on the left hand of Damascus. And he brought back all the goods, and also brought again his brother Lot, and his goods, and the women also, and the people. And the king of Sodom went out to meet him after his return from the slaughter of Chedorlaomer, and of the kings that were with him, at the valley of Shaveh, which is the king's dale." – Genesis 14:15–17

Abraham and his small band of man divided into separate units and launched a late-night raid in the heart of Chedorlaomer's territory. The trek to rescue Lot was over 100 miles. Upon their arrival, they massacred Chedorlaomer and all of his allies. How did they do this? Was it Abraham's brilliant military strategy? Was it his newfound courage in the face of adversity? Scripture provides the answer and a very important theme for our study:

> "And Melchizedek king of Salem brought forth bread and wine: and he was the priest of the most high God. And he blessed him, and said, Blessed be Abram of the most high God, possessor of

heaven and earth: **And blessed be the most high God, which hath delivered thine enemies into thy hand.** And he gave him tithes of all." – Genesis 14:18–20

Abraham won because God fought for him. As is the case throughout Scripture, whenever Nephilim were involved, *the Lord personally intervened in battles* to ensure their destruction. This of course is a picture of salvation as Jesus Christ, the promised Seed of the Woman, went to battle for all humanity on the cross – defeating Satan, sin, and the grave once and for all. It is very important to keep this theme in mind. God provided the Flood. God fought for Abram. And God continued to fulfill the prophecy by personally waging war against the Nephilim until they were extinct.

Genesis 14 also highlights a major reason God even permitted the Nephilim gene to survive on the ark. Humans are responsible for their own sinful decisions and thus bear their consequences. Sinful Ham *knew* what the stakes were when it came to choosing a wife before the Flood, and in his sinful arrogance he chose badly. Thus, Canaan clearly carried the gene. The return of the giants after the Flood also served as a witness to the unbelieving world. To the newly-formed postdiluvian nations, the Nephilim represented "gods on Earth." They were feared supermen among their human counterparts. So, when such mighty creatures were defeated by a small, rag-tag army it served as proof that God truly was on the side of those who believed in Him.

Abraham lived in a time before a written Bible existed. The Nephilim giants provided opportunities for God to demonstrate to the world time and time again that He was Lord of all. To quote Melchizedek, the Lord truly was "possessor of Heaven and Earth." The situation in Abraham's day appeared bleak for the Messianic bloodline. All the nations of the world were under rule of rebel angels. Nephilim giants were running rampant in the very land God promised to Abram. But the Lord was still on the throne and proved His authority and power over all these corrupted beings.

After this battle, Abraham came to a greater understanding of this:

"And the king of Sodom said unto Abram, Give me the persons, and take the goods to thyself. And Abram said to the king of Sodom, I have lift up mine hand unto the LORD, the most high God, the possessor of heaven and earth, That I will not take from a thread even to a shoelatchet, and that I will not take any thing that is thine, lest thou shouldest say, I have made Abram rich…." – Genesis 14:21–23

This was the first time Abram referred to the Lord as *El Elyon*, "the most high God," a declaration that of all the "gods" running around the earth at that time there was one Supreme God, the creator of all. Abram understood that depending wholly on God and not on the riches and power of this world was the way to salvation. He understood that the Lord would always provide a way for His people, and that ultimate way was the coming Messiah.

By now it should be apparent that the threat of Nephilim was very real for Abram, his wife, and future children. Rather than being obscure, fringe characters in Scripture, the giants were spread out in abundance throughout the Promised Land and played an important role in sacred history. They were tools in Satan's plot to undo God's plan of redemption.

Abram understood the important truth that the God of the Bible had power over all the Nephilim giants, fallen angels, and rebellious unbelieving humans. This would be a critical lesson for the people of Israel and for all who choose to follow God: Do you believe God's Word, or do you follow your own opinions? When trials come, do you cling to the truths of the Bible, or do you let your own philosophies, justifications, and "worldly wisdom" guide your decisions? Abram chose to trust God, and in this process the Lord was preparing Him to be the father of His nation. Shortly after Abram rescued Lot, the Lord promised Abram a future nation and homeland.

# GOD DECLARED ABRAHAM'S SEED RIGHTFUL HEIR OF THE LAND OF CANAAN

> "In the same day the LORD made a covenant with Abram, saying, Unto thy seed have I given this land, from the river of Egypt unto the great river, the river Euphrates: **The Kenites, and the Kenizzites, and the Kadmonites, And the Hittites, and the Perizzites, and the Rephaims, And the Amorites, and the Canaanites, and the Girgashites, and the Jebusites.**" – Genesis 15:18–21

The foundation was laid. With the whole world under the influence of false gods and idol worship, the true God established His own nation – *not* from the scattered pieces of the failed Tower of Babel global government but from one faithful man. And the Lord was going to place His country in His chosen area of the planet, which at that time happened to be the exact location where the giants had settled. The Nephilim had usurped the Promised Land, but God was going to restore it to Abraham and the Messianic bloodline after 400 years of occupation. During this time, the Nephilim would continue in their iniquity, filling the land with violence, until God saw fit to judge them with destruction.

The Lord prophesied that Abraham's descendants would form a great nation. In this prophecy God warned Abraham that his descendants would be strangers in lands that were not theirs and eventually suffer in bondage for 400 years before coming into their Promised Land. This sentence of slavery was fulfilled both in Canaan (which was not Abram's possession at the time; he was still a pilgrim there) and in Egypt, where the nation of Israel lived during the days of Joseph until the Exodus. God then promised that the Israelites would be provided for once they came out of their 400-year sojourn:

> "And also that nation, whom they shall serve, will I judge: and afterward shall they come out with great substance. And thou shalt

go to thy fathers in peace; thou shalt be buried in a good old age. But in the fourth generation they shall come hither again: for the iniquity of the Amorites is not yet full." – Genesis 15:14–16

This was fulfilled at the Exodus as the Israelites left with much gold, silver, and valuables from the Egyptian people. As they approached the Promised Land, it was the Amorites, whom God compared to cedars, under the leader of their Nephilim giant leader King Sihon, who were the initial aggressors trying to prevent their entry. Thus, the Nephilim nations were the main opposition to the Promised Land and the promised "seed of the woman" who would redeem humanity and defeat Satan. The battle lines were clearly drawn.

1 Peter 5:8 says of Satan: "Be sober, be vigilant; because your adversary the devil, as a roaring lion, walketh about, seeking whom he may devour."

## ABRAHAM FELL INTO SIN
## TRYING TO FULFILL THE PROPHECY

After trying to fulfill the prophecy "his own way" by impregnating Hagar, his maid, Abraham was reassured by God that he would indeed have a son with his wife, Sarah, despite their advanced ages (99 and 90 years old, respectively). This was God's original stated plan, and it *would* be fulfilled. In Genesis 17, God confirmed the covenant of the promised "seed" with Abraham:

> "And I will establish my covenant between me and thee and thy seed after thee in their generations for an everlasting covenant, to be a God unto thee, and to thy seed after thee. And I will give unto thee, and to thy seed after thee, the land wherein thou art a stranger, all the land of Canaan, for an everlasting possession; and I will be their God. And God said unto Abraham, Thou shalt keep my covenant therefore, thou, and thy seed after thee in their generations." – Genesis 17:7–9

The Promised Seed would indeed come through Abraham and his wife, Sarah. Circumcision was then instituted as a sign of the covenant for all the males in Abraham's lineage, again showing a separation between those who are of God and those who are of the heathen world.

## AN OATH TO PROTECT THE MESSIANIC BLOODLINE

"And Abraham was old, and well stricken in age: and the LORD had blessed Abraham in all things. And Abraham said unto his eldest servant of his house, that ruled over all that he had, Put, I pray thee, thy hand under my thigh: **And I will make thee swear by the LORD, the God of heaven, and the God of the earth, that thou shalt not take a wife unto my son of the daughters of the Canaanites, among whom I dwell: But thou shalt go unto my country, and to my kindred, and take a wife unto my son Isaac.**

And the servant said unto him, Peradventure the woman will not be willing to follow me unto this land: must I needs bring thy son again unto the land from whence thou camest? And Abraham said unto him, Beware thou that thou bring not my son thither again. the Lord God of heaven, which took me from my father's house, and from the land of my kindred, and which spake unto me, and that sware unto me, saying, Unto thy seed will I give this land; he shall send his angel before thee, and thou shalt take a wife unto my son from thence. And if the woman will not be willing to follow thee, then thou shalt be clear from this my oath: only bring not my son thither again. And the servant put his hand under the thigh of Abraham his master, and sware to him concerning that matter." – Genesis 24:1–9

In his final days of his life, Abraham made sure that his son Isaac, a child of divine promise, would not marry any Canaanite woman potentially carrying the Nephilim gene. Abraham was adamant in his instructions to Eleazer. Isaac was the key figure in the Messianic bloodline. The importance of Isaac in the world at that time cannot be overstated. His life and progeny were critical to the salvation of humanity. Abraham took this so seriously that he made his servant take an oath. Eleazer knew that Abraham was one of the few men on Earth who spoke to the Lord directly, so defying an oath with him was a very grave matter.

Abraham informed the servant that the angel of the Lord would go ahead of him to make the "bride search" successful. Once again, when it came to preserving the Holy Seed, God was directly involved. Abraham left nothing to chance and made sure that the potential bride would come from his own family, ensuring the Messianic bloodline would not be mingled with the Nephilim DNA of the Canaanites.

## ARBA – FATHER OF THE ANAKIM GIANTS

"And Sarah was an hundred and seven and twenty years old: these were the years of the life of Sarah. **And Sarah died in Kirjatharba; the same is Hebron in the land of Canaan**: and Abraham came to mourn for Sarah, and to weep for her." – Genesis 23:1–2

Sarah's death, a sad moment in Abraham's life, also gives more insight into the origin of the post-Flood Nephilim. She died in the city of Hebron, a very famous city in the Bible. Moses, the author of the book of Genesis, was sure to include the historical name of the city, which was Kirjatharba, which literally means "the city of Arba" or "the city of four." Arba was one of the oldest of the post-Flood Nephilim giants. The book of Joshua confirms that Arba was the father of this Nephilim bloodline:

> "And unto Caleb the son of Jephunneh he gave a part among the
> children of Judah, according to the commandment of the LORD to
> Joshua, **even the city of Arba the father of Anak, which city is
> Hebron.**" – Joshua 15:13

Though Arba was a "great man" among his giant family (Joshua 15:13), it was
his son Anak who would rename their Rephaim lineage "Anakim." In Genesis
14, the Anakim were the ethnic Nephilim group by which the other giant tribes
were compared. A 19th-century commentary on Arba's lineage stated:

> "That the Anakim were Nephilim is evident from the words 'sons of
> Anak which came of the Nephilim.' Now the father of Anak was Arba,
> or Arbah (Josh xv 13 xxi 11 Deut ix 2 Gen xxxv 27) and it is not a little
> remarkable that the Palestinian branch of the Nephilim were not called
> 'Arbahim' after him, but 'Anakim' after his son Anak. This cannot be
> accounted for by the supposition that Arba was not a person of
> consequence; for Joshua tells us (xiv 15) he was a 'great man' and
> moreover the chief city of the Anakim was named after him – Kirjath
> Arba. It can be accounted for only by the fact that the Anakim were
> not the children of Adam…." – *Genesis in Advance of Present Science –
> A Critical Investigation into Chapters I to IX*, Keegan Paul, Published
> by Trench & Company, 1883, pp. 268–269.

In all the descriptions of the postdiluvian giants, *there is no mention of angels'
having relations with women.* After the Flood, the giants who descended from
Ham gave birth to more genetically-diluted giants. This is how their bloodline
carried on. All postdiluvian giants were born "of giants," meaning their fathers
themselves were Nephilim. There are no recorded instances in Scripture of
angels' ever again attempting to take humans as wives. John Fleming's
commentary on the Nephilim, one of the most instructive books of the 19th
century on this topic, supports this idea:

"We entirely coincide in the opinion of those who think that, only for such a purpose, and only in consequence of the existence of an evil so extraordinary, would a remedy like that of the Deluge have been resorted to. A visitation, more limited in extent, and less terrible in its effects, would, otherwise, have probably appeared sufficient, in the view of the Supreme. The intention of Jehovah, of course was not to be frustrated: and hence we are compelled to reject the notion, that a like connexion [sp], between angelic and human beings, was formed in the period which succeeded the Flood." – *The Fallen Angels and the Heroes of Mythology*, Rev. John Fleming A.B., Dublin: Hodges, Foster, & Figgis, pp. 108–109.

"But though the Giants were destroyed the gigantic RACE(sp) remained. The children of the original Giants were Giants like their fathers: they were the grandsons of Angels – Giants at one remove – less by one degree than their parents, but greater by far than ordinary men. The heavenly blood still circulated in their veins and from them it was transmitted to posterity." – *The Last Vials: Being a Series of Essays Upon the Second Advent*, No. X, 22nd year, Sept. 1st, Robert A. Purdon, 1867, p. 6.

Anak, the son of Arba, begat more Nephilim who would play a major role in Israel under Moses' leadership, falling into sin and divine punishment. These postdiluvian giants were deadly adversaries in one of the most pivotal moments in the Old Testament. And their original home city, Hebron, would become one of the most important cities in the history of ancient Israel. Again, the impact of the Nephilim on biblical history cannot be overstated. Time and again, the giants threatened the survival of the human race, and the Lord, in His great love for all people, defeated them.

# CHAPTER 16

# KILL THE HEIR – TAKE THE INHERITANCE

"Hear another parable: There was a certain householder, which planted a vineyard, and hedged it round about, and digged a winepress in it, and built a tower, and let it out to husbandmen, and went into a far country: And when the time of the fruit drew near, he sent his servants to the husbandmen, that they might receive the fruits of it. And the husbandmen took his servants, and beat one, and killed another, and stoned another. Again, he sent other servants more than the first: and they did unto them likewise. But last of all he sent unto them his son, saying, They will reverence my son.

**But when the husbandmen saw the son, they said among themselves, This is the heir; come, let us kill him, and let us seize on his inheritance.** And they caught him, and cast him out of the vineyard, and slew him. When the lord therefore of the vineyard cometh, what will he do unto those husbandmen? They say unto him, **He will miserably destroy those wicked men, and will let out his vineyard unto other husbandmen, which shall render him the fruits in their seasons.**" – Jesus Christ, Matthew 21:33–41

In the above parable, the Lord Jesus Christ gave insight into the mentality of Satan and his wicked kingdom. Their plan, with respect to the Messianic bloodline, was to destroy anyone who proclaimed it and eliminate the heirs in the divine lineage any moment the opportunity arose. The Lord identified the sinful objective of their scheming: to "seize on his inheritance." In the days of Abraham, God made the stunning proclamation that the Messiah would come through Abraham's lineage. Satan had a specific target to focus on to prevent the prophecy's fulfillment. The cosmic war entered its next round.

## ISAAC ENDURED SPIRITUAL ATTACKS AGAINST THE MESSIANIC BLOODLINE

Isaac continued the Messianic lineage and was blessed by God. He was a faithful believer like his father, Abraham, and married a woman from Abraham's extended family, avoiding any genetic contamination. But trouble was on the horizon with his sons. After Isaac prayed to the Lord for his wife Rebekah to conceive, God prophesied the future of the twins she carried:

> "And the LORD said unto her, Two nations are in thy womb, and two manner of people shall be separated from thy bowels; **and the one people shall be stronger than the other people; and the elder shall serve the younger.**" – Genesis 25:23

Just as Canaan was prophesied to serve Shem and Japheth, so Esau, Isaac's eldest son, was cursed through a similar prophecy. After God's pronouncement it should have been evident to Isaac that Esau was going to be a source of trouble in some form. Rather than being cautious about his oldest son, however, Isaac favored him above Jacob (Genesis 25:28). When they were young men, Jacob, the heir to the prophecy, persuaded a famished Esau to sell him his birthright, which Esau agreed to, essentially for a meal

(Genesis 25:33). Esau's casual attitude towards the fate of humanity and the salvation of his own soul revealed his character. This was someone Satan could truly use.

## OUT OF FEAR ISAAC RISKED ANOTHER MAN TAKING REBEKAH JUST AS ABRAHAM DID WITH SARAH

In Genesis 26 another famine struck the land of Canaan, and Isaac took his family to the kingdom of Abimelech of the Philistines for provision. Here Isaac committed the same sin his father had and lied for fear that someone would violently take his wife from him:

> "And the men of the place asked him of his wife; and he said, She is my sister: for he feared to say, She is my wife; lest, said he, the men of the place should kill me for Rebekah; because she was fair to look upon. And it came to pass, when he had been there a long time, that Abimelech king of the Philistines looked out at a window, and saw, and, behold, Isaac was sporting with Rebekah his wife. And Abimelech called Isaac, and said, Behold, of a surety she is thy wife; and how saidst thou, She is my sister? And Isaac said unto him, Because I said, Lest I die for her. And Abimelech said, What is this thou hast done unto us? one of the people might lightly have lien with thy wife, and thou shouldest have brought guiltiness upon us. And Abimelech charged all his people, saying, He that toucheth this man or his wife shall surely be put to death." – Genesis 26:7–11

# GOD USED ISAAC TO REVEAL
# HIMSELF TO THE UNBELIEVING WORLD

Crisis averted, God then demonstrated His sovereignty to the Philistines through Isaac's supernatural prosperity:

> "Then Isaac sowed in that land, and received in the same year an hundredfold: and the LORD blessed him. And the man waxed great, and went forward, and grew until he became very great: … And the LORD appeared unto him the same night, and said, I am the God of Abraham thy father: fear not, for I am with thee, and will bless thee, and multiply thy seed for my servant Abraham's sake. And he builded an altar there, and called upon the name of the LORD, and pitched his tent there: and there Isaac's servants digged a well.
>
> Then Abimelech went to him from Gerar, and Ahuzzath one of his friends, and Phichol the chief captain of his army. And Isaac said unto them, Wherefore come ye to me, seeing ye hate me, and have sent me away from you? **And they said, We saw certainly that the LORD was with thee**: and we said, Let there be now an oath betwixt us, even betwixt us and thee, and let us make a covenant with thee; That thou wilt do us no hurt, as we have not touched thee, and as we have done unto thee nothing but good, and have sent thee away in peace: **thou art now the blessed of the LORD.**"
> – Genesis 26:12–13; 24–29

The Lord uses His faithful to witness to the world. In less than a year, Isaac's agricultural wealth and substance was so great that even the king acknowledged this man of God was more powerful than he. And by the end of the chapter, the Philistine king recognized Isaac as truly being the heir to the covenant of Abraham and "blessed of the Lord." This was the second aspect of the mission of the godly lineage: They were bearing witness to the

Gospel of Jesus Christ in the ancient world. The Lord was not restricting salvation to Abraham's family, for the Messiah would ultimately reconcile all humanity back to God (2 Corinthians 5:19). Any human who put his or her faith and trust in the Seed of the Woman had God's supernatural power manifesting in his or her life – even among the Philistines.

## ESAU'S SINS AGAINST ISAAC WERE A REMINDER OF CAIN'S EVIL WAYS

The Devil, of course, made a counterstrike through Esau. Having sold his birthright for a hot meal, Esau was lured into further sinful rebellion. Esau "despised his birthright" and was not truly a believer (Genesis 25:34). The loss of his birthright led him to a hatred of Jacob that drove Esau into sins similar to those of Cain's family before the Flood.

> "And Esau was forty years old when he took to wife Judith the daughter of Beeri the Hittite, and Bashemath the daughter of Elon the Hittite: Which were a grief of mind unto Isaac and to Rebekah." – Genesis 26:34–35

After all the effort Abraham made to keep his family from any involvement with the Nephilim-infested pagan nations, Esau married *two* daughters of Canaan. His parents were grieved at this development.

Though he was the firstborn of Isaac, Esau had no respect for the Lord as we see clearly in his blatant sin, which endangered the entire Messianic bloodline. From this point, the line leading to the Savior could not continue through him.

# REBEKAH DECEIVED ISAAC TO
# PROTECT THE HOLY SEED

Jacob disguised himself as Esau to receive the Abrahamic blessing from his father, Isaac, who by then was elderly and senile and unable to tell that the disguised Jacob was not Esau, the son he intended to bless. Isaac preferred Esau over Jacob and let his own thinking get in the way of the Lord's plan. God intended and prophesied to Isaac that Jacob would receive the blessing, even though he was the younger of the two sons.

In his later years Isaac lost his zeal for the Messianic bloodline. His foolish favoritism jeopardized the plan of salvation. But his wife, Rebekah, had not forgotten Jacob, who was *her* favorite son. Although such a preference was a selfish motivation, it did embolden her to deceive Isaac into mistaking Jacob for Esau and giving him the inherited blessing.

Although Rebekah and Isaac's scheme was deceitful, it served ultimately to fulfill God's plan. The Lord had announced to Rebekah from the time she was pregnant with the twins that Esau would serve his younger brother, Jacob, so she knew that God intended Jacob to receive the blessing. The result of this deception was that Esau's hatred of Jacob turned homicidal.

> "And Esau hated Jacob because of the blessing wherewith his father blessed him: and Esau said in his heart, The days of mourning for my father are at hand; then will I slay my brother Jacob. And these words of Esau her elder son were told to Rebekah: and she sent and called Jacob her younger son, and said unto him, Behold, thy brother Esau, as touching thee, doth comfort himself, purposing to kill thee. Now therefore, my son, obey my voice; arise, flee thou to Laban my brother to Haran; And tarry with him a few days, until thy brother's fury turn away;
>
> Until thy brother's anger turn away from thee, and he forget that which thou hast done to him: then I will send, and fetch thee from

thence: why should I be deprived also of you both in one day? And Rebekah said to Isaac, I am weary of my life because of the daughters of Heth: if Jacob take a wife of the daughters of Heth, such as these which are of the daughters of the land, what good shall my life do me?" – Genesis 27:41–46

Esau was prepared to murder his own brother for stealing his blessing. He planned this even though from the time Noah and his family exited the ark (Genesis 9) God instituted a death penalty for anyone who shed blood. This is why in verse 45 Rebekah tells Jacob that if Esau were to kill him, she would lose both sons "in one day." By law, a relative would be fully authorized to execute Esau on sight as a punishment for killing Jacob. Thus Esau, again knowing the future of humanity rested in his family, was willing to kill Jacob and then be killed even though neither of them had offspring who could carry on the Messianic bloodline. Satan had so filled this family with personal animosity and deceit that they were on the brink of mutual destruction.

Rebekah wisely sent Jacob to relatives in Haran where he could hide out from his wicked brother. But her worries were not over for there was the possibility of Jacob marrying a "daughter of Heth," another term for a Hittite. If Jacob made the same error as his brother, Esau, the Holy Seed would be jeopardized. Rebekah emphasized the gravity of the situation by saying her life would be utterly pointless if this took place. In her confession, we see a picture of the need for salvation in Christ. Truly, there is no point in life if one is not a part of the Messiah, which is achieved through faith in Christ for the forgiveness of sins. We are wise not to let these Old Testament statements on salvation be forgotten in antiquity because they certainly apply for all people today.

It was probably also not lost on Rebekah that this was precisely the tactic Satan employed against Eve when he pitted the evil Cain against his brother, Abel, leading to Abel's death and Cain's exile. The Devil often repeats the same tactics to lure humanity into sinful rebellion against the Lord.

In Genesis 28, Isaac finally took Rebekah's concern for the Messianic bloodline seriously:

> "And Isaac called Jacob, and blessed him, and charged him, and said unto him, **Thou shalt not take a wife of the daughters of Canaan.** Arise, go to Padanaram, to the house of Bethuel thy mother's father; and take thee a wife from thence of the daughters of Laban thy mother's brother. And God Almighty bless thee, and make thee fruitful, and multiply thee, that thou mayest be a multitude of people; And give thee the blessing of Abraham, to thee, and to thy seed with thee; that thou mayest inherit the land wherein thou art a stranger, which God gave unto Abraham. And Isaac sent away Jacob: and he went to Padanaram unto Laban, son of Bethuel the Syrian, the brother of Rebekah, Jacob's and Esau's mother. When Esau saw that Isaac had blessed Jacob, and sent him away to Padanaram, to take him a wife from thence; and that as he blessed him he gave him a charge, saying, Thou shalt not take a wife of the daughters of Canaan; And that Jacob obeyed his father and his mother, and was gone to Padanaram...." – Genesis 28:1–7

## GOD CONFIRMED THE MESSIANIC BLESSING WOULD PASS TO JACOB

Isaac, back in line with God's plans, charged Jacob not to take a wife from any of the offspring or nation of Canaan. He then sent him back to the house of Laban, his mother's extended family. With this command, Isaac blessed Jacob again with the Abrahamic blessing to receive the Promised Land and carry on the lineage to salvation. Although this would be the last time Jacob would ever see his mother, Rebekah's desire to spend time with her son paled in comparison to her duty to carry out God's will. The passage closes with a second charge from Isaac not take a wife from the Canaanites. Jacob was to avoid infiltration by the Nephilim bloodline at all costs. Jacob was willing to do anything in his power to obtain the birthright and blessings of the Lord. As he went to Padanaram in obedience to his righteous parents, he had a supernatural encounter:

> "And Jacob went out from Beersheba, and went toward Haran. And he lighted upon a certain place, and tarried there all night, because the sun was set; and he took of the stones of that place, and put them for his pillows, and lay down in that place to sleep. And he dreamed, and behold a ladder set up on the earth, and the top of it reached to heaven: and behold the angels of God ascending and descending on it. And, behold, the LORD stood above it, and said, I am the LORD God of Abraham thy father, and the God of Isaac: the land whereon thou liest, to thee will I give it, and to thy seed;
>
> And thy seed shall be as the dust of the earth, and thou shalt spread abroad to the west, and to the east, and to the north, and to the south: and in thee and in thy seed shall all the families of the earth be blessed. And, behold, I am with thee, and will keep thee in all places whither thou goest, and will bring thee again into this land; for I will not leave thee, until I have done that which I have spoken to thee of. And Jacob awaked out of his sleep, and he said, Surely the LORD is in this place; and I knew it not. And he was afraid, and said, How dreadful is this place! this is none other but the house of God, and this is the gate of heaven." – Genesis 28:10–17

In his dream, Jacob witnessed a supernatural ladder going to Heaven, and above it the Lord spoke to Him. Although it was a dream, God's message was true: *The Ultimate Prophecy would continue through Jacob.* At this critical moment, God provided supernatural assurance and comfort. This is the result of faith in God's Word. James 4:8 says "draw nigh to the Lord and he will draw nigh to you." A stronger and closer relationship will result from seeking God and trusting His Word over one's own heart.

Of course, the promised "seed" the Lord spoke of was Jesus Christ. And Jesus indeed cited this very dream of Jacob in John 1:

> "Jesus saw Nathanael coming to him, and saith of him, Behold an Israelite indeed, in whom is no guile! Nathanael saith unto him, Whence knowest thou me? Jesus answered and said unto him, Before that Philip called thee, when thou wast under the fig tree, I saw thee. Nathanael answered and saith unto him, Rabbi, thou art the Son of God; thou art the King of Israel. Jesus answered and said unto him, Because I said unto thee, I saw thee under the fig tree, believest thou? thou shalt see greater things than these. And he saith unto him, Verily, verily, I say unto you, **Hereafter ye shall see heaven open, and the angels of God ascending and descending upon the Son of man.**" – John 1:47–51

The Lord Jesus was pleased to meet Nathaniel because he was a righteous man. Jesus declared that in Nathan there was "no guile"! What a compliment to receive directly from God! Jesus then demonstrated His power by informing Nathaniel that He had seen him before they ever met (speaking to Jesus' omniscience). Nathaniel immediately responded by proclaiming, "Rabbi, thou art the Son of God; thou art the King of Israel." Very few people in the Gospels so readily acknowledged Jesus this way after just one statement. Jesus then promised Nathaniel he would see even "greater things" and cited the dream of Jacob's ladder. Jesus' pronouncement confirmed that the ladder in the dream was a symbolic foreshadow of Jesus Christ, the Son of God and true ladder between Earth and Heaven – the righteous, perfect answer to the false, satanic system of *"being as gods"* through the Nephilim incursion.

Jacob arrived at the home of Laban and fell in love with Rachel. Laban, using some of the same deceitful tactics Jacob once used, tricked Jacob into marrying Rachel's older sister Leah after laboring for seven years. After 14 years, Jacob married both Leah and Rebekah and fathered 11 children between his two wives and two handmaidens. But he sought to return to the

Promised Land where the Messianic bloodline was to reside. Once he was on his way, he remembered that Esau was there and was still looking to murder him and possibly his children. So, Jacob planned in desperation:

"And Jacob went on his way, and the angels of God met him. ²And when Jacob saw them, he said, This is God's host: and he called the name of that place Mahanaim. And Jacob sent messengers before him to Esau his brother unto the land of Seir, the country of Edom. And he commanded them, saying, Thus shall ye speak unto my lord Esau; Thy servant Jacob saith thus, I have sojourned with Laban, and stayed there until now: And I have oxen, and asses, flocks, and menservants, and womenservants: and I have sent to tell my lord, that I may find grace in thy sight. And the messengers returned to Jacob, saying, We came to thy brother Esau, and also he cometh to meet thee, and four hundred men with him." – Genesis 32:1–6

Jacob knew his life was in danger as Esau had amassed a small army to find him. He divided up his family and caravan in hopes that maybe one of the two could escape. He then sent a great deal of his wealth to Esau as a peace offering and sent his family to a distant town. He was taking the threat to his life and the promises of God most seriously. Jacob then took the most important step by praying to God for protection, repeating the promises God had made to him and his forefathers.

All alone, with no more wealth and his family in jeopardy, Jacob now encountered the Lord in person:

"And Jacob was left alone; and there wrestled a man with him until the breaking of the day. And when he saw that he prevailed not against him, he touched the hollow of his thigh; and the hollow of Jacob's thigh was out of joint, as he wrestled with him. And he said, Let me go, for the day breaketh. And he said, I will not let thee go, except thou bless me. And he said unto him, What is thy name? And he said, Jacob. And he said, Thy name shall be called no more Jacob, but Israel: for as a prince hast thou power with God and with men, and hast prevailed." – Genesis 32:24–28

For all Jacob's faults, one consistent theme ran through his life: He knew true success came from God, and he desperately sought the Lord. At this moment Jacob, whose name meant "deceiver," was renamed Israel, the nation that would give birth to the Messiah.

## THE ASSAULT OF DINAH – JACOB'S SONS PROTECT THE BLOODLINE

"And Dinah the daughter of Leah, which she bare unto Jacob, went out to see the daughters of the land. And when Shechem the son of Hamor the Hivite, prince of the country, saw her, he took her, and lay with her, and defiled her. And his soul clave unto Dinah the daughter of Jacob, and he loved the damsel, and spake kindly unto the damsel. And Shechem spake unto his father Hamor, saying, Get me this damsel to wife. And Jacob heard that he had defiled Dinah his daughter: now his sons were with his cattle in the field: and Jacob held his peace until they were come. And Hamor the father of Shechem went out unto Jacob to commune with him. And the sons of Jacob came out of the field when they heard it: and the men were grieved, and they were very wroth, because he had wrought folly in Israel in lying with Jacob's daughter: which thing ought not to be done." – Genesis 34:1–7

Jacob's 12 sons took the promise of the Messiah through the Holy Seed seriously. The sexual assault of their sister Dinah, at the hands of a Hivite named Schechem, was a grave offense. Going back to Noah's family tree in

Genesis 10, we see that the Hivites were sons of Canaan, the patriarch of the giants (Genesis 10:17). Satan seized upon an opportunity to infiltrate the nation of Israel through Dinah. Shechem's rape of Dinah and subsequent request for her hand in marriage ensured he had one less woman in the lineage of the Messiah to worry about. It provided a chance to corrupt the Messianic bloodline.

Jacob's sons were incensed at Shechem's behavior, and his father's offer to pay a dowry as remedy for the situation only added insult to injury. Jacob's sons responded by deceitfully accepting Hamor's offer but requiring that every male in the city be circumcised out of respect for Jewish custom prior to any marriage. This was a ruse designed to put the men in a weakened state as they recovered from the surgery and subsequent blood loss, making them no match for the sons of Israel who rose up and slaughtered them all.

This small episode again gives insight to how important preserving the lineage from mingling with the Canaanites was to the children of Israel. Their great-grandfather Abraham's strong warnings were not in vain – up to this point.

## REUBEN'S SIN

"And it came to pass, when Israel dwelt in that land, that Reuben went and lay with Bilhah his father's concubine: and Israel heard it." – Genesis 35:22

Jacob, now called Israel, lost the love of his life, Rachel. Just before her death, God reaffirmed His promises of blessings in the form of the Promised Land and the Messianic blessings that kings would come "from his loins" indicating that his descendants would rule. Adding to the prophetic implications of this passage, Rachel was buried in Bethlehem Ephrath, the same place where a little less than 2,000 years later, Jesus Christ, the Promised Messiah and a direct descendant of Israel, would be born (Genesis 35:19, Matthew 2:1).

On the heels of his loss, sinful temptation wrought havoc. Reuben, Jacob's firstborn son, committed fornication with Jacob's concubine Bilah, who was also the mother of two of Reuben's brothers (Dan and Naphtali). Satan thus continued the relentless attack on the Messianic bloodline. Sexual lust is one of the strongest forces in the world, and Satan uses it to achieve his ends. Remember that when Satan challenged the Lord Jesus Christ in the wilderness, Jesus called him "the tempter" (Matthew 4:3). The Devil sets up an environment of sinful temptation to lure us to choose sin over obedience to the Lord. Jacob chose to have a concubine, and years later Reuben walked right into the same trap, willingly.

As the firstborn son, Reuben was entitled to the prophetic birthright as he would be charged with carrying the Messianic seed into future generations and with it the promised blessings God originally made to Abraham. Once again sin and satanic influence threatened the Lord's plan of salvation. Reuben's fornication and disgrace of his father forfeited his claim to the birthright, as 1 Chronicles 5:1 confirms:

> "Now the sons of Reuben the firstborn of Israel, (for he was the firstborn; but forasmuch as he defiled his father's bed, his birthright was given unto the sons of Joseph the son of Israel: and the genealogy is not to be reckoned after the birthright)."

Since Satan could not kill Reuben, he settled on corrupting him. Certain stories in the Bible that seem minor or irrelevant in the "big picture" of Scripture were actually very significant in the ongoing battle to bring forth the Messiah. But, as always, Satan's minor victories will not foil God's plan of redemption. Since Reuben forfeited the birthright, it would be given to someone who was ready and willing to follow the Lord – the firstborn son of Jacob's second wife: Joseph. Satan picked up right where he left off with Reuben to attack Joseph, but he would not succeed in corrupting that man.

# THE LINEAGE OF ESAU AT
# MOUNT SEIR – GENESIS 36

Genesis 36 records the lineage of Esau, Jacob's older twin brother. In addition to selling his birthright, further confirmation of Esau's disobedience is that he married several Canaanite women:

> "Now these are the generations of Esau, who is Edom. Esau took his wives of the daughters of Canaan; Adah the daughter of Elon the Hittite, and Aholibamah the daughter of Anah the daughter of Zibeon the Hivite…." – Genesis 36:1–2

Esau had no respect for God, never repented, and had no interest in preserving the Messianic bloodline. Yet God still had mercy on him. He was the firstborn and favorite son of faithful Isaac. Esau still received a secondary blessing after Jacob's deception, which was fulfilled in Genesis 36 as Esau amassed great wealth and moved out of Canaan to the area of Mt. Seir. The mountain was named for Seir the Horite, who was a part of a nation inhabited by Nephilim hybrids. This cohabitation did not last long because God destroyed the Horites (or Horim):

> "When we turned, and took our journey into the wilderness by the way of the Red sea, as the LORD spake unto me: and we compassed mount Seir many days. And the LORD spake unto me, saying, Ye have compassed this mountain long enough: turn you northward. And command thou the people, saying, Ye are to pass through the coast of your brethren the children of Esau, which dwell in Seir; and they shall be afraid of you: take ye good heed unto yourselves therefore: Meddle not with them; for I will not give you of their land, no, not so much as a foot breadth; because I have given mount Seir unto Esau for a possession." – Deuteronomy 2:1–5

God honors his faithful servants. So even though Esau was a reprobate, his father, Isaac, was a faithful believer. Thus, the Lord preserved land for Esau's descendants, giving them common grace. Later in Deuteronomy 2 we learn what became of Seir and his Nephilim lineage:

> "As he did to the children of Esau, which dwelt in Seir, when he destroyed the Horims from before them; and they succeeded them, and dwelt in their stead even unto this day...." – Deuteronomy 2:22

*God personally engaged the Horim in combat* and conquered them allowing Esau's descendants to occupy Mt. Seir. Unfortunately, in due time their sinful rebellion would catch up with them.

## JOSEPH – FORESHADOW OF JESUS CHRIST THE MESSIAH

The story of "Joseph and the Coat of Many Colors" is one of the most popular Bible stories and packed with powerful doctrine. Here we will examine it from the perspective of the battle between the Holy Seed and the Nephilim. Satan successfully derailed Reuben's place in the Messianic bloodline, and the birthright was passed on to Joseph, the firstborn son of Jacob's true love, Rachel. Unable to conceive a child until late in life, Rachel gave birth to Joseph and later died giving birth to Benjamin. With her passing, Joseph became much more special to Jacob:

> "These are the generations of Jacob. Joseph, being seventeen years old, was feeding the flock with his brethren; and the lad was with the sons of Bilhah, and with the sons of Zilpah, his father's wives: and Joseph brought unto his father their evil report. Now Israel loved Joseph more than all his children, because he was the son of

his old age: and he made him a coat of many colours. And when his brethren saw that their father loved him more than all his brethren, they hated him, and could not speak peaceably unto him." – Genesis 37:2–4

The "coat of many colors" was more than just a fancy fashion statement or an expensive gift. It was a symbol of Jacob's love and Joseph's preeminence as the holder of the prophetic birthright. This is the first mention of clothes being made for a child since the Lord clothed Adam and Eve in the Garden. And just as those animal skins were a type of the sacrifice of the Messiah, so too the coat of Joseph was a foreshadow of the preeminence of Jesus Christ who is "the name above all names" (Philippians 2:9).

Despite being the eleventh of the 12 sons, Joseph moved to the position of preeminence as "firstborn" due to Reuben's folly. This honor did not sit well with his brothers. Adding salt to their wounds, Joseph received prophetic dreams from the Lord in which his brothers and even his father and mother were bowing down before him. Here again, the Tempter struck, this time inciting jealous rage in Joseph's brothers that was so strong they wanted to kill him. Satan used the same sinful temptation he used on Cain to murder his brother, Abel, and later, Jacob and Esau. (Note that Satan will frequently use the same tactics because naive humanity is slow to detect his devices.)

Sadly, Joseph's brothers took the bait and conspired to kill Joseph. Ironically, only the intervention of Reuben prevented their murderous plot:

"And when they saw him afar off, even before he came near unto them, they conspired against him to slay him. And they said one to another, Behold, this dreamer cometh. Come now therefore, and let us slay him, and cast him into some pit, and we will say, Some evil beast hath devoured him: and we shall see what will become of his dreams. And Reuben heard it, and he delivered him out of their hands; and said, Let us not kill him. And Reuben said unto them,

Shed no blood, but cast him into this pit that is in the wilderness, and lay no hand upon him; that he might rid him out of their hands, to deliver him to his father again. And it came to pass, when Joseph was come unto his brethren, that they stript Joseph out of his coat, his coat of many colours that was on him; And they took him, and cast him into a pit: and the pit was empty, there was no water in it." – Genesis 37:18–24

The war of the competing bloodlines took a turn in favor of the forces of evil. God replaced Reuben with Joseph as the continuation of the Messianic bloodline and blessing. And the Tempter, Satan, countered by using jealous rage to lure Joseph's brothers to try to murder him. The Devil continued his assault on the lineage that would ultimately destroy him.

Reuben, no doubt humbled from losing the birthright, reasoned with his brothers to spare Joseph's life. The first thing Joseph's brothers did once they attacked him was seize upon the coat of many colors. The coat symbolized the blessing that would lead to the future Messiah and Savior. Yet, all the brothers wanted to do was tear it off of Joseph. They were so blinded by their own sin that they were willing to turn their back on the brother who was the key to their salvation. A group of sinful Jewish leaders in Judea some 2,000 years later would do the same thing to one of their own, Jesus Christ. And many people do the same thing today – reject Jesus Christ despite hearing the clear Gospel message that He is the only way to salvation.

What Satan did not anticipate or fully comprehend was Joseph's faithfulness. The treachery of his brothers did not shake his faith in God. Sold into slavery, Joseph found himself in Egypt, in the home of Potiphar, the captain of the guard for the Pharaoh of Egypt. By God's grace Joseph excelled in his work and was soon put in charge of all of Potiphar's daily affairs. Scripture is clear that the Lord was with Joseph every step of the way. Satan, seeing that the Reuben's replacement as heir of Jacob was thriving, tried to tempt Joseph into sin with the same trap that tripped up his older brother Reuben:

"And it came to pass after these things, that his master's wife cast her eyes upon Joseph; and she said, Lie with me. But he refused, and said unto his master's wife, Behold, my master wotteth not what is with me in the house, and he hath committed all that he hath to my hand; There is none greater in this house than I; neither hath he kept back any thing from me but thee, because thou art his wife: how then can I do this great wickedness, and sin against God? And it came to pass, as she spake to Joseph day by day, that he hearkened not unto her, to lie by her, or to be with her." – Genesis 39:7–10

Potiphar's wife, burning with sexual lust, obsessed over Joseph. But her constant pleas for fornication had no effect on him. Joseph was faithful and obedient to the Lord and resisted the sinful temptation. With few options left, the Tempter continued to work on Potiphar's wife, driving her to such wrath at Joseph's rebuffs that she framed him for rape. This was yet another sad incident in which Joseph was attacked and suffered, though he had done no wrong. Joseph was thrown in prison for a crime he did not commit, foreshadowing the Messiah Jesus Christ who was falsely accused and crucified though He "knew no sin."

Consider Joseph's plight – falsely accused, a convicted rapist, and now an inmate in prison. It seemed the whole world was against him. The spiritually strongest son of Jacob may have resisted fornication with Potiphar's wife, but the Devil used the same woman to have Joseph imprisoned. If the other 10 sons of Israel could be thrown off course spiritually, perhaps the seed of Abraham would be undone and God's prophecy would fail. But Joseph had the Lord on his side. Even though he was suffering serious worldly problems, his faith in the Almighty God in Heaven was not shaken. And the Lord enabled Joseph to rise to even greater heights than anyone could imagine.

Thanks to Joseph's God-given gift for dream interpretation, the Pharaoh of Egypt summoned him to interpret a dream that deeply troubled him. Joseph correctly interpreted the dream to be a warning of seven years of an abundance of crops at harvest time followed by seven years of drought that were going to come upon Egypt and the surrounding nations of the known world at that time. Pharaoh was so impressed and astounded at Joseph's ability that he made him the second-highest-ranking ruler in the Egyptian empire. This put Joseph, whom the Devil thought he had disposed of, in one of the highest-ranking positions of authority in the world. Through this position, God used Joseph to take the planned salvation of the world through the Holy Seed to a new level.

## JUDAH TOOK CANAANITE WIVES AND JEOPARDIZED THE VERY TRIBE JACOB PROPHESIED WOULD BEAR THE MESSIAH

In the middle of Joseph's story, the Bible inserts a chapter that goes from Egypt all the way back to the land of Canaan and the actions of Joseph's brother Judah. Genesis 38 records an attempt to mingle Holy Seed with genetic corruption:

> "And it came to pass at that time, that Judah went down from his brethren, and turned in to a certain Adullamite, whose name was Hirah. **And Judah saw there a daughter of a certain Canaanite, whose name was Shuah; and he took her, and went in unto her.** And she conceived, and bare a son; and he called his name Er. And she conceived again, and bare a son; and she called his name Onan. And she yet again conceived, and bare a son; and called his name Shelah: and he was at Chezib, when she bare him. And Judah took a wife for Er his firstborn, whose name was Tamar." – Genesis 38:1–6

Having just lied to his father about Joseph's fate, Judah went "down from his brethren" and spent time instead with Hirah, a Canaanite merchant in Adullam. Away from his family's godly influence, Judah went astray.

Thinking of his own selfish desires, he traveled into the heart of Nephilim giant territory and "took" a wife and had three sons with her, fully mingling with the direct lineage of Canaan. It would be the tribe of Judah who eventually received the blessings of the Prophecy, and the Messiah would come through this specific tribe and lineage (Genesis 49:9–10). Judah compounded his mistake by arranging for Tamar, an Israelite woman, to marry his part-Canaanite son Er, further polluting the royal bloodline. Satan's temptation took Judah off mission and into a serious error that threatened the Holy Seed. But the Lord would not tolerate Judah's indiscretions:

> "**And Er, Judah's firstborn, was wicked in the sight of the LORD; and the LORD slew him**. And Judah said unto Onan, Go in unto thy brother's wife, and marry her, and raise up seed to thy brother. And Onan knew that the seed should not be his; and it came to pass, when he went in unto his brother's wife, that he spilled it on the ground, lest that he should give seed to his brother. And the thing which he did displeased the LORD: wherefore he slew him also. Then said Judah to Tamar his daughter in law, Remain a widow at thy father's house, till Shelah my son be grown: for he said, Lest peradventure he die also, as his brethren did. And Tamar went and dwelt in her father's house. And in process of time the daughter of Shuah Judah's wife died; and Judah was comforted, and went up unto his sheepshearers to Timnath, he and his friend Hirah the Adullamite." – Genesis 38:7–12

As were all the Nephilim and those who carried Nephilim genes, Er was "wicked in the sight of the Lord." This first son of Judah could have no part in the lineage that would lead to the Savior. And how did he die? *God killed him.* As would become a part of the Mosaic Law, if a married man died without having a child, his brother was to marry the widow. This law served to keep the nation of Israel growing while maintaining the genetic purity of the undefiled Messianic line. Onan, Judah's second son, violated this rule, leading to his death at the mighty hand of God. Why such harsh judgment? The Lord was correcting the sinful errors of Judah. His actions introduced the Nephilim – tainted genes of Canaan's descendants – into the nation of Israel. So, the Lord personally slew the offspring of this union. It is critical to remember that in these early stages of the plan of salvation, this small family was the critical instrument in God's hand. Twelve brothers were holders of the fate of the nation of Israel and the future of the entire world. God thus dealt with sinful mistakes such as Judah's sharply and swiftly. This serves to reveal God's grace in fiercely protecting humanity.

After the death of his second son, Judah took note of God's actions and sent Tamar, his fully Israelite daughter-in-law, away. The Lord was angered with Judah for marrying his sons off to Israelite women. Shortly afterwards, Judah's Canaanite wife died, thus ensuring he would have no more children with Nephilim genes born of that illicit union. The only son from this sinful marriage who was still alive was Shelah, and Judah decided that he was going to drop out of the matchmaking business and let Shelah remain single. Though it seems Judah was starting to figure things out, he still neglected one key aspect – repentance. Up until this point Judah had not repented to God for his disobedience. He was still trying to work things out through his own plan and not humbling himself before the Lord and seeking mercy.

Sadly, the Tempter struck again:

> "And it was told Tamar, saying, Behold thy father in law goeth up to Timnath to shear his sheep. And she put her widow's garments off from her, and covered her with a vail, and wrapped herself, and sat in an open place, which is by the way to Timnath; for she saw that Shelah was grown, and she was not given unto him to wife. When Judah saw her, he thought her to be an harlot; because she had covered her face. And he turned unto her by the way, and said, Go to, I pray thee, let me come in unto thee; (for he knew not that she was his daughter in law.) And she said, What wilt thou give me,

that thou mayest come in unto me? And he said, I will send thee a kid from the flock. And she said, Wilt thou give me a pledge, till thou send it? And he said, What pledge shall I give thee? And she said, Thy signet, and thy bracelets, and thy staff that is in thine hand. And he gave it her, and came in unto her, and she conceived by him." – Genesis 38:13–18

What was all this trickery about? Why is this story important enough to record in Scripture? From the perspective of the bloodlines of the Messiah and the Nephilim the reason is clear: God was once again correcting Judah's mistakes to protect the Holy Seed. Tamar knew that Judah was not going to let her marry his third and only remaining Canaanite son (lest God kill him as he slew his brothers who carried the genes of fallen angelic ancestors in their veins). And this displeased her because it was her only way to lawfully marry and be a part of the family of the great patriarch Abraham. Tamar was an Israelite and eligible to bear a child in the Messianic bloodline. This was a great honor and by law (since she was a widow) it was now her right. She deceived Judah by disguising herself as a prostitute.

Judah, still in the clutches of sinful rebellion, was easily seduced by the deception and continued his evil by hiring her for a night of fornication. Judah not only had sexual relations outside of marriage but added to his sin by giving his signet and staff – symbols of his status as an heir to Abraham, Isaac, and Jacob – to a woman he thought was a prostitute. The Bible does not omit the depraved character of many of its prominent figures. And Judah proved in this instance to be blinded by his sinful desires. Just as Judah's uncle Esau sold his birthright for a bowl of pottage a few decades earlier, Judah was now throwing away the sign of his inheritance in the Abrahamic blessing for a night of sex with a prostitute.

The signet, staff, and bracelets were a "deposit." Judah was supposed to make his actual payment to the woman with goats. When he tried to send them to her, "the harlot" was nowhere to be found. He then told his friends to keep the whole transaction quiet lest anyone discover his sin. As the book of Numbers states, however, "be sure your sin will find you out." Judah had a trail of sin with no repentance before God. And though he thought he had covered up his actions, it was all going to come to light.

> "And it came to pass about three months after, that it was told Judah, saying, Tamar thy daughter in law hath played the harlot; and also, behold, she is with child by whoredom. And Judah said, Bring her forth, and let her be burnt. When she was brought forth, she sent to her father in law, saying, By the man, whose these are, am I with child: and she said, Discern, I pray thee, whose are these, the signet, and bracelets, and staff. And Judah acknowledged them, and said, She hath been more righteous than I; because that I gave her not to Shelah my son. And he knew her again no more." – Genesis 38:24–26

Judah was informed that his daughter-in-law Tamar "played the harlot" and had a child out of wedlock. Notice Judah's rank hypocrisy as he immediately recommended that she be executed by burning her alive. Ignoring his own sexual sin once again, Judah condemned his daughter-in-law for the same act of evil he committed. But the signet and staff he had foolishly given to Tamar as compensation for her "harlotry" would prove her innocence and expose Judah before the public.

Tamar was a very shrewd woman and made sure she secured items that would prove her innocence. By divine law Judah was required to bear his third son to Tamar, who in sleeping with her father-in-law was seeking to exercise her lawful right to an heir. When he was openly exposed as an adulterer and whoremonger, Judah finally acknowledged his sin and admitted: "She hath been more righteous than I...."

This very interesting account demonstrated God's providential hand at work. The Lord's harsh judgment woke Judah up and ensured his youngest hybrid son did not marry and conceive children. The Lord took Tamar, a virgin, and set events in motion that resulted in Tamar's conceiving a rightful heir by Judah, thus preserving the Holy Seed. The end of the chapter describes the birth:

> "And it came to pass in the time of her travail, that, behold, twins were in her womb. And it came to pass, when she travailed, that the one put out his hand: and the midwife took and bound upon his hand a scarlet thread, saying, This came out first. And it came to pass, as he drew back his hand, that, behold, his brother came out: and she said, How hast thou broken forth? this breach be upon thee: therefore his name was called Pharez. And afterward came out his brother, that had the scarlet thread upon his hand: and his name was called Zarah." – Genesis 38:27–30

Yet another set of twins was born, and yet another "dispute" ensued right from the womb over who came out first and was thus entitled to the birthright of Judah (the importance of birthright was not lost on this family!). The midwife went so far as to tie a scarlet thread around the hand of the baby Zarah, who actually came out second. The significance of this birth episode for the bigger picture of the Messianic bloodline is clear: Order was restored in the house of Judah. Judah's remaining part-Canaanite son would never marry an Israelite woman. And Judah's youngest twin sons, who had no Canaanite/Nephilim genes in them, would continue the lineage of the Holy Seed. Satan had again been thwarted. The book of Matthew makes this clear:

> "The book of the generation of Jesus Christ, the son of David, the son of Abraham. Abraham begat Isaac; and Isaac begat Jacob; and Jacob begat [Judah] and his brethren; And [Judah] begat Phares and Zara of Thamar; and Phares begat Esrom; and Esrom begat Aram...." – Matthew 1:1–3

In the official lineage of Jesus Christ presented in Matthew 1, both twins are mentioned but Pharez's child Esrom is listed as the heir in the Messianic bloodline. Pharez, born of a son of Israel and an Israelite woman, maintained the purity of the line leading to Christ. So, Genesis 38, which seems to be a curious standalone story, in fact had major implications for the salvation plan of God and yet another victory for the Lord over the adversary.

# CHAPTER 17

# THE BIRTH OF GOD'S NATION

Despite being betrayed by his own brothers, sold into slavery, wrongfully convicted, and imprisoned, Joseph rose to become the second-most powerful man in the world. Pharaoh was so impressed with Joseph's ability to interpret dreams that he made him second in power over his kingdom (Genesis 41:40). His ascent in the Egyptian empire positioned him to rescue his family from famine and, more importantly, to engineer God's next step in protecting the Holy Seed. Joseph's prophetic dreams enabled him to prepare the nation of Egypt for the seven years of drought by directing them to store extra crops during the seven abundant years (Genesis 41:54). Joseph's meticulous instructions were carried out to the letter, and once the drought hit the world (leading to famine), Egypt was in a position of comfort and security.

Joseph and his family were rewarded with the city of Goshen as a homestead. God's sovereign plan took the family of the Prophecy out of the Promised Land and into Egypt. This was a time to build up the nation that would bring forth the Messiah. Jacob, deceived for decades thinking that his favored son and heir Joseph was dead, had a very interesting conversation after reuniting with his son:

> "And Joseph said unto his brethren, and unto his father's house, I will go up, and shew Pharaoh, and say unto him, My brethren, and my father's house, which were in the land of Canaan, are come unto me; And the men are shepherds, for their trade hath been to feed

> cattle; and they have brought their flocks, and their herds, and all
> that they have. And it shall come to pass, when Pharaoh shall call
> you, and shall say, What is your occupation? **That ye shall say,**
> **Thy servants' trade hath been about cattle from our youth even**
> **until now, both we, and also our fathers: that ye may dwell in**
> **the land of Goshen; for every shepherd is an abomination unto**
> **the Egyptians."** – Genesis 46:31–34

Why was this final detail about shepherds' being an abomination included in this passage? Why does that even matter? It provided a strategic advantage in the war of the bloodlines. Within the confines of the most powerful empire on the planet, Israel's offspring grew into a populous nation. Handling cattle was offensive and revolting in ancient Egyptian culture. Thus, the Egyptians had no desire to have social or marital relations with the Israelite people who were shepherds. This development provided the Israelites many generations to grow as a people – from 70 people to millions in the centuries that followed – with no outside interference or threat of genetic corruption. God used Joseph to provide a secure location for His infant nation to incubate and thrive. Thus, the lineage of the coming Messiah was preserved and flourished. Satan's window to target one man had closed. The family of Israel would grow into a thriving nation.

Two final prophecies in Genesis reminded this very young family of their place in God's plan to redeem the human race. On his deathbed, Jacob prophesied that the tribe of Judah would bring forth the Messiah. Decades later when Joseph was on his deathbed, his final words kept his family focused on their divine mission:

> "And Joseph said unto his brethren, I die: and God will surely visit
> you, and bring you out of this land unto the land which he sware
> to Abraham, to Isaac, and to Jacob. And Joseph took an oath of the
> children of Israel, saying, God will surely visit you, and ye shall
> carry up my bones from hence." – Genesis 50:24–25

Life in Egypt seemed pleasant to the children of Israel, but they were not to get comfortable. In his final words, Joseph kept his family on mission. God was going to visit them and bring them back to the Promised Land to take their inheritance from the Nephilim.

## FROM GENESIS TO GENOCIDE

With the Israelite population in the millions and his Nephilim armies dwindling, the Devil employed a new tactic to attack the Holy Seed – genocide:

> "Now there arose up a new king over Egypt, which knew not Joseph. And he said unto his people, Behold, the people of the children of Israel are more and mightier than we: Come on, let us deal wisely with them; lest they multiply, and it come to pass, that, when there falleth out any war, they join also unto our enemies, and fight against us, and so get them up out of the land… **And Pharaoh charged all his people, saying, Every son that is born ye shall cast into the river**, and every daughter ye shall save alive."
> – Exodus 1:8–10; 22

Many years after Joseph's death, a new Pharaoh who had no respect for Israel or their position of prominence assumed power. Threatened by the thriving immigrants within his borders, this Egyptian king issued a decree to murder all the male babies of the Israelites. In addition, he enslaved all their adults, subjecting them to inhumane treatment and hard labor. The Devil turned to human rulers to carry out his plan of wiping out the Seed of the Woman. If he could succeed in having every *male Israelite child* murdered, then potentially the Messiah would be dead or his lineage ruined.

God, in His infinite wisdom, made sure that the prophet Moses, then an infant, was saved – his mother prepared his own personal "ark" (yet another allusion to the Flood) to send Moses out of Goshen floating down a river (Exodus 2:3). By divine providence, the Pharaoh's daughter discovered and adopted Moses, raising him right under Pharaoh's nose as Egyptian royalty (Exodus 2:10). God called the adult Moses into action to prepare his people to reclaim the Promised Land from the Nephilim:

> "And when the LORD saw that he turned aside to see, God called unto him out of the midst of the bush, and said, Moses, Moses. And he said, Here am I. And he said, Draw not nigh hither: put off thy shoes from off thy feet, for the place whereon thou standest is holy ground. Moreover he said, I am the God of thy father, the God of Abraham, the God of Isaac, and the God of Jacob. And Moses hid his face; for he was afraid to look upon God. And the LORD said, I have surely seen the affliction of my people which are in Egypt, and have heard their cry by reason of their taskmasters; for I know their sorrows; And I am come down to deliver them out of the hand of the Egyptians, and to bring them up out of that land unto a good land and a large, unto a land flowing with milk and honey; **unto the place of the Canaanites, and the Hittites, and the Amorites, and the Perizzites, and the Hivites, and the Jebusites.**" – Exodus 3:4–8

From the first communication between the Lord and Moses, the mission was clear: It was time to remove the usurpers from the Promised Land and establish God's people there instead. The Nephilim who were entrenched in the land of Canaan had run out of time. The moment arrived to fulfill the divine promise to Abraham and remove the seed of Satan once and for all.

# GOD USED THE YEARS IN THE WILDERNESS TO SPIRITUALLY PREPARE ISRAEL FOR THE BATTLES TO COME IN THE LAND OF CANAAN

After the Exodus – in which God through a series of miracles punished Pharaoh until he freed the enslaved Israelite nation – the Lord revealed His divine Law to the Israelites in the wilderness. The second half of the book of Exodus and the book of Leviticus detail the "boot camp" for the Israelites before battle. To wage spiritual warfare effectively, you must know God's Word. God spent time with Moses and His people giving them the Ten Commandments and the 612 Mosaic laws. They were about to invade enemy territory that was filled with demonic activity, mystery religion, and the sinful influence of fallen angels. This was just as much a war of spiritual strength as of military might.

Their spiritual preparation complete, the Lord instructed the Israelites to count their population (Numbers 1:2–3). The Book of Numbers opens with a roll call of all the armies of the tribes of Israel to show God's faithfulness in building up their nation to prepare them for war. Moses was the first military leader in what would be a series of the only truly offensive wars the people of God would wage in the entire Bible.

# THE PROVOCATION – THE NEPHILIM CAUSED ISRAEL TO LOSE FAITH IN GOD AND SUFFER DEVASTATING CONSEQUENCES

Before the Israelites launched their attack the Lord commanded Moses to send 12 of their best men as spies into the land of Canaan to scout the Promised Land:

> "And the LORD spake unto Moses, saying, Send thou men, that they may search the land of Canaan, which I give unto the children

of Israel: of every tribe of their fathers shall ye send a man, every one a ruler among them… So they went up, and searched the land from the wilderness of Zin unto Rehob, as men come to Hamath. **And they ascended by the south, and came unto Hebron; where Ahiman, Sheshai, and Talmai, the children of Anak, were. (Now Hebron was built seven years before Zoan in Egypt.)** And they came unto the brook of Eshcol, **and cut down from thence a branch with one cluster of grapes, and they bare it between two upon a staff;** and they brought of the pomegranates, and of the figs." – Numbers 13:1–2; 21–23

The spies returned from the Promised Land carrying a cluster of grapes so large that two men had to carry it on a wooden pole! But that was not all they discovered:

"And they went and came to Moses, and to Aaron, and to all the congregation of the children of Israel, unto the wilderness of Paran, to Kadesh; and brought back word unto them, and unto all the congregation, and shewed them the fruit of the land. And they told him, and said, We came unto the land whither thou sentest us, and surely it floweth with milk and honey; and this is the fruit of it. **Nevertheless the people be strong that dwell in the land, and the cities are walled, and very great: and moreover we saw the children of Anak there.** The Amalekites dwell in the land of the south: and the Hittites, and the Jebusites, and the Amorites, dwell in the mountains: and the Canaanites dwell by the sea, and by the coast of Jordan.

And Caleb stilled the people before Moses, and said, Let us go up at once, and possess it; for we are well able to overcome it. But the men that went up with him said, We be not able to go up against the people; for they are stronger than we. And they brought up an evil report of the land which they had searched unto the children of Israel, saying, **The land, through which we have gone to** search it, is a land that eateth up the inhabitants thereof; and all the people that we saw in it are men of a great stature. And there we saw the giants, the sons of Anak, which come of the giants: and we were in our own sight as grasshoppers, and so we were in their sight." – Numbers 13:26–33

This was a major event in biblical history. The Israelites were on the cusp of entering the Promised Land. This was the time of salvation they had literally waited centuries for. God, having just destroyed the Egyptian empire, built the 12 tribes into a mighty fighting force. And yet 10 of the spies warned the Israelites not to enter the land of Canaan. Why? **Because they were scared of the Nephilim living there**. The sons of Anak were so imposing and their walled fortresses so massive that the 10 doubting spies had no faith in the Lord to defeat them! Only Joshua and Caleb believed that God could deliver on His promise of defeating the giants:

> "And all the congregation lifted up their voice, and cried; and the people wept that night. And all the children of Israel murmured against Moses and against Aaron: and the whole congregation said unto them, **Would God that we had died in the land of Egypt! or would God we had died in this wilderness!**... Then Moses and Aaron fell on their faces before all the assembly of the congregation of the children of Israel. And Joshua the son of Nun, and Caleb the son of Jephunneh, which were of them that searched the land, rent their clothes: And they spake unto all the company of the children of Israel, saying, The land, which we passed through to search it, is an exceeding good land. If the LORD delight in us, then he will bring us into this land, and give it us; a land which floweth with milk and honey." – Numbers 14:1–2; 5–8

Some scholars and Bible teachers have questioned whether the 10 spies were lying or exaggerating in their report and the sons of Anak were not actually giants. The Bible refutes this notion. The book of Deuteronomy proves the Anakim tribe were among the elite and most feared of the post-Flood Nephilim:

"The Emims dwelt therein in times past, a **people great, and many, and tall, as the Anakims; Which also were accounted giants [*rephaim*], as the Anakims**; but the Moabites called them Emims." – Deuteronomy 2:10–11

"That also was accounted a land of giants [*rephaim*]: giants dwelt therein in old time; and the Ammonites call them Zamzummims; **A people great, and many, and tall, as the Anakims**; but the LORD destroyed them before them; and they succeeded them, and dwelt in their stead...." – Deuteronomy 2:20–21

"Hear, O Israel: Thou art to pass over Jordan this day, to go in to possess nations greater and mightier than thyself, cities great and fenced up to heaven, **A people great and tall, the children of the Anakims, whom thou knowest, and of whom thou hast heard say, Who can stand before the children of Anak!**" – Deuteronomy 9:1–2

The sons of Anak were the tribe by whom other groups of Nephilim were measured. They resided in Hebron, which Scripture confirms was "built seven years before Zoan in Egypt" (Numbers 13:22). Hebron was the oldest city in the known world, and as we noted earlier it was originally known as Kirjath-Arba, in honor of Arba, the grandfather of Ahiman, Sheshai, and Talmai (Joshua 14:15).

Arba was a direct descendant of Canaan. He is introduced in Genesis 23 after the death of Sarah. He was one of the "sons of Heth" (Genesis 23:3) who built Kirjath-Arba, the city named in his honor. Heth was the second son of Canaan (Genesis 10:15) **and thus Arba, Anak, Ahiman, Sheshai, and Talmai were all part of the cursed lineage of Canaan**. Two commentaries support the connection between Canaan, Heth (whose descendants were called Hittites), and the Anakim:

> "A gigantic race descended through Anak, from Arba, one of 'the sons of Heth' (Gen 23:3), who seven years before the building of Zoan in Egypt (Num 13:22, Josh 15:13, 54) built Hebron which was hence called *KIRJATH ARBA* i.e., 'the city of Arba.' – *The System Bible Study: Or, The Busy People's Bible; Being an Effort to Give the Most Complete, the Most Concise, and the Most Useful Book of Classified Bible Helps,* The System Bible Company, Chicago Illinois, 1922, p. 18.

> "If Hebron was the city of the Hittites here intended, its chief at the time seems to have been Arba." – *A Critical and Exegetical Commentary on the Book of Genesis: With a New Translation,* James G. Murphy, Edinburgh: T&T Clark, 1893, p. 392.

Canaan's offspring occupied some of the more critical areas of the Promised Land. In Scripture, the area between Jerusalem and Kirjath-Arba (later known as Hebron) was dubbed "the Valley of The Rephaim":

> "And the border went up by the valley of the son of Hinnom unto the south side of the Jebusite; the same is Jerusalem: and the border went up to the top of the mountain that lieth before the valley of Hinnom westward, **which is at the end of the valley of the giants [rephaim] northward**...." – Joshua 15:8

This provides further confirmation that all of the giants were, like the Amorites, Zuzims, Emims, and other Nephilim tribes, genetically "Rephaim." Their particular tribal name was based on their location or, in the Anakim's case, on a legendary ancestor.

Just a few years earlier the Israelites had witnessed all the miracles of God, including parting the Red Sea and then destroying the Pharaoh of Egypt and all his armies in it. They were rescued from the most powerful empire on Earth by God's divine power alone. Time and time again, Yahweh demonstrated His superiority over all the other false deities and His enduring mercy and salvation towards His people Israel. And yet right at the border of the Promised Land they not only lost their faith but wanted to rid themselves of Moses and return to slavery in Egypt. Ahiman, Sheshai, and Talmai were so imposing (the spies said they themselves looked like grasshoppers in comparison), that *the Israelites did not even believe God could rescue them from a mere three enemies.* These Nephilim brothers revealed the heart of many Israelites: They lacked faith when they needed it most.

This act of rebellion angered the Lord so greatly that He threatened to wipe out all of Israel and restart the nation through Moses' seed (something Moses persuaded God not to do by pleading for His mercy in Numbers 14:11–12). As punishment for their rebellion, however, none of the Israelite adults over the age of 20 (and thus old enough to understand God's miracles and salvation in Egypt) were permitted to enter the Promised Land except for Joshua and Caleb, the faithful spies. God sentenced the Israelites to wander the wilderness for 40 years (one year for each day of the spies' mission) until the older generation had died off:

> "Because all those men which have seen my glory, and my miracles, which I did in Egypt and in the wilderness, and have tempted me now these ten times, and have not hearkened to my voice; Surely they shall not see the land which I sware unto their fathers, neither shall any of them that provoked me see it...." – Numbers 14:22–23

This was one of the worst days in Israel's history. Satan's cunning tactic of getting his Nephilim seed to occupy the Promised Land before the 12 tribes' arrival struck a disastrous blow.

In the New Testament, this event, known as "the provocation," is cited in the book of Hebrews as a picture of Christian salvation:

"For every house is builded by some man; but he that built all things is God. And Moses verily was faithful in all his house, as a servant, for a testimony of those things which were to be spoken after; But Christ as a son over his own house; whose house are we, if we hold fast the confidence and the rejoicing of the hope firm unto the end. Wherefore (as the Holy Ghost saith, To day if ye will hear his voice, **Harden not your hearts, as in the provocation, in the day of temptation in the wilderness: When your fathers tempted me, proved me, and saw my works forty years.** Wherefore I was grieved with that generation, and said, They do always err in their heart; and they have not known my ways. So I sware in my wrath, They shall not enter into my rest.) ... But with whom was he grieved forty years? was it not with them that had sinned, whose carcasses fell in the wilderness? And to whom sware he that they should not enter into his rest, but to them that believed not? **So we see that they could not enter in because of unbelief.**"
– Hebrews 3:4–11; 17–19

This passage explains the doctrine of salvation by grace through faith and points to this incident with the 10 doubting spies as a type and shadow of the challenge every single person faces in life. God offers Heaven (the true Promised Land) to all people. The Lord promises that He has made the way for us through Jesus Christ. Whether a person enters Heaven or dies in the wilderness of Hell is a matter of whether he will have faith in God or follow what his eyes see in this world. Lack of faith is what led to the Provocation and the punishment of a generation of Israelites. If they had faith, they would have been saved, which was all a part of their spiritual salvation as well.

Some 1,500 years later, Israel's encounter with three Nephilim brothers would serve as an object lesson in the New Testament for one of the fundamental doctrines of Christianity. Fear of the Nephilim caused the entire adult generations of Israel who came out of Egypt to die in the wilderness and not see the Promised Land. Satan knew that the Lord would rightfully punish even His own chosen people if they yielded to temptation to revolt against Him. But God was not done with Israel. Forty years later, when a new generation of Israelites matured, the time to strike back at the Nephilim finally arrived.

# CHAPTER 18

# WAR FOR THE PROMISED LAND

"The Lord is a man of war: the Lord is his name." – Exodus 15:3

When the 40-year wilderness punishment ended, the younger generation of Israelites were ready to wage war against the giant-infested Canaanite kingdoms. The Lord's strategy required them to pass through the land of Og and Sihon – imposing Nephilim kings who were "Gate Keepers" into God's country. Their kingdoms sat due east of the Dead Sea, Jordan River, and Sea of Galilee, controlling access into the Promised Land. Centuries earlier, this area was overrun with giants. During the Genesis 14 world war, Chedorlaomer killed most of the Rephaim in the land (Genesis 14:5). Despite the drastic decrease in number, these enemy nations were still formidable and awe-inspiring. The 12 tribes initially requested peaceful access through Sihon's territory:

> "And Israel sent messengers unto Sihon king of the Amorites, saying, Let me pass through thy land: we will not turn into the fields, or into the vineyards; we will not drink of the waters of the well: but we will go along by the king's high way, until we be past thy borders. And Sihon would not suffer Israel to pass through his border: but Sihon gathered all his people together, and went out against Israel into the wilderness: and he came to Jahaz, and fought against Israel." – Numbers 21:21–23

Sihon was so full of hatred for God's people that at their mere request to travel through his land he brought his entire army into the wilderness to attack the nation of Israel. This would prove to be his undoing:

> "And the LORD said unto me, Behold, I have begun to give Sihon and his land before thee: begin to possess, that thou mayest inherit his land. Then Sihon came out against us, he and all his people, to fight at Jahaz. **And the LORD our God delivered him before us; and we smote him, and his sons, and all his people.** And we took all his cities at that time, and utterly destroyed the men, and the women, and the little ones, of every city, we left none to remain: Only the cattle we took for a prey unto ourselves, and the spoil of the cities which we took. From Aroer, which is by the brink of the river of Arnon, and from the city that is by the river, even unto Gilead, there was not one city too strong for us: the LORD our God delivered all unto us...." – Deuteronomy 2:31–36

The book of Amos confirms that the Amorites were giants:

> "Yet destroyed I the Amorite before them, **whose height was like the height of the cedars**, and he was strong as the oaks; yet I destroyed his fruit from above, and his roots from beneath. Also I brought you up from the land of Egypt, and led you forty years through the wilderness, to possess the land of the Amorite." – Amos 2:9–10

In this passage God confirmed the massive size of the Amorite giants and His conquest of them. Sihon was so legendary his attack on Moab and its principal city, Heshbon, earned a proverb recorded in Scripture about the Nephilim king's victory:

> "For Heshbon was the city of Sihon the king of the Amorites, who had fought against the former king of Moab, and taken all his land

out of his hand, even unto Arnon. Wherefore they that speak in proverbs say, Come into Heshbon, let the city of Sihon be built and prepared: For there is a fire gone out of Heshbon, a flame from the city of Sihon: it hath consumed Ar of Moab, and the lords of the high places of Arnon. Woe to thee, Moab! thou art undone, O people of Chemosh: he hath given his sons that escaped, and his daughters, into captivity unto Sihon king of the Amorites. We have shot at them; Heshbon is perished even unto Dibon, and we have laid them waste even unto Nophah, which reacheth unto Medeba."
– Numbers 21:26–30

For all Sihon's military prowess, the mighty warrior giant fell before the Lord. Every step of the way, God went out in front of the Israelite army to fight the initial battle and severely cripple the enemy so they could finish the job (Deuteronomy 2:33 includes the detail that the 12 tribes *also killed Sihon's sons*, eliminating his genetic line). The Lord was specifically and personally involved in destroying the remaining Nephilim giants off the face of the earth, fulfilling the Genesis 3:15 prophecy of enmity between the divine and satanic seeds. Jesus Christ, in His pre-incarnate form, was waging war against the Nephilim. Years earlier God had assured the Israelites He would battle for them in the wilderness:

"And the LORD said unto Moses, Depart, and go up hence, thou and the people which thou hast brought up out of the land of Egypt, unto the land which I sware unto Abraham, to Isaac, and to Jacob, saying, Unto thy seed will I give it: **And I will send an angel before thee; and I will drive out the Canaanite, the Amorite, and the Hittite, and the Perizzite, the Hivite, and the Jebusite**: Unto a land flowing with milk and honey: for I will not go up in the midst of thee; for thou art a stiffnecked people: lest I consume thee in the way." – Exodus 33:1–3

# GOD SPECIFICALLY TARGETED THE DESCENDANTS OF CANAAN FOR EXTERMINATION

The seven nations God repeatedly targeted for extermination were all descendants of Canaan as listed Genesis 10:15–19 (the lone exception being the Perizzites whom scholars believe was a political name for the Horites, also descendants of Canaan). This was not a wholescale "genocide" but **a military campaign specifically aimed at the progeny of Canaan, the forefather of all the postdiluvian Nephilim.** This was why Canaan became such an infamous figure in ancient history that the entire Promised Land was named after him. Among his descendants were the last genetic remnant of the pre-Flood demigods.

Even in the case of the supernatural destruction of Sodom and Gomorrah, the inhabitants of those cities were direct descendants of Canaan (Genesis 10:19). Which is why, as stated earlier, in addition to their "exceeding wickedness" they were in league with the Nephilim of the Genesis 14 war.

Thus, the fate of the Amorites was *charem* – the ban of extermination. The conquest of Sihon commenced the war against giant-populated nations and nothing was left to chance. The Nephilim bloodline was "utterly destroyed" in this area. Sihon marched his armies into the field for open combat and was destroyed by the Angel of the Lord – the pre-incarnate Jesus Christ. God delivered up Sihon and his armies to be conquered by Moses and the Israelite warriors.

# AFTER DEFEATING SIHON THE ISRAELITES FACED KING OG OF BASHAN

Og of Bashan is one of the most famous of the post-Flood giants and was the second Nephilim king Moses and the Israelites battled en route to the Promised Land. In ancient times Og's bed was a famous relic:

> "For only Og king of Bashan remained of the remnant of giants; behold his bedstead was a bedstead of iron; is it not in Rabbath of the children of Ammon? nine cubits was the length thereof, and four cubits the breadth of it, after the cubit of a man." – Deuteronomy 3:11

The ancient Middle Eastern cubit measured anywhere from 18-22 inches meaning Og even by conservative estimates was approximately 13 feet tall. This was a massive man, and his bed even later was kept in Rabbath, the royal city of the Ammonites, for display like a prized museum collection. The awe and fascination with this legendary Nephilim king continued after his death.

Og was the last of the giants genetically closest to the original Rephaim and thus was still called "Rephaim" by the people of that area after the Babel dispersion. What remained were descendants who were not as tall or powerful as their ancestors. A 19th-century Bible attested to this notion:

> "'Only Og king of Bashan remained of the remnant of giants.' Instead of being translated "giants" the original should perhaps be retained as a proper name 'Rephaim.' Og was certainly a giant, but not the last of the giants, only the last of the gigantic race called the Rephaim."– *The Pictorial Bible: Being the Old and New Testaments According to the Authorized Version*, Volume 1, C. Knight; 1833, p. 447.

It is no wonder the Israelites said the lands of the giants "eateth the inhabitants up" (Numbers 13:32). Og and Sihon, the two gatekeepers of the Promised Land, were seemingly invincible forces in the ancient world. And yet they fell at the hands of the Israelites.

# THE NEPHILIM POSSESSED ADVANCED CONSTRUCTION ABILITY

Og's massive kingdom *consisted of 60 cities* (Deuteronomy 3:4). This was a staggering amount for a nation in about 1700 BC. Bashan was located in high country, which provided excellent pasture for grazing cattle. The many ravines and rocky hills provide a natural fortification ("The hill of God is as the hill of Bashan; an high hill as the hill of Bashan" – Psalm 68:15). Ashteroth, the capital city, was named after the chief goddess of the Nephilim. The main cities were "fenced with high walls, gates, and bars" (Deuteronomy 3:5). A commentary from one of the most prolific Christian publishers of the 19th century detailed the grandeur of this kingdom after the author took an expedition to the ruins of Bashan:

> "We have already alluded to the large blocks of basalt which are found scattered over the country east of Jordan and to the fact of the Rephaim having made use of these to build their houses and cities. Situated as they were on the very edge of the Desert, and exposed at all times to the attacks of the nomadic tribes, who were every year increasing in number, it was very important to them to have their towns well fortified. Many of their cities were very large and surrounded by walls, and so solidly built, that when the people were intrenched within their towns they might well be thought invincible." – *Cambridge Essays*, Vol. 4, John W. Parker, Cambridge University, 1858, p. 142.

The Nephilim possessed exceptional skill in building large structures. The testimony of scholars who in the 19th century made the voyage to the Middle East to view these ancient edifices in person also confirmed the superior construction of the giant-led nations of Og and Sihon:

> "…we almost might feel tempted, as many have been, to think that some mistake with regard to the numbers of these places had crept

into the text. But when we go to the very country, and find one after another great stone cities, walled and unwalled, with stone gates, and so crowded together that it becomes a matter of wonder how all the people could have lived in so small a tract of country; when we see houses built of such huge and massive stones that no force that could ever have been brought against them would have been sufficient to batter them down; when we find rooms in these houses so large and so lofty, that many of them would be considered fine rooms in a large house in Europe; and lastly, when we find some of these towns bearing the very name that cities in that country bore before the Israelites came out of Egypt, I think we cannot help feeling the strongest conviction that we have before us the cities of the giant Rephaim." – *A Cyclopædia of Biblical Geography, Biography, Natural History, and General Knowledge*, Vol. 1, J. Lawson and J.M. Wilson, A. Fullerton & Co., 1866, p. 141–142.

These revelations shed light on the many ancient monoliths that still exist today that contain individual bricks and slabs that weigh hundreds of tons. Were giants involved in their construction? In describing the giants' superhuman construction abilities, the Bible seems to confirm it was well within their power. And with discoveries like Gilgal Rephaim, archaeology is in agreement.

Upon hearing news of his fellow Nephilim king's defeat, Og did not hesitate to bring his armies to fight against the nation of Israel:

"Then we turned, and went up the way to Bashan: and Og the king of Bashan came out against us, he and all his people, to battle at Edrei. And the LORD said unto me, Fear him not: for I will deliver him, and all his people, and his land, into thy hand; and thou shalt do unto him as thou didst unto Sihon king of the Amorites, which dwelt at Heshbon." – Deuteronomy 3:1–2

In the face of this immense military force, their 60-city megalopolis, and hybrid king, the Lord told the Israelites "fear him not" (Deuteronomy 3:2). Og chose to leave his impenetrable headquarters and march his armies to Edrei to engage Moses and the Israelites. Why would this warrior king leave the security of his home city and expose his armies in the open battlefield? It was because God drove the giant out of Ashteroth Karnaim:

> "And I sent the hornet before you, which drave them out from before you, even the two kings of the Amorites; but not with thy sword, nor with thy bow." – Joshua 24:12.

A biblical commentary on the tactical advantage of the hornet stated:

> "It would seem [Joshua 24:12] that the hornet was sent into these impregnable cities by God, and so Og and his people were driven forth into the open field (v. 1), where they were overthrown by Moses and the Israelites in a pitched battle opposite Edrei. This signal victory and its circumstances evidently impressed the people deeply at this time, and its memory as the Psalms attest, lingered for ages after in the national mind." – *The Holy Bible According to the Authorized Version, AD 1611, With an Explanatory and Critical Commentary and a Revision of the Translation*, By Bishops and Other Clergy of the Anglican Church, Edited by F.C. Cook, M.A., Canon of Exeter, Vol. I – Part II. 1877, p. 813.

God, as promised, sent hornets to flush out Og and his armies before the Israelites advanced. Their high fences and massive walls could no longer protect them. The Lord then decimated the Nephilim king's forces, leaving Moses and his troops to subdue the remaining enemy forces:

"So the LORD our God delivered into our hands Og also, the king of Bashan, and all his people: and we smote him until none was left to him remaining. And we took all his cities at that time, there was not a city which we took not from them, threescore cities, all the region of Argob, the kingdom of Og in Bashan. All these cities were fenced with high walls, gates, and bars; beside unwalled towns a great many. And we utterly destroyed them, as we did unto Sihon king of Heshbon, utterly destroying the men, women, and children, of every city. But all the cattle, and the spoil of the cities, we took for a prey to ourselves." – Deuteronomy 3:3–7

The Israelites took no chances with this kingdom and wiped out all the people to prevent the spread of any latent Nephilim genes. God's instructions not to attack or even disturb the areas geographically adjacent to Og and Sihon's kingdoms further emphasizes the specific targeting of Canaan's lineage (Deuteronomy 2:37). This passage is also the first place in Scripture that refers to Mt. Hermon located on the northern border of Og's kingdom and the place the Book of Enoch identifies as the original landing spot of the Genesis 6 apostate angels.

The victories over Sihon and Og were recorded in an ancient Book of the Wars of the Lord (an ancient Jewish text not in existence today but referenced in the Old Testament and other historical documents). The Israelites overcame tremendous military odds and pulled off a stunning victory because the living God was on their side. The conquest of the Nephilim kings east of the Jordan river stood as a memorial and glorious testimony of God's deliverance throughout the Bible:

"Praise ye the LORD. Praise ye the name of the LORD; praise him, O ye servants of the LORD. Ye that stand in the house of the LORD, in the courts of the house of our God.... Whatsoever the LORD pleased, that did he in heaven, and in earth, in the seas, and all deep places. He causeth the vapours to ascend from the ends of the earth; he maketh lightnings for the rain; he bringeth the win out of his treasuries. Who smote the firstborn of Egypt, both of man and beast. Who sent tokens and wonders into the midst of thee, O Egypt, upon Pharaoh, and upon all his servants. Who smote great nations, and slew mighty kings; Sihon king of the Amorites, and Og king of Bashan, and all the kingdoms of Canaan: And gave their land for an heritage, an heritage unto Israel his people." – Psalm 135:1–2, 6–12

In the passage above, the psalmist extols the supernatural works of the Lord such as the plagues of Egypt during the Exodus. In this list, Sihon and Og are the only two kings mentioned by name. Their defeat ranked with the Lord's greatest miracles. Human or hybrid-human strength was no match for God. With the enormous corpse of the slain Og before them, the Israelites possessed the ultimate proof of Yahweh's power.

## JESUS CHRIST – THE ANGEL OF THE LORD – WAGED WAR AGAINST THE NEPHILIM KINGS

"Behold, I send an Angel before thee, to keep thee in the way, and to bring thee into the place which I have prepared. **Beware of him, and obey his voice, provoke him not; for he will not pardon your transgressions: for my name is in him.** But if thou shalt indeed obey his voice, and do all that I speak; then I will be an enemy unto thine enemies, and an adversary unto thine adversaries. For mine Angel shall go before thee, and bring thee in unto the Amorites, and the Hittites, and the Perizzites, and the Canaanites, the Hivites, and the Jebusites: and I will cut them off." – Exodus 23:20–23

This "Angel," the pre-incarnate Jesus Christ, literally waged wars against the Nephilim kingdoms. No normal angel could "pardon your transgressions," but the Messiah, as the Angel of the Lord, certainly could. The book of Exodus confirms that Jesus was the "Angel of the Lord" of the Old Testament:

> "And the angel of the LORD appeared unto him in a flame of fire out of the midst of a bush: and he looked, and, behold, the bush burned with fire, and the bush was not consumed. And Moses said, I will now turn aside, and see this great sight, why the bush is not burnt. And when the LORD saw that he turned aside to see, God called unto him out of the midst of the bush, and said, Moses, Moses. And he said, Here am I. And he said, Draw not nigh hither: put off thy shoes from off thy feet, for the place whereon thou standest is holy ground. Moreover he said, I am the God of thy father, the God of Abraham, the God of Isaac, and the God of Jacob. And Moses hid his face; for he was afraid to look upon God." – Exodus 3:2–6

The Angel of the Lord was the bodily manifestation of God on Earth in the Old Testament. Only Jesus Christ can fulfill this role, "for in him dwelleth all the fulness of the Godhead bodily" (Colossians 2:9). In the New Testament, Jesus Himself stated: "Not that any man hath seen the Father, save he which is of God, he hath seen the Father" (John 6:46), further confirming that no person in history saw God the Father. It was God the Son – Jesus Christ – making the in-person visitations to Earth and fighting before the people of Israel.

Psalm 44 credits God for waging the wars against the Canaanites on behalf of Israel:

> "We have heard with our ears, O God, our fathers have told us, what work thou didst in their days, in the times of old. How thou didst drive out the heathen with thy hand, and plantedst them; how thou didst afflict the people, and cast them out. For they

[Israel] got not the land in possession by their own sword, neither did their own arm save them: but thy right hand, and thine arm, and the light of thy countenance, because thou hadst a favour unto them." – Psalm 44:1–3

Many theologians and biblical commentaries affirm this interpretation:

"Here the angel who appeared in a flame of fire is declared to be God himself. No remark is therefore needed, to prove what the passage undeniably asserts, that Moses beheld God in the person of the angel or messenger of the LORD, and that the angel was the same as God; – He must therefore have been Christ, who was revealed as the 'Angel of the Covenant' in the succeeding history of Israel." – *Scriptural Views of Our Lord Jesus Christ, as the Creator, Upholder, and Redeemer of the World; Or Looking Unto Jesus*, John Fitz-Gerald, M.A., James Burns, 27, Portman Street, 1835, p. 306.

"That the Angel of the Lord who preceded the children of Israel from Egypt in the cloud and in the fire, was (agreeably to [Exodus 13:20–21 compared with 14:19–20; Numbers 14:6]) the LORD himself possessor of the incommunicable name… and who was in the [fullness] of time incarnate in the person of Jesus Christ, is the known undoubted faith of the Church of God, and needs not to be enlarged on here. This same Uncreated Angel, in whom was the name of the LORD, is promised by the mouth of Moses, in [Exodus 23:20– 23], to continue to precede the armies of Israel, and cut off the Canaanites before them: but with an awful caution annexed, that they should be careful not to provoke that august Presence, intolerant of any contact with sin." – *Observations on the Attempted Application of Pantheistic Principles to the Theory and Historic Criticism of the Gospel: Being the Christian Advocate's Publications for the Years 1840–1844*, Second Edition, W.H. Mills, D.D., F.R.A.S., Cambridge, Deighton, Bell & Co., 1861, pp. 353–354.

"We read 'Behold, I send an angel before thee, to keep thee in the way, and to bring thee into the place which I have prepared.' 'Mine angel shall go before thee and bring thee into the land of Canaan' (Exodus 23:20; 23). Surely this Angel of God was no other than Jehovah Jesus." – *Twelve Sermons Preached at Verulam District Church, Lambeth, London,* Third Series, The Rev. J. Battetrsby, Fisher & Sidstone, 23, Morgate Street, London, 1878, p. 17.

It was Jesus Christ who routed the armies of Og and Sihon. The triumph over these two Nephilim kings was one of many miraculous acts the Lord performed for Israel and humanity. Psalm 136 celebrated the legendary victory:

**"To him which smote great kings: for his mercy endureth for ever**: And slew famous kings: for his mercy endureth for ever: Sihon king of the Amorites: for his mercy endureth for ever: And Og the king of Bashan: for his mercy endureth for ever: And gave their land for an heritage: for his mercy endureth for ever:" – Psalm 136:17–21

The Israelites were "stiffnecked," complaining about their conditions in the wilderness, questioning Moses' leadership, and doubting God who brought them out of Egypt. But despite their sinful rebellion, God showed His great mercy towards them by serving as the "advance forces" to defeat a seemingly invincible foe. There is no limit to the mercy the Lord has for all people but especially for His saints. If you are a born-again Christian, never forget that no matter how far you sink into sin or backsliding, God is ever-ready and willing to forgive and remove that sin from your life and His memory just as He removed the Nephilim in Moses' day.

# THE NEPHILIM SURVIVED THE FLOOD TO SERVE AS EVIDENCE OF GOD'S POWER AND MERCY

The spectacular destruction of the kingdoms of Sihon and Og confirm why the Nephilim gene was permitted to pass through the ark: The military conquest of the postdiluvian giants at the hands of God was clear testimony and proof that the children of Israel served the true God of creation. The Gentile world was awed by the power of the God of Israel. Though the giants seemed unstoppable by any worldly measure, the 12 tribes of Israel, led by their God, annihilated them. Transitioning from Moses to his successor, Joshua, the might of Israel through Yahweh was evidenced in the testimony of Rahab of Jericho. Stupefied by the victories God provided to Israel, she risked her own life to protect two Jewish spies:

> "And she said unto the men, I know that the LORD hath given you the land, and that your terror is fallen upon us, and that all the inhabitants of the land faint because of you. For we have heard how the LORD dried up the water of the Red sea for you, when ye came out of Egypt; and what ye did unto the two kings of the Amorites, that were on the other side Jordan, **Sihon and Og, whom ye utterly destroyed. And as soon as we had heard these things, our hearts did melt, neither did there remain any more courage in any man, because of you: for the LORD your God, he is God in heaven above, and in earth beneath.**" – Joshua 2:9–11

# CROSSING JORDAN – THE CANAANITES QUAKED WITH FEAR AT THE ARRIVAL OF THE ISRAELITES IN THE PROMISED LAND

> "And I commanded you at that time, saying, the Lord your God hath given you this land to possess it: ye shall pass over armed before

your brethren the children of Israel, all that are meet for the war.... And I commanded Joshua at that time, saying, Thine eyes have seen all that the LORD your God hath done unto these two kings: so shall the LORD do unto all the kingdoms whither thou passest. Ye shall not fear them: for the LORD your God he shall fight for you." – Moses, Deuteronomy 3:18; 21–22

Moses disobeyed God and was denied entrance into the Promised Land (Numbers 20:12). Leadership of the nation of Israel passed to Joshua, who had faithfully followed Moses and learned firsthand what it meant to live a life of faith and godliness. In Deuteronomy 7, Moses delivered his final address to the nation of Israel, spiritually preparing them for the battles to come. The seven nations God promised to remove from the Land of Canaan awaited them. The time to reclaim the Promised Land had arrived. After reciting the Mosaic Law of the Old Covenant, Moses instructed his people on how to deal with the usurpers in the Promised Land:

> "When the LORD thy God shall bring thee into the land whither thou goest to possess it, and hath cast out many nations before thee, the Hittites, and the Girgashites, and the Amorites, and the Canaanites, and the Perizzites, and the Hivites, and the Jebusites, seven nations greater and mightier than thou; And when the LORD thy God shall deliver them before thee; thou shalt smite them, and utterly destroy them; thou shalt make no covenant with them, nor shew mercy unto them: **Neither shalt thou make marriages with them**; thy daughter thou shalt not give unto his son, nor his daughter shalt thou take unto thy son." – Deuteronomy 7:1–3

Though the descendants of Canaan were "greater and mightier" than the Israelites, the Lord would battle them, and that made all the difference. Moses, delivering instructions directly from God, commanded the people to wipe out the Canaanites, make no covenants, and avoid marrying them. The emphasis on having no intermingling with Canaan's descendants could not have been clearer. The Lord would not tolerate His own creation, humanity, tarnished with the seed of the false gods – the angelic ancestors of the Nephilim who in their wickedness tried to "play God" and create their own master race to dominate the earth and consume it.

In the days of Moses, many people in the Gentile world, lacking knowledge of Yahweh's Word, submitted to the power and influence of the Nephilim supermen. The Gentiles invoked God's wrath by joining the Nephilim in worship of their fallen angelic ancestors. As Moses continued his final pre-battle address, he warned about *the spiritual threat* the giant-infested nations posed as well:

> "For they will turn away thy son from following me, that they may serve other gods: so will the anger of the LORD be kindled against you, and destroy thee suddenly. But thus shall ye deal with them; ye shall destroy their altars, and break down their images, and cut down their groves, and burn their graven images with fire. For thou art an holy people unto the LORD thy God: the LORD thy God hath chosen thee to be a special people unto himself, above all people that are upon the face of the earth." – Deuteronomy 7:4–6

Upon vanquishing their foes, the children of Israel were to destroy any religious idol, structure, or edifice from the Canaanites. The Nephilim-populated nations promoted much of the idolatry of the ancient world. Leaving traces of their pagan practices invited the risk of falling into the worship of fallen angels and demons. An Israelite could just as easily become a "child of the Devil" by practicing pagan religion as by marrying into a family of giants. Marriage posed both a genetic *and spiritual danger*. This was yet another reason it was necessary to eliminate Canaan's Nephilim bloodline:

> "And thou shalt consume all the people which the LORD thy God shall deliver thee; thine eye shall have no pity upon them: neither

shalt thou serve their gods; for that will be a snare unto thee. If thou shalt say in thine heart, These nations are more than I; how can I dispossess them? Thou shalt not be afraid of them: but shalt well remember what the LORD thy God did unto Pharaoh, and unto all Egypt; The great temptations which thine eyes saw, and the signs, and the wonders, and the mighty hand, and the stretched out arm, whereby the LORD thy God brought thee out: so shall the LORD thy God do unto all the people of whom thou art afraid.

Moreover the LORD thy God will send the hornet among them, until they that are left, and hide themselves from thee, be destroyed. Thou shalt not be affrighted at them: for the LORD thy God is among you, a mighty God and terrible. And the LORD thy God will put out those nations before thee by little and little: thou mayest not consume them at once, lest the beasts of the field increase upon thee. But the LORD thy God shall deliver them unto thee, and shall destroy them with a mighty destruction, until they be destroyed. And he shall deliver their kings into thine hand, and thou shalt destroy their name from under heaven: there shall no man be able to stand before thee, until thou have destroyed them."
– Deuteronomy 7:16–24

These were the marching orders from God. Like a heroic general addressing his army on the eve of battle, the Creator of all used rousing speech to inspire the 12 tribes to be courageous before an enemy who appeared greater in stature and number. To the human eye, the odds were stacked against Israel, but God reassured them with the bold promises that *He and He alone would fight and defeat the enemy.* This included the infamous sons of Anak who had frightened the 10 spies and led an entire generation of Israelites to die in the wilderness:

"Hear, O Israel: Thou art to pass over Jordan this day, to go in to possess nations greater and mightier than thyself, cities great and fenced up to heaven, **A people great and tall, the children of the**

> Anakims, whom thou knowest, and of whom thou hast heard
> say, Who can stand before the children of Anak! Understand
> therefore this day, that the LORD thy God is he which goeth
> over before thee; as a consuming fire he shall destroy them, and
> he shall bring them down before thy face: so shalt thou drive
> them out, and destroy them quickly, as the LORD hath said
> unto thee." – Deuteronomy 9:1–3

The Lord acknowledged the legendary height, military prowess, and political might of Ahiman, Seshai, and Talmai. Their superhuman abilities and size inspired fear all over the world. The cities of Nephilim-polluted nations were monstrous citadels that were "fenced up to heaven" (Deuteronomy 9:1). There was a reason the Nephilim were "men of renown." And the Lord was going to personally deal with these fallen-angelic hybrids and destroy them.

## WHY WAS ISRAEL SELECTED TO BE GOD'S CHOSEN NATION?

The Israelites are often called "the chosen people." Why was this nation given such preeminence in the Old Testament? Was God truly playing favorites by having this particular ethnic group take the land from the Canaanites? Did the Lord just think highly of the Israelites and esteem them as a "superior people" or "master race" who "deserved" to live in the Promised Land more than other races? The next verses answer that question:

> "Speak not thou in thine heart, after that the LORD thy God hath
> cast them out from before thee, saying, For my righteousness the
> LORD hath brought me in to possess this land: **but for the
> wickedness of these nations the LORD doth drive them out
> from before thee.** Not for thy righteousness, or for the uprightness
> of thine heart, dost thou go to possess their land: but for the

wickedness of these nations the LORD thy God doth drive them out from before thee, and that he may perform the word which the LORD sware unto thy fathers, Abraham, Isaac, and Jacob. Understand therefore, that the LORD thy God giveth thee not this good land to possess it for thy righteousness; for thou art a stiffnecked people." – Deuteronomy 9:4–6

The Israelites were not given these victories because they were "so special" but rather to keep the promise God made to Abraham centuries earlier. Additionally, the Israelites *were the instrument of God's wrath upon the Nephilim hybrid nations.* When God made His covenant with Abraham, He told the patriarch that his offspring would spend 400 years as slaves under the authority of a foreign people because at that time "the iniquity of the Amorites is not yet full" (Genesis 15:16). The time had come for God to unleash his wrath on these peoples who not only rejected God but also murdered, stole, waged war, and established an elaborate system of idolatry with a host of pagan gods, goddesses, and occult ritual sacrifices. Much of the book of Deuteronomy outlines God's instructions on avoiding any cultural similarity with the pagan world Israel encountered in the Promised Land. The numerous rules regarding hair cutting, markings in skin, dietary restrictions, and the like were all aimed at differentiating the Israelites from the occult practitioners in the Promised Land.

## THE LORD EMBOLDENED JOSHUA TO VICTORY

Joshua was the human servant chosen to deliver God's battle plan for recapturing the Promised Land. The Lord inspired His chosen leader before the campaign was waged:

"Now after the death of Moses the servant of the LORD it came to pass, that the LORD spake unto Joshua the son of Nun, Moses' minister, saying, Moses my servant is dead; now therefore arise, go over this Jordan, thou, and all this people, unto the land which I do give to them, even to the children of Israel. Every place that the sole of your foot shall tread upon, that have I given unto you, as I said unto Moses. From the wilderness and this Lebanon even unto the great river, the river Euphrates, all the land of the Hittites, and unto the great sea toward the going down of the sun, shall be your coast. There shall not any man be able to stand before thee all the days of thy life: as I was with Moses, so I will be with thee: I will not fail thee, nor forsake thee.

Be strong and of a good courage: for unto this people shalt thou divide for an inheritance the land, which I sware unto their fathers to give them. Only be thou strong and very courageous, that thou mayest observe to do according to all the law, which Moses my servant commanded thee: turn not from it to the right hand or to the left, that thou mayest prosper withersoever thou goest." – Joshua 1:1–7

Three times God implored Joshua to "be strong" and of "good courage." The Lord reiterated the promise that the land of Canaan would indeed belong to the Israelites and that no one would ever be able to challenge Joshua on the field of battle. God inspired Joshua to trust His Word over his own eyes. No matter what awesome fortresses or giants lay ahead, Joshua was to be courageous – not in his own might, and not in his own strength. He was to have faith that God was with him every step of the way. Joshua's faith in God's Word would lead him to great victories over the Nephilim giants. And we will now look at some of the key moments in the war waged for the Promised Land.

# LIKE NOAH, GOD SAVED RAHAB – A FULLY-HUMAN BELIEVER IN A CORRUPTED SOCIETY

"I am convinced, she [cried],
the Lord, To Israel will perform his word,
And the fair plains of Canaan give;
Where his beloved [sons] shall live:
For all the people of our land,
In deep dejection trembling stand,
They having heard how God proceeds,
To make your way by dreadful deeds
The roaring sea his power divides,
And makes your passage thro the tides,
The giant Og and Sihon slain,
What hope to us can now remain?"

— John Fellows, "A Poem of Rahab," *The History of the Holy Bible as Contained in the Old and New Testaments*, Vol. II, London, 1778, pp. 339–340.

In preparation for his opening battle Joshua sent two spies to scout Jericho. These men worked undercover to examine the inner workings of the city. To avoid detection at night they lodged in the place of business of the harlot Rahab. Risking her own life, Rahab lied to the king of Jericho's soldiers who were searching for the Israelite invaders. Her protection of the spies and testimony as to *why* she helped them illustrate the importance of the conquest of the giants:

"And she said unto the men, I know that the LORD hath given you the land, and that your terror is fallen upon us, and that all the inhabitants of the land faint because of you. For we have heard how the LORD dried up the water of the Red sea for you, when ye came out of Egypt; and what ye did unto the two kings of the Amorites, that were on the other side Jordan, Sihon and Og, whom ye utterly destroyed. And as soon as we had heard these things, our hearts did melt, neither did there remain any more courage in any man, because of you: for the LORD your God, he is God in heaven above, and in earth beneath. Now therefore, I pray you, swear unto me by the LORD, since I have shewed you kindness, that ye will also shew kindness unto my father's house, and give me a true token: And that ye will save alive my father, and my mother, and my brethren, and my sisters, and all that they have, and deliver our lives from death." – Joshua 2:9–13

Rahab lived in Jericho, one of the most fortified cities in the world. Archeological findings confirm that the city was impregnable:

"The mound, or 'tell' of Jericho was surrounded by a great earthen rampart, or embankment, with a stone retaining wall at its base. The retaining wall was some four to five meters (12–15 feet) high. On top of that was a mudbrick wall two meters (six feet) thick and about six to eight meters (20–26 feet) high.4 At the crest of the embankment was a similar mudbrick wall whose base was roughly 14 meters (46 feet) above the ground level outside the retaining wall (see diagram). This is what loomed high above the Israelites as they marched around the city each day for seven days. Humanly speaking, it was impossible for the Israelites to penetrate the impregnable bastion of Jericho." – The Walls of Jericho Archaeology Confirms: They Really Did Come A–tumblin' Down, by Bryant Wood on March 1, 1999. http://www.answersingenesis.org/articles/cm/v21/n2/the–walls–of–jericho#fnList_1_4

The outer and inner walls of the city were 6-feet and 12-feet thick, respectively. The construction was in line with the militarized metropolis of

King Og. And this is precisely where God commenced his campaign in the land of Canaan.

In addition to the rousing pre-battle speech to the 12 tribes, God also manifested supernaturally to show the entire nation that He was with them. At the Jordan River, the Lord parted the waters for the Israelites to enter the Promised Land just as their ancestors had done at the Red Sea after fleeing Egypt:

> "And the LORD said unto Joshua, This day will I begin to magnify thee in the sight of all Israel, that they may know that, as I was with Moses, so I will be with thee. And thou shalt command the priests that bear the ark of the covenant, saying, When ye are come to the brink of the water of Jordan, ye shall stand still in Jordan. And Joshua said unto the children of Israel, Come hither, and hear the words of the LORD your God. **And Joshua said, Hereby ye shall know that the living God is among you, and that he will without fail drive out from before you the Canaanites, and the Hittites, and the Hivites, and the Perizzites, and the Girgashites, and the Amorites, and the Jebusites**. Behold, the ark of the covenant of the LORD of all the earth passeth over before you into Jordan. Now therefore take you twelve men out of the tribes of Israel, out of every tribe a man. And it shall come to pass, as soon as the soles of the feet of the priests that bear the ark of the LORD, the LORD of all the earth, shall rest in the waters of Jordan, that the waters of Jordan shall be cut off from the waters that come down from above; and they shall stand upon an heap.
>
> And it came to pass, when the people removed from their tents, to pass over Jordan, and the priests bearing the ark of the covenant before the people; And as they that bare the ark were come unto Jordan, and the feet of the priests that bare the ark were dipped in the brim of the water, (for Jordan overfloweth all his banks all the

> time of harvest,) That the waters which came down from above stood and rose up upon an heap very far from the city Adam, that is beside Zaretan: and those that came down toward the sea of the plain, even the salt sea, failed, and were cut off: and the people passed over right against Jericho. And the priests that bare the ark of the covenant of the LORD stood firm on dry ground in the midst of Jordan, and all the Israelites passed over on dry ground, until all the people were passed clean over Jordan." – Joshua 3:7–17

God never asks for "blind faith" in His children. He wants all believers to know that He is true to His Word and promises. Just as He has fulfilled all promises made in the past, so too will He continue to deliver on every promise He gives to those who believe and put faith and trust in Him in the future. The Lord did not want only to inspire Joshua but to provide clear supernatural proof to the people of Israel that Joshua was indeed divinely selected to lead them in battle. It provided irrefutable evidence to all the people that the Creator was on their side and victory was at hand.

The miracle was also a message to the enemy. God finished His instructions to Joshua on the great crossing of the river saying: "For the LORD your God dried up the waters of Jordan from before you, until ye were passed over, as the LORD your God did to the Red sea, which he dried up from before us, until we were gone over: **That all the people of the earth might know the hand of the LORD, that it is mighty**: that ye might fear the LORD your God for ever" (Joshua 4:23–24).

The Jordan River miracle was not lost on the Nephilim-led nations in Canaan:

> "And it came to pass, when all the kings of the Amorites, which were on the side of Jordan westward, and all the kings of the Canaanites, which were by the sea, heard that the LORD had dried up the waters of Jordan from before the children of Israel, until we were passed

over, **that their heart melted, neither was there spirit in them any more, because of the children of Israel**." – Joshua 5:1

The postdiluvian Nephilim were the most feared force on Earth. And yet, when they received word that Israelites crossed over a supernaturally-parted Jordan River, they and their human subjects were horrified. By exterminating the Nephilim, the Lord was not only saving the human race but proving to the population that the true God of the universe was with Israel and not with the pagan false gods of the Nephilim-led nations.

## THE CONQUEST OF JERICHO – PARALLELS WITH THE LAST DAYS BEFORE THE FLOOD

"Now Jericho was straitly shut up because of the children of Israel: none went out, and none came in. And the LORD said unto Joshua, See, I have given into thine hand Jericho, and the king thereof, and the mighty men of valour." – Joshua 6:1–2

As Joshua and Israel approached the stronghold of the Canaanites, their enemies quaked in fear behind their massive walls. Joshua then executed the unconventional battle strategy given directly by God:

"And Joshua rose early in the morning, and the priests took up the ark of the LORD. And seven priests bearing seven trumpets of rams' horns before the ark of the LORD went on continually, and blew with the trumpets: and the armed men went before them; but the reward came after the ark of the LORD, the priests going on, and blowing with the trumpets. And the second day they compassed the city once, and returned into the camp: so they did six days. And it came to pass on the seventh day, that they rose early about the dawning of the day, and compassed the city after the same manner seven times: only on that day they compassed the city seven times. And it came to pass at the seventh time, when the priests blew with the trumpets, Joshua said unto the people, Shout; for the LORD hath given you the city." – Joshua 6:12–16

For six days the Israelites marched around Jericho in silence. At the end of each march the priests issued a single trumpet blast. Then, on the seventh day, the people circled the city seven times and shouted, and the Lord supernaturally destroyed the impenetrable walls of Jericho. This very interesting battle plan holds parallels with the Flood. The people of Jericho were well aware that the Israelites had prevailed over Egypt at the Exodus. This tiny nation of slaves had won a battle over the preeminent empire in the world. The Canaanites in Jericho also knew of the victories God gave Israel over Nephilim kings Og and Sihon. They had a powerful witness of the might and power of the Lord of the people of Israel.

The Israelites literally came to the doorstep of Jericho. But did the Canaanites repent? Did they seek peace with the Lord? No. They shut themselves in and put their trust in their walls to protect them from God – this despite the fact that for six days the Israelites did not attack. Their armies were led by the priests bearing the Ark of the Covenant and blowing trumpets. Despite this opportunity, the Canaanites chose to remain in their city, and their mighty walls crumbled allowing for their destruction.

Notice the parallels to the Flood of Noah's day. Noah preached the Gospel for over a century to the sinful world and they would not listen. He built the ark in the sight of the people – a clear sign of the impending doom that was coming to them, and yet they ignored him. Then, once the ark was completed, God told Noah to go inside for seven days. No longer would the rebellious sinners of the pre-Flood world hear Noah's calls to repent and believe in the Savior. There was simply silence for seven days. In similar fashion, God instructed Joshua and the 12 tribes to remain silent seven days.

No one was to make a sound as they circled Jericho. Then, on the seventh day, just as it was in the days of Noah the Lord punished the Nephilim-infested evildoers in devastating fashion:

> "So the people shouted when the priests blew with the trumpets: and it came to pass, when the people heard the sound of the trumpet, and the people shouted with a great shout, that the wall fell down flat, so that the people went up into the city, every man straight before him, and they took the city. And they utterly destroyed all that was in the city, both man and woman, young and old, and ox, and sheep, and ass, with the edge of the sword. But Joshua had said unto the two men that had spied out the country, Go into the harlot's house, and bring out thence the woman, and all that she hath, as ye sware unto her. And the young men that were spies went in, and brought out Rahab, and her father, and her mother, and her brethren, and all that she did; and they brought out all her kindred, and left them without the camp of Israel. And they burnt the city with fire, and all that was therein: only the silver, and the gold, and the vessels of brass and of iron, they put into the treasury of the house of the LORD." – Joshua 6:20–24

The Lord eradicated the walls of Jericho, leaving them vulnerable to an attack by the Israelite forces. Rahab, a believer who was genetically fully human, was spared along with all her family. Just as Noah was "perfect in his generations" despite living in a world overrun by the giants, so Rahab's lineage avoided the taint of Nephilim DNA. This we know because Rahab eventually became a part of the lineage of the Messiah, being the great-grandmother of King David and a direct ancestor of Jesus Christ (Matthew 1:5–6).

When we contrast this with the treatment of the rest of the Canaanites, it is clear that this "genocide" was the result of something far greater than hatred between enemies. It was a systematic removal of the cursed, satanic hybrid seed of Canaan from the earth. Joshua reinforced the condemned status of the hybrid Canaanites by cursing the city:

"And Joshua adjured them at that time, saying, Cursed be the man before the LORD, that riseth up and buildeth this city Jericho: he shall lay the foundation thereof in his firstborn, and in his youngest son shall he set up the gates of it." – Joshua 6:26

Just as Cain and Canaan before them, the descendants of the satanic bloodline were cursed by God's anointed.

## THE BATTLE OF AI –
## ANOTHER SUPERNATURAL CONQUEST

At the battle of Ai, Joshua employed a very clever strategy. After bringing a small force to the main entrance to the city, the Israelites retreated from the Canaanite armies, feigning defeat. The ruse lured the enemy out of its secure defensive position within the city. Once the Canaanites chased after the supposedly conquered Jewish forces, separate units, stationed in the rear of Ai, launched an ambush. While this type of strategy made Joshua a master tactician in the eyes of historians, he was merely following God's instructions. The Lord still fought the enemy directly to ensure victory:

"And Joshua and all Israel made as if they were beaten before them, and fled by the way of the wilderness. And all the people that were in Ai were called together to pursue after them: and they pursued after Joshua, and were drawn away from the city. And there was not a man left in Ai or Bethel, that went not out after Israel: and they left the city open, and pursued after Israel. **And the LORD said unto Joshua, Stretch out the spear that is in thy hand toward Ai; for I will give it into thine hand.** And Joshua stretched out the spear that he had in his hand toward the city.

And the ambush arose quickly out of their place, and they ran as soon as he had stretched out his hand: and they entered into the city, and took it, and hasted and set the city on fire. And when the men of Ai looked behind them, they saw, and, behold, the smoke of the city ascended up to heaven, and they had no power to flee this way or that way: and the people that fled to the wilderness turned back upon the pursuers. And when Joshua and all Israel saw that the ambush had taken the city, and that the smoke of the city ascended, then they turned again, and slew the men of Ai." – Joshua 8:15–21

The Lord empowered the ambush units to victory. And the Canaanites were eradicated:

"And it came to pass, when Israel had made an end of slaying all the inhabitants of Ai in the field, in the wilderness wherein they chased them, and when they were all fallen on the edge of the sword, until they were consumed, that all the Israelites returned unto Ai, and smote it with the edge of the sword. And so it was, that all that fell that day, both of men and women, were twelve thousand, even all the men of Ai. For Joshua drew not his hand back, wherewith he stretched out the spear, until he had utterly destroyed all the inhabitants of Ai." – Joshua 8:24–26

Also noteworthy is that Joshua is another form of the name Yeshua, the name of the Savior. The book of Joshua contains an abundance of Messianic foreshadowing. Just as Joshua led the Israelites into the Promised Land of Canaan, so too does Jesus Christ lead all believers into the true Promised Land – Heaven and the Millennial Kingdom. Joshua did the will of God the Father as did Jesus. So even in type and shadow, we see that God personally waged war against the giants to wipe them off the face of the earth.

# JOSHUA RECLAIMED THE LAND FOR GOD

At the end of the battle Joshua claimed the newly-acquired territory for Yahweh. He erected an altar in Shechem, the valley that lay between Mt. Ebal and Mt. Gerazim:

> "Then Joshua built an altar unto the LORD God of Israel in mount Ebal, As Moses the servant of the LORD commanded the children of Israel, as it is written in the book of the law of Moses, an altar of whole stones, over which no man hath lift up any iron: and they offered thereon burnt offerings unto the LORD, and sacrificed peace offerings. And he wrote there upon the stones a copy of the law of Moses, which he wrote in the presence of the children of Israel. And all Israel, and their elders, and officers, and their judges, stood on this side the ark and on that side before the priests the Levites, which bare the Ark of the Covenant of the LORD, as well the stranger, as he that was born among them; half of them over against mount Gerizim, and half of them over against mount Ebal; as Moses the servant of the LORD had commanded before, that they should bless the people of Israel.

> "And afterward he read all the words of the law, the blessings and cursings, according to all that is written in the book of the law. There was not a word of all that Moses commanded, which Joshua read not before all the congregation of Israel, with the women, and the little ones, and the strangers that were conversant among them." – Joshua 8:30–35

This very peculiar event was done according to instructions Moses gave in Deuteronomy 27. Six tribes of Israel were instructed to recite the curses of the Mosaic Law on Mt. Ebal while the other six stood on Mt. Gerazim and recited the blessings of the Law. Having won yet another military victory through the supernatural power of the Lord, Joshua showed his obedience by following Moses' command to erect altars at Mt. Ebal and Mt. Gerazim. The altars were made of "whole stones," large rocks that were uncut and not carved. This was the antithesis of the Tower of Babel, the walls of Jericho, and all the other man-made structures that were revered in the pagan world.

The whole stones represented God's power as creator and man's need to rely fully on the Lord for salvation. Joshua provided leadership not just in battle but in right worship and reverence for God.

The recording and public recital of the books of Moses was a declaration that the Promised Land was dedicated to the God of Israel. It was a bold testimony of God's Word to all the remaining people of Canaan. Just as Moses gathered the entire nation after the Exodus to recite God's Word to them, so Joshua, now in the Promised Land, taught the book of the Law to Israel and all "the strangers" or foreigners who had joined them. It is God's Word that Satan so strongly hates and opposes because the Gospel is literally "the power of God unto salvation" (Romans 1:16). The Word of God convicts persons of their sin. It stirs the sorrow and desire for forgiveness that can come only through the Messiah. It exposes the dark, sinful ways and deceptions of the world. Thus, in response to this great and glorious day for all believers, Satan immediately stirred up the enemies of God.

## THE KING OF JERUSALEM – FORESHADOW OF THE ANTICHRIST

"Now it came to pass, when Adonizedec king of Jerusalem had heard how Joshua had taken Ai, and had utterly destroyed it; as he had done to Jericho and her king, so he had done to Ai and her king; and how the inhabitants of Gibeon had made peace with Israel, and were among them; ² That they feared greatly, because Gibeon was a great city, as one of the royal cities, and because it was greater than Ai, and all the men thereof were mighty.

> Wherefore Adonizedec king of Jerusalem, sent unto Hoham king of
> Hebron, and unto Piram king of Jarmuth, and unto Japhia king of
> Lachish, and unto Debir king of Eglon, saying, Come up unto me,
> and help me, that we may smite Gibeon: for it hath made peace with
> Joshua and with the children of Israel. Therefore the five kings of the
> Amorites, the king of Jerusalem, the king of Hebron, the king of
> Jarmuth, the king of Lachish, the king of Eglon, gathered themselves
> together, and went up, they and all their hosts, and encamped before
> Gibeon, and made war against it." – Joshua 10:1–5

Having lost the Gibeonites and another city in the Promised Land, the
enemies of Israel prepared a counterstrike. This is the mentality of the unsaved
– relentless hostility towards God and His Word. Romans 8:7 states: "Because
the carnal mind is enmity against God: for it is not subject to the law of God,
neither indeed can be." Nonbelievers are at constant war with God because
they reject His Word and authority. In the spirit of the Nephilim, this
hostility was magnified to even greater depravity, which is why Satan attacks
God's Word and instills doubt and hatred for it in the hearts and minds of
society. What Joshua did threatened Satan's entire agenda for corrupting
humanity:

> "But if our gospel be hid, it is hid to them that are lost: In whom
> the god of this world hath blinded the minds of them which believe
> not, lest the light of the glorious gospel of Christ, who is the image
> of God, should shine unto them." – 2 Corinthians 4:3–4

To keep the Canaanites under their sway, the giant-mixed nations formed a
confederacy to retaliate against Israel. Up until Joshua 10, Israel had been the
aggressor in the war for the Promised Land. By capturing Jericho, Joshua
controlled the center of the land of Canaan, providing Israel with a strategic
advantage. The Canaanites then launched their own counteroffensive.

Despite Israel's destruction of the Egyptian army, their conquest of Sihon and Og, the supernatural crumbling of the walls of Jericho, and the murder of every citizen at Ai, the Canaanite nations showed no intention of retreat or surrender. They still craved war with God as the satanic spirit of their fallen angelic ancestors burned within them. To their dismay, the Lord was prepared for combat:

> "So Joshua ascended from Gilgal, he, and all the people of war with him, and all the mighty men of valour. And the LORD said unto Joshua, Fear them not: for I have delivered them into thine hand; there shall not a man of them stand before thee. Joshua therefore came unto them suddenly, and went up from Gilgal all night. **And the LORD discomfited them before Israel, and slew them with a great slaughter at Gibeon, and chased them along the way that goeth up to Bethhoron, and smote them to Azekah, and unto Makkedah.** And it came to pass, as they fled from before Israel, and were in the going down to Bethhoron, that the LORD cast down great stones from heaven upon them unto Azekah, and they died: they were more which died with hailstones than they whom the children of Israel slew with the sword." – Joshua 10:7–11

The Lord slaughtered Adonizedec and his confederacy. He fought these nations directly and, as the enemy retreated, rained hailstones on them. Joshua's forces were once again "cleaning up the mess" after the main battle was won. God's witness to the world was clear, and He executed His just punishment of the wicked on this same day when Joshua told the sun to "stand still" and it stood still in the sky for a day until all of the enemies were killed.

The kings of this confederacy also bore a signature of the Nephilim – ruling in groups of five. The most prominent Anakim family included Arba, his son Anak, and three grandsons – Ahiman, Seshai, and Talmai. The Philistines, whose territory was home to the last remnant of the giants, were ruled by five lords (1 Samuel 6:4). Goliath and his four kinsmen were the last giants on Earth (1 Chronicles 20:6–8). With their armies routed, the five kings of southern Canaan retreated in fear from the Lord and Joshua. They hid in caves but were soon discovered and brought before the Jewish servant of God:

> "Then said Joshua, Open the mouth of the cave, and bring out those five kings unto me out of the cave. And they did so, and brought forth those five kings unto him out of the cave, the king of Jerusalem, the king of Hebron, the king of Jarmuth, the king of Lachish, and the king of Eglon. And it came to pass, when they brought out those kings unto Joshua, that Joshua called for all the men of Israel, and said unto the captains of the men of war which went with him, Come near, put your feet upon the necks of these kings. And they came near, and put their feet upon the necks of them.
>
> And Joshua said unto them, Fear not, nor be dismayed, be strong and of good courage: for thus shall the LORD do to all your enemies against whom ye fight. And afterward Joshua smote them, and slew them, and hanged them on five trees: and they were hanging upon the trees until the evening." – Joshua 10:22–26

In this dramatic display, Joshua, whose Hebrew name *Yeshua* foreshadowed the coming Messiah, proclaimed the victory for God. This was Israel's ultimate display of faith in the Creator. In the heart of Nephilim territory, Joshua, a child of slaves, stood triumphant with his foot on the necks of Satan's forces. The days of Nephilim dominance on the planet were coming to an end. With the supernatural hailstorm and the earth literally stopping its rotation, the Gentile world was on notice: The God of Israel was indeed the Creator.

> "And that day Joshua took Makkedah, and smote it with the edge of the sword, and the king thereof he utterly destroyed, them, and

all the souls that were therein; he let none remain: and he did to the king of Makkedah as he did unto the king of Jericho. ²⁹ Then Joshua passed from Makkedah, and all Israel with him, unto Libnah, and fought against Libnah: ³⁰ And the LORD delivered it also, and the king thereof, into the hand of Israel; and he smote it with the edge of the sword, and all the souls that were therein; he let none remain in it; but did unto the king thereof as he did unto the king of Jericho. ³¹ And Joshua passed from Libnah, and all Israel with him, unto Lachish, and encamped against it, and fought against it:

³² And the LORD delivered Lachish into the hand of Israel, which took it on the second day, and smote it with the edge of the sword, and all the souls that were therein, according to all that he had done to Libnah. ³³ Then Horam king of Gezer came up to help Lachish; and Joshua smote him and his people, until he had left him none remaining.

³⁴ And from Lachish Joshua passed unto Eglon, and all Israel with him; and they encamped against it, and fought against it: ³⁵ And they took it on that day, and smote it with the edge of the sword, and all the souls that were therein he utterly destroyed that day, according to all that he had done to Lachish. ³⁶ And Joshua went up from Eglon, and all Israel with him, unto Hebron; and they fought against it: ³⁷ And they took it, and smote it with the edge of the sword, and the king thereof, and all the cities thereof, and all the souls that were therein; he left none remaining, according to all that he had done to Eglon; but destroyed it utterly, and all the souls that were therein.

³⁸ And Joshua returned, and all Israel with him, to Debir; and fought against it: ³⁹ And he took it, and the king thereof, and all the cities thereof; and they smote them with the edge of the sword, and utterly destroyed all the souls that were therein; he left none remaining: as he

had done to Hebron, so he did to Debir, and to the king thereof; as he had done also to Libnah, and to her king. [40] So Joshua smote all the country of the hills, and of the south, and of the vale, and of the springs, and all their kings: he left none remaining, but utterly destroyed all that breathed, as the LORD God of Israel commanded. [41] And Joshua smote them from Kadeshbarnea even unto Gaza, and all the country of Goshen, even unto Gibeon. [42] And all these kings and their land did Joshua take at one time, because the LORD God of Israel fought for Israel. [43] And Joshua returned, and all Israel with him, unto the camp to Gilgal." – Joshua 10:28–43

In these battles, God and the Israelites exterminated the Nephilim gene pool. No person carrying the Nephilim DNA was to be left. This was the fulfillment of the curse Noah placed on Canaan centuries earlier. A 19th-century commentary described the *cherem* thusly:

"The word itself, used actively, means the devotement of anything by Jehovah, His putting it under a ban, the result of which is destruction; [compare 1 Kings 20:42] 'Because thou hast let go out of thy hand a man whom I appointed to utter destruction.'" – *The Book of Joshua: With Notes, Maps, and Introduction*, edited by George Frederick Maclear, 1880, p. 59.

The last vestiges of the Nephilim were under siege. The Lord in His infinite love for all people undid Satan's schemes to corrupt the Messianic bloodline. This "genocide," as Bible detractors and skeptics often call it, was a necessary military campaign to save all human beings from extinction at the hands of a corrupt superhuman race. God showed the world that through faith in Him even the mightiest kings of the world would fall. Israel was a young nation. All the elders, military veterans, and people who had been involved in any type of conflict at the Exodus had died in the wilderness. Using a bunch of "green recruits," God led them to the greatest military victories of antiquity.

# THE FINAL BATTLE FOR THE LAND OF CANAAN

Joshua 11 details the final effort of the Canaanites:

> "And it came to pass, when Jabin king of Hazor had heard those things, that he sent to Jobab king of Madon, and to the king of Shimron, and to the king of Achshaph, and to the kings that were on the north of the mountains, and of the plains south of Chinneroth, and in the valley, and in the borders of Dor on the west, And to the Canaanite on the east and on the west, and to the Amorite, and the Hittite, and the Perizzite, and the Jebusite in the mountains, and to the Hivite under Hermon in the land of Mizpeh. And they went out, they and all their hosts with them, much people, even as the sand that is upon the sea shore in multitude, with horses and chariots very many. And when all these kings were met together, they came and pitched together at the waters of Merom, to fight against Israel." – Joshua 11:1–5

Aware that the five kings far south of him had fallen, Jabin, the king of Hazor and supreme ruler of northern Canaan, wasted no time assembling a massive coalition of the remaining kingdoms in the north. The kingdoms in Jabin's confederacy stretched from Chinneroth, which was adjacent to the Jordan River in the northeastern section of Canaan, all the way west to Dor, a coastal city on the shores of the Mediterranean Sea. This passage introduces chariots – advanced military technology at that time – into biblical history. This last stand by the Canaanites revealed not just a large population but their absolute fixation on destroying God's people. Consumed with hatred for God's faithful, they gave no thought to diplomacy and immediately marshaled their forces for war. This would prove to be grave error:

> "And the LORD said unto Joshua, Be not afraid because of them: **for tomorrow about this time will I deliver them up all slain before**

**Israel**: thou shalt hough their horses, and burn their chariots with fire. So Joshua came, and all the people of war with him, against them by the waters of Merom suddenly; and they fell upon them. And the LORD delivered them into the hand of Israel, who smote them, and chased them unto great Zidon, and unto Misrephothmaim, and unto the valley of Mizpeh eastward; and they smote them, until they left them none remaining." – Joshua 11:6–8

Like many foolish leaders, King Jabin ignored Israel's victories over Egypt, Og, Sihon, Jericho, and other giant-led nations. Mobilizing all the forces of the northern kingdoms, they waited in open space to battle the Israelites.

The armies of the northern confederacy were vast, comprising "much people, even as the sand that is upon the sea shore in multitude, with horses and chariots very many." In the face of this challenge, God proved again that He truly was a "man of war." The Angel of the Lord led the charge, slaughtering the enemy and leaving Israel to track down those in retreat. Jabin's remaining forces split into three factions, one heading northwest to "the great Zidon," an ancient title for the city of Sidon. Another group fled to Misrephothmaim – the salt pits near Sidon. The third group ran to Mizpeh, further north and east, at the foot of Mt. Hermon. Joshua led the Israelite reinforcements and slew all the enemies attempting escape.

An ever-obedient servant of God, Joshua continued the campaign through the north for seven more years, conquering the final remaining cities of the Nephilim:

"And Joshua did unto them as the LORD bade him: he houghed their horses, and burnt their chariots with fire. And Joshua at that time turned back, and took Hazor, and smote the king thereof with the sword: for Hazor beforetime was the head of all those kingdoms. And they smote all the souls that were therein with the edge of the sword, utterly destroying them: there was not any left to breathe: and he burnt Hazor with fire. And all the cities of those kings, and all the kings of them, did Joshua take, and smote them with the edge of the sword, and he utterly destroyed them, as Moses the servant of the LORD commanded... So Joshua took the whole land, according to all that the LORD said unto Moses; and Joshua gave it for an inheritance unto Israel according to their divisions by their tribes. And the land rested from war...." – Joshua 11:9–12, 23

As God promised Abraham, Isaac, and Jacob, He took the land of Canaan back from the usurpers and gave it to the people of Israel. Not only had the Holy Seed prevailed but the Holy Land was no longer in the hands of the enemy.

## THE 33 KINGS OF CANAAN WERE SYMBOLIC OF THE ONE-THIRD OF ANGELS WHO REBELLED AGAINST GOD

Joshua 12 lists all the kings God and the armies of Israel defeated – "all the kings thirty and one," and Moses had defeated Kings Og and Sihon. All told 33 kings of the Nephilim giant-infested Promised Land were conquered. The number 33 or 1/3 is significant in Scripture because it is associated with the original angelic rebellion against God:

"And there appeared a great wonder in heaven; a woman clothed with the sun, and the moon under her feet, and upon her head a crown of twelve stars: And she being with child cried, travailing in birth, and pained to be delivered. And there appeared another wonder in heaven; and behold a great red dragon, having seven heads and ten horns, and seven crowns upon his heads. **And his tail drew the third part of the stars of heaven, and did cast them to the earth: and the dragon stood before the woman which**

**was ready to be delivered, for to devour her child as soon as it was born.**" – Revelation 12:1–4

In John's vision of Satan's plan to prevent the birth of the Messiah, the stars the Devil cast to Earth represent the one third of the angels who joined with him in rebellion against God. Number patterns in the Bible are not coincidental. When the Lord Jesus was on the cross, two of the three people executed that day went to paradise. One of them, or 1/3, mocked the Lord and went to Hell and everlasting punishment. Adam had three sons (Cain, Abel, and Seth), one of whom was "of that wicked one." Noah had three sons – one of whom (Ham) was wicked and begat the patriarch of the post-Flood giants. The post-Flood giants, by the satanic spiritual influence indwelling them, arranged themselves to have 33 rulers among them.

## THE PROMISED LAND
## GIVEN TO VICTORIOUS ISRAEL

"And the LORD gave unto Israel all the land which he sware to give unto their fathers; and they possessed it, and dwelt therein. And the LORD gave them rest round about, according to all that he sware unto their fathers: and there stood not a man of all their enemies before them; the LORD delivered all their enemies into their hand. There failed not ought of any good thing which the LORD had spoken unto the house of Israel; all came to pass." – Joshua 21:43–45

Joshua's conquest was the greatest military campaign in the Bible. While Israel would fight battles in the centuries that followed, none compared to the sheer aggression, relentless pursuit, and numerous victories of the servant Joshua. A true foreshadow of Yeshua, the Seed of the Woman, Joshua humbly obeyed God who fought for Israel and humanity. The genetic threat the giants posed to humanity was almost completely removed from the earth. Any designs Satan had on defeating God's people with his super soldiers were dashed. But at that point in history, not all the giants were dead.

# UNFINISHED BUSINESS –
## SOME CANAANITES WERE NEVER CONQUERED

> "Now Joshua was old and stricken in years; and the LORD said unto him, Thou art old and stricken in years, and there remaineth yet very much land to be possessed." – Joshua 13:1

With the prophecy of the Promised Land fulfilled, there was much to rejoice over. But human error, sin, and recklessness would once again creep into the plan of God. The Nephilim giants were routed but not completely vanquished. This would prove to be a costly error.

> "And at that time came Joshua, and cut off the Anakims from the mountains, from Hebron, from Debir, from Anab, and from all the mountains of Judah, and from all the mountains of Israel: Joshua destroyed them utterly with their cities. There was none of the Anakims left in the land of the children of Israel: **only in Gaza, in Gath, and in Ashdod, there remained**." – Joshua 11:21–22

The Anakims were on the run and had lost all their cities. Some of them escaped to the cities of Gaza, Ashdod, and Gath where centuries later a Nephilim named Goliath would emerge. In this passage we see the beginning of an unfortunate pattern in which Israel spared small pockets of Canaanites in defiance of God's clear command:

> "Nevertheless the children of Israel expelled not the Geshurites, nor the Maachathites: but the Geshurites and the Maachathites dwell

among the Israelites until this day." – Joshua 13:13

"As for the Jebusites the inhabitants of Jerusalem, the children of Judah could not drive them out; but the Jebusites dwell with the children of Judah at Jerusalem unto this day." – Joshua 15:63

"And they drave not out the Canaanites that dwelt in Gezer: but the Canaanites dwell among the Ephraimites unto this day, and serve under tribute." – Joshua 16:10

"Yet the children of Manasseh could not drive out the inhabitants of those cities; but the Canaanites would dwell in that land. Yet it came to pass, when the children of Israel were waxen strong, that they put the Canaanites to tribute, but did not utterly drive them out." – Joshua 17:12–13

How easy it is to receive a blessing from God and then rest on one's laurels. How quickly do we remember to pray fervently when we are in crisis and then get lax once the crisis has passed? The Israelites were humans subject to like passions as people today. With the many victories and the Promised Land in their hands, they repeatedly failed to follow God's instruction to exterminate any trace of Canaanites from the land. God wanted to rid the world once and for all of the threat of the giants. But Israel allowed them to remain in small numbers. This would prove to be a costly error because in so doing they gave Satan a small foothold in the Promised Land – one that he would surely exploit.

# ONE FINAL MISSION –
# CALEB'S REVENGE ON THE SONS OF ANAK

Caleb, the faithful spy of Numbers 13 who implored the Israelites not to fear the sons of Anak and enter the Promised Land, eventually faced them in combat. He and Joshua were the last living adults who were part of the Exodus from Egypt. They witnessed the mighty miracles of God. They endured the punishment of the 40 years of wilderness journey after the Provocation. And they fought side by side as the 33 kings of the Promised Land were defeated and the giants were pushed to the brink of extinction. Though advanced in years, Caleb led his tribe against the sons of Anak:

> "And unto Caleb the son of Jephunneh he gave a part among the children of Judah, according to the commandment of the LORD to Joshua, even the city of Arba the father of Anak, which city is Hebron. And Caleb drove thence the three sons of Anak, Sheshai, and Ahiman, and Talmai, the children of Anak…" – Joshua 15:13–14

> "And afterward the children of Judah went down to fight against the Canaanites, that dwelt in the mountain, and in the south, and in the valley. And Judah went against the Canaanites that dwelt in Hebron: (now the name of Hebron before was Kirjatharba:) **and they slew Sheshai, and Ahiman, and Talmai**… And they gave Hebron unto Caleb, as Moses said: and he expelled thence the three sons of Anak." – Judges 1:9–10, 20

At long last, Sheshai, Ahiman, and Talmai, the giants who caused the older generation of Israel to doubt God, were dead. The grizzled war veteran Caleb led an expedition to capture Hebron, the stronghold of the Anakim built by their giant forefather, Arba, and executed the giants who caused a generation of Caleb's kinsmen and friends to die in the wilderness. He and his family were awarded Hebron as part of their allotment for valor.

## JOSHUA'S FINAL ADDRESS TO THE 12 TRIBES

In his final years of life, the elderly Joshua assembled the nation of Israel to deliver a final address. As their earthly leader he knew all too well that the war was not over. He testified to God's greatness and faithfulness in an appeal to inspire his people to completely wipe out the Canaanites and the Nephilim gene from the land:

> "And Joshua called for all Israel, and for their elders, and for their heads, and for their judges, and for their officers, and said unto them, I am old and stricken in age: And ye have seen all that the LORD your God hath done unto all these nations because of you; for the LORD your God is he that hath fought for you. Behold, I have divided unto you by lot these nations that remain, to be an inheritance for your tribes, from Jordan, with all the nations that I have cut off, even unto the great sea westward. And the LORD your God, he shall expel them from before you, and drive them from out of your sight; and ye shall possess their land, as the LORD your God hath promised unto you.
>
> Be ye therefore very courageous to keep and to do all that is written in the book of the law of Moses, that ye turn not aside therefrom to the right hand or to the left; That ye come not among these nations, these that remain among you; neither make mention of the name of their gods, nor cause to swear by them, neither serve them, nor bow yourselves unto them: But cleave unto the LORD your God, as ye have done unto this day. For the LORD hath driven out from before you great nations and strong: but as for you, no man hath been able to stand before you unto this day. One man of you shall chase a thousand: for the LORD your God, he it is that fighteth for you, as he hath promised you. Take good heed therefore unto yourselves, that ye love the LORD your God." – Joshua 23:2–11

Faith and reliance on God leads to a closeness with Him and constant spiritual revelation. Joshua understood that although the number of Canaanites may have dwindled they still presented a very real spiritual threat. The lure of false gods and idolatry remained as long as Canaanites were alive. Joshua understood this and did his best to warn the Israelites of the dire consequences if they ever joined themselves spiritually to seed of the serpent:

"Else if ye do in any wise go back, and cleave unto the remnant of these nations, even these that remain among you, and shall make marriages with them, and go in unto them, and they to you: **Know for a certainty that the LORD your God will no more drive out any of these nations from before you; but they shall be snares and traps unto you, and scourges in your sides, and thorns in your eyes, until ye perish from off this good land which the LORD your God hath given you**. And, behold, this day I am going the way of all the earth: and ye know in all your hearts and in all your souls, that not one thing hath failed of all the good things which the LORD your God spake concerning you; all are come to pass unto you, and not one thing hath failed thereof.

Therefore it shall come to pass, that as all good things are come upon you, which the LORD your God promised you; so shall the LORD bring upon you all evil **things, until he have destroyed you from off this good land which the LORD your God hath given you**. When ye have transgressed the covenant of the LORD your God, which he commanded you, and have gone and served other gods, and bowed yourselves to them; then shall the anger of the LORD be kindled against you, and ye shall perish quickly from off the good land which he hath given unto you." – Joshua 23:12–16

And with that Satan now had his next plan of attack. His hybrid army, small in number and the genetic threat all but eliminated, the strategy shifted to *spiritual corruption*. Sinful angels were never again going to marry human women. If an Israelite man were seduced by an idolatrous Canaanite woman, however, she could lead him into worship of fallen angels and demons. The Devil not only had an opening but knew that severe punishment awaited Israel if they disobeyed Joshua's words – a punishment so harsh they could lose the Promised Land! On the cusp of a devastating defeat, the adversary of humanity saw a way to recapture the Holy Land and see his sworn enemies perish. The plan was simple: Seduce the nation of Israel to rebel against the God who created them and instead follow the religion of the Nephilim.

# CHAPTER 19

# THE RELIGION OF THE NEPHILIM

"And the Philistine [Goliath] cursed David by his gods."
– 1 Samuel 17:43

The Nephilim were the originators of the pagan religions of the Old Testament. Though Joshua's conquest nearly exterminated the giant population, their spiritual practices lived on through their human subjects in the land of Canaan. Once the Israelites controlled the Promised Land, they faced a new challenge – resisting the allure of pagan beliefs. Joshua received a prophecy from God, and in his final words recorded in Scripture the great warrior, speaking by inspiration of the Holy Spirit, delivered the heavenly message:

> "Now therefore fear the LORD, and serve him in sincerity and in truth: and put away the gods which your fathers served on the other side of the flood, and in Egypt; and serve ye the LORD. And if it seem evil unto you to serve the LORD, choose you this day whom ye will serve; whether the gods which your fathers served that were on the other side of the flood, or the gods of the Amorites, in whose land ye dwell: but as for me and my house, we will serve the LORD." – Joshua 24:14–15

The choice God offered them was a simple one: "choose this day whom ye will serve." The Israelites had no excuse to doubt God. They witnessed the miracles. They saw Jesus Christ, the Angel of the Lord, literally fight tens of thousands of enemies, slaughtering them before their eyes and leaving the armies of Israel to chase down those in fearful retreat. God gave them the Promised Land with cities, vineyards, and lush farmland intact – demonstrating His abundant love for His chosen nation. All Israel had to do was continue to trust in God and not let their hearts turn to the fallen idols and gods of their enemies. The Bible details time and time again that the false religions were all centered in the cities the Nephilim once dominated.

## FOLLOWING JOSHUA'S DEATH THE ISRAELITES STOPPED ENFORCING THE *CHEREM* AGAINST THE CANAANITES, WHICH WAS THE FIRST STEP TOWARDS THEIR SPIRITUAL CORRUPTION

The book of Judges records Israel's history in the years after the death of Joshua. Without their faithful leader, the victorious warrior nation stumbled.

"And the spies saw a man come forth out of the city, and they said unto him, Shew us, we pray thee, the entrance into the city, and we will shew thee mercy. And when he shewed them the entrance into the city, they smote the city with the edge of the sword; **but they let go the man and all his family**. And the man went into the land of the Hittites, and built a city, and called the name thereof Luz: which is the name thereof unto this day. Neither did Manasseh drive out the inhabitants of Bethshean and her towns, nor Taanach and her towns, nor the inhabitants of Dor and her towns, nor the inhabitants of Ibleam and her towns, nor the inhabitants of Megiddo and her towns: but the Canaanites would dwell in that land. And it came to pass, when Israel was strong, that they put the Canaanites to tribute, and did not utterly drive them out. Neither did Ephraim drive out the Canaanites that dwelt in Gezer; but the Canaanites dwelt in Gezer among them. Neither did Zebulun drive out the inhabitants of Kitron, nor the inhabitants of Nahalol; but the Canaanites dwelt among them, and became tributaries." – Judges 1:24–30

Whether it was an arbitrary act of mercy, a desire to collect tax revenue, or just plain laziness, the tribes of Israel repeatedly failed to eliminate the final pockets of Canaan's descendants that remained in their respective lots of the Promised Land. And those "small sins" would lead to major catastrophe.

## THE ISRAELITES REBELLED AND WORSHIPED ASHTAROTH – GODDESS OF THE POST-FLOOD GIANTS

"… and there arose another generation after them, which knew not the LORD, nor yet the works which he had done for Israel. And the children of Israel did evil in the sight of the LORD, and served Baalim: And they forsook the LORD God of their fathers, which brought them out of the land of Egypt, and followed other gods, of the gods of the people that were round about them, and bowed themselves unto them, and provoked the LORD to anger. And they forsook the LORD, and served Baal and Ashtaroth."
– Judges 2:10–13

While the false god Baal is mentioned many times in Scripture, *Ashtaroth is the first pagan god mentioned in the Bible*: "And in the fourteenth year came Chedorlaomer, and the kings that were with him, and smote the Rephaims in Ashteroth Karnaim" (Genesis 14:5). During the world war of Genesis 14 the Bible records the Rephaim living in a city named in honor of Ashtaroth:

"The principal town of the Rephaim at the time of the eastern invasion was Ashteroth Karnaim, that is, the town dedicated to the horned Ashtoreth (the Moon and Venus), and was hence called 'the house of Ashtarte.'" – *A Historical and Critical Commentary on the Old Testament*, M. M. Kalisch, 1858, p. 224.

The worship of the sun, moon, and stars was strictly forbidden in Scripture (Deuteronomy 4:19). The first instance of this sin in the Bible was among the corrupted descendants of the giant-occupied nations. By Abraham's day, the goddess Ashtoreth was not only worshiped but there was a city erected in her honor. King Og made Ashteroth Karnaim his stronghold in Bashan. The lure into spiritual corruption was just as powerful as the genetic threat the Nephilim posed.

Mankind looked to the heavens with sinful ambition from the days of Nimrod – whose grandfather Ham could certainly have shared the history of the antediluvian world where the sons of God and hybrid supermen ruled with technological and military superiority. No doubt some in the post-Flood world yearned to return to those days. Thus, the idolatrous practices of the giants spread through the Promised Land. Many centuries later, in the days of King David, the worship only increased. After King Saul died, the Philistines beheaded him and "put his armour in the house of Ashtaroth" (1 Samuel 31:10). In giant-led nations, the worship of false gods was rampant.

The Lord, of course, retains complete authority over the sun, moon, stars, and all the host of heaven. God "made two great lights" (the sun and moon) as well as the stars (Genesis 1:16). He set a "tabernacle for the sun" (Psalm 19:4). The heavens declare the glory of God, their creator (Psalm 19:1). Joshua, trusting in God's power, commanded the sun to "stand still." During the Great Tribulation to come, the Lord will remove the light of the sun, moon, and stars to signal that the end times have commenced (Revelation 6:12–13).

In the wilderness, God repeatedly warned the Israelites of the many idolatrous practices of the Nephilim-led nations in Canaan:

"When thou art come into the land which the LORD thy God giveth thee, thou shalt not learn to do after the abominations of those nations. There shall not be found among you any one that maketh his son or his daughter to pass through the fire, or that useth divination, or an observer of times, or an enchanter, or a witch. Or a charmer, or a consulter with familiar spirits, or a wizard, or a necromancer. For all that do these things are an abomination unto the LORD: and because of these abominations the LORD thy God doth drive them out from before thee. Thou shalt be perfect with the LORD thy God. For these nations, which thou shalt possess, hearkened unto observers of times, and unto diviners: but as for thee, the LORD thy God hath not suffered thee so to do." – Deuteronomy 18:9–14

Indwelled with the corrupted spirit of their fallen angelic ancestors, the post-Flood Nephilim trod an accelerated path to spiritual rebellion against the Lord. Angels in the Bible are often synonymous with stars and thus ancestor worship (in the case of the Nephilim) most likely found its origin in the land of Canaan as the giants after the Flood sought to commune with their fallen, wicked angelic ancestors.

The lure of idolatry was so strong that it threatened to corrupt the entire nation of Israel and the lineage of the Holy Seed. Yet despite God's stern warnings, Israel failed to remove their enemies and thus fell into the snare of their false religions.

## CHOOSE THIS DAY WHOM YOU WILL SERVE

"Now these are the nations which the LORD left, to prove Israel by them, even as many of Israel as had not known all the wars of Canaan; Only that the generations of the children of Israel might

> know, to teach them war, at the least such as before knew nothing thereof; Namely, five lords of the Philistines, and all the Canaanites, and the Sidonians, and the Hivites that dwelt in mount Lebanon, from mount Baalhermon unto the entering in of Hamath. **And they were to prove Israel by them, to know whether they would hearken unto the commandments of the LORD, which he commanded their fathers by the hand of Moses.**" – Judges 3:1–4

The generation of Israelites in the book of Judges were either children or not yet born during Joshua's war for the Promised Land. After allowing the remnant Canaanite nations to remain in the Promised Land, God used these enemies to "teach war" to the inexperienced and rebellious Israelites. These final enemies would also test the faith of the Israelites – a test they failed most miserably.

> "And the children of Israel dwelt among the Canaanites, Hittites, and Amorites, and Perizzites, and Hivites, and Jebusites: **And they took their daughters to be their wives, and gave their daughters to their sons, and served their gods.** And the children of Israel did evil in the sight of the LORD, and forgat the LORD their God, and served Baalim and the groves." – Judges 3:5–7

Forgetting all their history and God's commands, the Israelites intermarried with the remaining descendants of Canaan. Shortly afterwards, that sin led to their adoption of the giants' pagan religions.

# THE GROVES – A PAGAN CORRUPTION OF THE GARDEN OF EDEN

"And Abraham planted a grove in Beersheba, and called there on the name of the LORD, the everlasting God." – Genesis 21:33

The first time a grove is mentioned in Scripture is in a positive, God-honoring sense (Genesis 21:33). Abraham, in respect and worship of the true and living God, planted a grove. Idolaters, however, soon used the grove for their own purposes to worship false gods. The grove was a replica of the Garden of God in Eden. The desire to "reclaim Eden" still burned in the hearts of those who served the Devil. Pagan idols were placed in the midst of the trees of the grove with the hope of conjuring a spirit to receive insight or power. Like all pagan practices grove worship was an attempt to access the heavenly realm without honoring the creator of Heaven. As one commentary on the Garden of Eden stated:

> "It is, therefore morally certain that the Tree or Grove worship found existing in Canaan by Joshua and the Israelites was the same that had been practised there from the very first settlement of the aboriginal Canaanites. But the Canaanites migrated direct from the cradle of the human family – their ancestor Canaan being the grandson of Noah. The origin of Tree and Grove worship in the land of Canaan is thus traced back to the very family who issued from the Ark and to whom all the traditions of Paradise were familiar as household words. Is it possible to believe that it had any other origin but those very traditions?" – *Traditions of Eden: Or, Proofs of the Historical Character of the Pentateuch*, Henry Shepheard, 1871 p. 159.

The use of groves became such a perversion of the Garden of God that it was eventually banned under the Law of Moses (Deuteronomy 16:21). By the time recorded in the book of Judges, Israel had fallen so deep into idolatry that when God commanded the faithful judge Gideon to cut down a grove to Baal the 12 tribes wanted to execute him for desecrating their place of false worship (Judges 6:30).

## THE WORSHIP OF THE HOST OF HEAVEN

> "If I beheld the sun when it shined, or the moon walking in brightness; And my heart hath been secretly enticed, or my mouth hath kissed my hand: This also were an iniquity to be punished by the judge: for I should have denied the God that is above." – Job 31:26–28

Another sin the Israelites ensnared themselves in was the worship of the host of heaven. Deification of the sun, moon, and stars was one of the primary principles of pagan religion in the land of Canaan. The Bible repeatedly draws a connection between angels and celestial bodies, so the half-human, half-angel giants were naturally drawn to commune and worship their fully-angelic ancestors. The "morning stars sang together" at the creation of the earth (Job 38:7). In Revelation, the Devil, when cast down to Earth, pulls down "the third part of the stars of Heaven" with him. In the book of Judges, after Barak and Deborah led the Israelites to victory over the wicked Sisera, Deborah's song of praise proclaimed, "the stars in their courses fought against Sisera" (Judges 5:20). There is a mysterious connection between angels, who are invisible to the human eye, and the stars and heavenly bodies we view in the sky each night. The Bible uses the title "host of heaven" interchangeably for both. A 19th-century Christian magazine wrote of this connection:

> "But soon there mingled with this thought – perhaps the two had been, as it were, born together –that besides this visible host there was one of invisible warriors – the guardians of the just, the

chastisers of evil–doers, that these were the rulers of the stars themselves. The 'angels of God that did his pleasure' were also his 'host.'" – "The Lord of Saboath," E. H. Plumptre, as published in *The Sunday Magazine*, Strahan and Company, 1869, p. 149.

Yahweh is called "the Lord of Hosts" in Scripture. *Saboath* is the Hebrew term for host. The title designates God as sovereign over all angels. When Joshua encountered Jesus Christ before the battle of Jericho, the Lord referred to Himself as "captain of the host of the LORD" (Joshua 5:14). King David lauded God for "the work of thy fingers, the moon and the stars, which thou hast ordained" (Psalm 8:3). Centuries later the Lord Jesus Christ referred to this verse stating, "But if I *with the finger of God* cast out devils, no doubt the kingdom of God is come upon you" (Luke 11:20). Christ created not only the vast solar systems but the angels who are aligned with them. The seraphim who surround the throne of God sing of His authority over all angelic beings: "… Holy, holy, holy, is the LORD of hosts: the whole earth is full of his glory" (Isaiah 6:1–3).

The Nephilim sought to defy God's authority by instituting star worship. In fact, sabianism or zabianism (a spin on the Hebrew *Saboath*) became the term for the worship of heavenly bodies. The Israelites foolishly adopted these satanic practices and were chastised by the prophets for their sin. Amos, who prophesied shortly before the conquest of the Northern Kingdom, specifically pointed to their worship of the host of heaven as a principal abomination they committed before the eyes of God:

> "Seek the LORD, and ye shall live; lest he break out like fire in the house of Joseph, and devour it, and there be none to quench it in Bethel. Ye who turn judgment to wormwood, and leave off righteousness in the earth, Seek him that maketh the seven stars and Orion, and turneth the shadow of death into the morning, and maketh the day dark with night: that calleth for the waters of the sea, and poureth them out upon the face of the earth: the Lord is his name:

That strengtheneth the spoiled against the strong, so that the spoiled shall come against the fortress. They hate him that rebuketh in the gate, and they abhor him that speaketh uprightly. …Have ye offered unto me sacrifices and offerings in the wilderness forty years, O house of Israel? **But ye have borne the tabernacle of your Moloch and Chiun your images, the star of your god,** which ye made to yourselves. Therefore will I cause you to go into captivity beyond Damascus, saith the LORD, whose name is The God of hosts." – Amos 5:6–10, 25–27

This passage is rich with insight into the divine realm. In his rebuke, Amos reminded the 12 tribes that the God of Abraham created "the seven stars," an ancient reference to the constellations Pleiades and Orion. The Lord causes the sun to rise and set. He has authority over the stars, moon, and sun and thus should be worshiped. Yet right alongside the sacrifice and oblation to the Lord, the Israelites compromised their faith by worshiping Moloch and Chiun, whom Amos identifies as "the star of your god." The Apostle Stephen referred to this passage in the book of Acts:

"Then God turned, and gave them up to worship the host of heaven; as it is written in the book of the prophets…." – Acts 7:42

Reverend John Lightfoot, a churchman, rabbinical scholar, and Vice Chancellor of Cambridge University, affirmed the notion that angels are linked or rule over the stars and planets in space:

"That Stephen [saith], God gave them up to worship *all the host of heaven:* now if [Chiun] betoken but one Idol, or one Planet, this cometh very short of the intent that he aimeth at their worshiping of all." – *The Works of the Reverend and Learned John Lightfoot,* Volume 1, John Lightfoot, 1684, p. 784.

# THE NEPHILIM WERE
# WORSHIPING THEIR ANCESTORS

The giants – both first-generation Nephilim and their later postdiluvian descendants – were in awe of their angelic forefathers. In Ezekiel 32 the giants ask the fallen angels who are sent to the pit: "Be thou in the depth of the pit: to whom art thou superior?" (Ezekiel 32:21 LXX). In the end times the Nephilim pose a question to both the Antichrist and Satan – the souls of the dead pre-Flood Rephaim kings – asking, "Art thou also become weak as we? art thou become like unto us?" (Isaiah 14:10). On both occasions, the giants, who once ruled the world, were stunned that angels could possibly be defeated and sentenced to Hell. Nimrod sought to raise his tower to Heaven, inspiring humanity in its extreme arrogance. The practice of "kissing the hand," which Job referred to in the passage quoted above, was yet another sign of the wicked legacy of false religion the Nephilim usurpers birthed in Canaan. A 19th-century Christian preacher and scholar commented on this ritual:

> "The ancient heathens were accustomed to kiss the hands, the feet, the knees, or even the mouths of the gods. It was also accounted a part of devotion to kiss the doors of the temples, the pillars and the posts of the gates. Among idolaters, in times as remote as the days of Job, it seems to have been a customary act of worship to their distant or unseen deities to kiss the hand. To this there is an evident allusion in [Job 31:26–27]." – *The Faiths of the World: An Account of All Religions and Religious Sects, Their Doctrines, Rites, Ceremonies, and Customs*, Volume 2, Rev. James Gardner, A. Fullarton & Company, 1858, p. 276.

## ISRAEL'S DESIRE FOR A KING LED TO GREATER SPIRITUAL CALAMITY

"And said unto him, Behold, thou art old, and thy sons walk not in thy ways: **now make us a king to judge us like all the nations**. But the thing displeased Samuel, when they said, Give us a king to judge us. And Samuel prayed unto the LORD. And the LORD said unto Samuel, Hearken unto the voice of the people in all that they say unto thee: **for they have not rejected thee, but they have rejected me, that I should not reign over them**." – 1 Samuel 8:5–7

In the Garden of Eden Satan enticed Eve with the notion of man-centered salvation ("ye shall be as gods"). He deceived her into imagining she could be as a god and achieve immortality by disobeying God. This same spirit inspired the notion of a king, a human sovereign ruler over all people. The first king recorded in the Bible was the Assyrian, the fallen angelic monarch of the antediluvian world (Ezekiel 31:6). After the Flood Nimrod, the grandson of Ham, reestablished monarchy as he attempted to rule the entire world population from Babel. Nimrod demonstrated not just the military might but the spiritual influence kings held over their subjects. He persuaded the populace of the known world to unite in defying the Lord. Generations later, during the wars for the Promised Land, the various giant-led nations in the land of Canaan had 33 kings who then submitted to Og, Sihon, Adonibezek and Jabin, the supreme rulers of the regions of the land of Canaan.

In God's plan for earthly government, there was to be no human or angelic king over nations. The Lord Himself ruled ancient Israel. Judges were appointed to interpret God's law and make right judgments over them when disputes or criminal allegations arose. The judges, however, were not kings or rulers, which Judges 8 makes clear when the Israelites wanted to make Gideon their king:

"Then the men of Israel said unto Gideon, Rule thou over us, both thou, and thy son, and thy son's son also: for thou hast delivered us from the hand of Midian. **And Gideon said unto them, I will not rule over you, neither shall my son rule over you: the LORD shall rule over you**." – Judges 8:22–23

How quickly the sinful flesh will turn to human solutions and forget the salvation and power of God. By the end of the book of Judges, the Israelites insisted on a king so that they could mirror the heathen nations around them. Decades of seduction by Canaanite culture led them to want to further emulate their sworn enemies. This was the danger of the spiritual corruption that took place once the 12 tribes settled in the Promised Land (and was yet another critical reason for the extermination of the giant-populated nations). The spiritual practices of the remnant Nephilim proved a true snare for the Israelites and led their hearts astray from the worship of God.

The prophet Samuel pleaded with God when the people requested a human king:

"But the thing displeased Samuel, when they said, Give us a king to judge us. And Samuel prayed unto the LORD. **And the LORD said unto Samuel, Hearken unto the voice of the people in all that they say unto thee: for they have not rejected thee, but they have rejected me, that I should not reign over them**. According to all the works which they have done since the day that I brought them up out of Egypt even unto this day, wherewith they have forsaken me, and served other gods, so do they also unto thee." – 1 Samuel 8:6–8

Despite the prophet's warning that appointing a king would have disastrous consequences, the Israelites insisted on appointing a monarch (1 Samuel 8:11–18). King Saul, the first human king of the 12 tribes, was an unrepentant man of dubious faith. His reckless actions and defiance of God led him ultimately to consult with a witch (1 Samuel 28:7). Before this time, no leader in Israel's history practiced the occult. Yet it took only one instance of tribulation for Saul to employ satanic means to lead his people. This was the grave danger kings posed. Their decisions led the nation either closer to or farther away from God. Tragically, in most instances it was the latter.

King Solomon, the third king of Israel, epitomized the dangerous influence of monarchy. Not surprising, his descent into spiritual rebellion came *through marriage*. Solomon "loved many strange women, together with the daughter of Pharaoh, women of the Moabites, Ammonites, Edomites, Zidonians, and Hittites" (1 Kings 11:1). With 700 hundred wives and 300 concubines, Solomon took the violation of God's requirement of monogamy to the extreme. These women led Solomon into all manner of pagan practices as he served Ashtoreth, sacrificed to pagan gods, and permitted their worship. This brazen defiance led to the nation of Israel splitting into two kingdoms – the 10 northern tribes who would be known as Israel or Ephraim, and the two southern tribes of Judah and Benjamin.

Jeroboam, the first king of the northern tribes, was so wicked that he erected golden calves and told his people "behold thy gods, O Israel, which brought thee up out of the land of Egypt" (1 Kings 12:28). The golden calf – an abomination so offensive that God executed thousands for participating in a prior construction of it in the days of Moses – was now being credited with leading the Israelites through the Exodus! Though the Devil's Nephilim armies were wiped out, their spiritual legacy poisoned the hearts and minds of the 12 tribes. The spiritual apostasy of the Northern Kingdom led to catastrophic judgment. 2 Kings 17 records their fate:

> "Then the king of Assyria came up throughout all the land, and went up to Samaria, and besieged it three years. In the ninth year of Hoshea the king of Assyria took Samaria, and carried Israel away into Assyria, and placed them in Halah and in Habor by the river

of Gozan, and in the cities of the Medes. For so it was, that the children of Israel had sinned against the LORD their God, which had brought them up out of the land of Egypt, from under the hand of Pharaoh king of Egypt, and had feared other gods, And walked in the statutes of the heathen, whom the LORD cast out from before the children of Israel, and of the kings of Israel, which they had made.

**"And the children of Israel did secretly those things that were not right against the LORD their God, and they built them high places in all their cities, from the tower of the watchmen to the fenced city. And they set them up images and groves in every high hill, and under every green tree: And there they burnt incense in all the high places, as did the heathen whom the LORD carried away before them; and wrought wicked things to provoke the LORD to anger:**

"For they served idols, whereof the LORD had said unto them, Ye shall not do this thing. Yet the LORD testified against Israel, and against Judah, by all the prophets, and by all the seers, saying, Turn ye from your evil ways, and keep my commandments and my statutes, according to all the law which I commanded your fathers, and which I sent to you by my servants the prophets. Notwithstanding they would not hear, but hardened their necks, like to the neck of their fathers, that did not believe in the LORD their God.

"And they rejected his statutes, and his covenant that he made with their fathers, and his testimonies which he testified against them; and they followed vanity, and became vain, and went after the heathen that were round about them, concerning whom the LORD had charged them, that they should not do like them. And they left all the commandments of the LORD their God, and made them molten images, even two calves, and made a grove, and worshipped all the host of heaven, and served Baal. And they caused their sons and their daughters to pass through the fire, and used divination and enchantments, and sold themselves to do evil in the sight of the LORD, to provoke him to anger. **Therefore the LORD was very angry with Israel, and removed them out of his sight: there was none left but the tribe of Judah only.**" – 2 Kings 17:5–18

The Northern Kingdom fell into all of the idolatrous practices of the Canaanites. The vestiges of antediluvian religion were its undoing. And the Assyrian Empire, one of the many Gentile nations wholly given over to paganism, would be God's weapon of judgment against the 10 tribes of the north. The Southern Kingdom fared no better. Despite having several faithful kings, Judah also fell prey to the spiritual seduction of Nephilim pagan spirituality. Following the horrible example of his father, Solomon, Rehoboam dragged the Southern Kingdom into the same wickedness as its northern counterpart:

"And Rehoboam the son of Solomon reigned in Judah. Rehoboam was forty and one years old when he began to reign, and he reigned seventeen years in Jerusalem, the city which the LORD did choose out of all the tribes of Israel, to put his name there. And his mother's name was Naamah an Ammonitess. And Judah did evil in the sight of the LORD, and they provoked him to jealousy with their sins which they had committed, above all that their fathers had done. For they also built them high places, and images, and groves, on every high hill, and under every green tree. And there were also sodomites in the land: **and they did according to all the abominations of the nations which the LORD cast out before the children of Israel.**" – 1 Kings 14:21–24

Judah adopted the religion of the Nephilim whom the Lord had defeated. What Satan could not accomplish with brute military force was achieved through spiritual infiltration. King Ahab, who reigned during the ministry of the prophet Elijah, established an occult council comprising 450 prophets of Baal and 400 prophets of the groves who ate at the table of his wife, Queen Jezebel (1 Kings 18:19). Ahab instituted Baal worship as the official state religion. Jezebel ordered mass executions of godly prophets, forcing Elijah and the remaining faithful men in the land to live as fugitives (1 Kings 18:13). The nation was so wholly given over to satanic occult practices that Elijah suspected he was the only faithful believer remaining in the country.

The final king, who brought on the ultimate judgment of Judah, was Manesseh who practiced every abominable deed God *specifically* forbade of the Israelites:

> "Manasseh was twelve years old when he began to reign, and reigned fifty and five years in Jerusalem. And his mother's name was Hephzibah. And he did that which was evil in the sight of the LORD, after the abominations of the heathen, whom the LORD cast out before the children of Israel. For he built up again the high places which Hezekiah his father had destroyed; and he reared up altars for Baal, and made a grove, as did Ahab king of Israel; and worshipped all the host of heaven, and served them. And he built altars in the house of the LORD, of which the LORD said, In Jerusalem will I put my name. And he built altars for all the host of heaven in the two courts of the house of the LORD.

> And he made his son pass through the fire, and observed times, and used enchantments, and dealt with familiar spirits and wizards: he wrought much wickedness in the sight of the LORD, to provoke him to anger. And he set a graven image of the grove that he had made in the house, of which the LORD said to David, and to Solomon his son, In this house, and in Jerusalem, which I have chosen out of all tribes of Israel, will I put my name for ever: Neither will I make the feet of Israel move any more out of the land

which I gave their fathers; only if they will observe to do according to all that I have commanded them, and according to all the law that my servant Moses commanded them. But they hearkened not: **and Manasseh seduced them to do more evil than did the nations whom the LORD destroyed before the children of Israel.**" – 2 Kings 21:1–9

The Israelites were so thoroughly corrupt that their sins were even worse than those of the Nephilim-led nations in the days of Moses and Joshua. Thus, the wrath of God was kindled. Manasseh "seduced" the people into rebellion and went beyond any other king in his wickedness by taking a statue of an idol from a grove and placing it in the holy temple of God. Once again Satan found his way into God's temple. And once again the Lord responded with swift judgment. This would be the end of the Southern Kingdom as God pronounced that they would lose the Promised Land. The prophet Ezekiel, who wrote his book during the Babylonian conquest of Judah, captured how far from faithful trust in the Lord the Southern Kingdom had fallen:

"Again the word of the LORD came unto me, saying, Son of man, cause Jerusalem to know her abominations, And say, Thus saith the Lord GOD unto Jerusalem; **Thy birth and thy nativity is of the land of Canaan; thy father was an Amorite, and thy mother an Hittite**. And as for thy nativity, in the day thou wast born thy navel was not cut, neither wast thou washed in water to supple thee; thou wast not salted at all, nor swaddled at all." – Ezekiel 16:1–4

"Behold, therefore I have stretched out my hand over thee, and have diminished thine ordinary food, and delivered thee unto the will of them that hate thee, the daughters of the Philistines, which are ashamed of thy lewd way. Thou hast played the whore also with the Assyrians, because thou wast unsatiable; yea, thou hast played the harlot with them, and yet couldest not be satisfied. Thou hast moreover multiplied thy fornication in the land of Canaan unto

Chaldea; and yet thou wast not satisfied therewith. How weak is thine heart, saith the LORD GOD, seeing thou doest all these things, the work of an imperious whorish woman...." – Ezekiel 16:27–30

"As I live, saith the Lord GOD, Sodom thy sister hath not done, she nor her daughters, as thou hast done, thou and thy daughters." – Ezekiel 16:48

Corrupted by idolatry, the Southern Kingdom was now equal to the Canaanites in the eyes of God. Spiritually, the chosen people of the Lord were so far from the saving faith in the Messiah that they were even worse than the enemies God removed from the Promised Land for them. In the rebuke from God, note the metaphoric language all centered on marriage and intimate relations – but in the sinful, Genesis 6-sense when the Devil corrupted marriage to the extreme. The Israelites were called "whore," "harlot," and "adultress" – all descriptive allusions to worshiping any other god but Yahweh. Judah was even worse than the city of Sodom (direct offspring of Canaan). And the wicked kings of both the Northern and Southern Kingdoms were at the epicenter of this spiritual infidelity. Trusting the leadership of "great men and women" (who by nature were corrupt sinners) over God Himself was just one of the many deceptions Satan spread to humanity. Soon Judah was conquered by Nebuchadnezzar, the king of Babylon.

The kings of the Israelites foolishly adopted Nephilim Canaanite religion, and it led to their most severe punishment. King Manasseh not only set up an idol in the temple but also sacrificed his own children – a practice that originated with the Nephilim.

## THE VALLEY OF THE SON OF HINNOM – THE NEPHILIM CONNECTION TO PAGAN CHILD SACRIFICE

"And he caused his children to pass through the fire in the valley of the son of Hinnom: also he observed times, and used enchantments, and used witchcraft, and dealt with a familiar spirit, and with wizards: he wrought much evil in the sight of the LORD, to provoke him to anger." – 2 Chronicles 33:6

"And the border came down to the end of the mountain that lieth before the valley of the son of Hinnom, and which is in the valley of the giants [rephaim] on the north." – Joshua 18:16

"Before occupying the land of Bashan it seems that the Rephaim had dwelt in the interior of Canaan, as they left their name to 'the Valley of Rephaim,' – a valley to the southwest of Jerusalem, on the right hand of the road which leads from Jerusalem to Bethlehem. It is a continuation of the ill-famed 'Valley of the son of Hinnom' which in later times became known as 'Gehenna'...." – *Correspondences of Canaan: A Study of the Spiritual Geography and History of and History of the Land and Nations of the Word*, Carl Theophilus Odhner, Academy Book Room, Bryn Athyn, PA, 1911, p. 60.

One of the more abominable acts in Scripture was the sacrifice of children in service to pagan gods. Many of the kings of Israel committed these murders.

"Ahaz was twenty years old when he began to reign, and he reigned sixteen years in Jerusalem: but he did not that which was right in the sight of the LORD, like David his father: For he walked in the ways of the kings of Israel, and made also molten images for Baalim. Moreover he burnt incense in the valley of the son of Hinnom, **and** burnt his children in the fire, after the abominations of the heathen whom the LORD had cast out before the children of Israel." – 2 Chronicles 28:1–3

Situated just outside the gates of Jerusalem, the Valley of the Son of Hinnom was the center of pagan child sacrifice and was also known as the valley of the Rephaim. Many contemporary biblical maps, commentaries, and sermons erroneously place the valley of the son of Hinnom on the southwest of Jerusalem. While it does stretch to the southwest of Jerusalem, it actually wraps around the entire southern border to the east of Jerusalem as the Scriptures confirm:

> "Thus saith the LORD, Go and get a potter's earthen bottle, and take of the ancients of the people, And of the ancients of the priests; And go forth unto the valley of the son of Hinnom, which is *by the entry of the east gate*, and proclaim there the words that I shall tell thee…." – Jeremiah 19:1–2

> "It appears, however, to be certain, that the name 'Hinnom' was also applied to the eastern ravine in ancient times: thus the Prophet Jeremiah (ixix 2) says, 'Go forth into the Valley of the Son of Hinnom, which is by the East Gate' — which implies that the 'Hinnom Valley' is that which passes the East Gate of the City, and intervenes between the City and Olivet. It is equally clear that the same valley was called Kidron." – *Haydn's Bible Dictionary*, London: Ward, Lock, & Co., Warwick House, Dorsett Buildings, Salisbury Square, E.C., Charles Boutrell, 1878, p. 388.

"Kidron" was not a separate valley but was a term used for the eastern portion of the Valley of the Son of Hinnom in ancient times. Modern scholarship has incorrectly treated the two as separate valleys. This is significant for our study because the East Gate led directly into the temple. And thus, due east of the presence of God and His holy temple was a place of ultimate sinful rebellion and punishment. Just as being "east of Eden" in the days of Adam, Eve, and Cain was a removal from God's presence, so too was this valley. When God instructed the prophet Jeremiah to take an earthen vessel to the Valley of the Son of Hinnom, it was to pronounce the ultimate judgment upon the 12 tribes:

"And say, Hear ye the word of the LORD, O kings of Judah, and inhabitants of Jerusalem; Thus saith the LORD of hosts, the God of Israel; Behold, I will bring evil upon this place, the which whosoever heareth, his ears shall tingle. Because they have forsaken me, and have estranged this place, and have burned incense in it unto other gods, whom neither they nor their fathers have known, nor the kings of Judah, and have filled this place with the blood of innocents; They have built also the high places of Baal, to burn their sons with fire for burnt offerings unto Baal, which I commanded not, nor spake it, neither came it into my mind:

**Therefore, behold, the days come, saith the LORD, that this place shall no more be called Tophet, nor The valley of the son of Hinnom, but The valley of slaughter. And I will make void the counsel of Judah and Jerusalem in this place**; and I will cause them to fall by the sword before their enemies, and by the hands of them that seek their lives: and their carcases will I give to be meat for the fowls of the heaven, and for the beasts of the earth. And I will make this city desolate, and an hissing; every one that passeth thereby shall be astonished and hiss because of all the plagues thereof. …And the houses of Jerusalem, and the houses of the kings of Judah, shall be defiled as the place of Tophet, because of all the houses upon whose roofs they have burned incense unto all the host of heaven, and have poured out drink offerings unto other gods." – Jeremiah 19:3–9, 13

The Southern Kingdom of Judah, the last vestige of God's nation in the Promised Land, grew so wicked that they sacrificed their own children in worship of fallen angels and demons. Satan's long-game strategy of spiritual infiltration succeeded. The people of Judah would be conquered, slaughtered, and burned just as their own children were in pagan sacrifice. The vile spiritual influence of the ancient giant religions was the Israelites' ultimate undoing.

The Valley of the Son of Hinnom was an ancient stronghold for the Canaanites. The idolatry the giants left behind was so alluring that it dragged the people of Israel into brazen rebellion against God and ultimately their loss of the Promised Land. The Valley of the Son of Hinnom, or *ge enna* in Greek, had a specific place of sacrifice called Topheth. It is believed to have derived its name from the Hebrew word *toph*, or drum. Loud drums were played to drown out the cries of children being sacrificed in Tophet's fire. Gehenna soon became synonymous with Hell itself in Scripture:

> "For Tophet is ordained of old; yea, for the king it is prepared; he hath made it deep and large: the pile thereof is fire and much wood; the breath of the LORD, like a stream of brimstone, doth kindle it." – Isaiah 30:33

In this address to the Assyrian Empire, which had conquered the northern tribes of Israel, the prophet Isaiah proclaimed, "Tophet is ordained of old." This was an allusion to antediluvian judgment and immediately moves the verse from literal to metaphorical. The king of Assyria did not die in the Valley of the Son of Hinnom; thus, the "king" for whom the metaphorical Tophet was prepared could not have been he. Additionally, the sacrificial flames of the literal Tophet were maintained by pagan idolaters, not by the breath of the Lord. The conclusion from this metaphorical usage is that the Lord Himself used this place of ancient Rephaim sacrifice as a symbol for Hell.

In the New Testament, the Lord Jesus Christ referenced "Gehenna" on 12 occasions. For example:

> "But I say unto you, That whosoever is angry with his brother without a cause shall be in danger of the judgment: and whosoever shall say to his brother, Raca, shall be in danger of the council: but whosoever shall say, Thou fool, shall be in danger of hell [*ge enna*] fire." – Matthew 5:22

> "And if thy hand offend thee, cut it off: it is better for thee to enter into life maimed, than having two hands to go into hell [*ge enna*], into the fire that never shall be quenched...." – Mark 9:43

> "But I will forewarn you whom ye shall fear: Fear him, which after he hath killed hath power to cast into hell [*ge enna*]; yea, I say unto you, Fear him." – Luke 12:5

These verses underscore the powerful symbolic nature of Gehenna or the Valley of the Son of Hinnom in ancient Jewish culture. It became a shorthand reference to the torments of Hell and the Lake of Fire. Hence Jesus' warning that people should fear the one who "after he hath killed hath power to cast into hell." The Lord also confirmed that the Lake of Fire, the place of final judgment for all unbelievers, was "prepared for the devil and his angels" (Matthew 25:41), confirming Isaiah's statement that Tophet was "prepared of old." The place of Canaanite pagan sacrifice was the closest thing to Hell on Earth in the ancient world.

From the Flood of Noah's day, to an entire generation of Israelites dying in the wilderness for 40 years, to the spiritual corruption in the days of the Judges that set the nation on a path to its own destruction, the giants and their subject nations were one of Satan's most powerful tools in his war against the Holy Seed. They also stood, however, as a testimony to God's power and might. Because when even one faithful servant trusted in God, he could overcome the mightiest giant – even in the case of a young boy named David.

# CHAPTER 20

# THE LAST STAND OF THE NEPHILIM

King David conquered the final remnant of Nephilim on Earth. The last of the Anakim descendants were on the western coast of the Promised Land – forced to the coast of the Mediterranean Sea after Joshua's conquest. During the generation of the Judges, Israel allowed the last few giants to remain in this land, which was the territory of the Philistines. But King David, whom God called "a man after my own heart," was a faithful warrior in the tradition of Joshua and Moses and would see that the final giants were vanquished. Starting with Goliath.

## GOLIATH AND HIS RELATIVES WERE THE LAST OF THE GIANTS

"In David's time, the accounts say, there were rephaim, that is to say, giant people, living in Gath and they mention none elsewhere." – *A Dictionary of the Bible Dealing with Its Language, Literature, and Contents, including the Biblical Theology*, Vol. II Feign–Kinsman, James Hastings, 1911, p. 166.

Goliath is the most popular giant of all time – owing no doubt to the fact that he is the only giant in the Bible who is actually quoted. His standing among the Philistine armies reflected the relationship the Nephilim in Canaan had with the partially mingled or fully human counterparts they lived among: The giants were in charge. The satanic spirit within him permeated his nation that was steeped in demonic idolatry. In 1 Samuel 16 the Lord rejected Saul as king and had the prophet Samuel anoint David. Immediately following this divine coronation, the Philistines marshaled for battle against the Israelites and Goliath dictated the terms of war to all involved – namely one-on-one combat for the rulership of both nations.

## THE ULTIMATE PROPHECY ON DISPLAY IN THE VALLEY OF ELAH

The timing of this legendary duel was no coincidence. In the preceding chapter, the prophet Samuel anointed the teenage David to be king while the rebellious Saul still sat on the throne. The Holy Spirit of God departed from Saul and indwelled David. This was a spiritual coronation, and the enemies of God and the Messiah marshaled their human servants to war against Israel before this new king could assume power. Little did they know, David himself would be at the center of the battle.

David, carrying the DNA of the bloodline that would lead to Messiah, and Goliath, descendant of the sons of God of Genesis 6, faced off in one-on-one combat. This was yet another stunning fulfillment of Genesis 3:15. With their enmity at its peak, the Seed of the Woman conquered the seed of the Devil. The Philistines were positioned "between Shochoh and Azekah, in Ephesdammim" (1 Samuel 17:1), due west of Jerusalem. Led by the Nephilim warrior, they were headed straight for the location of the antediluvian Eden. The iron tip of Goliath's spear weighed roughly 30 pounds, and its shaft was the size of an ancient loom used to make fabric. He was a superhuman soldier who rendered the entire army of Israel paralyzed with fear.

Like Moses and Joshua before him, David was a devoted solider of the Lord. His own remarks entering the battle underscored the theme of God's purpose in the war against the giants:

"And as he talked with them, behold, there came up the champion, the Philistine of Gath, Goliath by name, out of the armies of the Philistines, and spake according to the same words: and David heard them....And David spake to the men that stood by him, saying, What shall be done to the man that killeth this Philistine, and taketh away the reproach from Israel? **for who is this uncircumcised Philistine, that he should defy the armies of the living God?**" – 1 Samuel 17:23, 26–28

In David's mind Goliath's size and weaponry were irrelevant. What mattered was that he was a demon-worshiping pagan railing against the very creator of the universe. The battle was not even close – a giant stood no chance trying to fight the Lord. David's courage grew from his understanding that God would be fighting the battle that day:

"And David said to Saul, Let no man's heart fail because of him; thy servant will go and fight with this Philistine. And Saul said to David, Thou art not able to go against this Philistine to fight with him: for thou art but a youth, and he a man of war from his youth. And David said unto Saul, Thy servant kept his father's sheep, and there came a lion, and a bear, and took a lamb out of the flock: And I went out after him, and smote him, and delivered it out of his mouth: and when he arose against me, I caught him by his beard, and smote him, and slew him. Thy servant slew both the lion and the bear: and this uncircumcised Philistine shall be as one of them, seeing he hath defied the armies of the living God. David said moreover, the Lord that delivered me out of the paw of the lion, and out of the paw of the bear, he will deliver me out of the hand of this Philistine. And Saul said unto David, Go, and the LORD be with thee." – 1 Samuel 17:32–37

# "HE SHALL BRUISE THY HEAD" – DAVID FORESHADOWED THE MESSIAH

As prophesied in Genesis 3:15, David, a foreshadow of the Messiah, Jesus Christ, killed Goliath with a wound to the head. The Bible confirms that David was a type and shadow of the prophesied Seed of the Woman:

- David was of the tribe of Judah – the tribe from which Jesus Christ was born.
- David in Hebrew means "beloved." When Jesus was baptized in the Jordan River, God the Father spoke from Heaven and called Jesus "my beloved son."
- David was born in Bethlehem (Ruth 4:18-22; 1 Samuel 16). Jesus was born in Bethlehem (Luke 2:4).
- Several Old Testament Messianic prophecies used the name "David" to refer to Jesus. For example, Ezekiel 37:25: "And they shall dwell in the land that I have given unto Jacob my servant, wherein your fathers have dwelt; and they shall dwell therein, even they, and their children, and their children's children for ever: **and my servant David shall be their prince for ever**." Among other passages are Jeremiah 30:9; Ezekiel 34:23; Ezekiel 34:24; Ezekiel 37:24; Hosea 3:5.
- Prior to becoming king, David worked as a shepherd. Jesus called Himself the "good Shepherd" (John 10:11; 10:14).
- David was 30 years old when he began to reign as king (2 Samuel 5:4). Jesus was 30 years old when He began His earthly ministry (Luke 3:3).
- The Messiah was prophesied to sit on the throne of King David (Isaiah 9:7, Isaiah 16:5; Isaiah 22:22).

Like Moses and Joshua before him, David was a great servant of God and a warrior. Even as a youth, David embraced the war between the two bloodlines and fought valiantly. This is the fight Jesus Christ would ultimately finish during His incarnation on Earth. But until the Messiah arrived, there would be open warfare between the forces of God and of Satan. And David continued the fight against the remainder of Goliath's family.

*David's Mighty Men Versus the Last of the Nephilim*

> "In these cities of the Philistines some families of the gigantic Anakim remained for hundreds of years, even until the time of David, for of this monstrous stock came the giant Goliath of Gath, whose height was six cubits and one span, about ten feet and a half. The stripling David slew the boasting monster, but many years afterwards the aged king was met in battle by four other giants of the same accursed race...." – *Correspondence of Canaan, a Study of the Spiritual Geography and History of the Lands and Nations of the Word*, Carl Theophilus Odhner, Academy Book Room, 1911, p. 56.

As God prophesied David bruised the head of Goliath, killing him with one stone to the forehead. According to the book of Revelation, the battle between Jesus Christ and the Assyrian in the end times will play out in similar, swift fashion with the Lord's conquering the Antichrist (Revelation 19:11–21). But as the quote above noted, Goliath was not the last giant to walk the earth. Five giants remained and they all fell at the hands of David's "mighty men," a select group of elite soldiers who waged a relentless campaign against the last of the Canaanites.

# ISHBIBENOB

> "And Ishbibenob, which was of the sons of the giant [*rapha*], the weight of whose spear weighed three hundred shekels of brass in weight, he being girded with a new sword, thought to have slain

> David. But Abishai the son of Zeruiah succoured him, and smote
> the Philistine, and killed him. Then the men of David sware unto
> him, saying, Thou shalt go no more out with us to battle, that thou
> quench not the light of Israel." – 2 Samuel 21:16–17

King David pursued the Philistine armies to the point of pure exhaustion and
Ishbibenob, one of Goliath's relativess, seized the opportunity to try to
assassinate the king of Israel. The head of his spear was "three hundred shekels
of brass" or 7½ pounds – recalling the description of Goliath's weaponry.
Like his brother, Ishbibenob used oversized weapons to match his
superhuman strength. But Abishai, one of the mighty men, swept in to save
David's life and killed this Nephilim descendant.

The text also properly identifies Ishbibenob as one of the "sons of the giant."
The Bible confirms once again that the postdiluvian giants were not the direct
offspring of angels but were rather a genetically diluted form of their hybrid
ancestors. They were sons of the Rephaim. The Septuagint describes these
final Nephilim as "descendants of the giants in Geth, the family of Rapha" (2
Samuel 21:22 LXX).

## CONQUEST OF THE REMNANT

> "And it came to pass after this, that there was again a battle with
> the Philistines at Gob: then Sibbechai the Hushathite slew Saph,
> which was of the sons of the giant. And there was again a battle in
> Gob with the Philistines, where Elhanan the son of Jaareoregim, a
> Bethlehemite, slew the brother of Goliath the Gittite, the staff of
> whose spear was like a weaver's beam. And there was yet a battle in
> Gath, where was a man of great stature, that had on every hand six
> fingers, and on every foot six toes, four and twenty in number; and
> he also was born to the giant. And when he defied Israel, Jonathan

the son of Shimeah the brother of David slew him. These four were born to the giant in Gath, and fell by the hand of David, and by the hand of his servants." – 2 Samuel 21:18–22

In rapid succession, the remnant of the giants was vanquished. There is some debate as to whether these giants were the siblings of Goliath whom David had slain as a teen. The textual evidence, however, indicates it is more likely that they were merely relatives of Goliath. The Septuagint translation of the text reads: "And there was a battle in Rom with the Philistines; and Eleanan son of Ariorgim the Bethleemite slew Goliath the Gittite; and the staff of his spear *was* as a weaver's beam" (2 Kings 21:19 LXX). This was no error; rather it is likely that this was another giant named after the legendary Goliath who died decades earlier:

> "The words *'the brother of'* are conjecturally inserted in the EV from [1 Chron]. They are not found here in the Hebrew text, or in any of the ancient versions. The parallel passage in 1 Chr. xx 5 reads *and Elhanan the son of Jair slew Lahmi the brother of Goliath the Gittite.* Now (1) the reading *Jair* is certainly preferable to *Jaare–oregim.* Oregim, the word for weavers in the line below, was inserted by a careless scribe, and the Hebrew letters of *Jair* transposed so as to read *Jaare.* (2) The letters of the words *Belh lchemitc* Goliath which stand together in the Heb. text so closely resemble those of *Lahmi the brother of Goliath* that it is almost certain that one reading is an accidental corruption of the other. But which is the original it is not easy to decide. There is no difficulty in supposing that another giant beside the one slain by David bore the name of Goliath." – *The Cambridge Bible for Schools and Colleges, The Second Book of Samuel,* Edited by A.F. Kilpatrick, Cambridge University Press, 1908, p. 197.

Also of note is the giant who was born with six fingers and toes. This was possibly a distinguishing feature of many giants (similar to their oversized armaments). And perhaps this is how Noah so readily identified Canaan, the father of the postdiluvian Nephilim.

## A SUPERNATURAL BATTLE

How was it that David's "mighty men" were able to conquer Nephilim descendants in one-on-one combat? The same way David as a mere teen was able to slay Goliath – by divine empowerment. King David's "special forces" soldiers vanquished the last of the seed of Satan and achieved many other superhuman exploits. David, a true type and shadow of Jesus Christ, "the Son of David," and his mighty men, forerunners of the disciples and apostles, were endowed with extraordinary fighting prowess. A 19th-century Bible commentary illuminated this foreshadowing:

> "The mention of the four heroes of David who overcame 'the sons of the giant' invites a comparison of the spiritual victories achieved by the Four Evangelists, and by all Evangelical champions who fight the good fight of faith preached in the Four Gospels, and thus overcome the world, the flesh, and the devil. Whatever victory is gained by them, not due to themselves, but it is achieved by the co-operation of Christ working in them and by them: and so the enemies of the Christian Church fall by the hand of the Divine: 'David and by the hand of his servants….'" – *The Book of Samuel in the Authorized Version; with Notes and Introduction*, C.H.R. Wordsworth, D.D., New Edition, Rivingtons, Waterloo Place, 1878, p. 122.

# "THE EGYPTIAN"

"Benaiah the son of Jehoiada, the son of a valiant man of Kabzeel, who had done many acts; he slew two lionlike men of Moab: also he went down and slew a lion in a pit in a snowy day. And he slew an Egyptian, a man of great stature, five cubits high; and in the Egyptian's hand was a spear like a weaver's beam; and he went down to him with a staff, and plucked the spear out of the Egyptian's hand, and slew him with his own spear. These things did Benaiah the son of Jehoiada, and had the name among the three mighties." – 1 Chronicles 11:22–24

The last of the Nephilim was a Rephaim descendant from Egypt. Benaiah, one of David's commandos, was fresh off killing two "lionlike men of Moab" and an actual lion before encountering the Egyptian. The man was five cubits or 8 feet 9 inches tall (using the Egyptian cubit) and, like Goliath and his kin, carried a spear the size of a weaver's beam. Benaiah had little trouble overpowering this final giant and killing him with his own weapon. These individual duels marked the end of the presence of the Nephilim on Earth. Giants make no further appearances in biblical history. The only references to Nephilim in the Bible after the books of 2 Samuel and 1 Chronicles are in esoteric and prophetic passages. King David finally completed the job tasked to Israel centuries earlier – ridding the earth of the corrupted genes of the giants.

## THE DEATH OF THE NEPHILIM IMMEDIATELY FORCED SATAN INTO ACTION

A biblical indicator that the Nephilim were no more is that immediately following the deaths of the sons of the giant in Gath and the Egyptian, the Devil himself is recorded as personally inciting sin in Israel:

"And Satan stood up against Israel, and provoked David to number Israel. And David said to Joab and to the rulers of the people, Go, number Israel from Beersheba even to Dan; and bring the number of them to me, that I may know it. And Joab answered, the Lord make his people an hundred times so many more as they be: but, my lord the king, are they not all my lord's servants? why then doth my lord require this thing? why will he be a cause of trespass to Israel?

Nevertheless the king's word prevailed against Joab. Wherefore Joab departed, and went throughout all Israel, and came to Jerusalem....And God was displeased with this thing; therefore he smote Israel." – 1 Chronicles 21:1–4; 7

With his supermen exterminated, the Devil took direct action against Israel. David's numbering of his soldiers was an act of vanity and pride in his own power. The Lord had delivered David and the 12 tribes through all their military conflicts. For David then to engage in such a pointless exercise was an insult to the Lord. Israel suffered through a plague that killed 70,000 men because of David's sin (1 Chronicles 21:14). The Devil was forced into new tactics as the Nephilim were finally destroyed. This was also the end of any Philistine military aggression in Israel's history.

## AFTER 70 YEARS OF SLAVERY IN BABYLON THE 12 TRIBES RETURNED TO THE PROMISED LAND

The books of Ezra and Nehemiah chronicle the return of the Southern Kingdom to the Promised Land after the 70 years of captivity in Babylon. The Lord promised mercy to the Israelites after 70 years, and Gentile kings beginning with King Cyrus of Persia arranged for the captives to return to their homeland. Ezra details the lineages of Israelites who returned to the

Promised Land – making sure the chronicle of the lineage leading to the Messiah was maintained. A campaign to build the second temple in Jerusalem was underway, and the people were truly joyful to be returning to the land of their fathers. But the issue of marrying into Canaanite bloodlines persisted:

> "Now when these things were done, the princes came to me, saying, The people of Israel, and the priests, and the Levites, have not separated themselves from the people of the lands, doing according to their abominations, even of the Canaanites, the Hittites, the Perizzites, the Jebusites, the Ammonites, the Moabites, the Egyptians, and the Amorites. **For they have taken of their daughters for themselves, and for their sons: so that the holy seed have mingled themselves with the people of those lands**: yea, the hand of the princes and rulers hath been chief in this trespass. And when I heard this thing, I rent my garment and my mantle, and plucked off the hair of my head and of my beard, and sat down astonied. Then were assembled unto me every one that trembled at the words of the God of Israel, because of the transgression of those that had been carried away; and I sat astonied until the evening sacrifice." – Ezra 9:1–4

At this point it should be clear why the news of these marriages so devastated Ezra that he tore off his mantle, ripped the hair out of his scalp and beard, and sat in silence until evening. Just when there was finally a glimmer of hope that the Messianic lineage could return to the Promised Land, the Israelites entered the illicit marriages that caused so much sin in the first place. And the priests, princes, and rulers – trusted "fine leaders" – were chief in leading the rebellion. Fortunately, Ezra did not sit idle in his despair. As a true godly servant, he pleaded for mercy from the Creator:

> "And said, O my God, I am ashamed and blush to lift up my face to thee, my God: for our iniquities are increased over our head, and

our trespass is grown up unto the heavens. Since the days of our fathers have we been in a great trespass unto this day; and for our iniquities have we, our kings, and our priests, been delivered into the hand of the kings of the lands, to the sword, to captivity, and to a spoil, and to confusion of face, as it is this day. And now for a little space grace hath been shewed from the LORD our God, to leave us a remnant to escape, and to give us a nail in his holy place, that our God may lighten our eyes, and give us a little reviving in our bondage.

And now, O our God, what shall we say after this? for we have forsaken thy commandments, Which thou hast commanded by thy servants the prophets, saying, The land, unto which ye go to possess it, is an unclean land with the filthiness of the people of the lands, with their abominations, which have filled it from one end to another with their uncleanness." – Ezra 9:6–11

In blunt language, Ezra confessed the many sins of his people, particularly citing the marriages God warned them to avoid centuries earlier. Rather than revolt, the people were convicted of their sin and responded with repentant hearts:

"Now when Ezra had prayed, and when he had confessed, weeping and casting himself down before the house of God, there assembled unto him out of Israel a very great congregation of men and women and children: for the people wept very sore. And Shechaniah the son of Jehiel, one of the sons of Elam, answered and said unto Ezra, We have trespassed against our God, and have taken strange wives of the people of the land: yet now there is hope in Israel concerning this thing. **Now therefore let us make a covenant with our God to put away all the wives, and such as are born of them, according to the counsel of my lord, and of those that tremble at the commandment of our God; and let it be done according**

**to the law**. Arise; for this matter belongeth unto thee: we also will be with thee: be of good courage, and do it. Then arose Ezra, and made the chief priests, the Levites, and all Israel, to swear that they should do according to this word. And they sware." – Ezra 10:1–5

This time, the Israelites had a humble heart in the face of God's judgment. They had learned the excruciating lessons from prior generations. The book of Ezra closes with a list of all the lineages of men who put away their wives. To no surprise, Nehemiah records the spiritual revival in Israel. The book of the Law was read to the people daily. Sacrifices resumed. The blessed hope in the Seed of the Woman was restored. And five centuries later, the Messiah whom Satan worked so feverishly to stop, destroy, and prevent, would be born in the Promised Land. Satan's conqueror was on His way.

# CHAPTER 21

# DEMONS – SPIRITS OF THE DEAD NEPHILIM

"These angels, then, who have fallen from heaven, and haunt the air, and the earth, and are no longer able to rise to heavenly things, and the souls of the giants, which are the demons who wander about the world, perform actions similar, the one (that is the demons) to the natures they have received, the other (that is the angels) to the appetites they have indulged." – Athenogaras in about 177 AD, as quoted in *The Fallen Angels and the Heroes of Mythology*, Rev. John Fleming A.B., Dublin: Hodges, Foster, & Figgis, p. 148.

A major assertion in the Book of Enoch is that demons are the spirits of the dead Nephilim:

"And now, the giants, who are produced from the spirits and flesh, shall be called evil spirits upon the earth, and on the earth shall be their dwelling. Evil spirits have proceeded from their bodies; because they are born from men and from the holy Watchers is their beginning and primal origin; they shall be evil spirits on earth, and evil spirits shall they be called. [As for the spirits of heaven, in heaven shall be their dwelling, but as for the spirits of the earth which were born upon the earth, on the earth shall be their dwelling.] And the spirits of the giants afflict, oppress, destroy, attack, do battle, and work destruction on the earth, and cause trouble: they take no food, but nevertheless hunger and thirst, and cause offences. And these spirits shall rise up against the children of men and against the women, because they have proceeded from them." – 1 Enoch 15:8–12

Though this is a very exciting and thought-provoking declaration, it is of little importance without biblical confirmation. Can we establish by Scripture alone that demons are in fact the souls of the dead giants? In this chapter, we will seek to prove that indeed it can be.

## THE DIFFERENCE BETWEEN ANGELS AND DEMONS

Though commentaries, sermons, and books on the Bible often treat angels and demons as interchangeable, Scripture reveals that they are quite distinct from each other. Consider the following.

*Angels Have Bodies – Demons Do Not*

As we have seen in earlier chapters, angels have corporeal bodies. Abraham fed angels and cleaned their feet (Genesis 18). The righteous angels who saved Lot were able to touch him and his family, close doors, and needed a place to spend the night (Genesis 19). The angel Gabriel, whom Daniel called "the man Gabriel," flew through the sky and landed to touch the prophet, demonstrating his physical existence (Daniel 9). The angels who sinned in the days of Noah are bound in chains (Jude). The Apostle Paul said certain types of angels could visit your home and you would never even know it was not an earth-born human (Hebrews 13:2).

Demons, on the other hand, do not have bodies. In the Old Testament they are referred to as "familiar spirits." In the New Testament they are called "unclean spirits." To prove He was truly resurrected to a glorified body the Lord Jesus Christ told His disciples, "Behold my hands and my feet, that it is I myself: handle me, and see; *for a spirit hath not flesh and bones*, as ye see me have" (Luke 24:39). All through the Gospels, demons desperately seek bodies of human beings to inhabit, and sometimes hundreds of them occupy the body of one person:

> "For he said unto him, Come out of the man, thou unclean spirit. And he asked him, What is thy name? And he answered, saying, My name is Legion: for we are many" – Mark 5:8–9

In another passage in which Jesus described demons, He refers to their disembodied state as well as *their aversion to water*:

> "When the unclean spirit is gone out of a man, **he walketh through dry places, seeking rest; and finding none, he saith, I will return unto my house whence I came out.** And when he cometh, he findeth it swept and garnished. Then goeth he, and taketh to him seven other spirits more wicked than himself; and they enter in, and dwell there: and the last state of that man is worse than the first." – Luke 11:24–26

So not only can multiple unclean spirits enter a human body but when they are not possessing a human being they seek to reside in the "dry places" or desert areas. Additionally, aside from the demonic context, the word "unclean" is used only two other times in the New Testament. In both instances the word refers to sinful personal relationships (1 Corinthians 7:14; Acts 10:28).

*Both Good and Evil Angels Receive a Level of Respect – Demons Do Not*

> "For we wrestle not against flesh and blood, but against principalities, against powers, against the rulers of the darkness of this world, against spiritual wickedness in high places." – Ephesians 6:12

Paul invoked formal titles in deference to the various official ranks of fallen angels in God's heavenly government. Sons of God, watchers, holy ones, principalities, and powers are some of the various titles angels hold in Heaven. In the book of Jude apostate Christians were criticized for "speaking evil of dignities" – a stern correction to any believer who would mock or speak harshly of fallen angels. Jude continued his point in the very next verse in which he relays an interaction between the archangel Michael and Satan:

> "Yet Michael the archangel, when contending with the devil he disputed about the body of Moses, durst not bring against him a railing accusation, but said, the Lord rebuke thee." – Jude 1:9

Even an archangel refrained from speaking disrespectfully to the Devil. No such deference is required for demons. They are called "unclean," "foul," and "devils." Demons are not superior in rank to humans and are often subject to the whims and commands of human beings. In God's warnings about the sinful practices of the Canaanites, He characterized demons as being subject to the authority of witches and wizards:

> "Regard not them that have familiar spirits, neither seek after wizards, to be defiled by them: I am the Lord your God." – Leviticus 19:31

# CONSISTENT WITH GOD'S APPROACH TO THE NEPHILIM THROUGHOUT THE OLD TESTAMENT, THE MOSAIC LAW PRESCRIBED THE *CHEREM* OR DEATH PENALTY FOR ANYONE WHO CONSULTED WITH FAMILIAR SPIRITS.

"And the soul that turneth after such as have familiar spirits, and after wizards, to go a whoring after them, I will even set my face against that soul, and will cut him off from among his people." – Leviticus 20:6

"A man also or woman that hath a familiar spirit, or that is a wizard, shall surely be put to death: they shall stone them with stones: their blood shall be upon them." – Leviticus 20:27

*Demonic Activity in the Old Testament*

Judges 9 records the first demonic activity in Scripture:

"When Abimelech had reigned three years over Israel, **Then God sent an evil spirit between Abimelech and the men of Shechem**; and the men of Shechem dealt treacherously with Abimelech: That the cruelty done to the threescore and ten sons of Jerubbaal might come, and their blood be laid upon Abimelech their brother, which slew them; and upon the men of Shechem, which aided him in the killing of his brethren." – Judges 9:22–24

God punished the wicked Abimelech by sending an "evil spirit" or *ra ruwach* in Hebrew. This is different from *malak*, the Hebrew term for angels in the Old Testament. The evil spirit was something altogether different from an angel or the human spirit. It was wholly evil and possessed none of the remnants of God's goodness all humans receive at birth (Romans 2:14–15). The first account of a man possessed by a demon was King Saul, the first ruler of Israel. Saul was a wicked, foolish leader who offered sacrifices to God in flagrant violation of the command that such offerings be made only by Levite priests (Saul was a Benjamite). He later starved his own armies by making them take a pointless oath. When God commanded him to enforce the *cherem* against the Amalekites, Saul disobeyed, sparing their king and livestock. All his sinful rebellion led to the Holy Spirit's presence departing from Saul and a demonic spirit taking him over:

> "But the Spirit of the LORD departed from Saul, and an evil spirit from the LORD troubled him. And Saul's servants said unto him, Behold now, an evil spirit from God troubleth thee. Let our lord now command thy servants, which are before thee, to seek out a man, who is a cunning player on an harp: and it shall come to pass, when the evil spirit from God is upon thee, that he shall play with his hand, and thou shalt be well." – 1 Samuel 16:14–16

This is a very fascinating passage of Scripture. Once again the evil spirit is called *ra ruwach* in Hebrew. The Old Testament authors seemed certain that these beings were different from angels (*malak* in Hebrew). The Jewish historian Josephus, who used the Greek Septuagint, wrote of Saul's possession:

> "…but as for Saul, some strange and demoniacal disorders came upon him, and brought upon him such suffocations as were ready to choke him; for which the physicians could find no other remedy but this, That if any person could charm those passions by singing, and playing upon the harp, they advised them to inquire for such a one, and to observe when these demons came upon him and disturbed him, and to take care that such a person might stand over him, and play upon the harp, and recite hymns to him… And when he was come, Saul was pleased with him, and made him his armor–

bearer, and had him in very great esteem; for he charmed his passion, and was the only physician against the trouble he had from the demons, whensoever it was that it came upon him, and this by reciting of hymns, and playing upon the harp, and bringing Saul to his right mind again." – *Antiquities of the Jews* 8.2, Josephus, about 150 AD. *Antiquities of the Jews*, Book VI, 3:1-2, Flavius Josephus, as recorded in *The Works of Flavius Josephus*, William Whiston, Vol. 1, 1843, p. 165-166.

The first-century Jewish historian recognized this episode as demon possession. Only music played by a believer in God could free Saul from the clutches of the evil spirit. The harp, invented by Jabal (with angelic assistance), one of the members of the antediluvian first family of the Nephilim, became a tool to repel the spirits of the giants.

The night before his death, King Saul rebelled against God a final time by seeking guidance from a woman with a familiar spirit. Disguising himself, Saul pleaded with the witch to call up the spirit of the deceased prophet Samuel to devise a battle plan against the Philistines:

"Then said Saul unto his servants, Seek me a woman that hath a familiar spirit [*owb*], that I may go to her, and enquire of her. And his servants said to him, Behold, there is a woman that hath a familiar spirit at Endor. And Saul disguised himself, and put on other raiment, and he went, and two men with him, and they came to the woman by night: and he said, I pray thee, divine unto me by the familiar spirit, and bring me him up, whom I shall name unto thee." – 1 Samuel 28:7–8

Demonic spirits were sources of knowledge and could help a person "divine" or know the future. In this passage, the term translated "familiar spirit" in Hebrew is *owb* or a "ghost" or "spirit of a dead one" and not "angel" [*malak*].

Demonic spirits were thought to be "brought up" from beneath the earth's surface, something the witch of Endor confirmed:

> "Then said the woman, Whom shall I bring up unto thee? And he said, Bring me up Samuel. And when the woman saw Samuel, she cried with a loud voice: and the woman spake to Saul, saying, Why hast thou deceived me? for thou art Saul. And the king said unto her, Be not afraid: for what sawest thou? And the woman said unto Saul, I saw gods [*elohim*] ascending out of the earth." – 1 Samuel 28:11–13

This passage reveals a critical distinction. Angels occupy the air and heavens (the lone exception being the sinning angels of Genesis 6 who are presently bound in the abyss and will not return until the Great Tribulation). Demons come from within the earth in Hell. Through some means, certain demonic spirits are granted access to the earth's surface to interact with and menace humanity. God put a strict ban on consulting demons, and Saul ultimately died for this sin:

> "So Saul died for his transgression which he committed against the LORD, even against the word of the LORD, which he kept not, and also for asking counsel of one that had a familiar spirit, to enquire of it; And enquired not of the LORD: therefore he slew him, and turned the kingdom unto David the son of Jesse." – 1 Chronicles 10:13–14

Theologians in prior centuries recognized the distinction between "devil" and "evil spirit" in the Old Testament. The latter was a spirit of the deceased giants:

> "It is unfortunate that our translation makes no distinction between the Devil and a Demon, which can very clearly be distinguished from each other in the originals, both Hebrew and Greek: Satan

both in Hebrew and Greek, and διαβάλλω, in Greek is never found in the plural number when applied to the Evil Spirit; δαίμων and δαιμονίζομαι are so frequently. In Jewish theology these two classes are distinct Satan, being a pure Spirit of like nature with the angels, while the *Shedim,* or demons, are half human. These last are identified with the Nephilim, or 'Fallen ones,' the giants, the children of the sons of God and the daughters of men (Gen 6:2); half angelic, half human, in many Jewish writings most conspicuously in the Book of Enoch." – *The Christian Remembrancer, A Quarterly Review*, Vol. LI, William Scott, Francis Garden, James Bowling Mosley, 1866, p. 273.

## NEW TESTAMENT DEMONIC ACTIVITY

In the New Testament, occult practitioners accessed the spirit realm by calling up demons to do their bidding. Acts 16 provides an example:

"And it came to pass, as we went to prayer, **a certain damsel possessed with a spirit of divination** met us, which brought her masters much gain by soothsaying: The same followed Paul and us, and cried, saying, These men are the servants of the most high God, which shew unto us the way of salvation. And this did she many days. But Paul, being grieved, turned and said to the spirit, I command thee in the name of Jesus Christ to come out of her. And he came out the same hour." – Acts 16:16–18

The demon in this passage helped the wicked masters of the young lady earn money by "soothsaying" or predicting the future. The Apostle Paul had no difficulty commanding the demon to leave the woman. In fact, Acts 19 shows that even Paul's discarded handkerchiefs could cast out demons. Jesus granted the disciples divine spiritual power to cast out demons. After using this power, they were amazed that demons listened to their commands, to which Jesus replied: "Notwithstanding in this rejoice not, that the spirits are subject unto you; but rather rejoice, because your names are written in heaven" (Luke 10:20).

Earlier, we examined the biblical principle that the sinful nature of Adam passed down through all of humanity via fathers with the exception of Jesus Christ (who was begotten of God). It only follows logically then that fallen angelic fathers passed their spiritual nature on to their Nephilim children. As hybrids, Nephilim were a different race from humans and angels and thus had a different spirit altogether. Upon death, the demon spirit lived on, still obsessed with sinful rebellion. A biblical commentary on this subject arrived at the same conclusion:

> "As it is entirely contrary to Scripture that the dead could thus be called up, we see the reason why these witches were not suffered to be in Israel. They were supposed to have a familiar (Hebrew *ob* – of the dead) spirit; but this powerful spirit does not come from the dead in Sheol, but has descended from father to child, and can be traced to no other source than to the sons of God; a spirit of power and might which has become defiled – unclean" – *The Sons of God and Their Inheritance*, Emma J. Penney, 1921, p 74.

## DEMONS MASQUERADED AS THE GODS OF THE PAGAN RELIGIONS

These disembodied spirits assumed the role of pagan gods and idols in ancient times:

> "So the LORD alone did lead him, and there was no strange god with him…. [15] But Jeshurun waxed fat, and kicked: thou art waxen fat, thou art grown thick, thou art covered with fatness; then he

forsook God which made him, and lightly esteemed the Rock of his salvation. They provoked him to jealousy with strange gods, with abominations provoked they him to anger. **They sacrificed unto devils, not to God; to gods whom they knew not,** *to new gods that came newly up,* **whom** your fathers feared not." – Deuteornomy 32:12, 15–17

"And they served their idols: which were a snare unto them. Yea, they sacrificed their sons and their daughters unto devils [*shedim*], And shed innocent blood, even the blood of their sons and of their daughters, **whom they sacrificed unto the idols of Canaan**: and the land was polluted with blood." – Psalm 106:36–38

The ultimate destruction of the Northern and Southern Kingdoms of Israel resulted from the demonic worship they adopted in Canaan. While the stone- or wood-carved idol of the Canaanite was a useless figure, a demonic entity did ultimately receive the worship that sinful man directed towards it. In Deuteronomy 32, God confirmed that these idols were "new gods that came newly up," signifying that they were not a part of the original creation. These new gods were located in the heart of the earth, thus the need for them to "come up" to interact with humanity.

The Hebrew word for "devils" or "demons" is *shedim*. The ancient Israelites sinned in treating these demons as gods. These devils were the spirits of the deceased Nephilim. The book of Isaiah confirms this:

"O LORD our God, **other lords beside thee have had dominion over us**: but by thee only will we make mention of thy name. They are dead [*rephaim*], they shall not live; they are deceased, they shall not rise: therefore hast thou visited and destroyed them, and made all their memory to perish." – Isaiah 26:13–14

426 · RYAN PITTERSON

The prophet Isaiah acknowledged that his people were sinfully worshiping "other lords" – namely the *rephaim* or spirits of dead giants. Unlike the fallen angels who were swallowed alive into the abyss, however, the Rephaim are deceased spirits who will never be resurrected to bodily form ("they shall not rise"). As they were not a part of God's creation, they have no hope of resurrection and remain disembodied spirits. They are sentenced to Hell and on occasion visit the surface of the earth impersonating gods and luring sinners into spiritual adultery.

The Apostle Paul acknowledged the difference between the worship of angels and devils:

> "What say I then? that the idol is any thing, or that which is offered in sacrifice to idols is any thing? **But I say, that the things which the Gentiles sacrifice, they sacrifice to devils**, and not to God: and I would not that ye should have fellowship with devils. Ye cannot drink the cup of the Lord, and the cup of devils: ye cannot be partakers of the Lord's table, and of the table of devils." – 1 Corinthians 10:19–21

With respect to angels Paul wrote:

> "Let no man beguile you of your reward in a voluntary humility and worshipping of angels, **intruding into those things which he hath not seen**, vainly puffed up by his fleshly mind...." – Colossians 2:18

Paul classified angels and devils as separate classes of beings – angels were unseen while encounters with demons were commonplace. Even those who challenged Paul during his ministry came to the same distinction between demons and angels:

"And there arose a great cry: and the scribes that were of the Pharisees' part arose, and strove, saying, We find no evil in this man: **but if a spirit or an angel hath spoken to him**, let us not fight against God." - Acts 23:9

Prophecy informs us that even in the end times demonic spirits will still lure people into idolatry:

"Now the Spirit speaketh expressly, that in the latter times some shall depart from the faith, giving heed to seducing spirits, and doctrines of devils…." – 1 Timothy 4:1

"Beloved, believe not every spirit, *but try the spirits* whether they are of God: because many false prophets are gone out into the world." – 1 John 4:1

Demons seek to spiritually corrupt humanity and lead them into idolatry. The many false teachers and heretics who preach erroneous doctrines while using the name of the Lord Jesus Christ are under the control or influence of demonic spirits (the spirits "seduce" these false preachers, again using the sexual language often associated with the Nephilim). In the end times, the Antichrist, False Prophet, and Satan will all release demons to entice world leaders to join in the battle of Armageddon:

"And I saw three unclean spirits like frogs come out of the mouth of the dragon, and out of the mouth of the beast, and out of the mouth of the false prophet. **For they are the spirits of devils [*daimon*]**, working miracles, which go forth unto the kings of the earth and of the whole world, to gather them to the battle of that great day of God Almighty." – Revelation 16:13–14

Justin Martyr, writing in the first century AD, arrived at a similar conclusion regarding the origin of demons and their nefarious spiritual agenda:

> "But the angels transgressed this appointment. and were captivated by love of women, and begat children who are those that are called demons; and besides, they afterwards subdued the human race to themselves, partly by magical writings, and partly by fears and the punishments they occasioned, and partly by teaching them to offer sacrifices, and incense, and libations, of which things they stood in need after they were enslaved by lustful passions; and among men they sowed murders, wars, adulteries, intemperate deeds, and all wickedness." – *The Second Apology of Justin, for the Christians, Addressed to the Roman Senate*, Justin Martyr, Chapter V, as quoted in *Ante-Nicene Christian Library, Translations of the Writings of the Fathers Down to AD 325,* Vol. II, Rev. Alexander Roberts, D.D., James Donaldson, 1868, pp. 75–76.

Given the distinctions between angels and demons, the only logical conclusion is that demons are (as the book of Isaiah described them) the spirits of the Rephaim – the once legendary Nephilim of the antediluvian world. Although the Bible does not give many details, it is certain that the spiritual state of the Nephilim was truly unique as they were the offspring of the heavenly and earthly realms. Giants were a satanic imitation of the prophesied Seed of the Woman who would one day save humanity. And the spiritual nature of their fallen angelic fathers was wholly corrupted and steeped in sin. As demons, they were permitted through various means to re-enter the earthly realm, serving humans and luring the unsuspecting into sin and false religion. Angels and demons in Scripture are quite different. And the greatest demonstration of the unique status of demons is revealed in their interactions with the Lord Jesus Christ.

> "Now to him that is of power to stablish you according to my gospel, and the preaching of Jesus Christ, according to the

revelation of the mystery, which was kept secret since the world began...." – Romans 16:25

"And to make all men see what is the fellowship of the mystery, which from the beginning of the world hath been hid in God, who created all things by Jesus Christ: To the intent that now unto the principalities and powers in heavenly places might be known by the church the manifold wisdom of God...." – Ephesians 3:9–10

" Unto whom it was revealed, that not unto themselves, but unto us they did minister the things, which are now reported unto you by them that have preached the gospel unto you with the Holy Ghost sent down from heaven; which things the angels desire to look into." – 1 Peter 1:12

# CHAPTER 22

# JESUS CHRIST AND THE NEPHILIM

> "And there was in their synagogue a man with an unclean spirit; and he cried out, Saying, Let us alone; what have we to do with thee, thou Jesus of Nazareth? art thou come to destroy us? I know thee who thou art, the Holy One of God." – Mark 1:23–24

In the days of Jesus Christ's incarnation on Earth, there was an astounding amount of demonic activity. Whether they were called "unclean spirits" or "devils," these disembodied spirits had a number of encounters with the Lord and always knew His true identity:

> "And unclean spirits, when they saw him, fell down before him, and cried, saying, Thou art the Son of God. And he straitly charged them that they should not make him known." – Mark 3:11–12

> "And in the synagogue there was a man, which had a spirit of an unclean devil, and cried out with a loud voice, Saying, Let us alone; what have we to do with thee, thou Jesus of Nazareth? art thou come to destroy us? I know thee who thou art; the Holy One of God. And Jesus rebuked him, saying, Hold thy peace, and come out of him. And when the devil had thrown him in the midst, he came out of him, and hurt him not. And they were all amazed, and spake among themselves, saying, What a word is this! for with

authority and power he commandeth the unclean spirits, and they come out. And the fame of him went out into every place of the country round about." – Luke 4:33–37

These passages reveal a lot about the relationship between demons and the Lord Jesus Christ. In the face of the Angel of the Lord who had conquered and killed them in the Old Testament, the spirits of the dead giants were completely aware of the true identity of the incarnate Jesus Christ of the New Testament. In the latter passage, the unclean spirit conceded he was no match for Jesus whatsoever saying, "art thou come to destroy us" and referred to Jesus as "the Holy One" – a title used in the Old Testament to signify Him both as God and Messiah (2 Kings 19:22, Psalm 16:10; Psalm 89:18).

The demons were under the authority of Jesus and responded immediately to His command to leave the possessed victim. Another subtle hint that these foul spirits are those of the Nephilim is that they once again serve as a testimony of the Gospel and God's sovereign power over all creation. Jesus' authority over demons was an unprecedented event and gave proof that He was indeed the Son of God. At every critical point in history, the giants were a means for God to demonstrate His power to the unbelieving world.

## ALLUSIONS TO THE JUDGMENT OF THE NEPHILIM IN DEMON ENCOUNTERS

In several encounters between Christ and demons there are references to the Flood:

"And they came over unto the other side of the sea, into the country of the Gadarenes. And when he was come out of the ship, immediately there met him out of the tombs a man with an unclean spirit, Who had his dwelling among the tombs; and no man could bind him, no, not with chains: Because that he had been often bound with fetters and chains, and the chains had been plucked asunder by him, and the fetters broken in pieces: neither could any man tame him. And always, night and day, he was in the mountains, and in the tombs, crying, and cutting himself with stones." – Mark 5:1–5

The Gadarenes were located in what was once Bashan, the home of legendary Rephaim king Og. The poor possessed man in this account was near some tombs when his possession took place. This hearkens back to the Old Testament prohibition against necromancy and other occult practices. What was the man who was embodied by possibly 2,000 demons doing in a graveyard? The Bible never says why he was at the tombs, but if he was there for occult purposes that would explain why he was vulnerable to demon possession. Also of note was that this possessed man, like a giant, was so supernaturally strong that "no man could bind him, no not with chains." The angelic fathers of the antediluvian Nephilim were of course *bound with chains* in the abyss where they remain today until the judgment of the great day.

The nature of an unclean spirit is unrepressed rage and sinful insanity. The demons within the man had driven him to nakedness (Luke 8:27) and screaming and cutting himself with stones all day. Akin to the condition of humanity before the Flood, this man was consumed with imaginations of violence continually. Luke's account reveals even more and shows a connection to the Nephilim:

> "And Jesus asked him, saying, What is thy name? And he said, Legion: because many devils were entered into him. And they besought him that he would not command them to go out into the deep." – Luke 8:30–31

The word for "deep" in verse 31 is "Hades," the Old Testament *Abaddon* or place of punishment for the angels who sinned. The demons are not only aware of the existence of the abyss but beg Jesus not to send them to the prison of their angelic forefathers.

> "Now there was there nigh unto the mountains a great herd of swine feeding. And all the devils besought him, saying, Send us into the swine, that we may enter into them. And forthwith Jesus gave them leave. And the unclean spirits went out, and entered into the swine: and the herd ran violently down a steep place into the sea, (they were about two thousand;) and were choked in the sea." – Mark 5:11–13

In stunning fashion, Jesus permitted the demons to enter into the bodies of pigs (ritually unclean animals that God forbade the Israelites from eating or even touching in some instances). The herd charged "violently" into a deep portion of the sea and drowned. This was a reenactment of the flood judgment. The giants who once ruled the earth were wiped out by choking on the waters of the Flood. This passage provides some of the most compelling evidence of the link between the demons of the New Testament and the giants of the Old Testament.

## THE UNPARDONABLE SIN –
## NEW TESTAMENT VERSION OF THE *CHEREM*

One of the more mysterious passages in the Bible concerns the "unpardonable sin" – the one sin in the Bible for which the Lord Jesus Christ said there would be no forgiveness. It occurred when the Pharisees, upon seeing Jesus cast out a demon, accused Jesus Himself of being possessed: "And the scribes which came down from Jerusalem said, He hath Beelzebub, and by the prince of the devils casteth he out devils" (Mark 3:22).

> "No man can enter into a strong man's house, and spoil his goods, except he will first bind the strong man; and then he will spoil his

house. Verily I say unto you, All sins shall be forgiven unto the sons of men, and blasphemies wherewith soever they shall blaspheme: But he that shall blaspheme against the Holy Ghost hath never forgiveness, but is in danger of eternal damnation. **Because they said, He hath an unclean spirit.**" – Mark 3:27–30

Accusing the Savior of the world of having a demon within Him was the one sin for which there would be no forgiveness. This is in line with God's zero-tolerance policy towards the giants all throughout Scripture. For 4,000 years of history, Satan attempted to corrupt and pollute the lineage of the Messiah. All the genealogies in Scripture testify to his grand failure to do so. As to His humanity, Jesus Christ was born of a wholly human bloodline. To slander the Savior of humanity with an accusation that He, the Creator of all, was possessed by the spirit of a dead giant was a sin that would receive no pardon.

## JESUS' POWER OVER DEMONS HELPED PROVE HE WAS MESSIAH

The accounts of demon possession in the Gospels implicitly identify the unclean spirits as being the corrupted souls of the Nephilim giants. By some means, these demons are periodically granted access to the human realm. Their persistent goal is to corrupt human beings into sin, possess them, and destroy them. In first-century Judea, devils appeared to be at their peak of manifestations on Earth. This should be no surprise as the spirits of the deceased giants once again served as a testimony to the power of God and the truth of the Gospel.

Time and time again, eyewitnesses were amazed that Jesus Christ had full authority over demons. In every encounter with a demoniac, the Lord Jesus Christ commanded the demons at will, and in utter fear and dread they obeyed Him. This was unprecedented and served as proof that Jesus was indeed the Son of God:

"As they went out, behold, they brought to him a dumb man possessed with a devil. And when the devil was cast out, the dumb spake: **and the multitudes marvelled, saying, It was never so seen in Israel.**" – Matthew 9:32–33 [emphasis added]

"Then was brought unto him one possessed with a devil, blind, and dumb: and he healed him, insomuch that the blind and dumb both spake and saw. **And all the people were amazed, and said, Is not this the son of David?**" – Matthew 12:22–23

"And in the synagogue there was a man, which had a spirit of an unclean devil, and cried out with a loud voice, Saying, Let us alone; what have we to do with thee, thou Jesus of Nazareth? art thou come to destroy us? I know thee who thou art; the Holy One of God. And Jesus rebuked him, saying, Hold thy peace, and come out of him. And when the devil had thrown him in the midst, he came out of him, and hurt him not. **And they were all amazed, and spake among themselves, saying, What a word is this! for with authority and power he commandeth the unclean spirits, and they come out.** And the fame of him went out into every place of the country round about." – Luke 4:33–37

As was the case from the days of Enoch, the giants served as evidence that God is the true ruler of all. The demonic spirits frightened many people living in Judea in the first century. They turned rational human beings into virtual animals via possession and afflicted children with disease. And yet, Jesus cast them out with just a word. After Jesus removed the legion of demons from the man at the Gadarenes, the miracle served the greater purpose of being a testimony to Christ's divinity:

"Then they went out to see what was done; and came to Jesus, and found the man, out of whom the devils were departed, sitting at the feet of Jesus, clothed, and in his right mind: and they were afraid. They also which saw it told them by what means he that was possessed of the devils was healed. Then the whole multitude of the country of the Gadarenes round about besought him to depart from them; for they were taken with great fear: and he went up into the ship, and returned back again. Now the man out of whom the devils were departed besought him that he might be with him: but Jesus sent him away, saying, **Return to thine own house, and shew how great things God hath done unto thee. And he went his way, and published throughout the whole city how great things Jesus had done unto him**." – Luke 8:35–39

When the Pharisees accused the Lord of having a demon He confirmed His divine power to them:

"But he, knowing their thoughts, said unto them, Every kingdom divided against itself is brought to desolation; and a house divided against a house falleth. If Satan also be divided against himself, how shall his kingdom stand? because ye say that I cast out devils through Beelzebub. And if I by Beelzebub cast out devils, by whom do your sons cast them out? therefore shall they be your judges. But if I with the finger of God cast out devils, no doubt the kingdom of God is come upon you." – Luke 11:17–20

Jesus Christ's authority over demonic spirits proved He was unique among all of humanity. That, along with His many other miracles, confirmed that He was the Seed of the Woman, the prophesied Holy One of God. He was the fulfillment of Genesis 3:15. He was the Giant Slayer of Numbers, Deuteronomy, and Joshua. He was the Angel, with the name of Yahweh in Him, who went before David into battle against Goliath. The demons were well aware of this, and trembled (James 2:19).

## JESUS PROCLAIMED HIS VICTORY TO THE APOSTATE ANGELS IN THE ABYSS

In addition to confronting the demons during his earthly ministry, Jesus Christ also confronted the sinful sons of God imprisoned in the abyss. In the three days between His death on the cross and His triumphant resurrection, Christ went into *Hades* and the lowest Hell to speak with the sinful angels of Genesis 6:

> "For Christ also hath once suffered for sins, the just for the unjust, that he might bring us to God, being put to death in the flesh, but quickened by the Spirit: **By which also he went and preached unto the spirits in prison; Which sometime were disobedient, when once the longsuffering of God waited in the days of Noah, while the ark was a preparing,** wherein few, that is, eight souls were saved by water." – 1 Peter 3:18–20

In yet another stunning account (not found in any extra-biblical text), the Holy Bible records that Jesus Christ went and spoke with the apostate angels who spawned the Nephilim. Bound in chains for thousands of years at that point, what a shock it must have been to those rebels to see the Son of God proclaim victory over the very Devil with whom they had foolishly allied themselves. The New Testament has two Greek words translated "preach" in the King James Version. *Kērussō*, the word used in the above verse, means "to be a herald, officiate as a herald." It was more of a public proclamation than an invitation to forgiveness. The Lord proclaimed His conquest of the sinful forces of Satan and his kingdom. A popular Christian apologetic book written in the early 20th century expounded on Jesus' preaching in the bowels of Hell:

> "If we so interpret it here, the preaching was not at all to men who had been wicked in the days of Noah but to supernatural beings who had been disobedient in the days of Noah and who were now in prison in consequence of this disobedience. Are there any

Scripture passages that hint that there were supernatural beings who were disobedient in the days of Noah and who were consequently in prison? There are. In Genesis 6:1 we are told that 'the sons of God saw the daughters of men that they were fair, and they took them wives of all which they chose.'

Many commentators understand the descendants of Seth, a godly man, to be "the sons of God" in this passage. But if we are to interpret scripture by scripture they seem rather to have been angelic beings. There seems to be a clear reference to this passage in Jude 6, where we are told of 'angels which kept not their own principality but left their proper habitation' and in consequence were kept in everlasting chains in darkness until the judgment of the great day...." – *Difficulties in the Bible, Alleged Errors and Contradictions*, Rev. R.A. Torrey, Moody Press, 1907.

Why would Jesus need to make such an announcement? It was a preparation for the fulfillment of Scripture. The book of Philippians describes the exaltation of Jesus after His victory on the cross:

"Who, being in the form of God, thought it not robbery to be equal with God: [7] But made himself of no reputation, and took upon him the form of a servant, and was made in the likeness of men: And being found in fashion as a man, he humbled himself, and became obedient unto death, even the death of the cross. Wherefore God also hath highly exalted him, and given him a name which is above every name: That at the name of Jesus every knee should bow, of things in heaven, and things in earth, **and things under the earth**...." – Philippians 2:6–10

Under the cloud of supernatural darkness, the sinful sons of God were unaware of what was transpiring during their imprisonment until Jesus published His majestic victory and the redemption of humanity through His sacrifice. And whether it was at that moment or in the future, they will indeed bow before Him.

# IMMORTAL HUMANS –
# THE RETURN OF THE SONS OF GOD

"But as many as received him, **to them gave he power to become the sons of God,** even to them that believe on his name: Which were born, not of blood, nor of the will of the flesh, nor of the will of man, but of God." – John 1:12–13

In the death, burial, and resurrection of Jesus Christ, God defeated Satan and restored order to His heavenly kingdom. By taking on the sins of humanity and offering Himself as a sacrifice, Jesus Christ provided a way of atonement for all humans who believe in Him, and thus they could receive a newborn spirit from God. A born-again Christian is no longer an Earth-realm being. He is a "Son of God," meaning a divine creation. The immortality Satan promised Adam and Eve could never be achieved through human effort. It could be attained only through Jesus Christ. And in salvation, a new generation of sons of God were raised up, all born-again Christians. The sinful angels of the original satanic rebellion were to be replaced with the newly born sons of God. If you are a born-again believer this is who you are today.

"That ye may be blameless and harmless, the sons of God, without rebuke, in the midst of a crooked and perverse nation, among whom ye shine as lights in the world...." – Philippians 2:15

Live for God today, battle with your flesh that is still earthly, and let the world see the glory of the Gospel through your words and deeds. But understand that all born-again Christians are destined to be equal to the holy angels and judges of the wicked sinful sons of God. The full fruition of this replacement will happen at the Rapture when all believers receive their glorified bodies:

> "And if Christ be in you, the body is dead because of sin; but the Spirit is life because of righteousness. But if the Spirit of him that raised up Jesus from the dead dwell in you, he that raised up Christ from the dead shall also quicken your mortal bodies by his Spirit that dwelleth in you. Therefore, brethren, we are debtors, not to the flesh, to live after the flesh. For if ye live after the flesh, ye shall die: but if ye through the Spirit do mortify the deeds of the body, ye shall live. **For as many as are led by the Spirit of God, they are the sons of God.**" – Romans 8:10–14

The body of a believer is "dead" in that it no longer rules over that person. A Christian is led by the newborn spirit in him or her birthed from God. Thus, believers are "sons of God" in title. And soon all of God's Kingdom will be united in Heaven with Christ ruling over them and leading them back to Earth to reclaim the planet for the Millennial Kingdom: "For the earnest expectation of the creature waiteth for the manifestation of the sons of God" (Romans 8:19).

Just as the Israelites received the kingdoms from the giant-infested Canaanites, so too shall believers receive the kingdom from the Devil, his fallen angels, demons, and wicked children. "And because ye are sons, God hath sent forth the Spirit of his Son into your hearts, crying, Abba, Father. Wherefore thou art no more a servant, but a son; and if a son, then an heir of God through Christ" (Galatians 4:6–7).

By being "in Christ" a believer is spiritually united with the Lord and thus rightfully entitled to the blessings of the millennial and eternal Kingdom of God. This is what God promised from the first chapters of the Bible. The entire war fought for thousands of years will culminate with God's true children, wretched sinners who believe in Him through faith, being redeemed, restored, and glorified with divine, immortal bodies and spirits. Why? Because of love:

> "Behold, what manner of love the Father hath bestowed upon us, that we should be called the sons of God: therefore the world knoweth us not, because it knew him not. **Beloved, now are we the sons of God, and it doth not yet appear what we shall be: but we know that, when he shall appear, we shall be like him; for we shall see him as he is.**" – 1 John 3:1–2

# CONCLUSION

Jesus Christ is the central figure of the Bible, the universe, and human history. Lord willing, it is now evident that alongside the prophecy of the Seed of the Woman, there was also a prophecy of the seed of Satan. And woven throughout the Bible is the account of the ongoing war between two bloodlines that has yet to reach its culmination. The Nephilim giants were some of Satan's most powerful soldiers in this war, as they played critical roles all throughout the Bible, even into the New Testament. And from the Bible and the Bible alone, we can discern that God's intention to birth a creation in His image would not be stopped by Satan's efforts to corrupt and destroy creation. But this war is far from over.

The Nephilim and the angels who sinned will still play a role in the end times, which a prophecy from the book of Daniel makes clear:

> "And whereas thou sawest iron mixed with miry clay, **they shall mingle themselves with the seed of men**: but they shall not cleave one to another, even as iron is not mixed with clay. And in the days of these kings shall the God of heaven set up a kingdom, which

shall never be destroyed: and the kingdom shall not be left to other people, but it shall break in pieces and consume all these kingdoms, and it shall stand for ever." – Daniel 2:43–44

The Bible predicts that on the cusp of Christ's return to Earth to fight the Battle of Armageddon and reclaim the planet there will once again be an effort to mingle the seed of humanity with that of the heavenly. The angels who sinned will return to Earth along with the spirits of the Nephilim. And the ultimate seed of Satan, the Antichrist, who has a direct connection to the Nephilim before the Flood, will emerge from the bottomless pit to deceive the sinning world into believing he is god. We will cover all these topics in the next study.

**"But as the days of Noah were, so shall also the coming of the Son of man be."** – Jesus Christ

Made in the USA
Columbia, SC
06 May 2021